THE HANDMAID'S TALE

MARGARET ATWOOD

ART & ADAPTATION
RENÉE NAULT

NAN A. TALESE
DOUBLEDAY
New York

Copyright © 2019 O.W. Toad Ltd.

Adapted by Renée Nault and Margaret Atwood. Art by Renée Nault

All rights reserved. Published in the United States by Nan A. Talese/Doubleday, a division of Penguin Random House LLC, New York.

www.nanatalese.com

Doubleday is a registered trademark of Penguin Random House LLC.
Nan A. Talese and the colophon are trademarks of Penguin Random House LLC.

Lettering and book design by Jennifer Lum
Printed and bound in China

Cover art: Renée Nault
Cover design: Jennifer Lum

LIBRARY OF CONGRESS CATALOGING-IN-PUBLICATION DATA
Names: Atwood, Margaret, 1939- author. | Nault, Renee, artist, adapter. |
  Graphic novel adaptation of: Atwood, Margaret, 1939- Handmaid's tale.
Title: The handmaid's tale / Margaret Atwood ; art & adaptation, Renee Nault.
Description: First edition. | New York : Nan A. Talese, [2019].
Identifiers: LCCN 2018037724 (print) | LCCN 2018038144 (ebook) | ISBN
  9780385544856 (ebook) | ISBN 9780385539241 (hardback)
Subjects: LCSH: Atwood, Margaret, 1939- Handmaid's tale-Adaptations. |
  Misogyny-Comic books, strips, etc. | Women-Comic books, strips, etc. |
  Graphic novels. | BISAC: COMICS & GRAPHIC NOVELS / Literary. | COMICS &
  GRAPHIC NOVELS / Science Fiction. | GSAFD: Fantasy fiction. | Dystopias.
Classification: LCC PN6733.A89 (ebook) | LCC PN6733.A89 H36 2019 (print) |
  DDC 741.5/971-dc23
LC record available at https://lccn.loc.gov/2018037724

10 9 8 7 6 5 4 3 2

First Edition

I

NIGHT

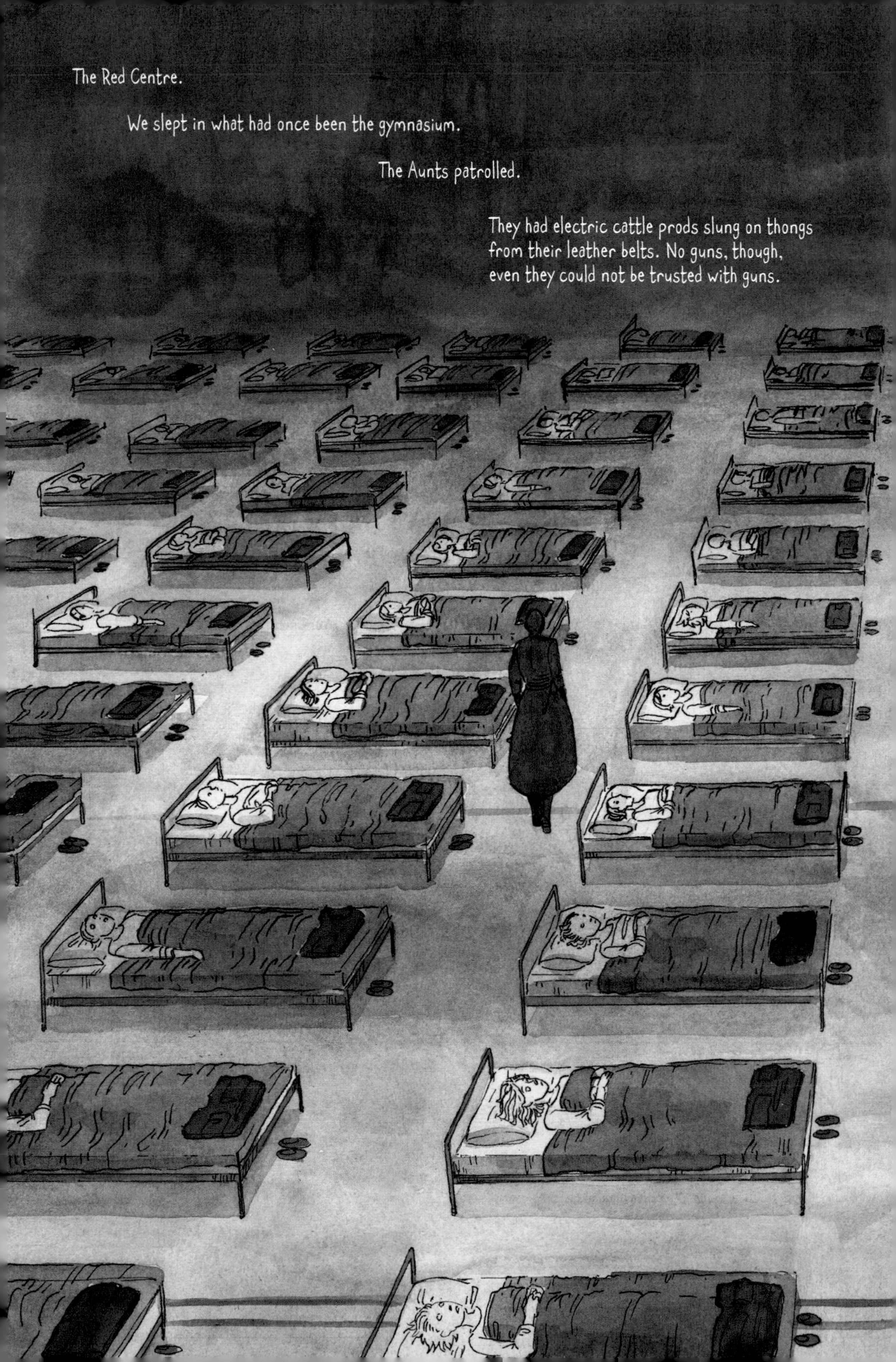
The Red Centre.
We slept in what had once been the gymnasium.
The Aunts patrolled.
They had electric cattle prods slung on thongs from their leather belts. No guns, though, even they could not be trusted with guns.

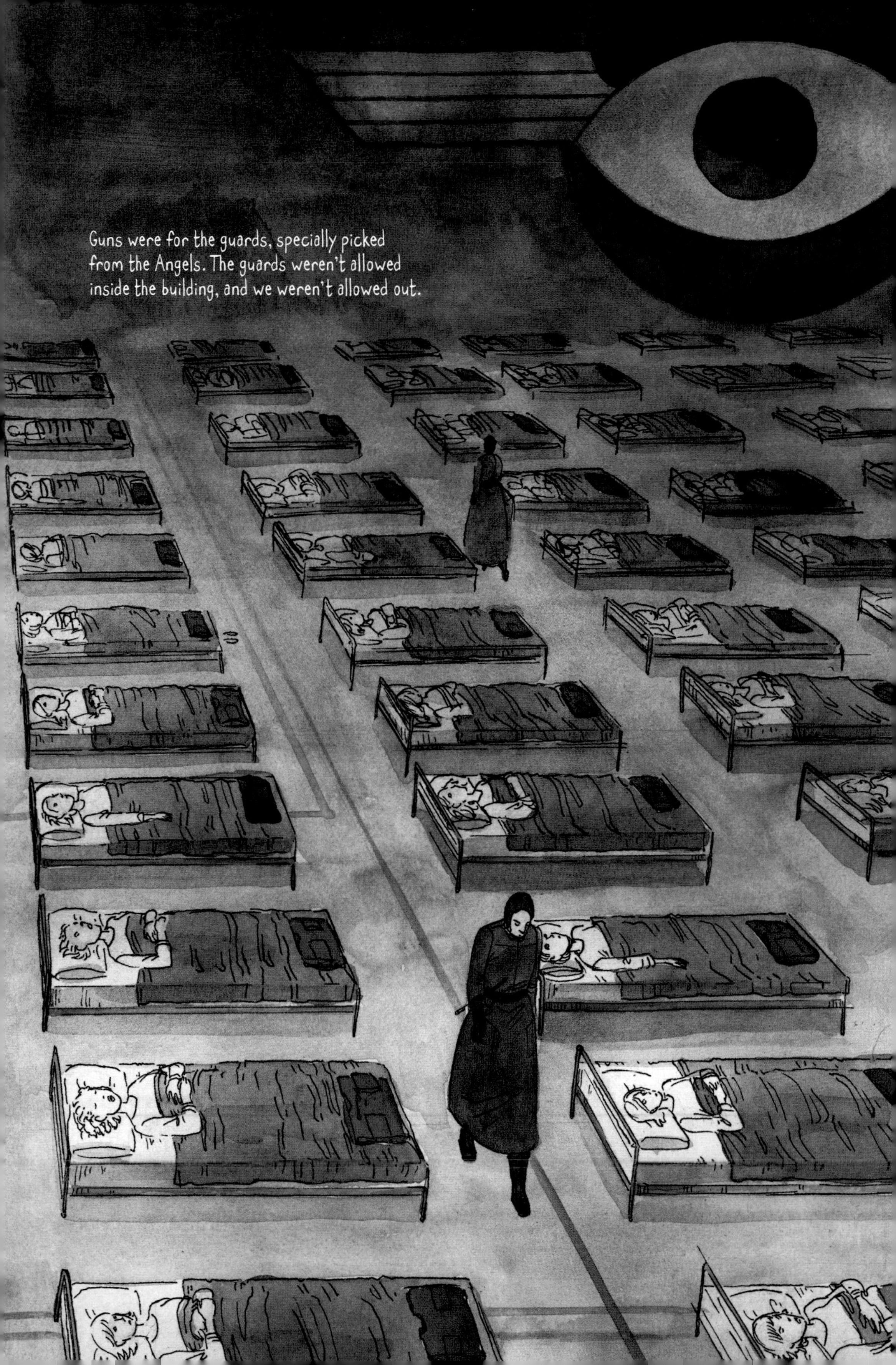
Guns were for the guards, specially picked from the Angels. The guards weren't allowed inside the building, and we weren't allowed out.

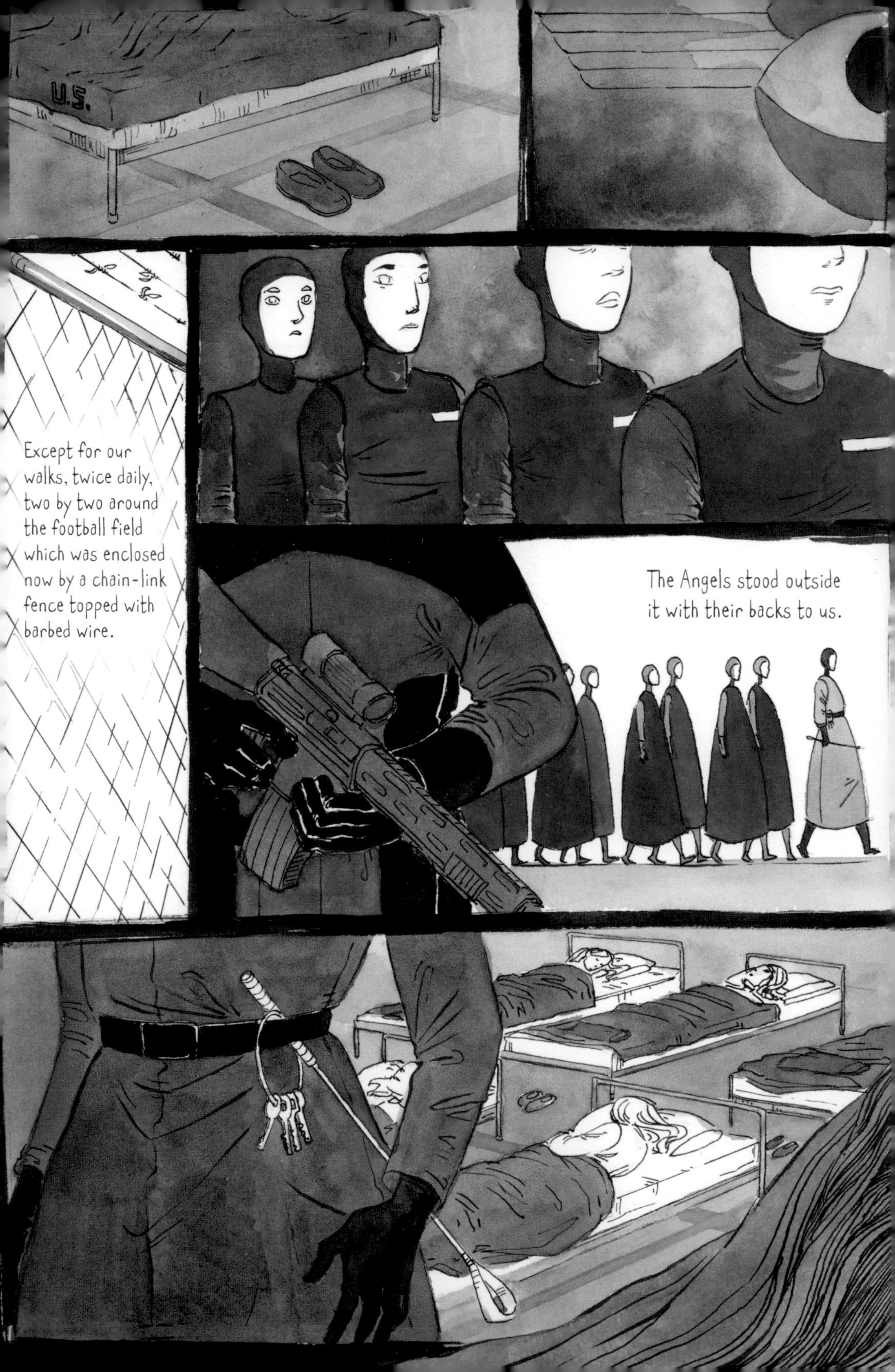

U.S.
Except for our walks, twice daily, two by two around the football field which was enclosed now by a chain-link fence topped with barbed wire.
The Angels stood outside it with their backs to us.

We learned to whisper almost without sound.

In the semi-darkness we could stretch out our arms, when the Aunts weren't looking, and touch each other's hands across space.

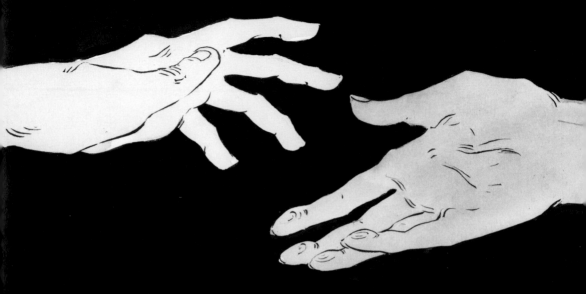

We learned to lip-read, our heads flat on the beds, turned sideways, watching each other's mouths. In this way we exchanged names, from bed to bed:

Alma.

Janine.

Dolores.

Moira.

June.

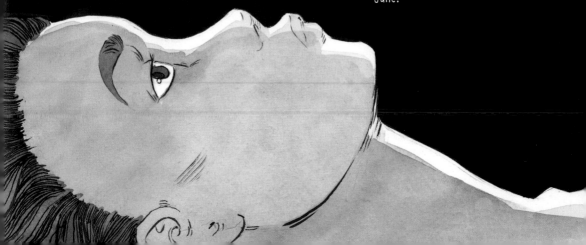

II

SHOPPING

The Commander's House.

My name is Offred now, and here is where I live.

A chair,

a table,

a lamp.

Above, on the white ceiling, a relief ornament in the shape of
a wreath, and in the centre of it a blank space, plastered over,
like the place in a face where the eye has been taken out. There
must have been a chandelier, once. They've removed anything
you could tie a rope to.

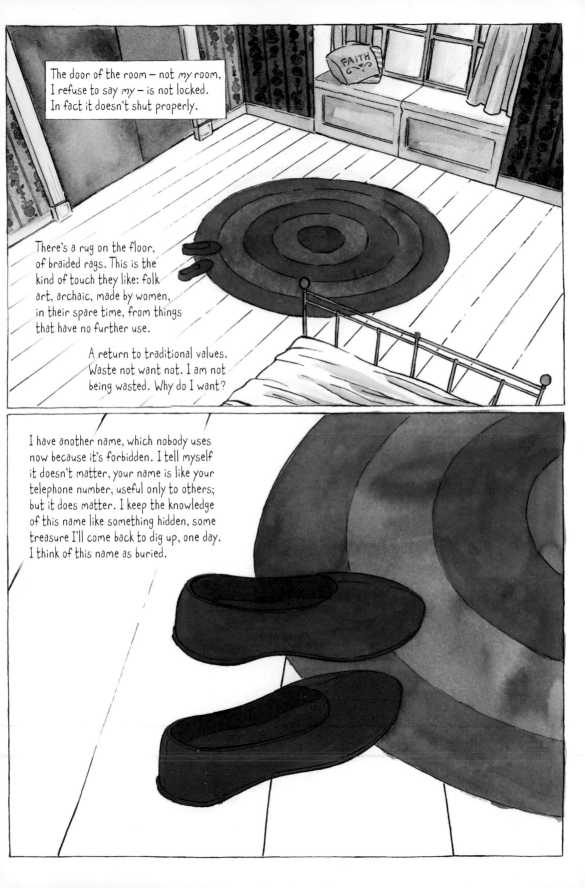

The door of the room — not *my* room, I refuse to say *my* — is not locked. In fact it doesn't shut properly.

There's a rug on the floor, of braided rags. This is the kind of touch they like: folk art, archaic, made by women, in their spare time, from things that have no further use.

A return to traditional values. Waste not want not. I am not being wasted. Why do I want?

I have another name, which nobody uses now because it's forbidden. I tell myself it doesn't matter, your name is like your telephone number, useful only to others; but it does matter. I keep the knowledge of this name like something hidden, some treasure I'll come back to dig up, one day. I think of this name as buried.

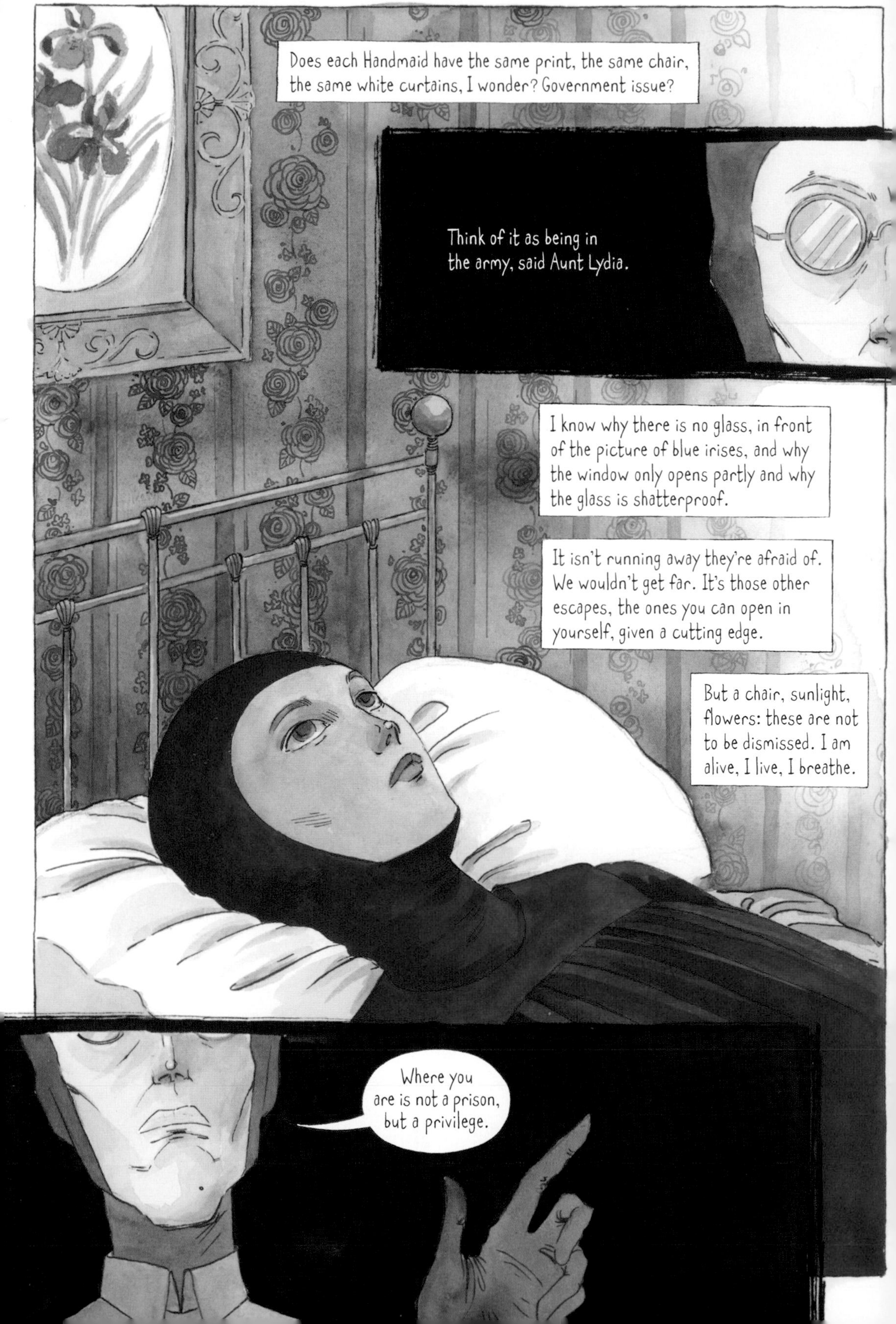
Does each Handmaid have the same print, the same chair, the same white curtains, I wonder? Government issue?
Think of it as being in the army, said Aunt Lydia.
I know why there is no glass, in front of the picture of blue irises, and why the window only opens partly and why the glass is shatterproof.
It isn't running away they're afraid of. We wouldn't get far. It's those other escapes, the ones you can open in yourself, given a cutting edge.
But a chair, sunlight, flowers: these are not to be dismissed. I am alive, I live, I breathe.
Where you are is not a prison, but a privilege.

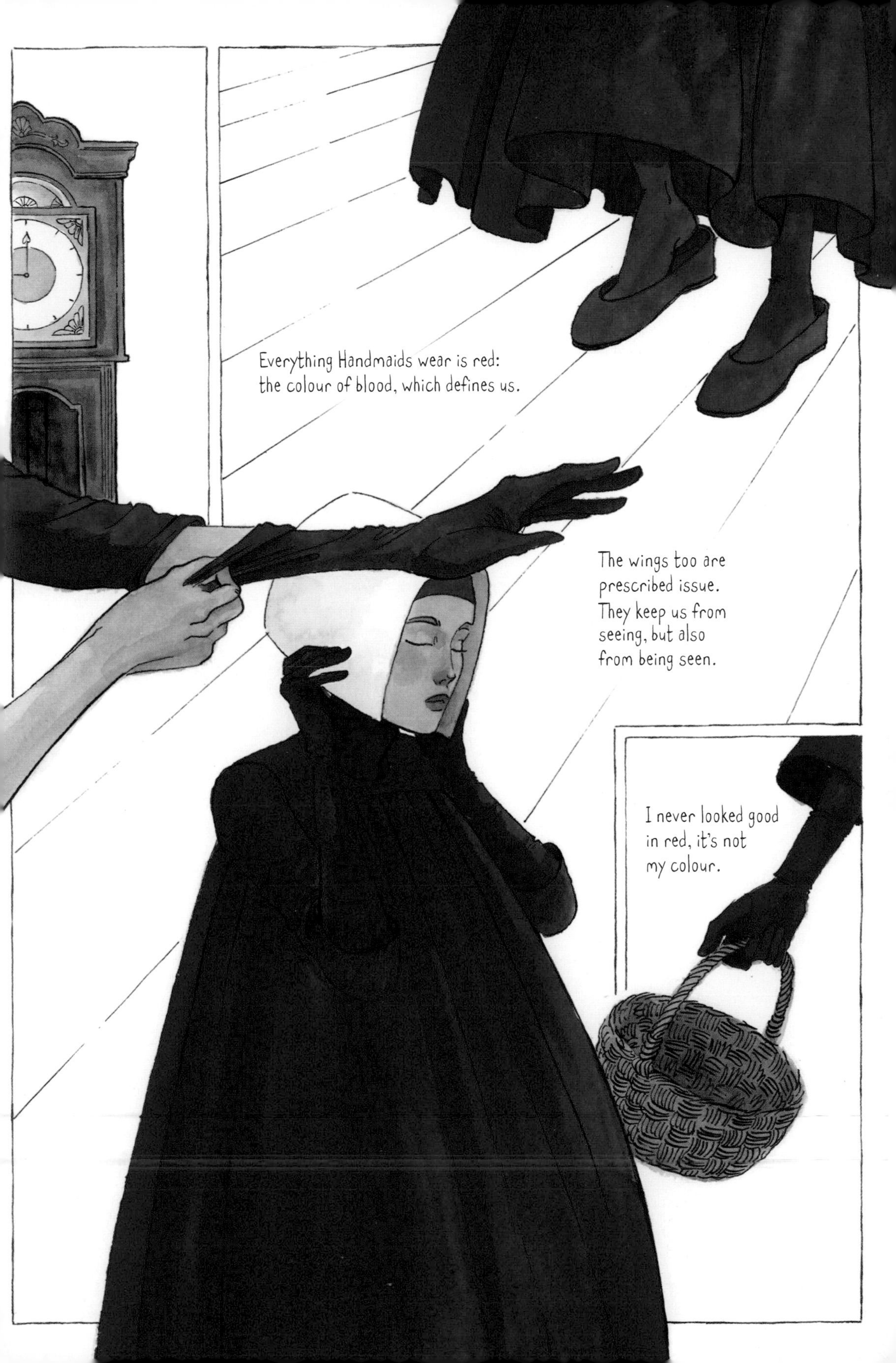
Everything Handmaids wear is red:
the colour of blood, which defines us.
The wings too are
prescribed issue.
They keep us from
seeing, but also
from being seen.
I never looked good
in red, it's not
my colour.

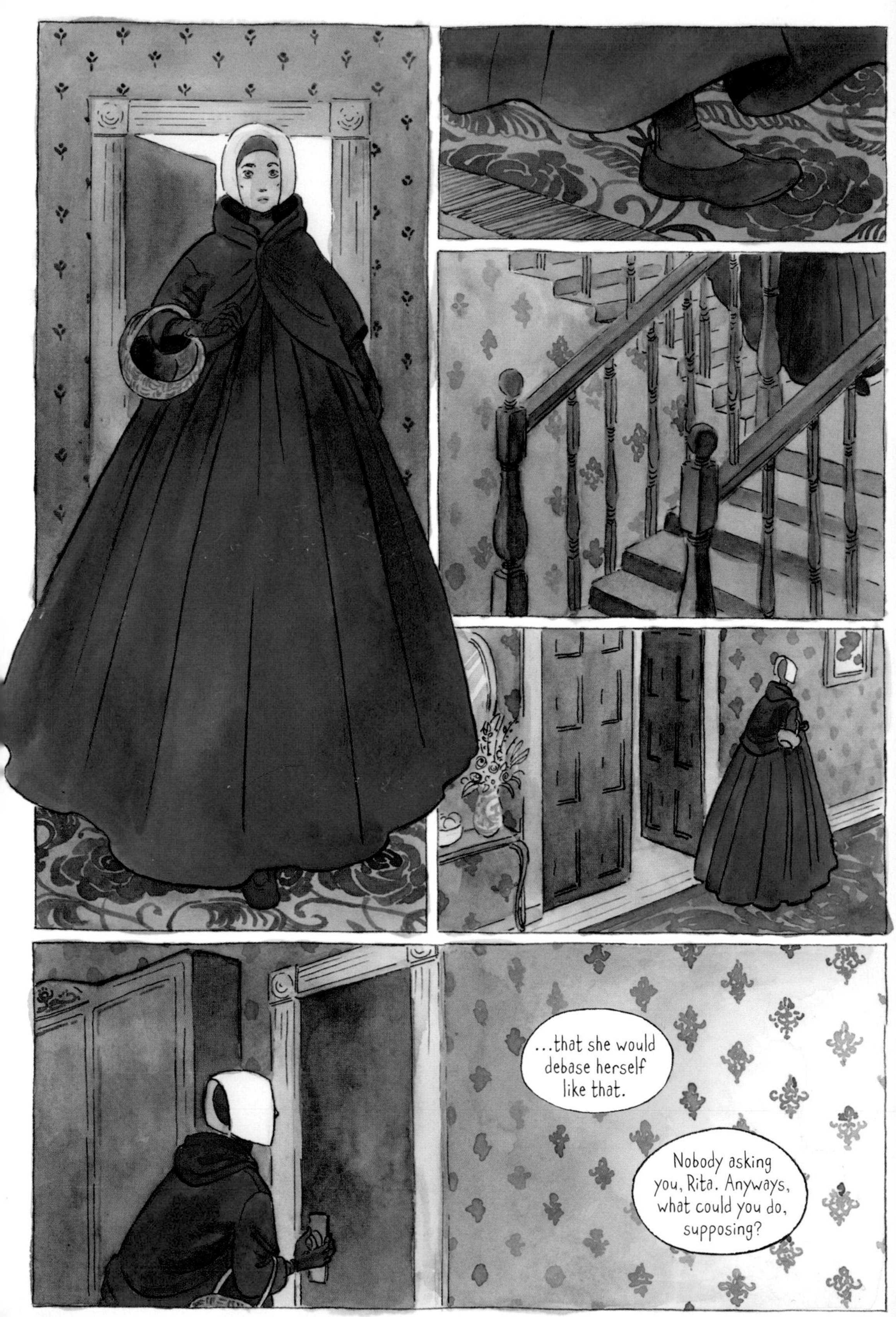
...that she would debase herself like that.
Nobody asking you, Rita. Anyways, what could you do, supposing?

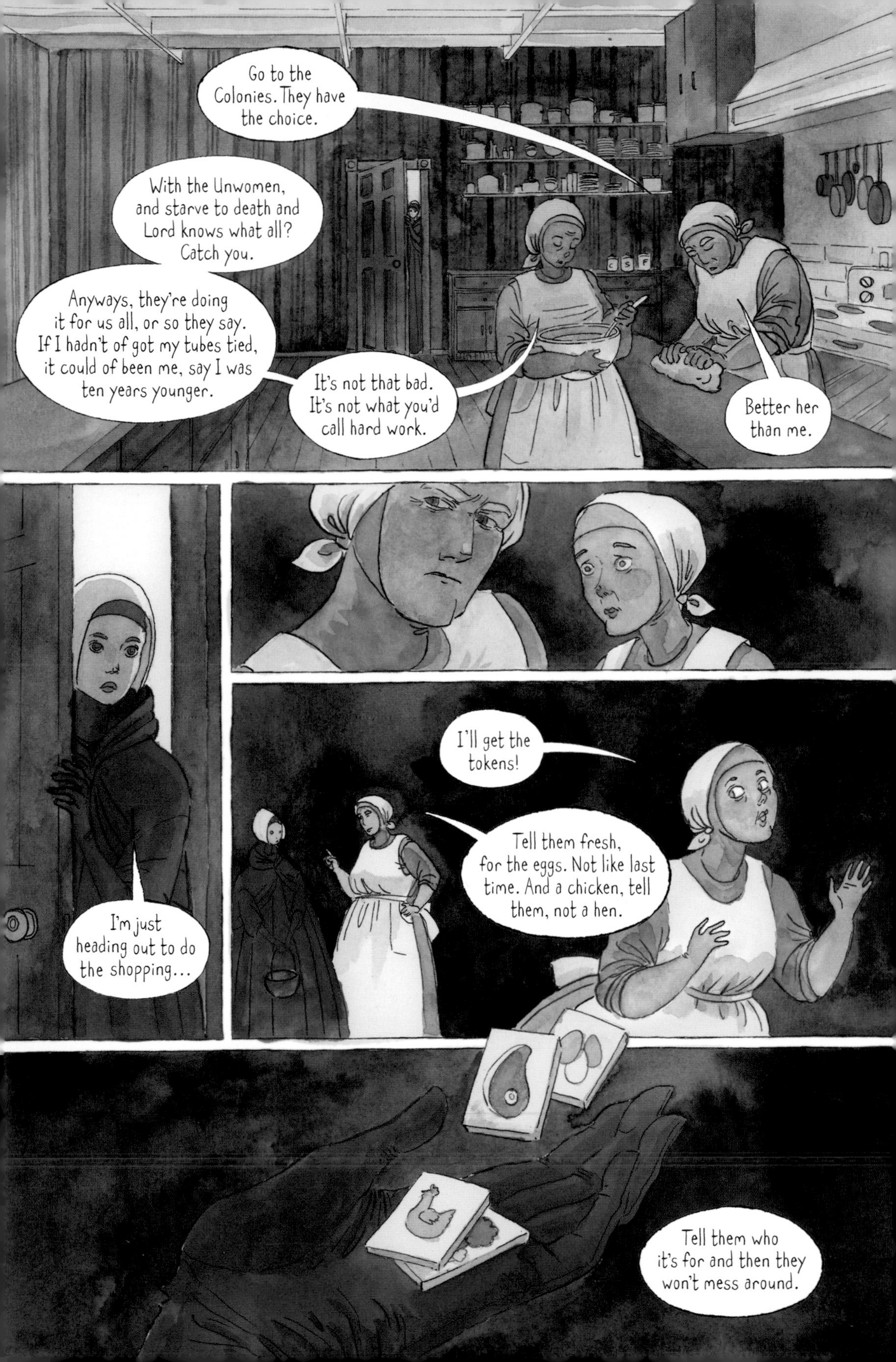
Go to the Colonies. They have the choice.
With the Unwomen, and starve to death and Lord knows what all? Catch you.
Anyways, they're doing it for us all, or so they say. If I hadn't of got my tubes tied, it could of been me, say I was ten years younger.
It's not that bad. It's not what you'd call hard work.
Better her than me.
I'm just heading out to do the shopping...
I'll get the tokens!
Tell them fresh, for the eggs. Not like last time. And a chicken, tell them, not a hen.
Tell them who it's for and then they won't mess around.

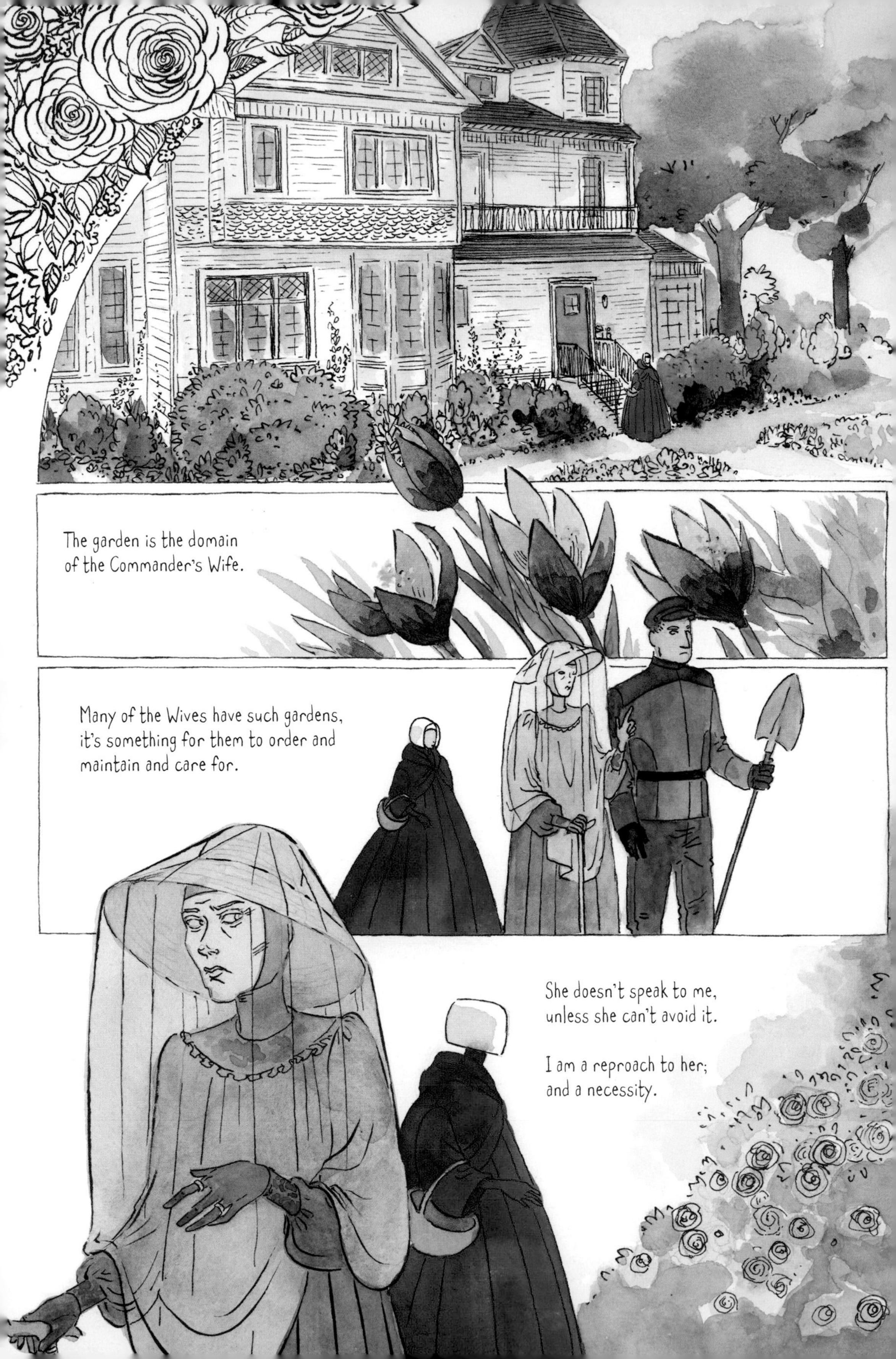
The garden is the domain of the Commander's Wife.
Many of the Wives have such gardens, it's something for them to order and maintain and care for.
She doesn't speak to me, unless she can't avoid it.
I am a reproach to her; and a necessity.

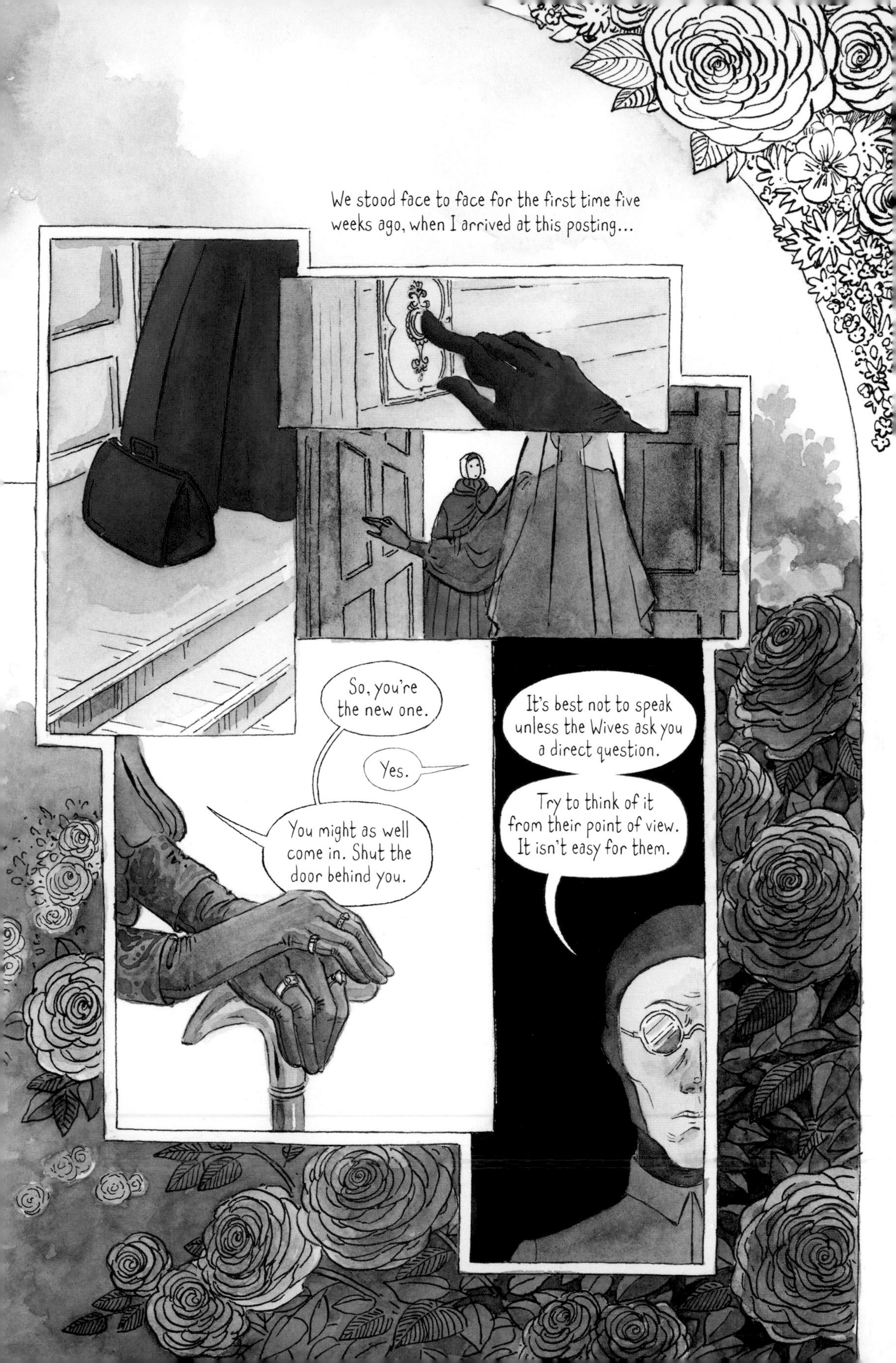
We stood face to face for the first time five weeks ago, when I arrived at this posting...
So, you're the new one.
Yes.
You might as well come in. Shut the door behind you.
It's best not to speak unless the Wives ask you a direct question.
Try to think of it from their point of view. It isn't easy for them.

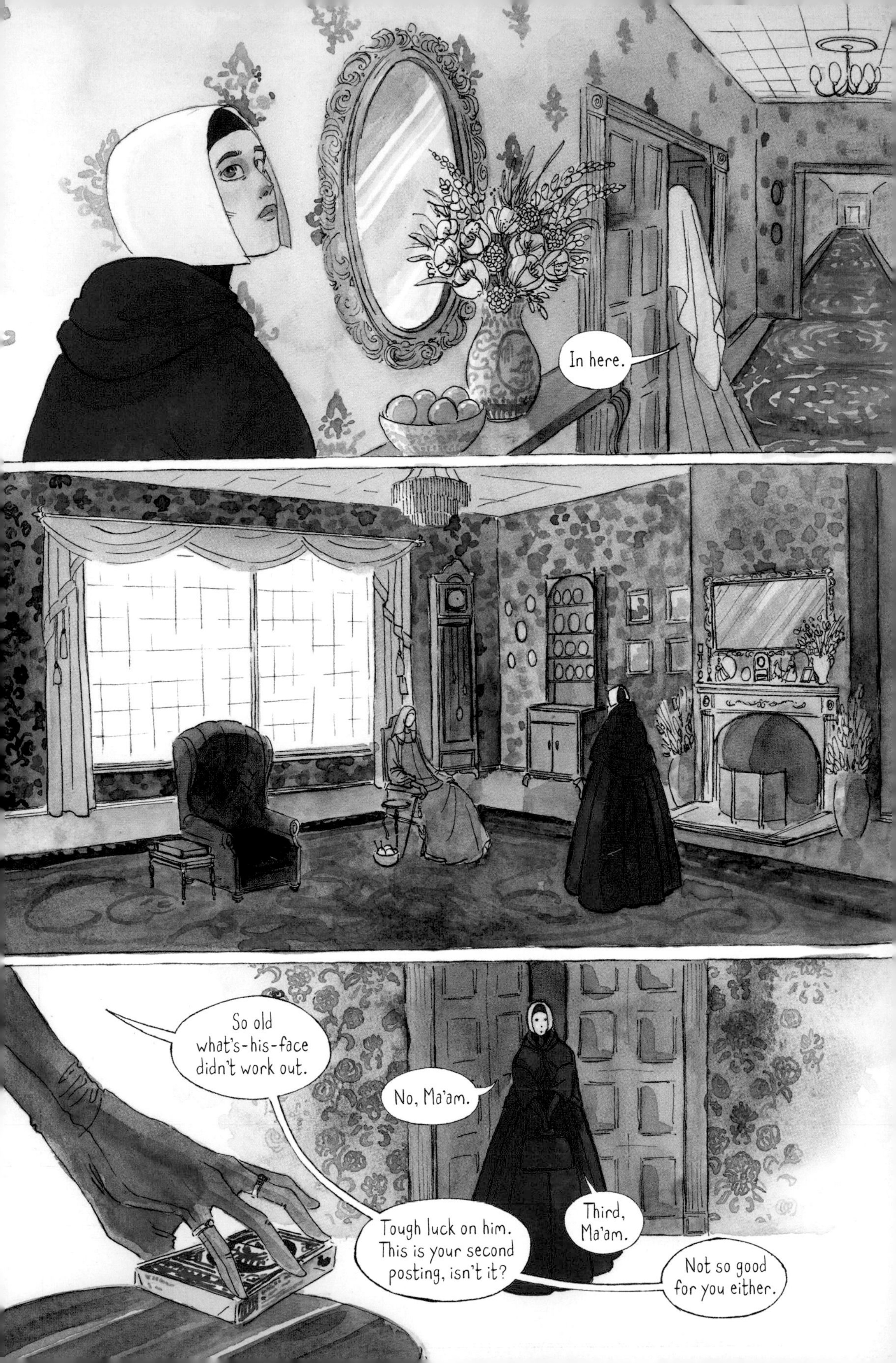
In here.
So old what's-his-face didn't work out.
No, Ma'am.
Tough luck on him. This is your second posting, isn't it?
Third, Ma'am.
Not so good for you either.

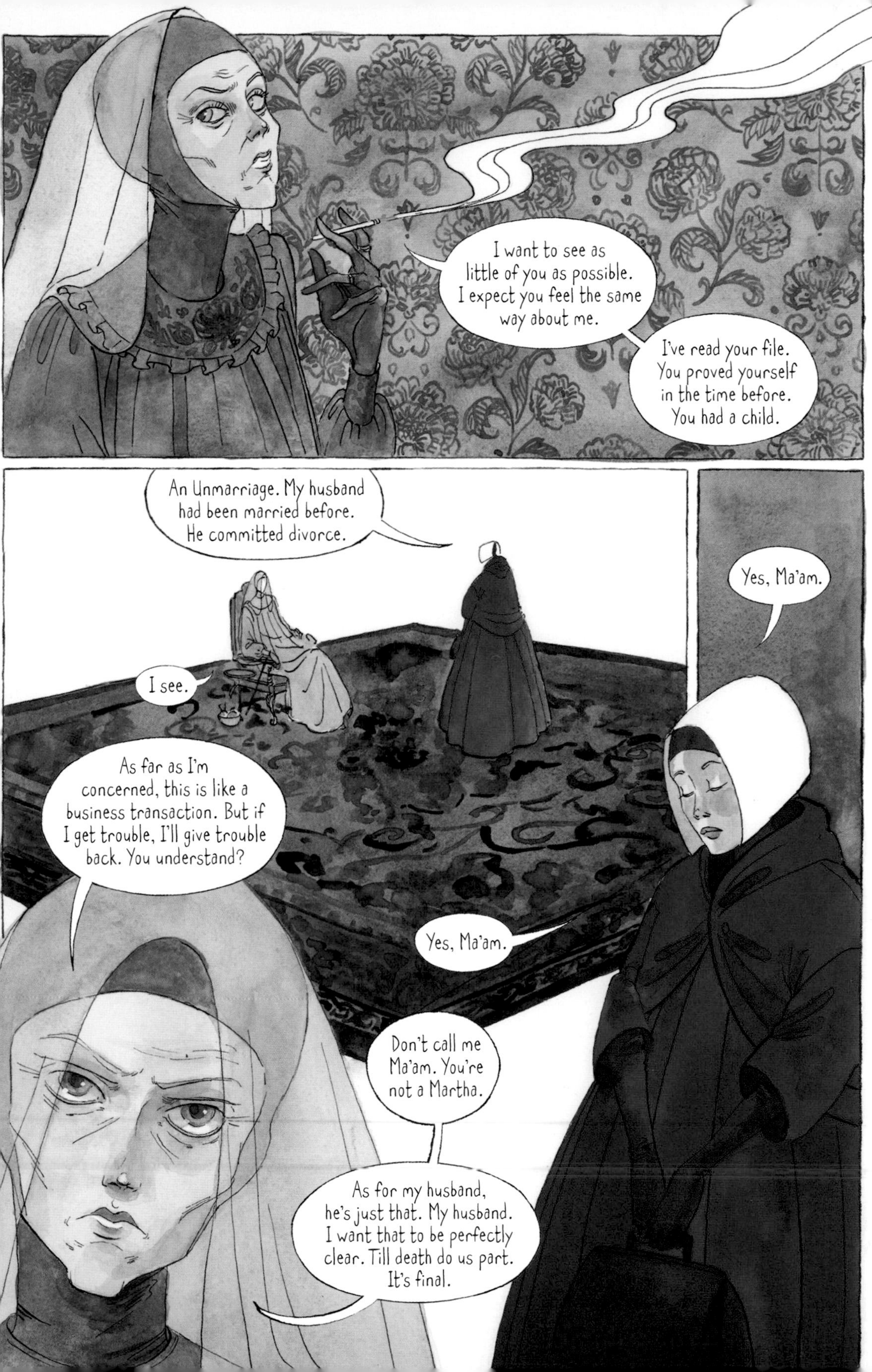

I want to see as little of you as possible. I expect you feel the same way about me.
I've read your file. You proved yourself in the time before. You had a child.
An Unmarriage. My husband had been married before. He committed divorce.
I see.
Yes, Ma'am.
As far as I'm concerned, this is like a business transaction. But if I get trouble, I'll give trouble back. You understand?
Yes, Ma'am.
Don't call me Ma'am. You're not a Martha.
As for my husband, he's just that. My husband. I want that to be perfectly clear. Till death do us part. It's final.

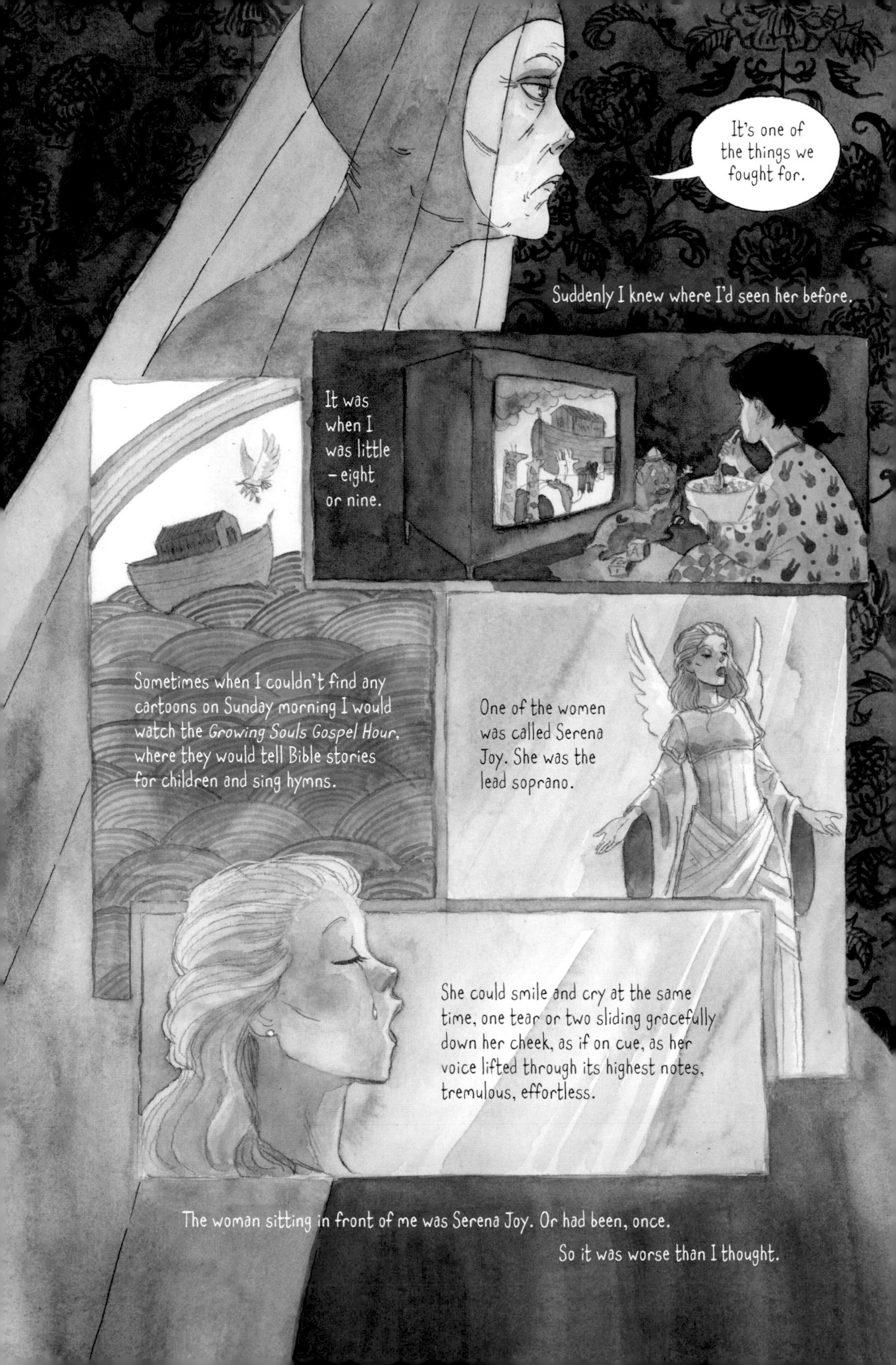
It's one of the things we fought for.
Suddenly I knew where I'd seen her before.
It was when I was little – eight or nine.
Sometimes when I couldn't find any cartoons on Sunday morning I would watch the *Growing Souls Gospel Hour*, where they would tell Bible stories for children and sing hymns.
One of the women was called Serena Joy. She was the lead soprano.
She could smile and cry at the same time, one tear or two sliding gracefully down her cheek, as if on cue, as her voice lifted through its highest notes, tremulous, effortless.
The woman sitting in front of me was Serena Joy. Or had been, once.
So it was worse than I thought.

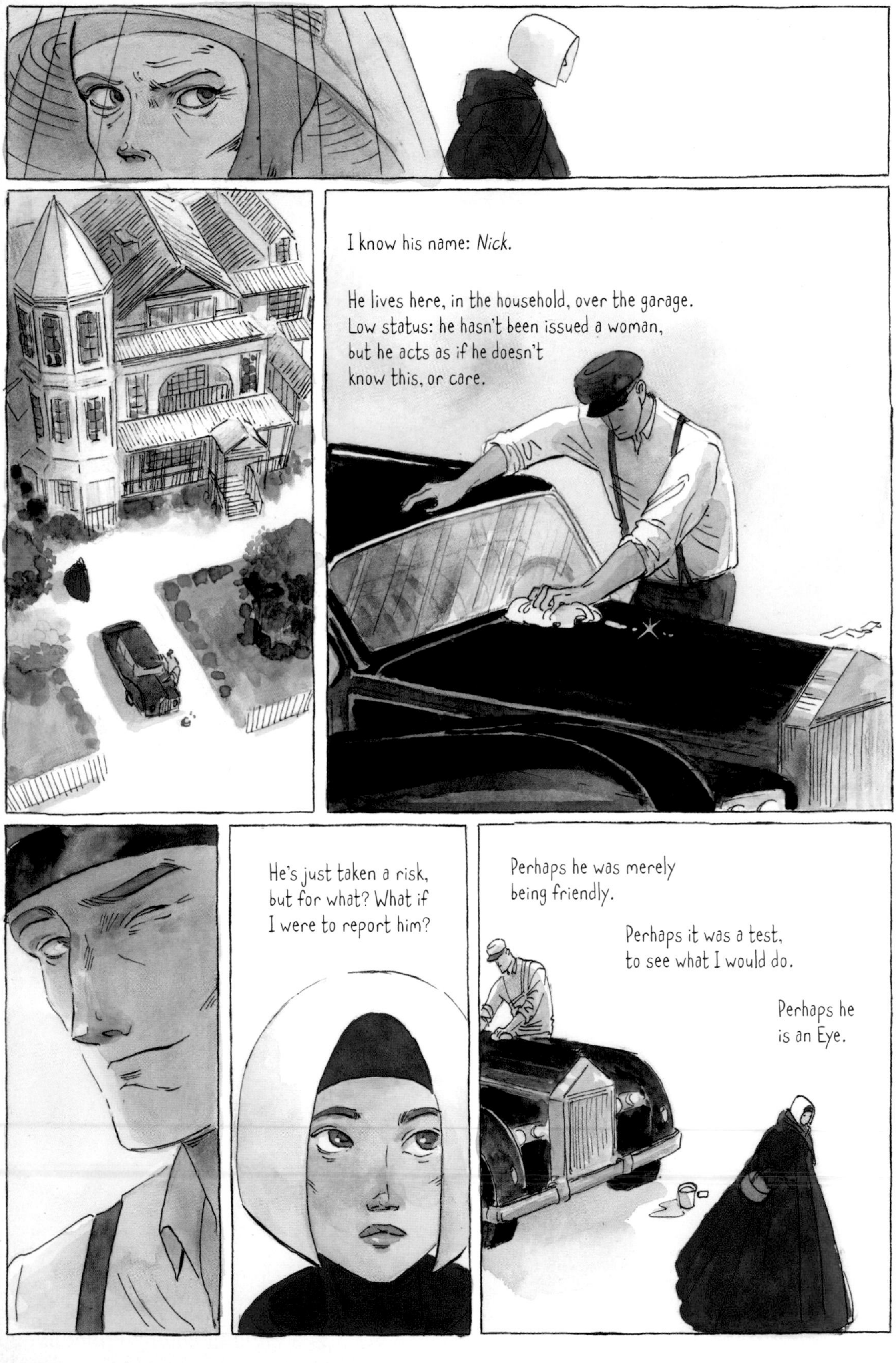
I know his name: *Nick.*
He lives here, in the household, over the garage.
Low status: he hasn't been issued a woman,
but he acts as if he doesn't
know this, or care.
He's just taken a risk,
but for what? What if
I were to report him?
Perhaps he was merely
being friendly.
Perhaps it was a test,
to see what I would do.
Perhaps he
is an Eye.

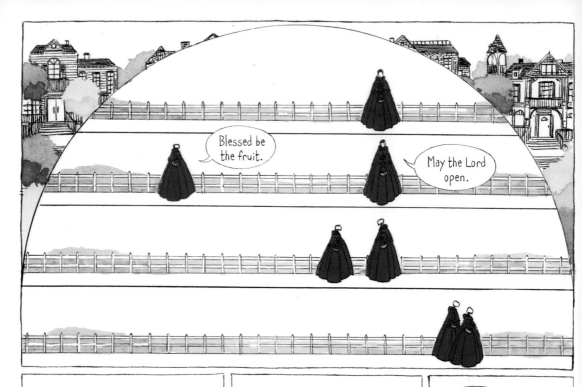

Blessed be the fruit.

May the Lord open.

We aren't allowed to go out except in twos. This is supposed to be for our protection.

The truth is that she is my spy, as I am hers.

This woman has been my partner for two weeks. I don't know what happened to the one before. Her name is Ofglen, and that's all I know about her.

The war is going well, I hear.

Praise be.

We've been sent good weather.

I think of her as a woman for whom every act is done for show. She does such things to look good.

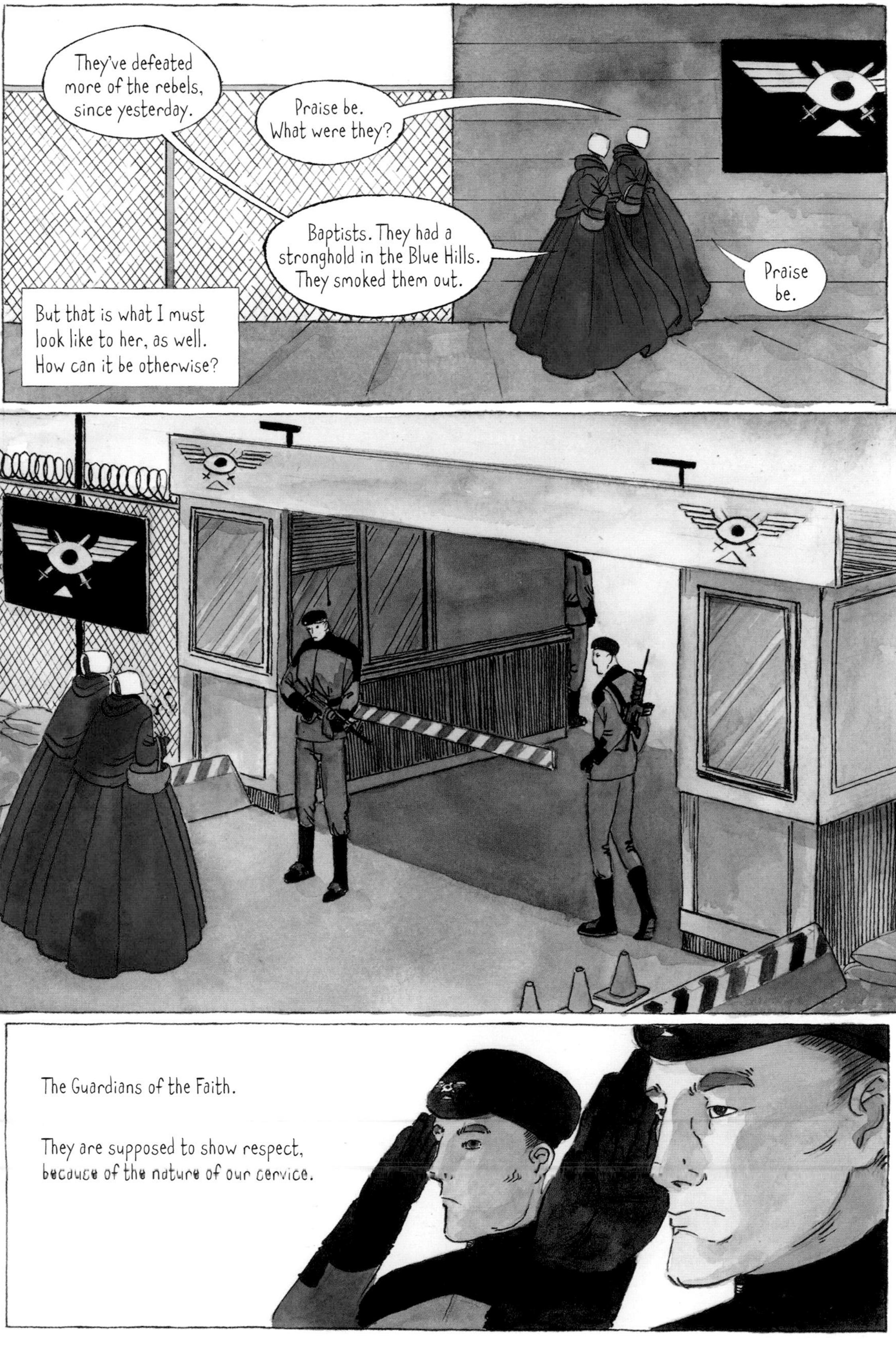
They've defeated more of the rebels, since yesterday.
Praise be. What were they?
Baptists. They had a stronghold in the Blue Hills. They smoked them out.
Praise be.
But that is what I must look like to her, as well. How can it be otherwise?
The Guardians of the Faith.
They are supposed to show respect, because of the nature of our service.

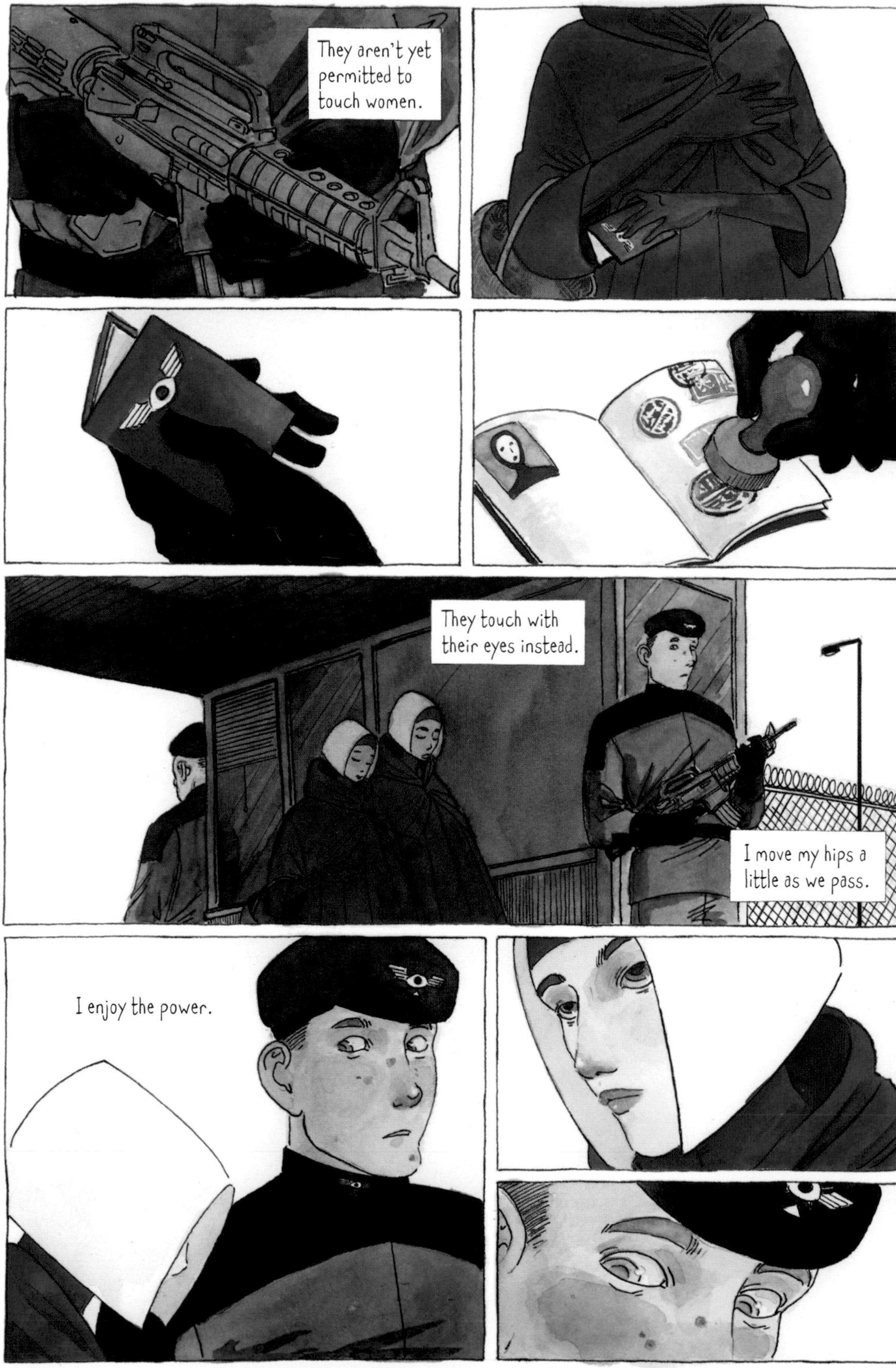
They aren't yet permitted to touch women.
They touch with their eyes instead.
I move my hips a little as we pass.
I enjoy the power.

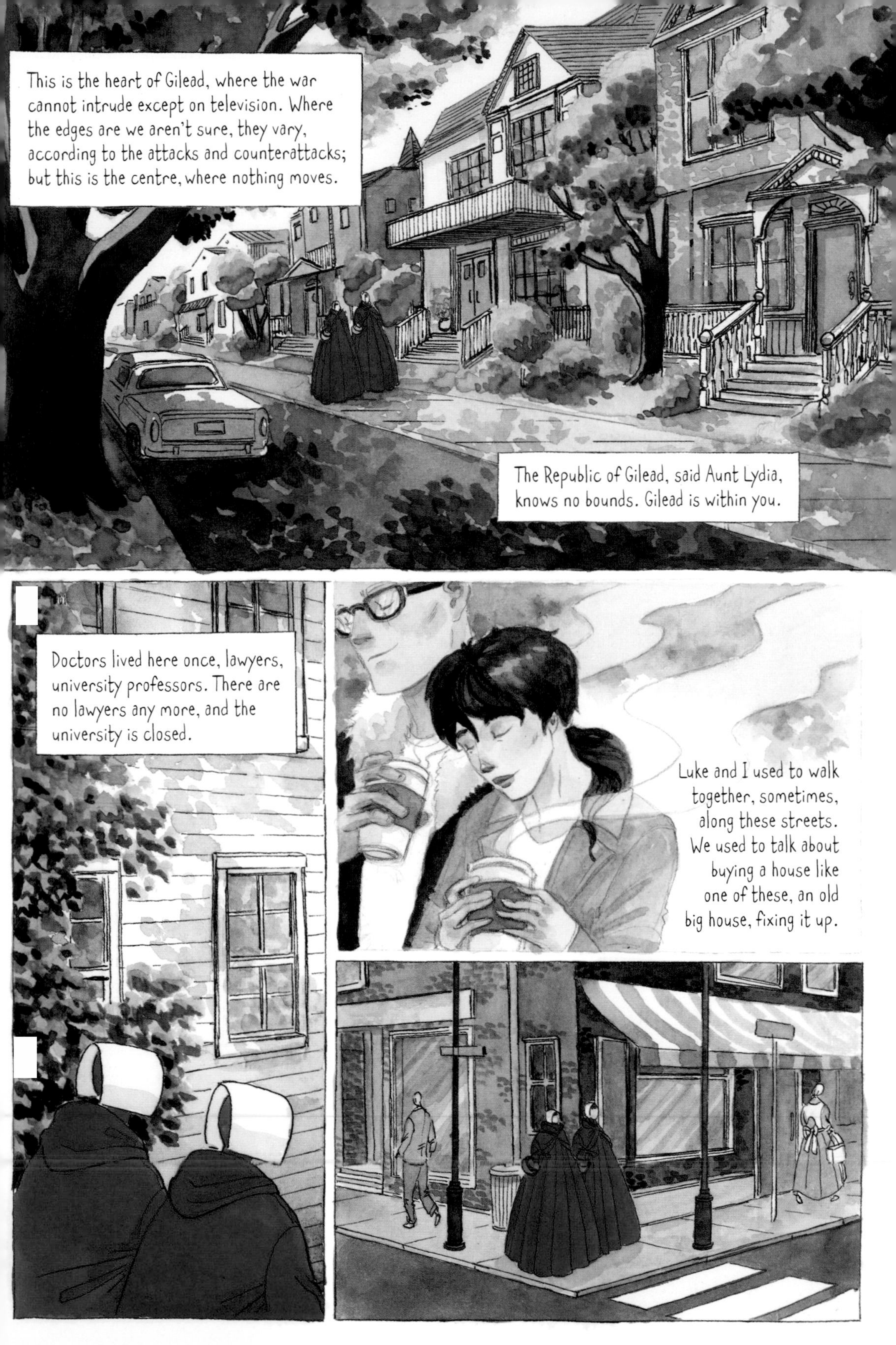
This is the heart of Gilead, where the war cannot intrude except on television. Where the edges are we aren't sure, they vary, according to the attacks and counterattacks; but this is the centre, where nothing moves.
The Republic of Gilead, said Aunt Lydia, knows no bounds. Gilead is within you.
Doctors lived here once, lawyers, university professors. There are no lawyers any more, and the university is closed.
Luke and I used to walk together, sometimes, along these streets. We used to talk about buying a house like one of these, an old big house, fixing it up.

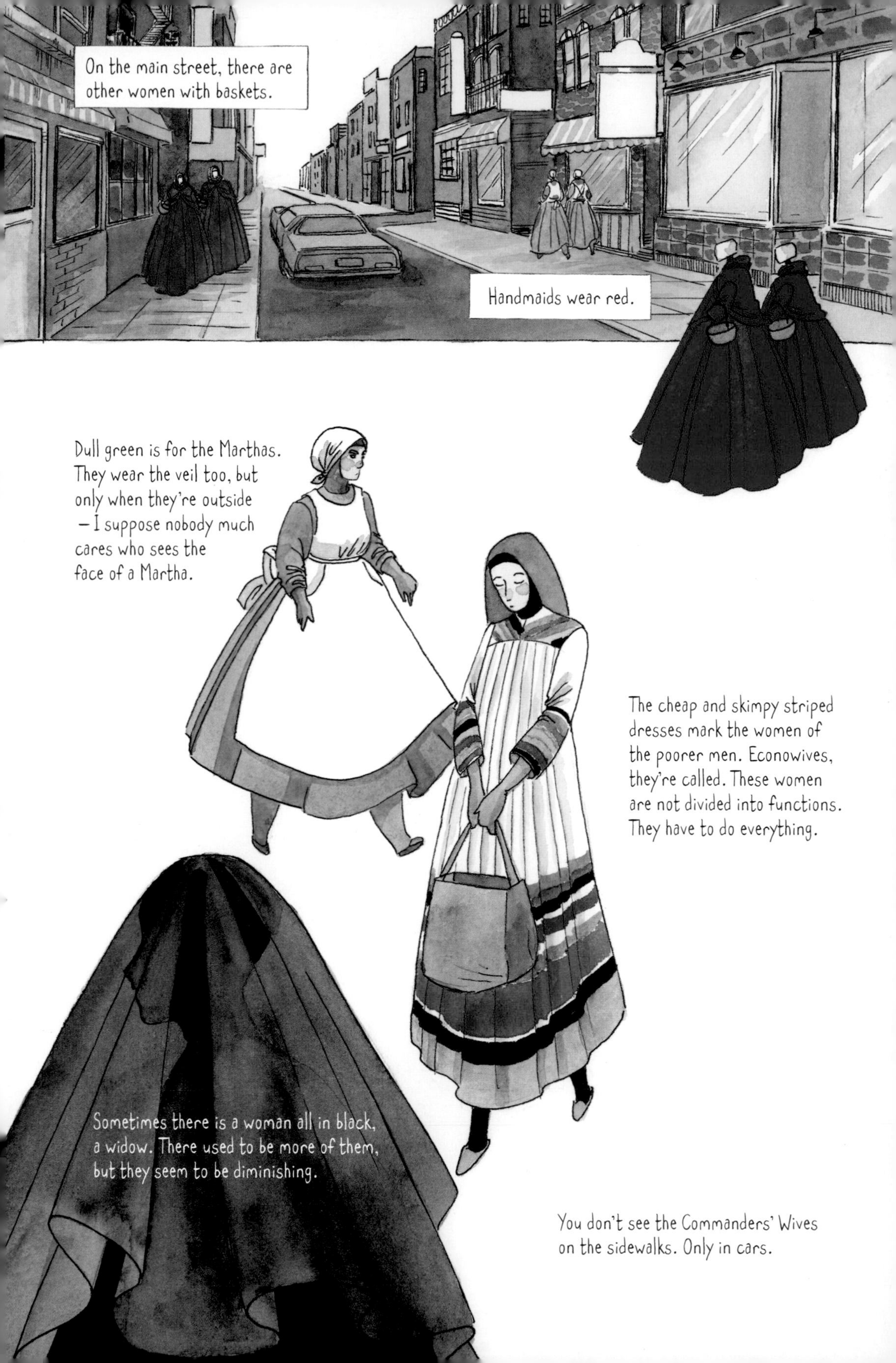
On the main street, there are other women with baskets.
Handmaids wear red.
Dull green is for the Marthas. They wear the veil too, but only when they're outside —I suppose nobody much cares who sees the face of a Martha.
The cheap and skimpy striped dresses mark the women of the poorer men. Econowives, they're called. These women are not divided into functions. They have to do everything.
Sometimes there is a woman all in black, a widow. There used to be more of them, but they seem to be diminishing.
You don't see the Commanders' Wives on the sidewalks. Only in cars.

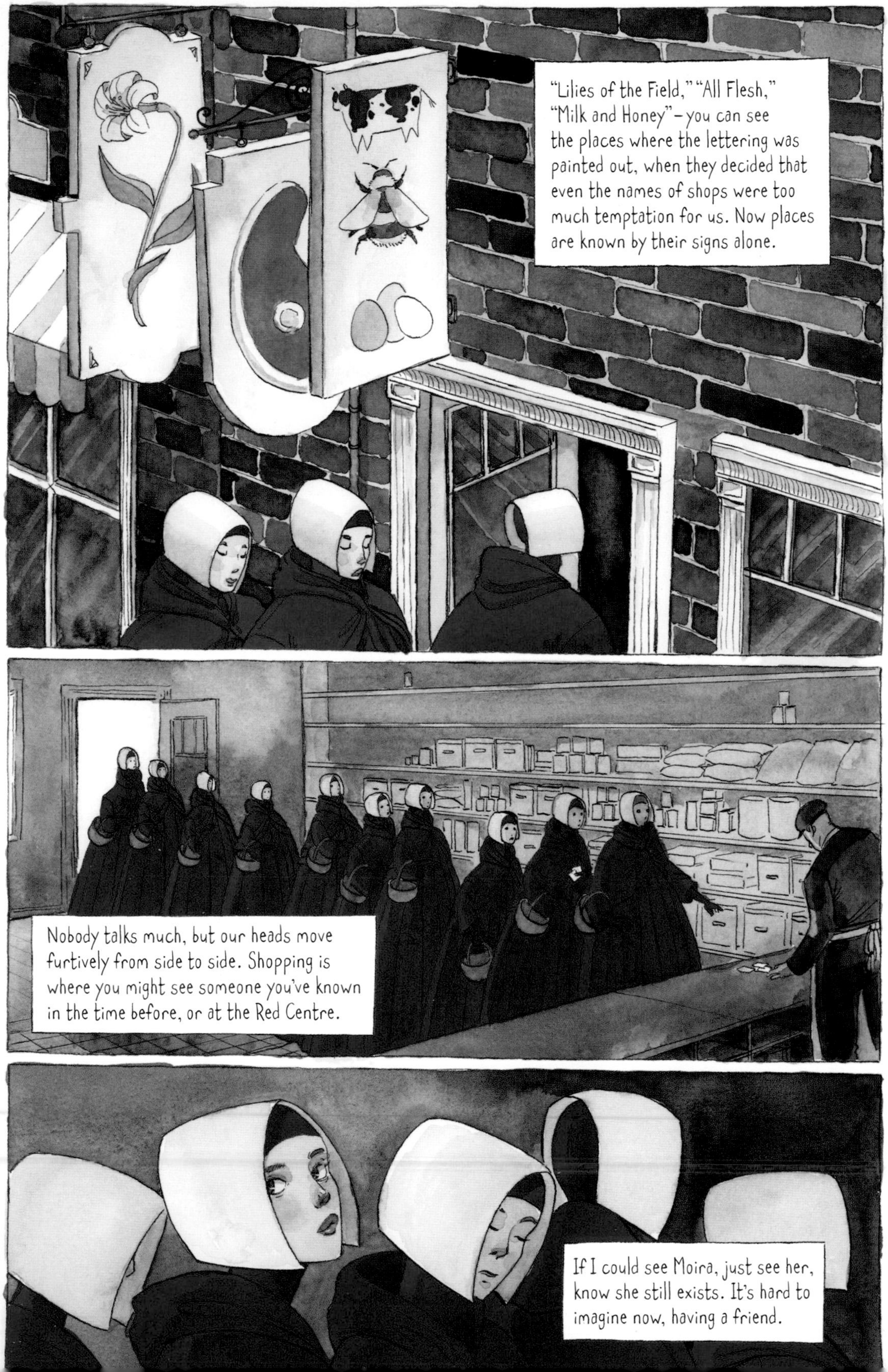
"Lilies of the Field," "All Flesh," "Milk and Honey" – you can see the places where the lettering was painted out, when they decided that even the names of shops were too much temptation for us. Now places are known by their signs alone.
Nobody talks much, but our heads move furtively from side to side. Shopping is where you might see someone you've known in the time before, or at the Red Centre.
If I could see Moira, just see her, know she still exists. It's hard to imagine now, having a friend.

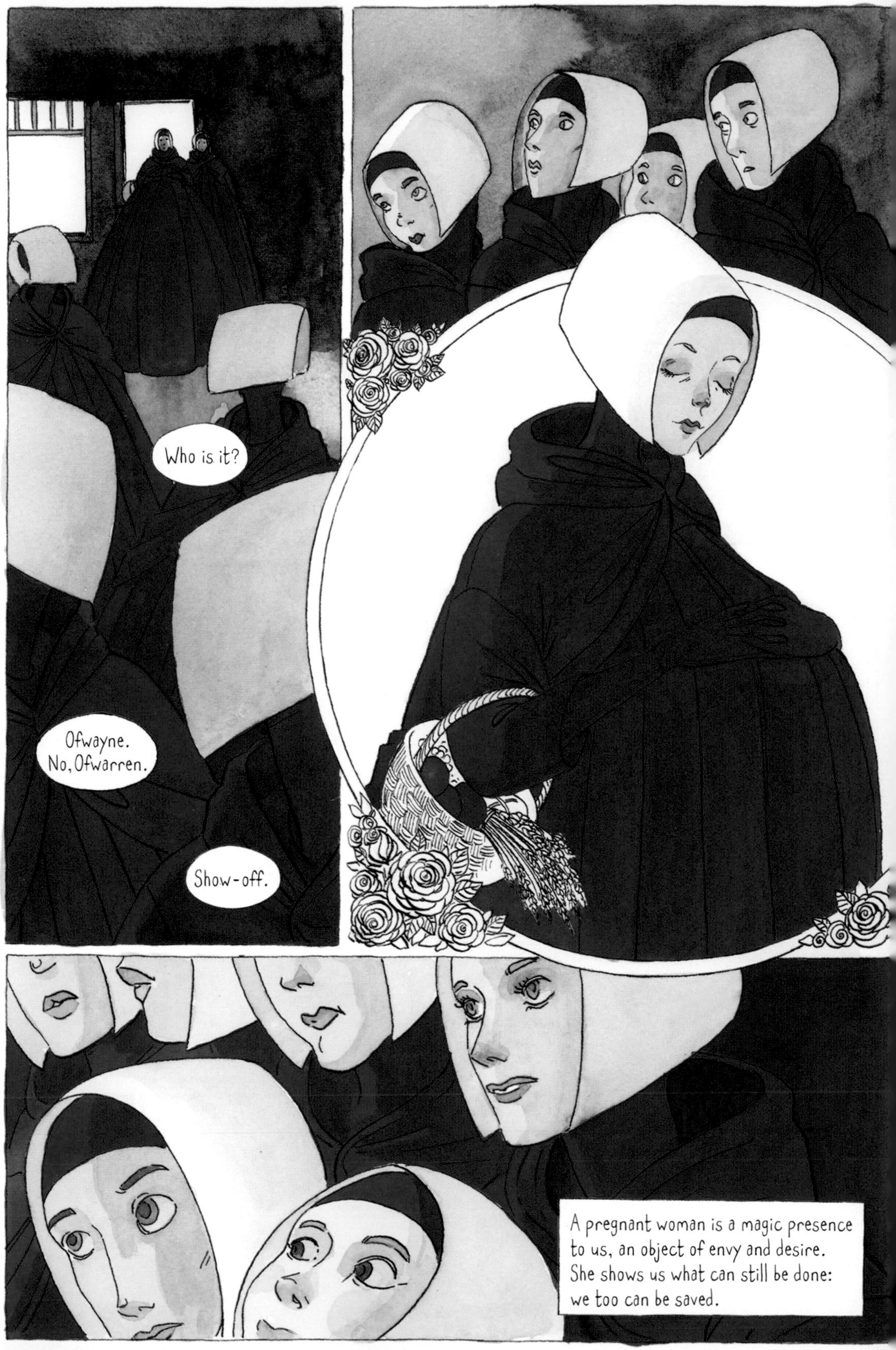

Who is it?
Ofwayne. No, Ofwarren.
Show-off.
A pregnant woman is a magic presence to us, an object of envy and desire. She shows us what can still be done: we too can be saved.

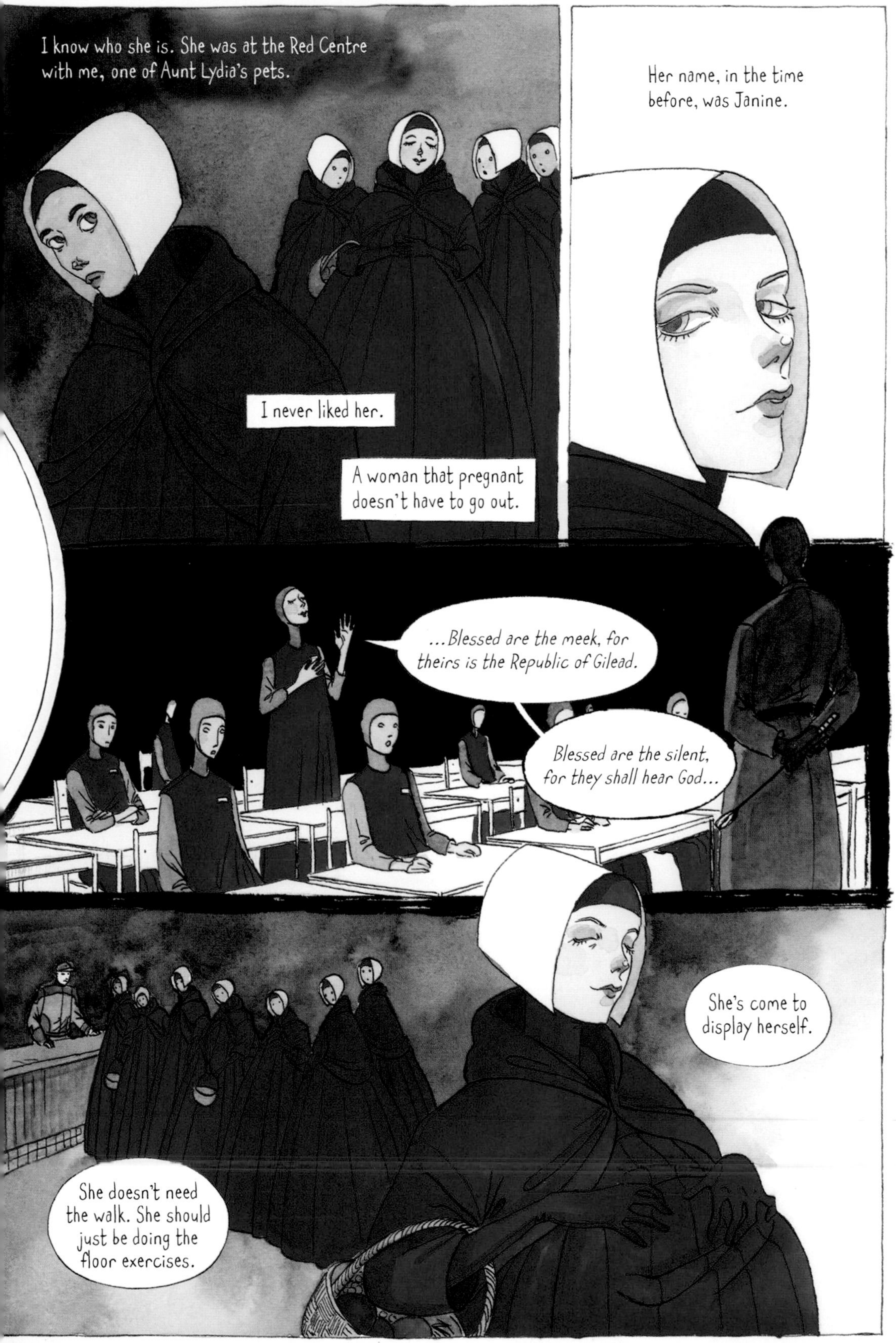
I know who she is. She was at the Red Centre with me, one of Aunt Lydia's pets.
Her name, in the time before, was Janine.
I never liked her.
A woman that pregnant doesn't have to go out.
...Blessed are the meek, for theirs is the Republic of Gilead.
Blessed are the silent, for they shall hear God...
She's come to display herself.
She doesn't need the walk. She should just be doing the floor exercises.

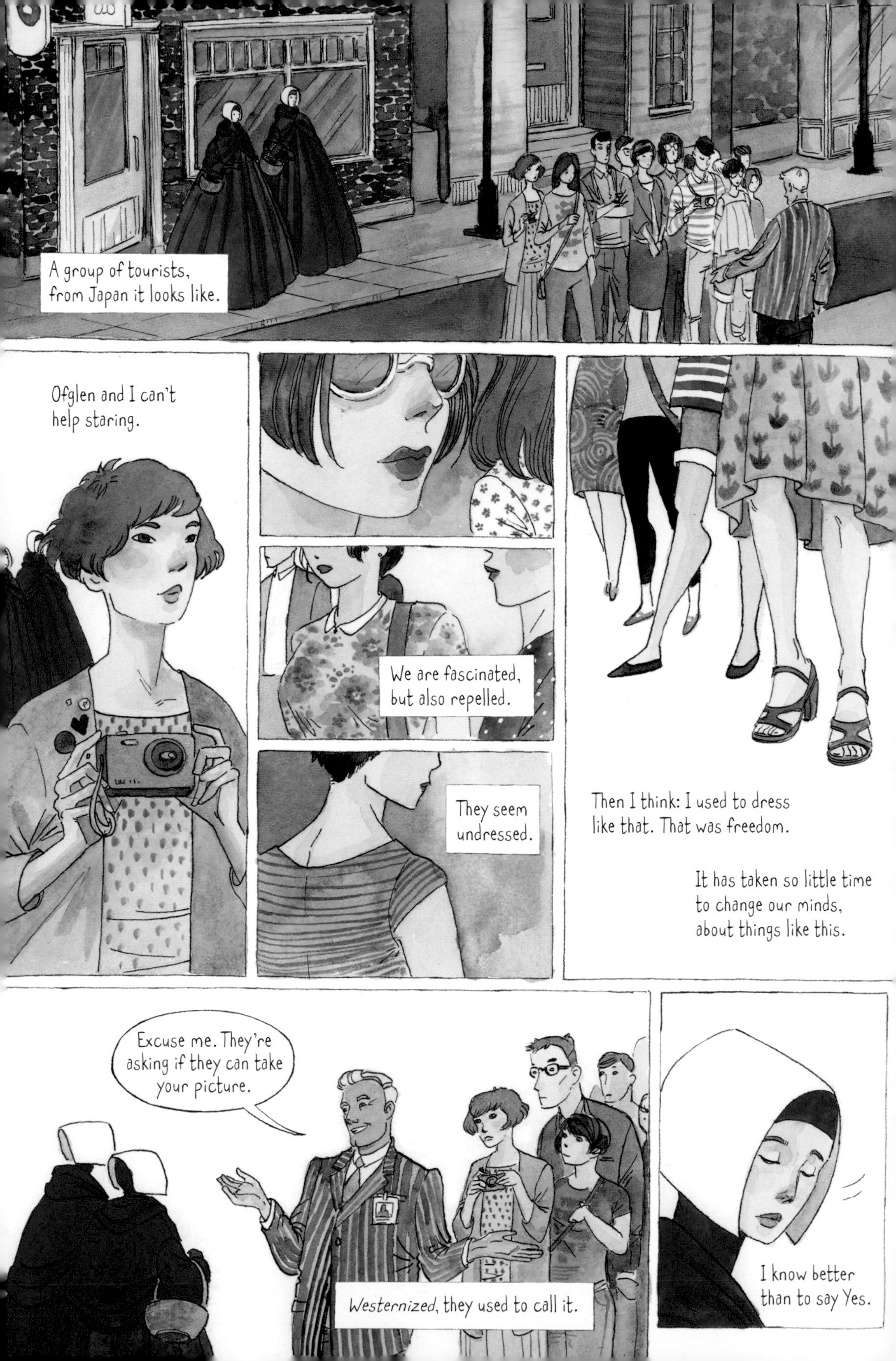
A group of tourists, from Japan it looks like.
Ofglen and I can't help staring.
We are fascinated, but also repelled.
They seem undressed.
Then I think: I used to dress like that. That was freedom.
It has taken so little time to change our minds, about things like this.
Excuse me. They're asking if they can take your picture.
Westernized, they used to call it.
I know better than to say Yes.

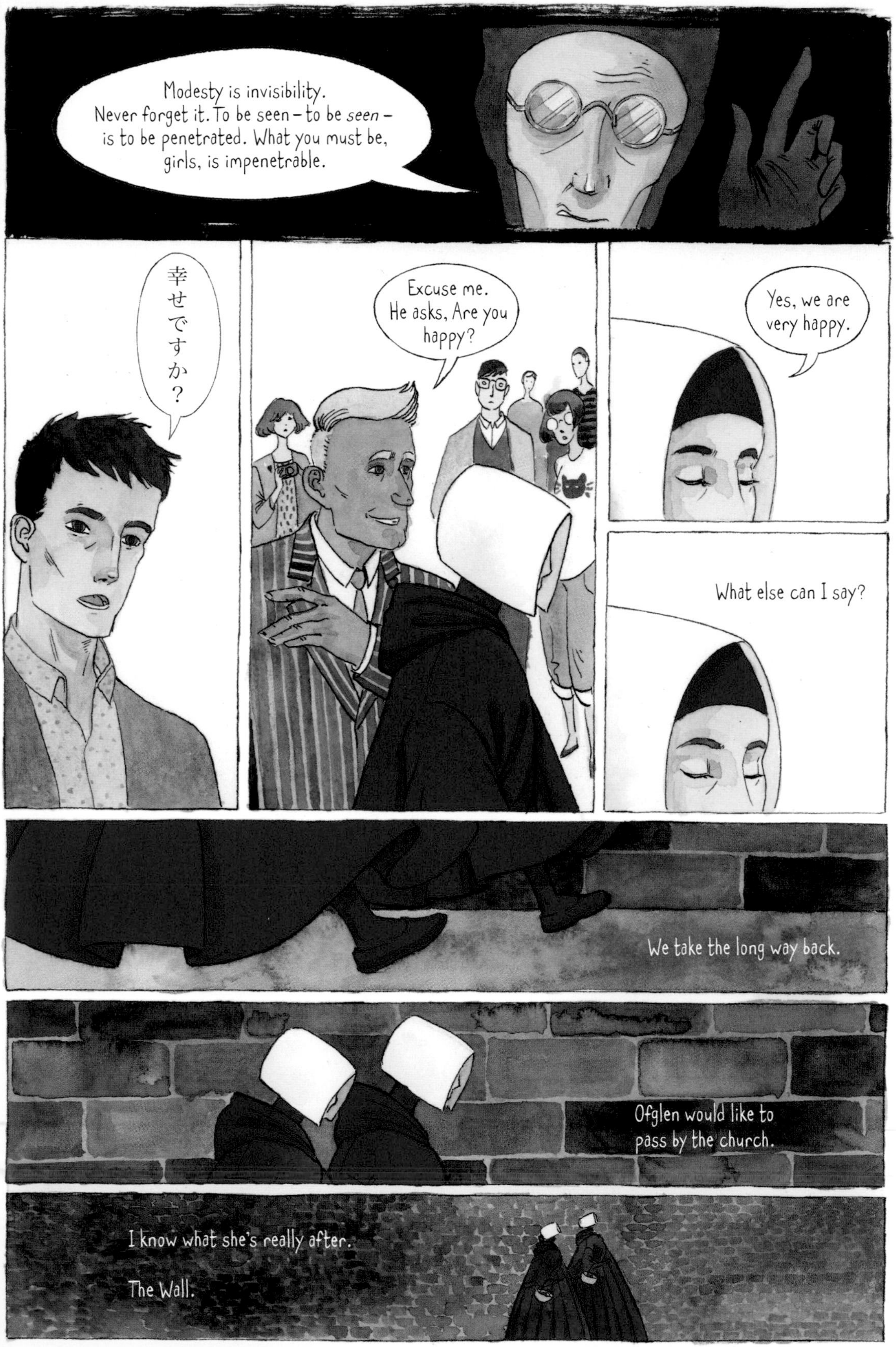
Modesty is invisibility. Never forget it. To be seen – to be *seen* – is to be penetrated. What you must be, girls, is impenetrable.
幸せですか？
Excuse me. He asks, Are you happy?
Yes, we are very happy.
What else can I say?
We take the long way back.
Ofglen would like to pass by the church.
I know what she's really after.
The Wall.

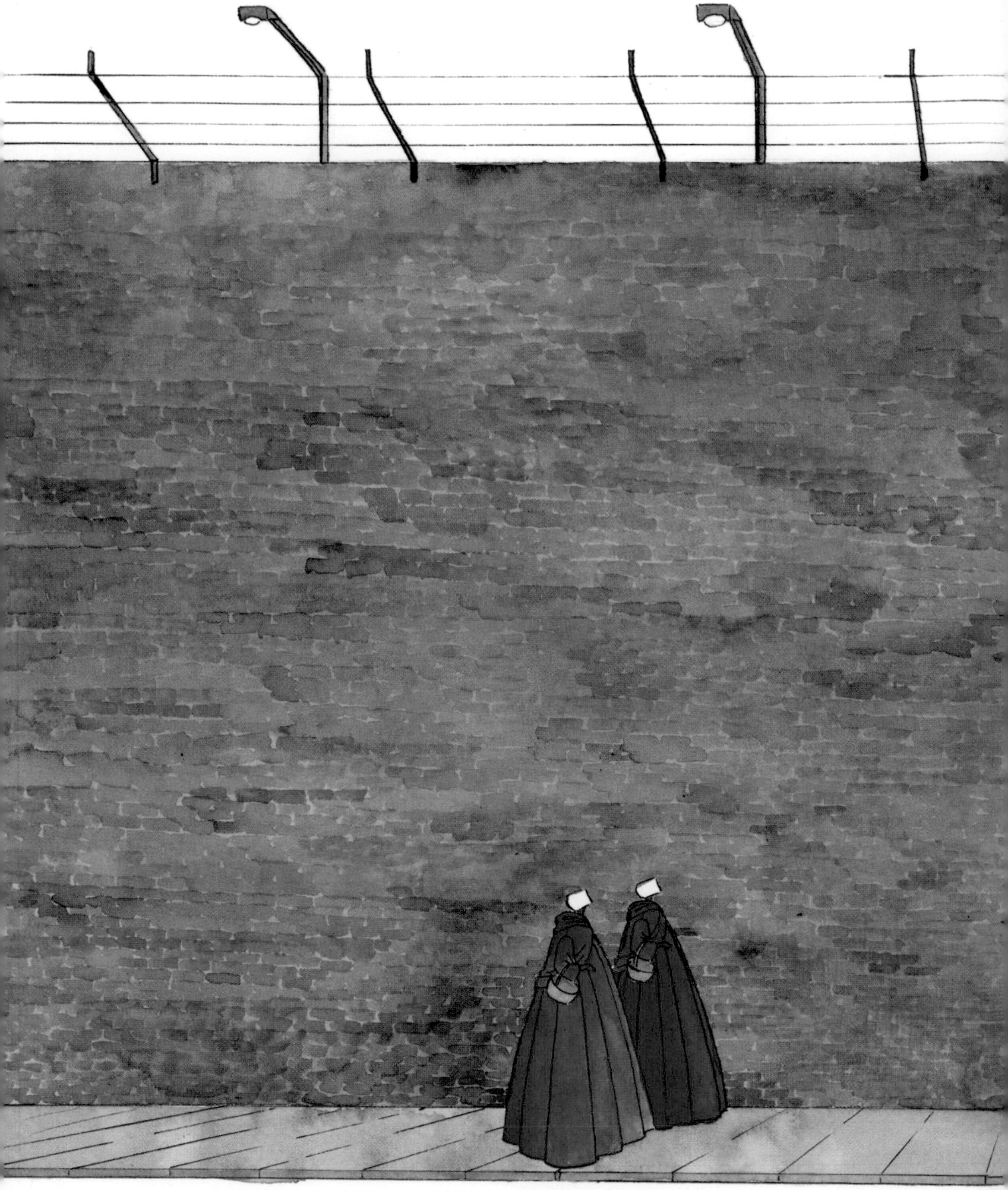

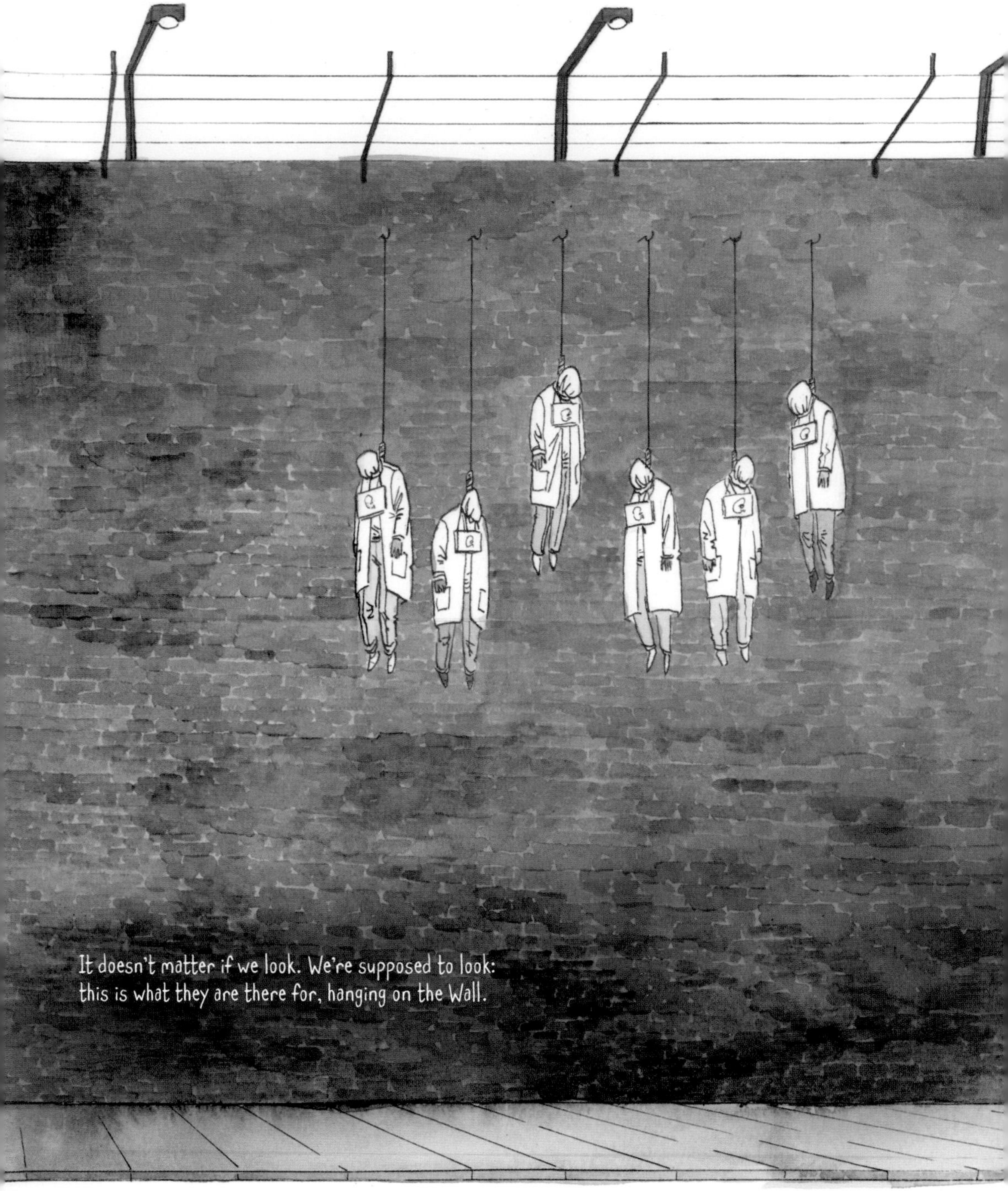
It doesn't matter if we look. We're supposed to look:
this is what they are there for, hanging on the Wall.

Sometimes they'll be there for days, until there's a new batch, so as many people as possible will have the chance to see them.

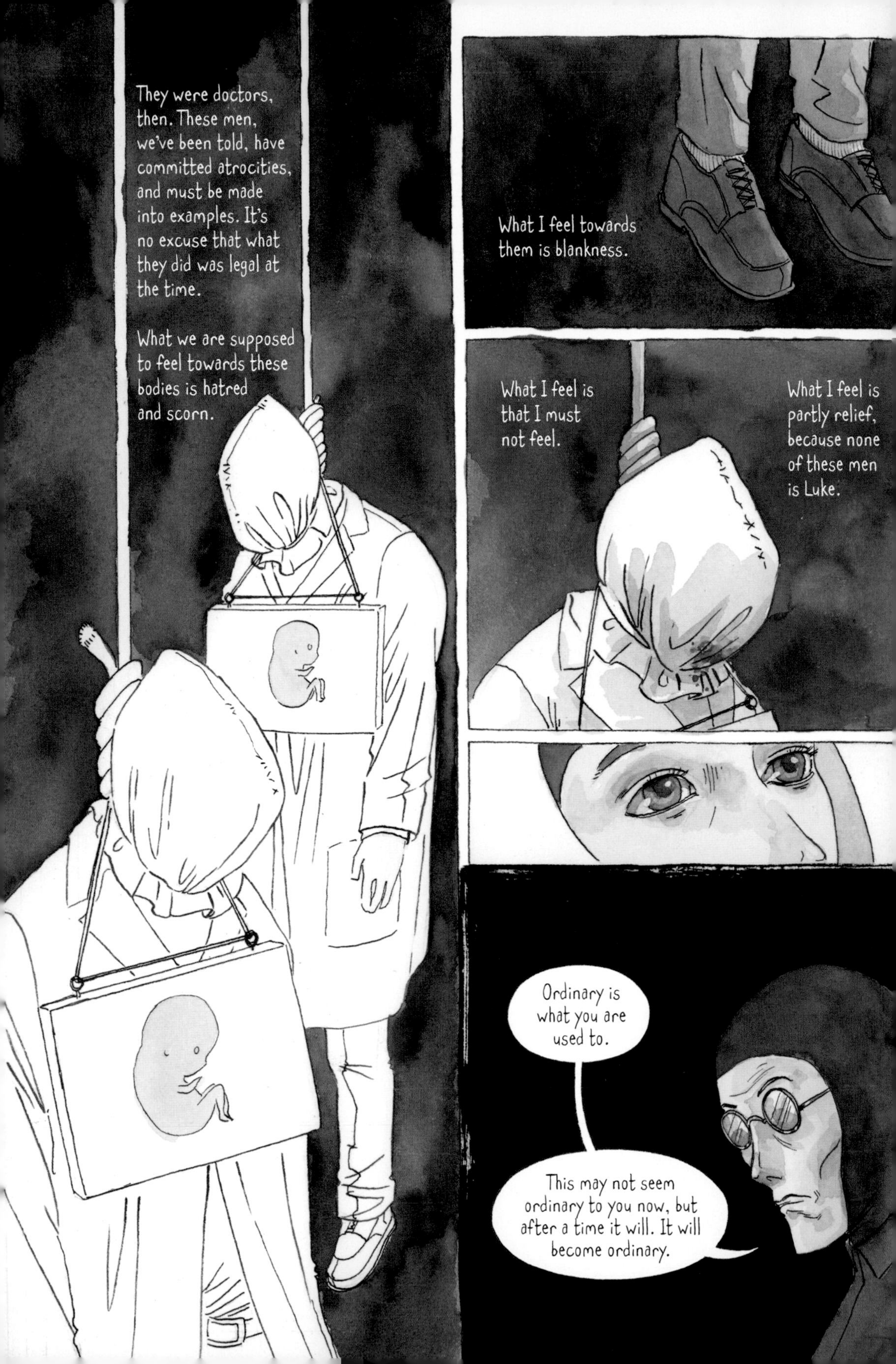

They were doctors, then. These men, we've been told, have committed atrocities, and must be made into examples. It's no excuse that what they did was legal at the time.
What we are supposed to feel towards these bodies is hatred and scorn.
What I feel towards them is blankness.
What I feel is that I must not feel.
What I feel is partly relief, because none of these men is Luke.
Ordinary is what you are used to.
This may not seem ordinary to you now, but after a time it will. It will become ordinary.

III

NIGHT

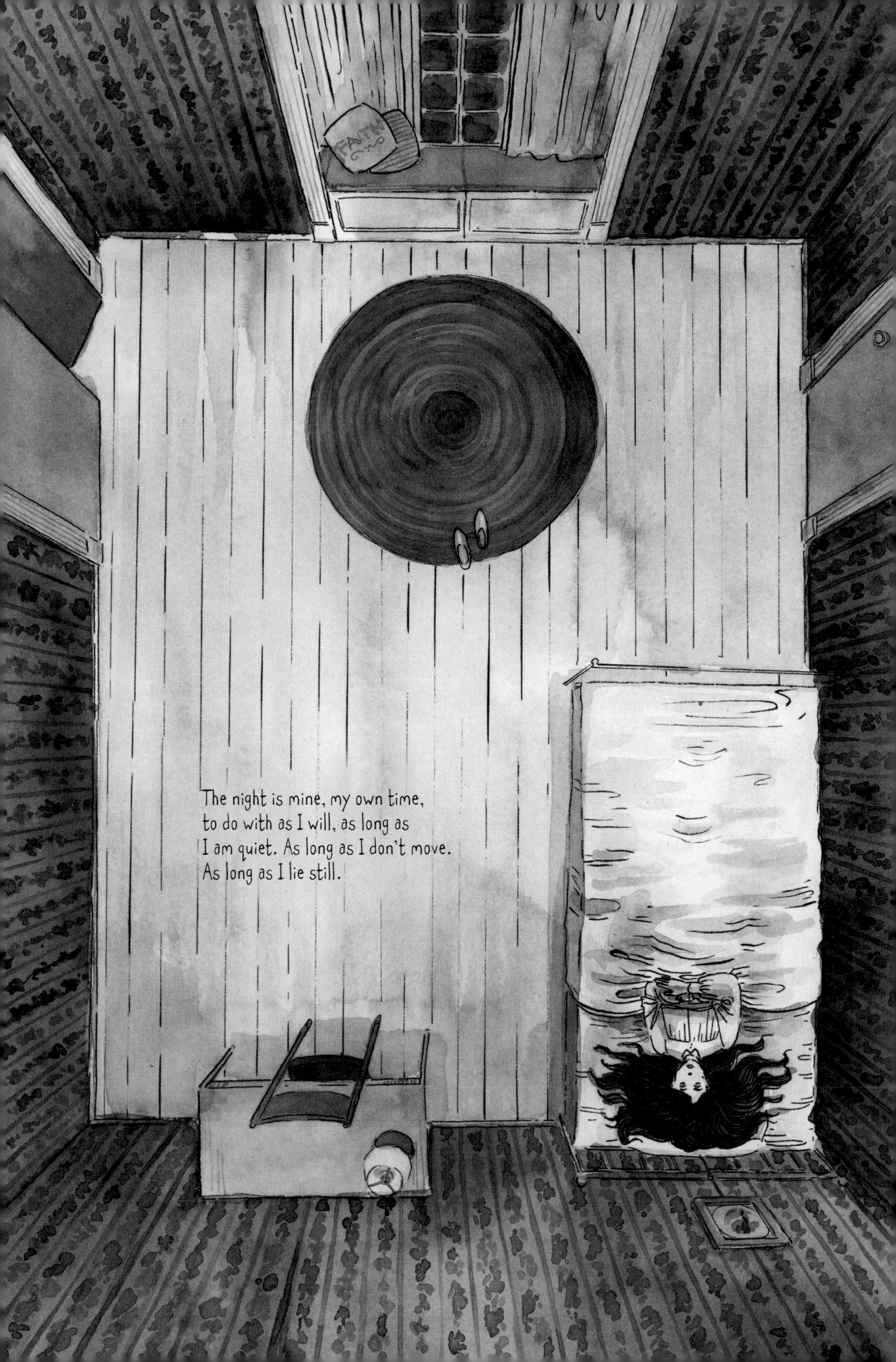
FAITH
The night is mine, my own time,
to do with as I will, as long as
I am quiet. As long as I don't move.
As long as I lie still.

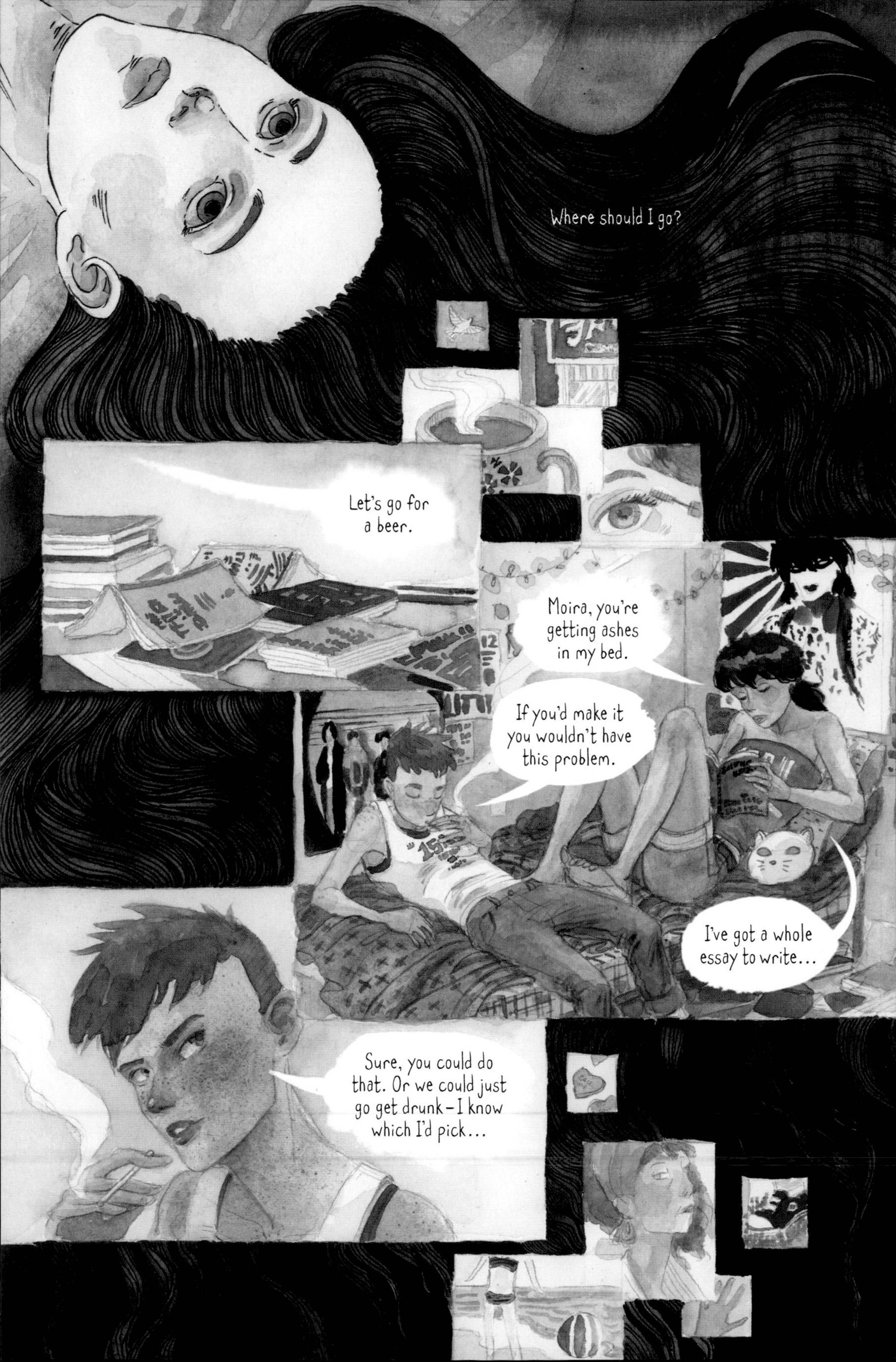
Where should I go?
Let's go for a beer.
Moira, you're getting ashes in my bed.
If you'd make it you wouldn't have this problem.
I've got a whole essay to write...
Sure, you could do that. Or we could just go get drunk—I know which I'd pick...

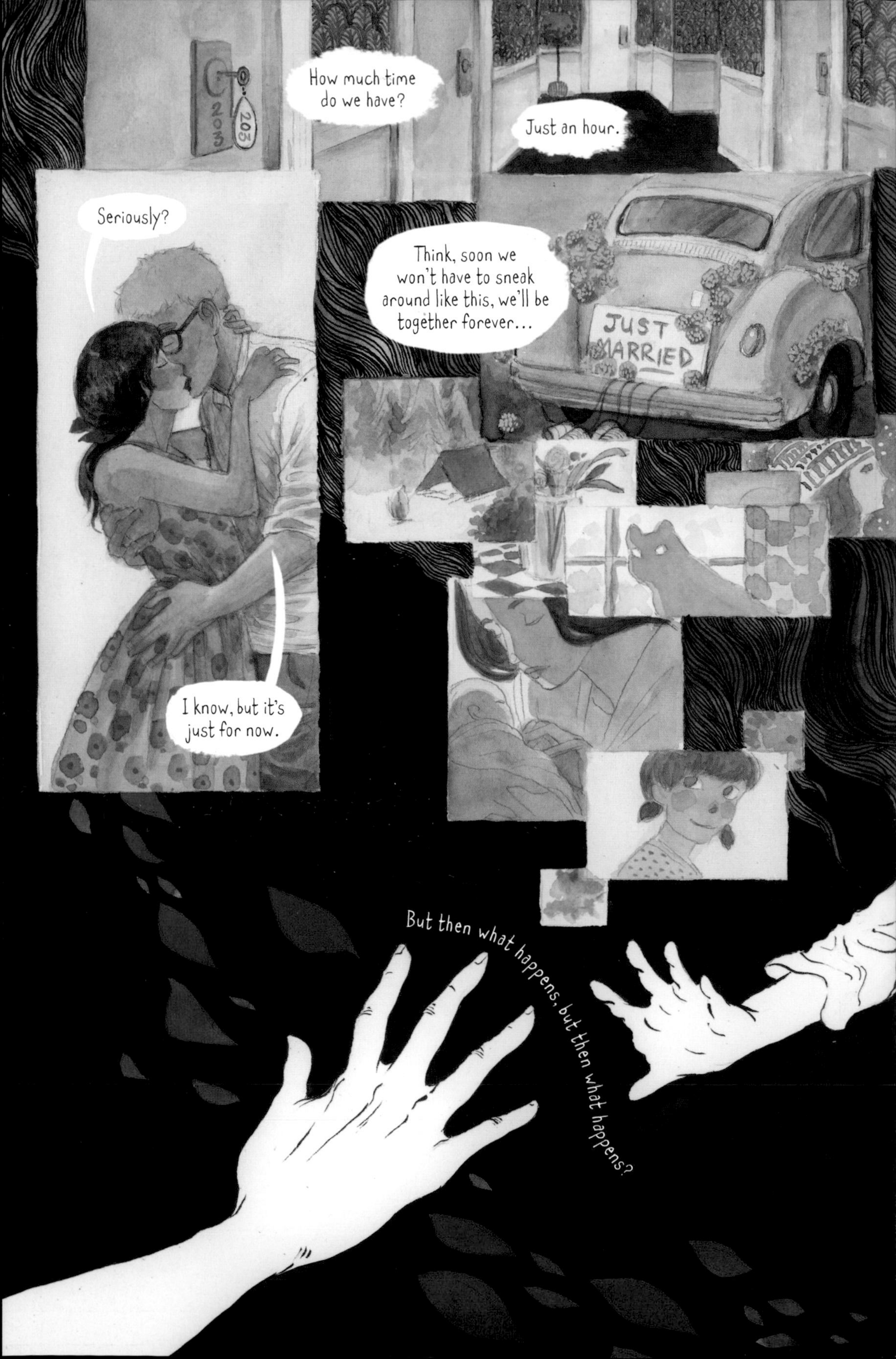
203
203
How much time do we have?
Just an hour.
Seriously?
I know, but it's just for now.
Think, soon we won't have to sneak around like this, we'll be together forever...
JUST MARRIED
But then what happens, but then what happens?

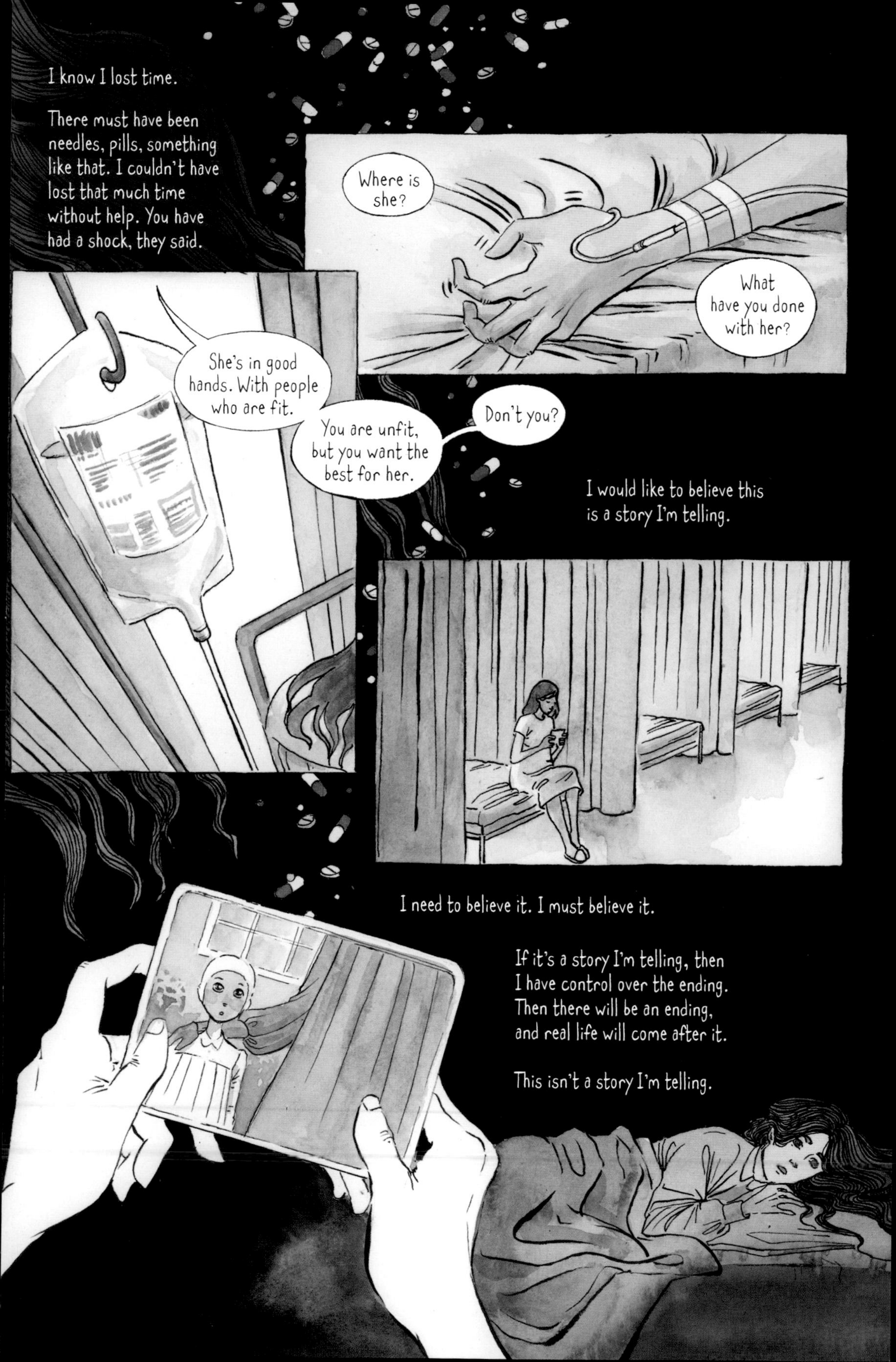
I know I lost time.
There must have been needles, pills, something like that. I couldn't have lost that much time without help. You have had a shock, they said.
Where is she?
What have you done with her?
She's in good hands. With people who are fit.
You are unfit, but you want the best for her.
Don't you?
I would like to believe this is a story I'm telling.
I need to believe it. I must believe it.
If it's a story I'm telling, then I have control over the ending. Then there will be an ending, and real life will come after it.
This isn't a story I'm telling.

IV

WAITING ROOM

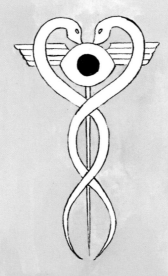

I'm taken to the doctor's once a month, for tests: urine, hormones, cancer smear, blood test; the same as before, except that now it's obligatory.

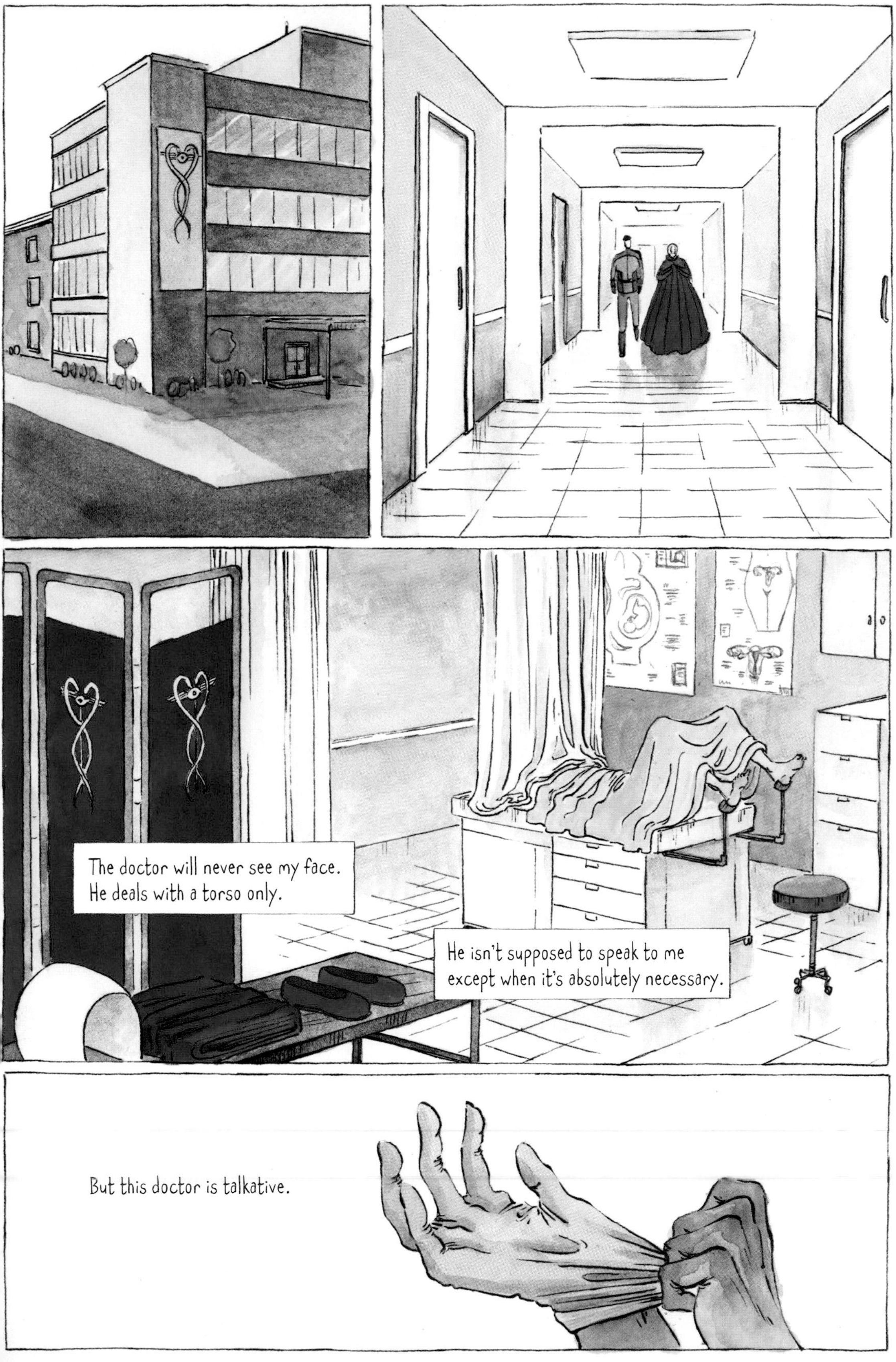
The doctor will never see my face.
He deals with a torso only.
He isn't supposed to speak to me
except when it's absolutely necessary.
But this doctor is talkative.

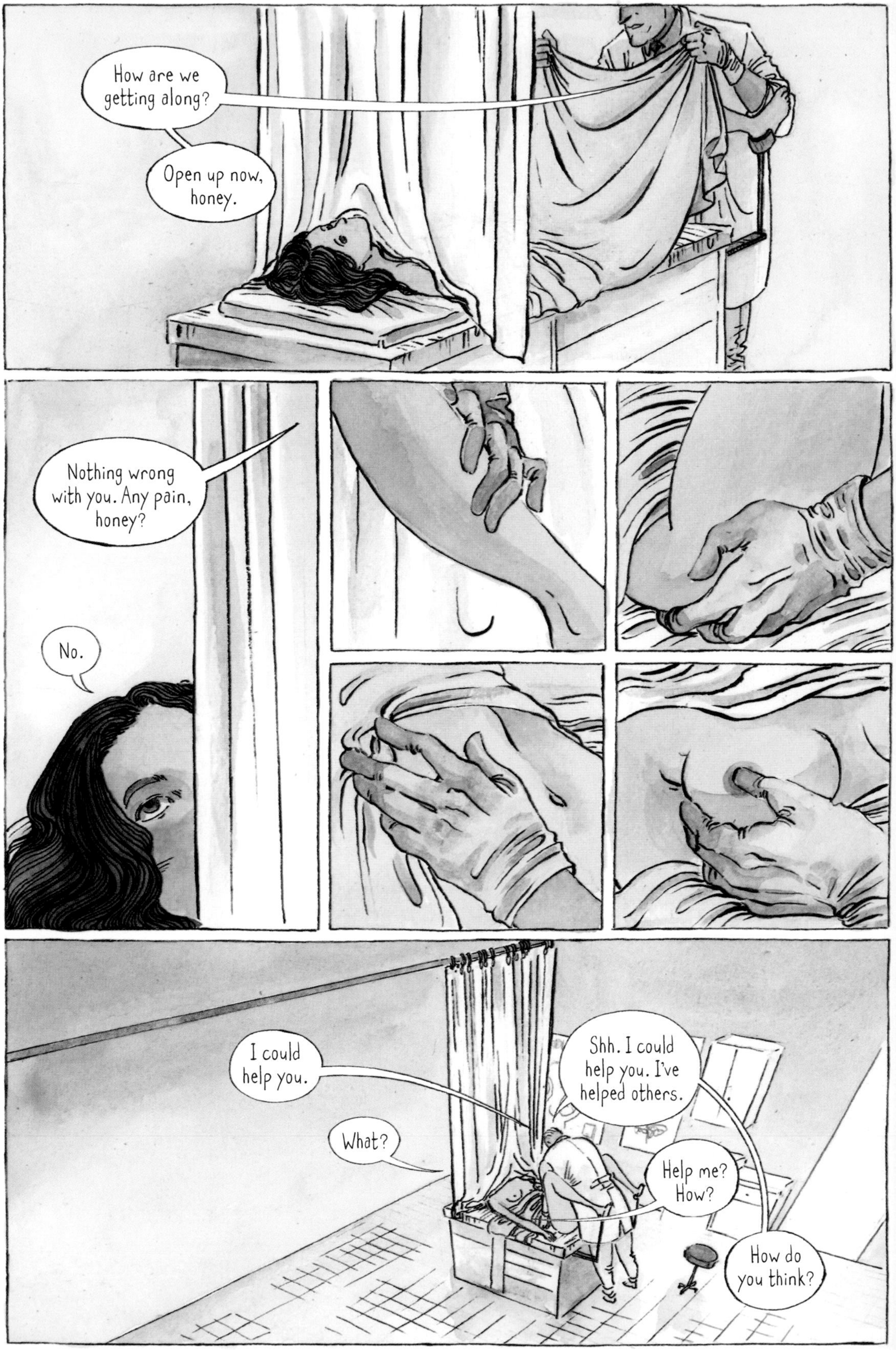
How are we getting along?
Open up now, honey.
Nothing wrong with you. Any pain, honey?
No.
I could help you.
What?
Shh. I could help you. I've helped others.
Help me? How?
How do you think?

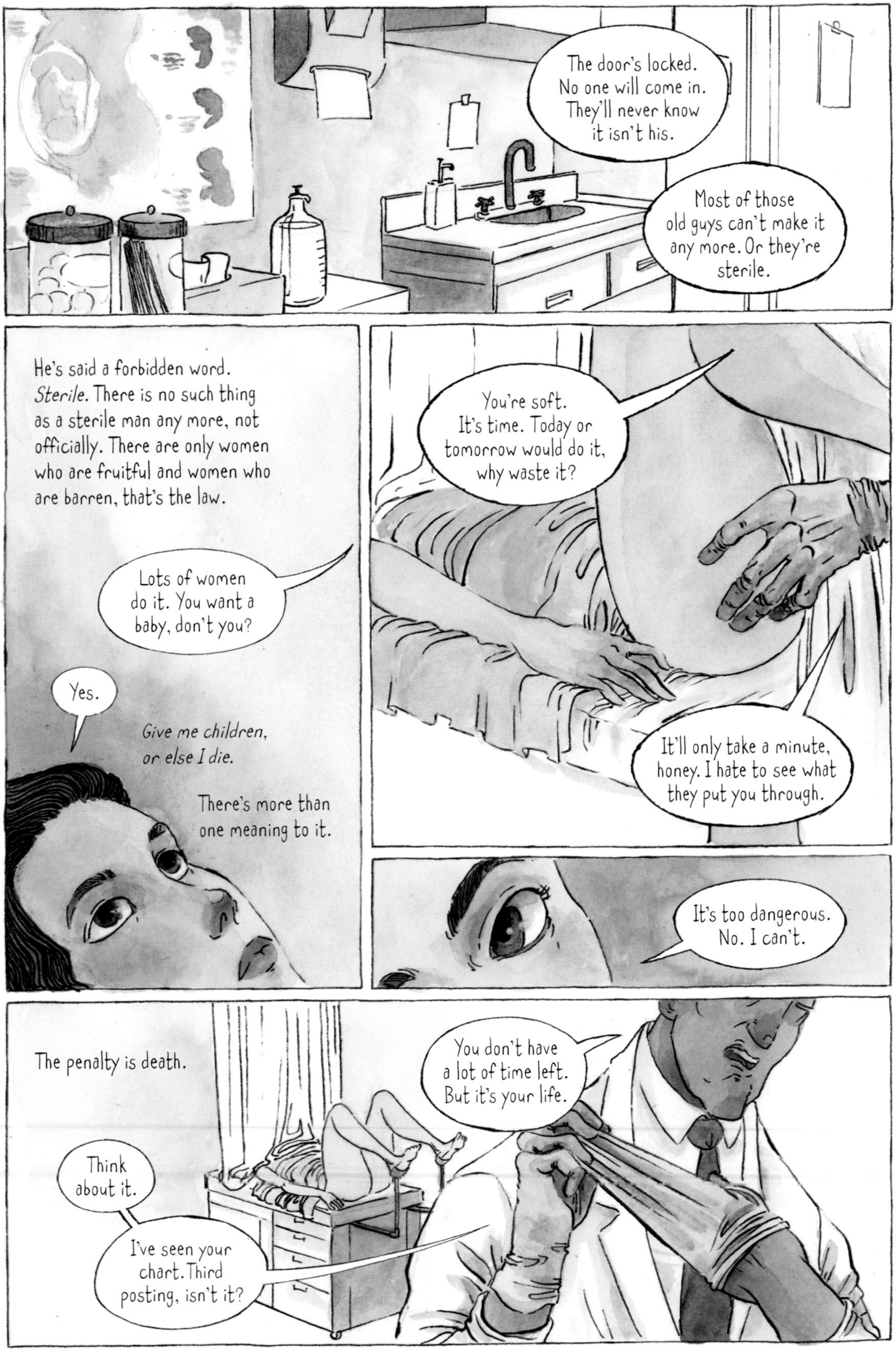
The door's locked. No one will come in. They'll never know it isn't his.
Most of those old guys can't make it any more. Or they're sterile.
He's said a forbidden word. *Sterile*. There is no such thing as a sterile man any more, not officially. There are only women who are fruitful and women who are barren, that's the law.
You're soft. It's time. Today or tomorrow would do it, why waste it?
Lots of women do it. You want a baby, don't you?
Yes.
Give me children, or else I die.
There's more than one meaning to it.
It'll only take a minute, honey. I hate to see what they put you through.
It's too dangerous. No. I can't.
The penalty is death.
You don't have a lot of time left. But it's your life.
Think about it.
I've seen your chart. Third posting, isn't it?

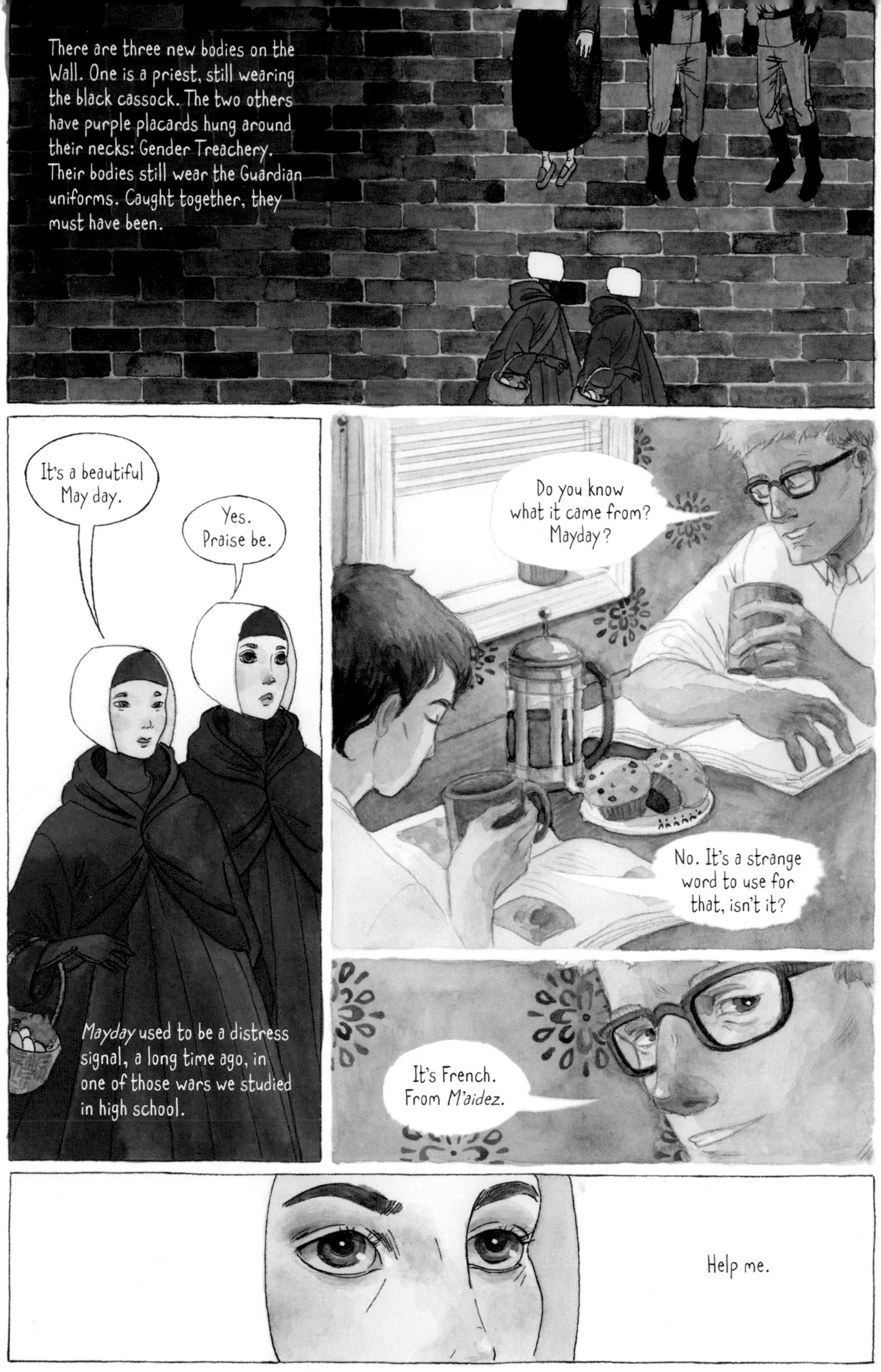
There are three new bodies on the Wall. One is a priest, still wearing the black cassock. The two others have purple placards hung around their necks: Gender Treachery. Their bodies still wear the Guardian uniforms. Caught together, they must have been.
It's a beautiful May day.
Yes. Praise be.
Mayday used to be a distress signal, a long time ago, in one of those wars we studied in high school.
Do you know what it came from? Mayday?
No. It's a strange word to use for that, isn't it?
It's French. From *M'aidez*.
Help me.

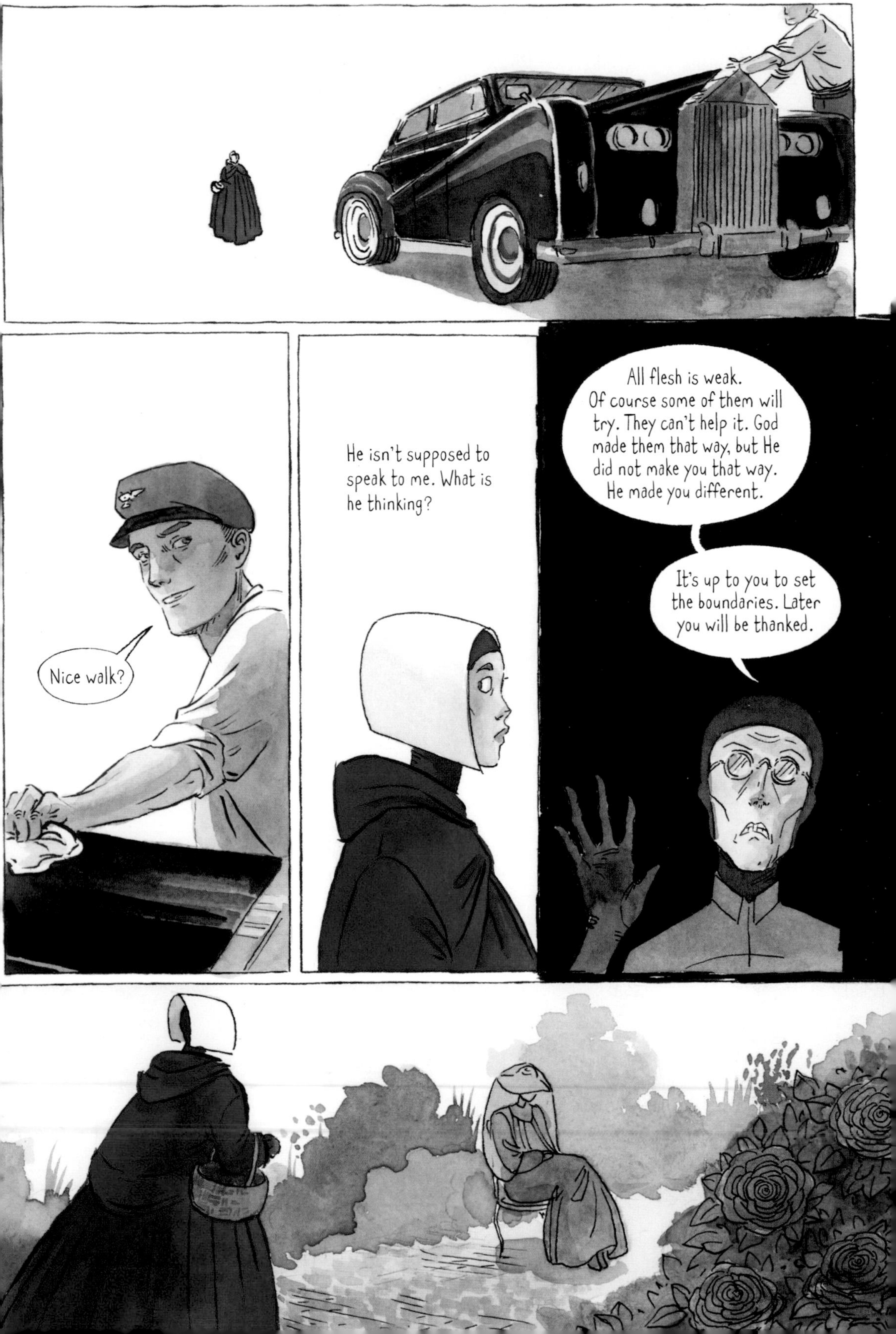
Nice walk?
He isn't supposed to speak to me. What is he thinking?
All flesh is weak. Of course some of them will try. They can't help it. God made them that way, but He did not make you that way. He made you different.
It's up to you to set the boundaries. Later you will be thanked.

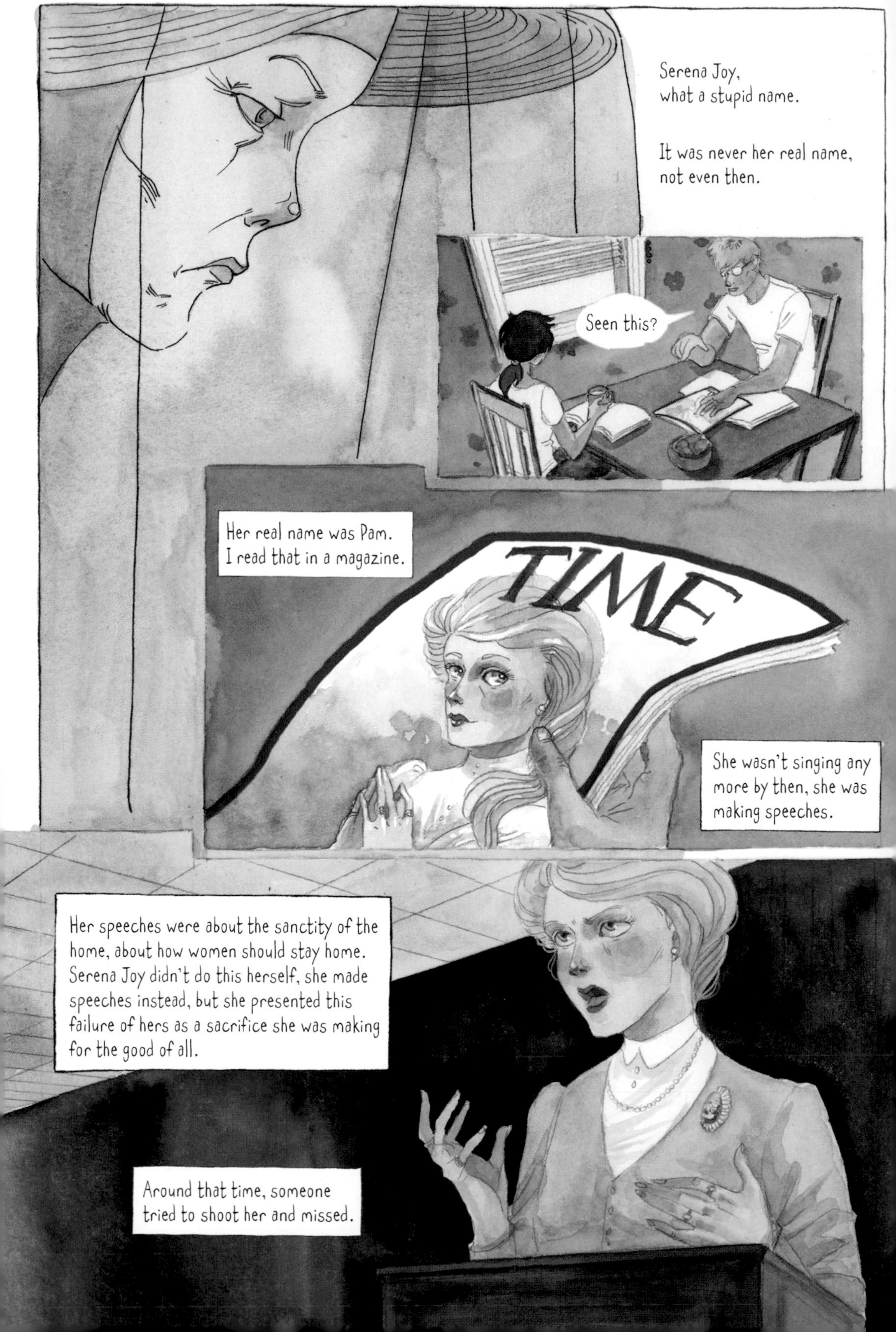
Serena Joy,
what a stupid name.
It was never her real name,
not even then.
Seen this?
Her real name was Pam.
I read that in a magazine.
TIME
She wasn't singing any more by then, she was making speeches.
Her speeches were about the sanctity of the home, about how women should stay home. Serena Joy didn't do this herself, she made speeches instead, but she presented this failure of hers as a sacrifice she was making for the good of all.
Around that time, someone tried to shoot her and missed.

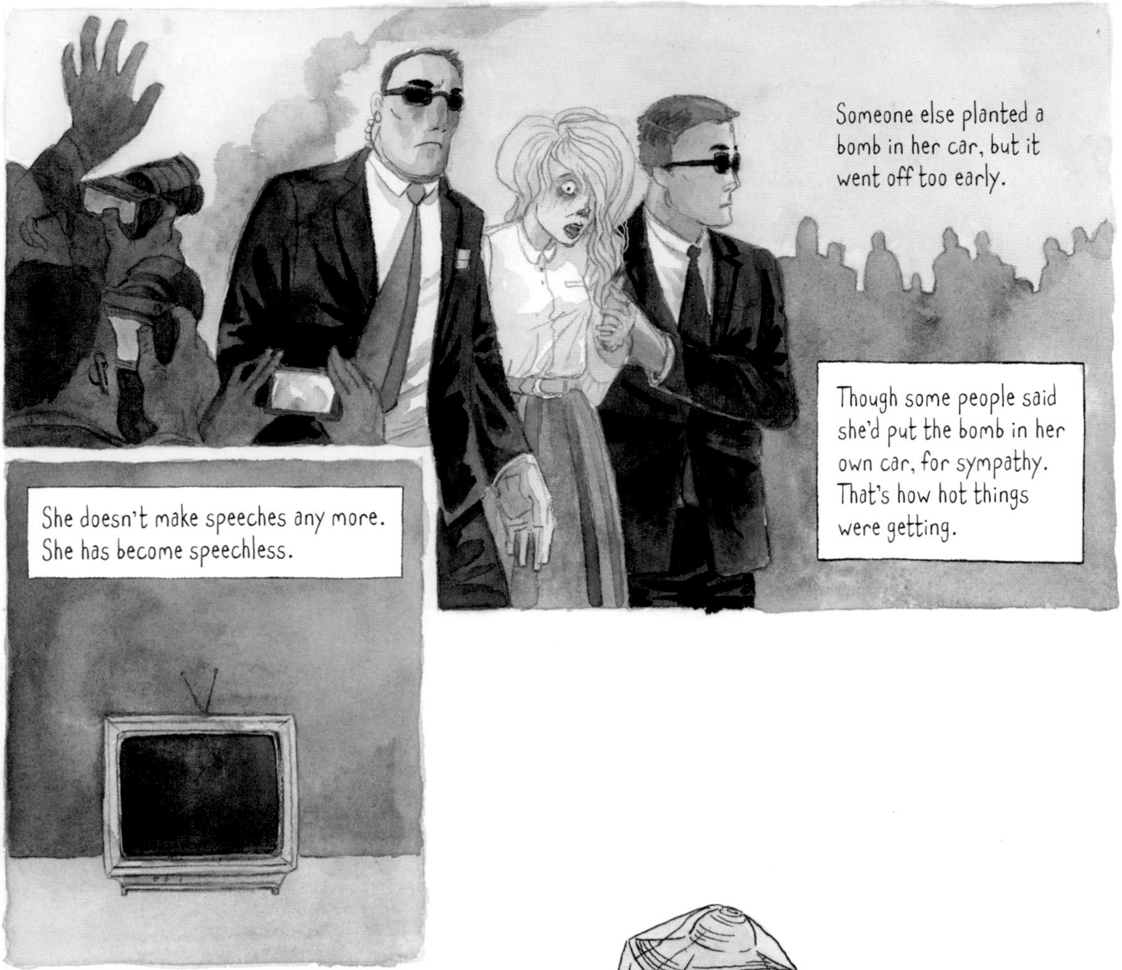
Someone else planted a bomb in her car, but it went off too early.
Though some people said she'd put the bomb in her own car, for sympathy. That's how hot things were getting.
She doesn't make speeches any more. She has become speechless.

She stays in her home, but it doesn't seem to agree with her.

How furious she must be, now that she's been taken at her word.

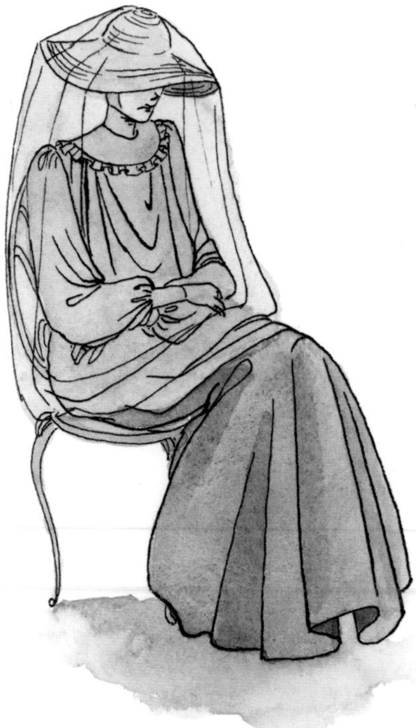

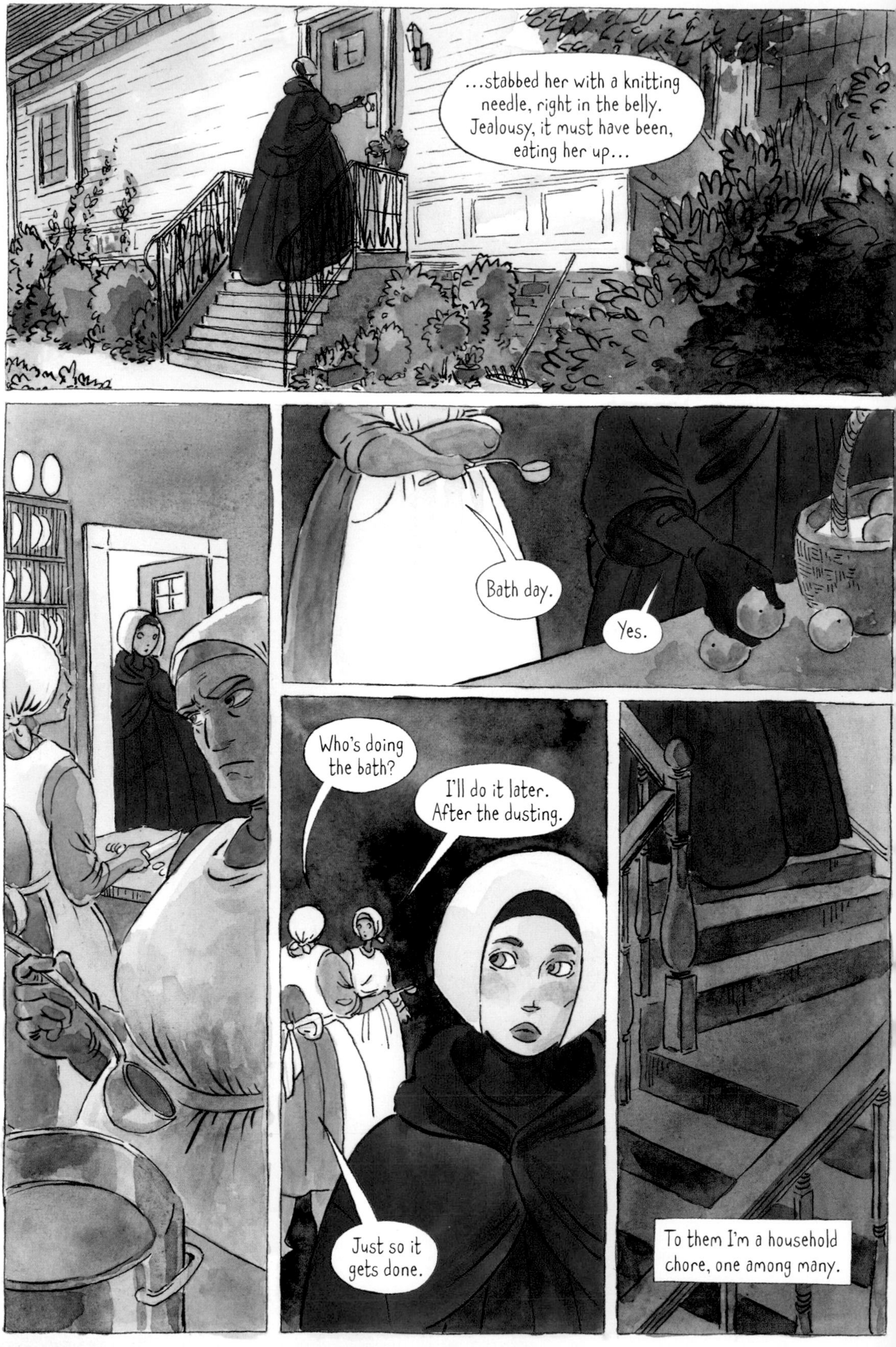
...stabbed her with a knitting needle, right in the belly. Jealousy, it must have been, eating her up...
Bath day.
Yes.
Who's doing the bath?
I'll do it later. After the dusting.
Just so it gets done.
To them I'm a household chore, one among many.

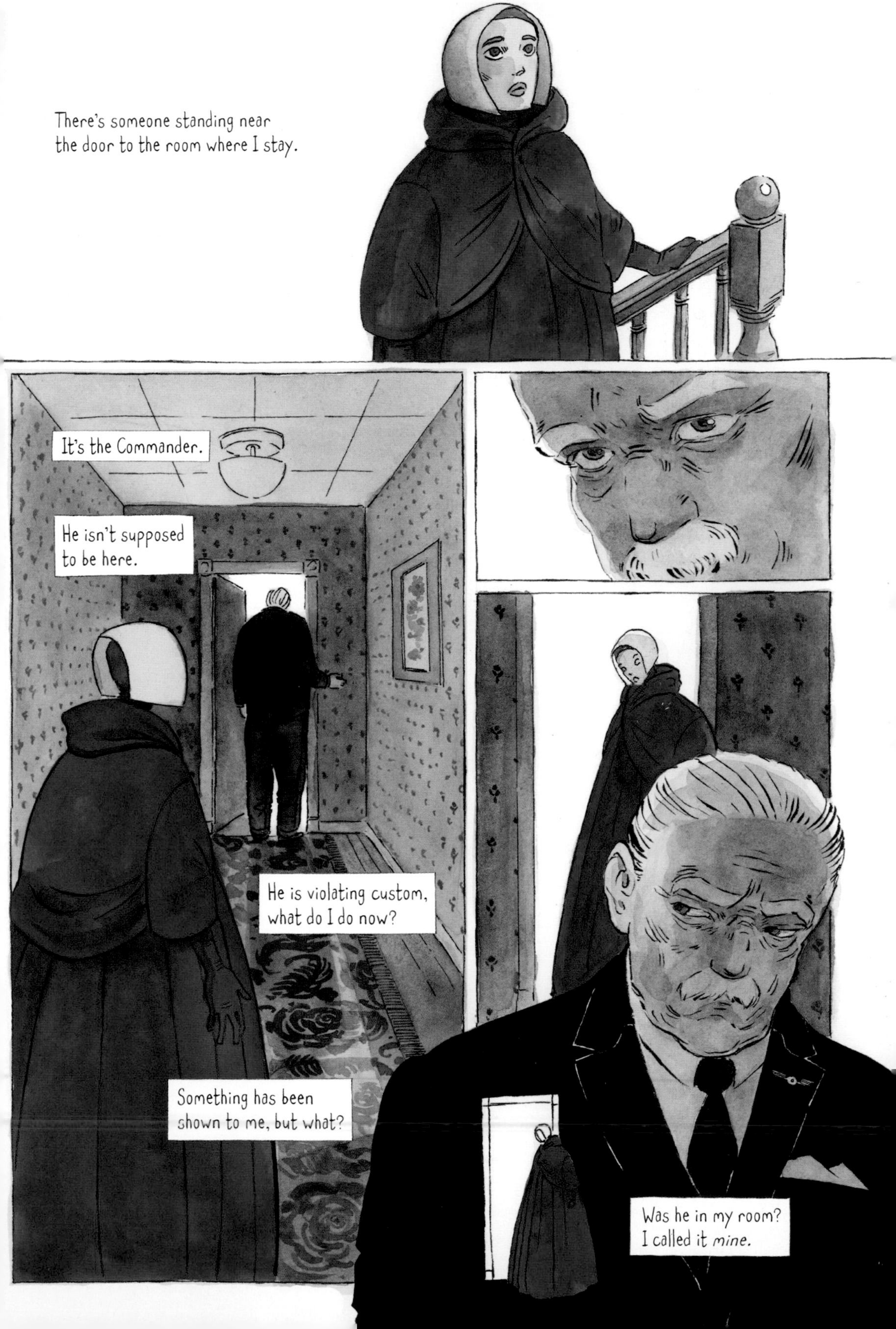
There's someone standing near the door to the room where I stay.
It's the Commander.
He isn't supposed to be here.
He is violating custom, what do I do now?
Something has been shown to me, but what?
Was he in my room? I called it *mine*.

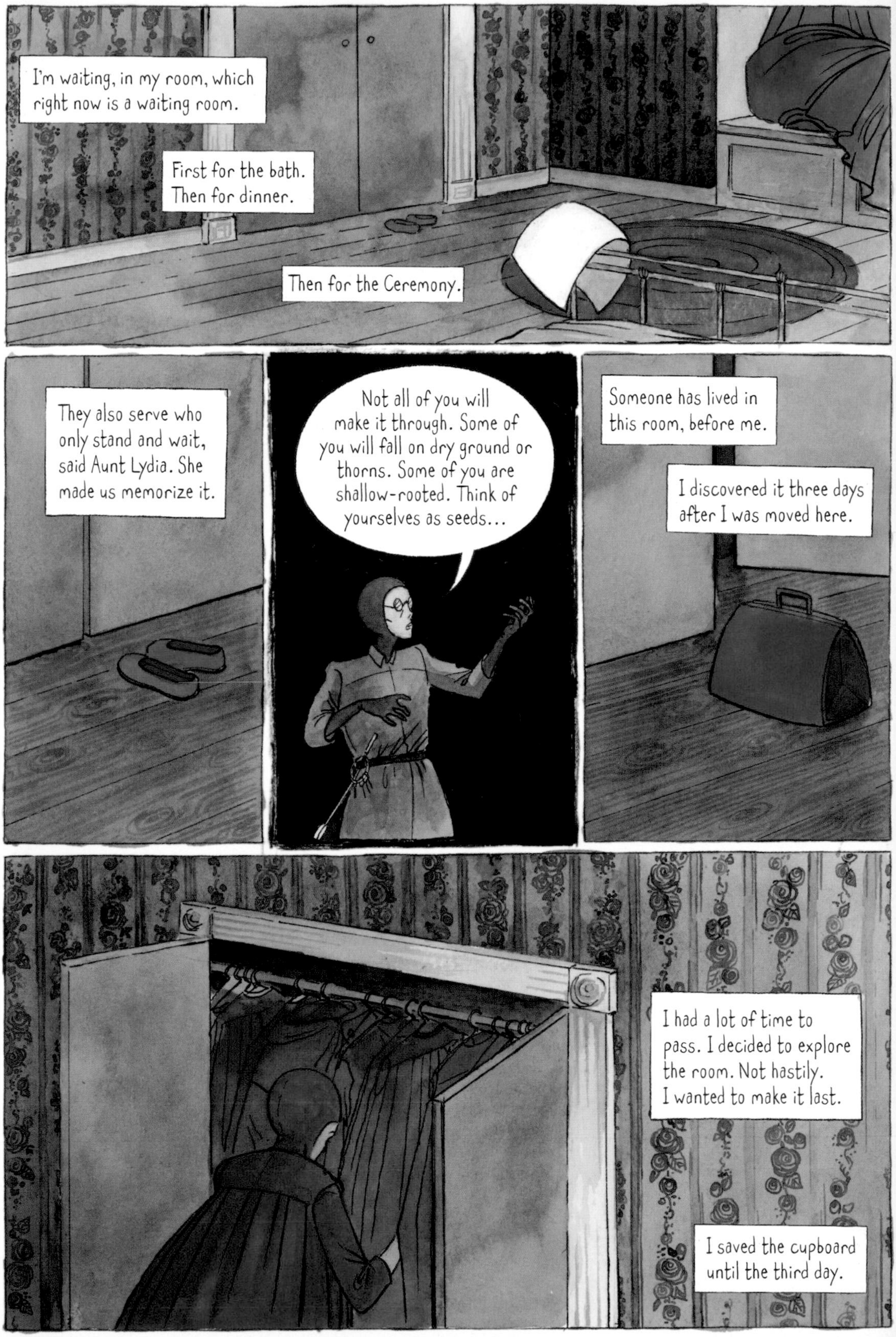
I'm waiting, in my room, which right now is a waiting room.
First for the bath. Then for dinner.
Then for the Ceremony.
They also serve who only stand and wait, said Aunt Lydia. She made us memorize it.
Not all of you will make it through. Some of you will fall on dry ground or thorns. Some of you are shallow-rooted. Think of yourselves as seeds...
Someone has lived in this room, before me.
I discovered it three days after I was moved here.
I had a lot of time to pass. I decided to explore the room. Not hastily. I wanted to make it last.
I saved the cupboard until the third day.

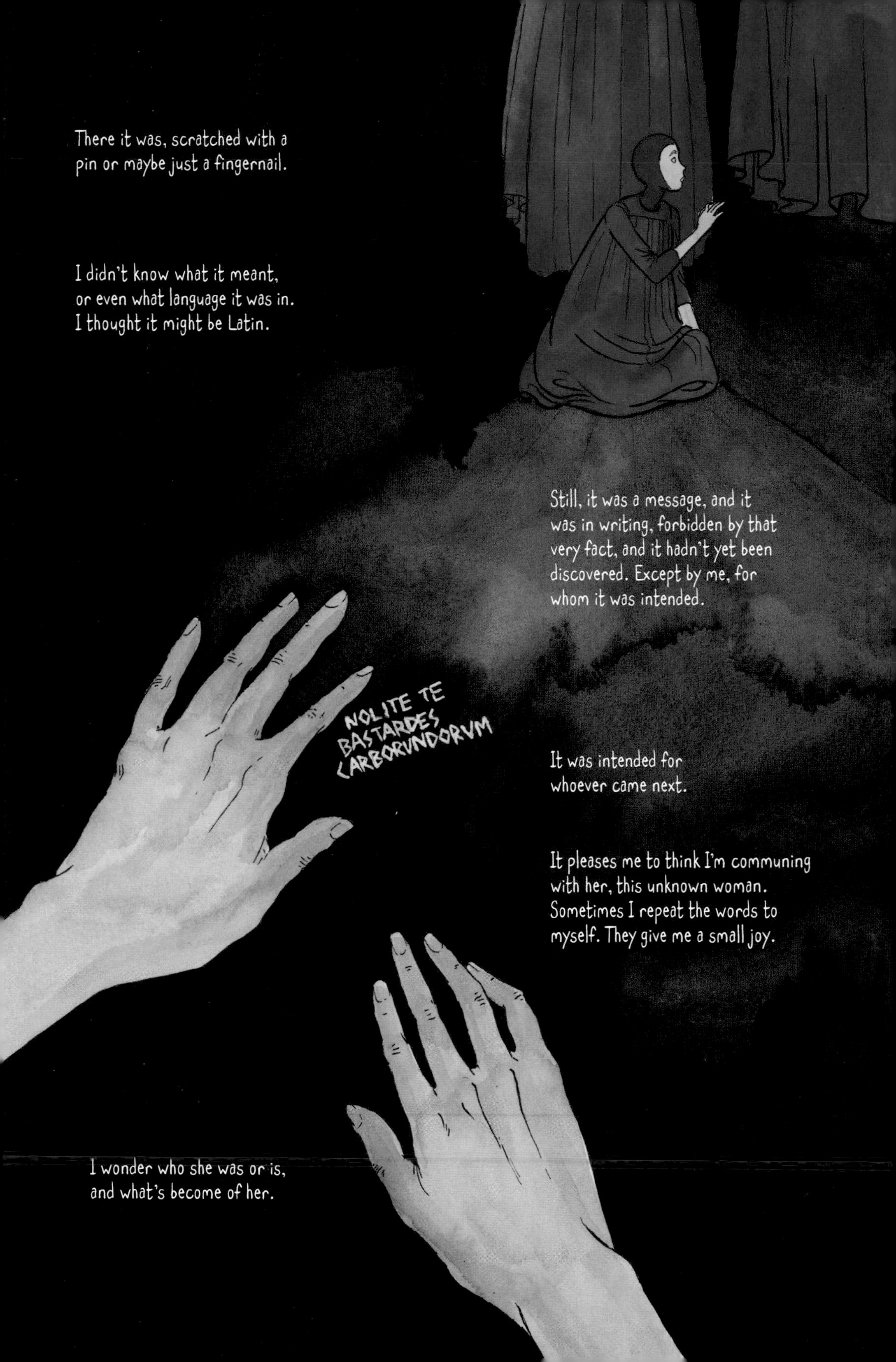
There it was, scratched with a pin or maybe just a fingernail.
I didn't know what it meant, or even what language it was in. I thought it might be Latin.
Still, it was a message, and it was in writing, forbidden by that very fact, and it hadn't yet been discovered. Except by me, for whom it was intended.
NOLITE TE BASTARDES CARBORUNDORUM
It was intended for whoever came next.
It pleases me to think I'm communing with her, this unknown woman. Sometimes I repeat the words to myself. They give me a small joy.
I wonder who she was or is, and what's become of her.

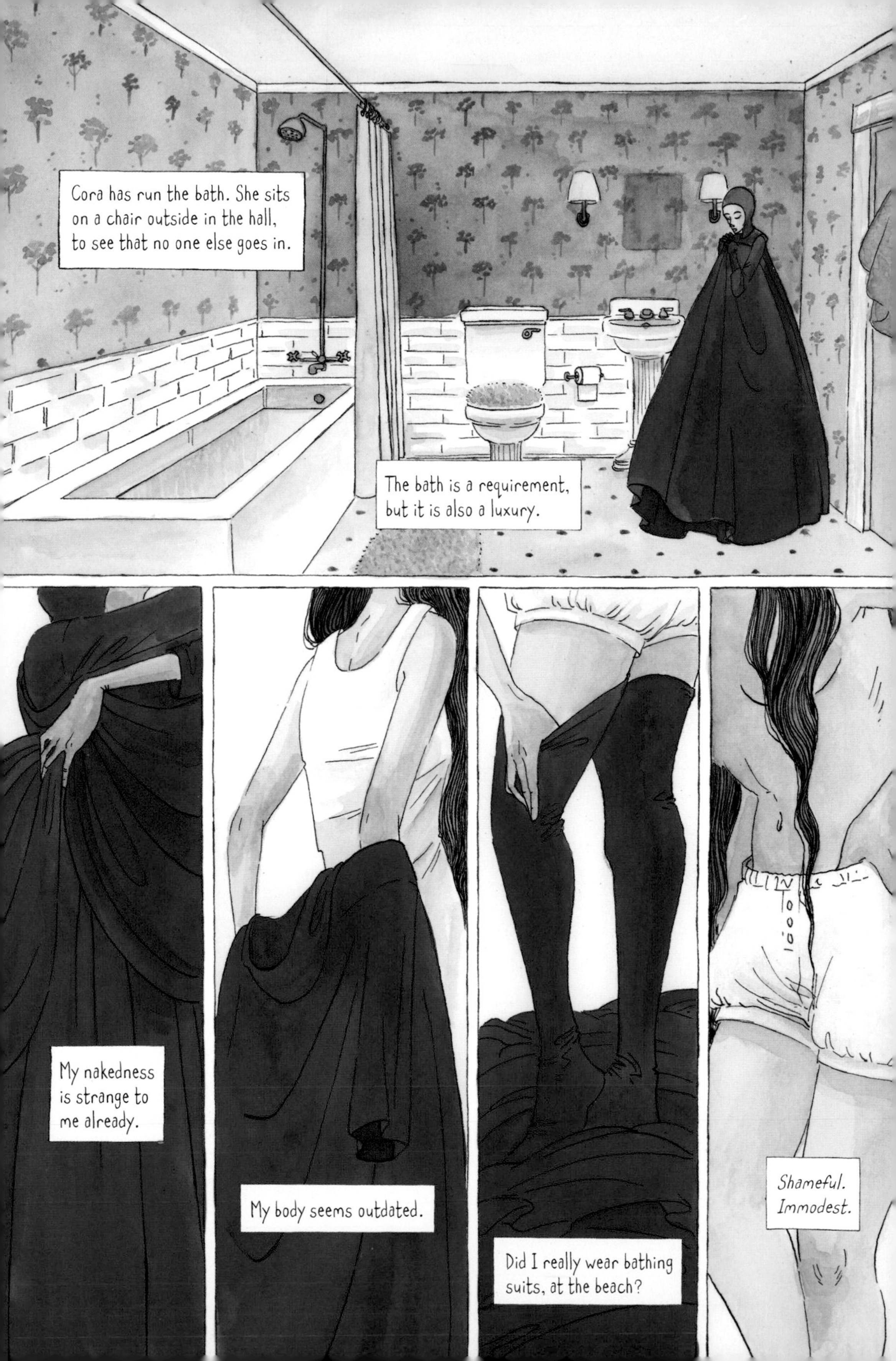
Cora has run the bath. She sits on a chair outside in the hall, to see that no one else goes in.
The bath is a requirement, but it is also a luxury.
My nakedness is strange to me already.
My body seems outdated.
Did I really wear bathing suits, at the beach?
Shameful. Immodest.

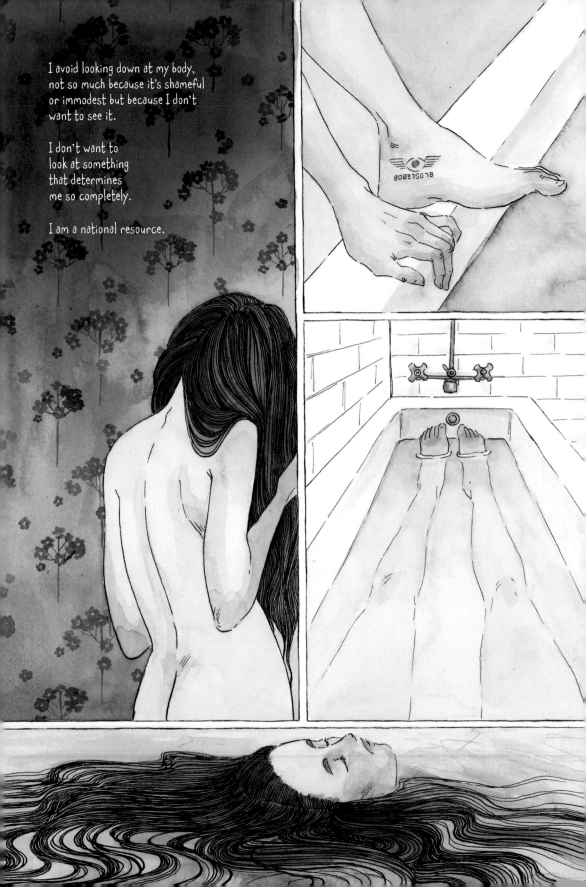

I avoid looking down at my body, not so much because it's shameful or immodest but because I don't want to see it.

I don't want to look at something that determines me so completely.

I am a national resource.

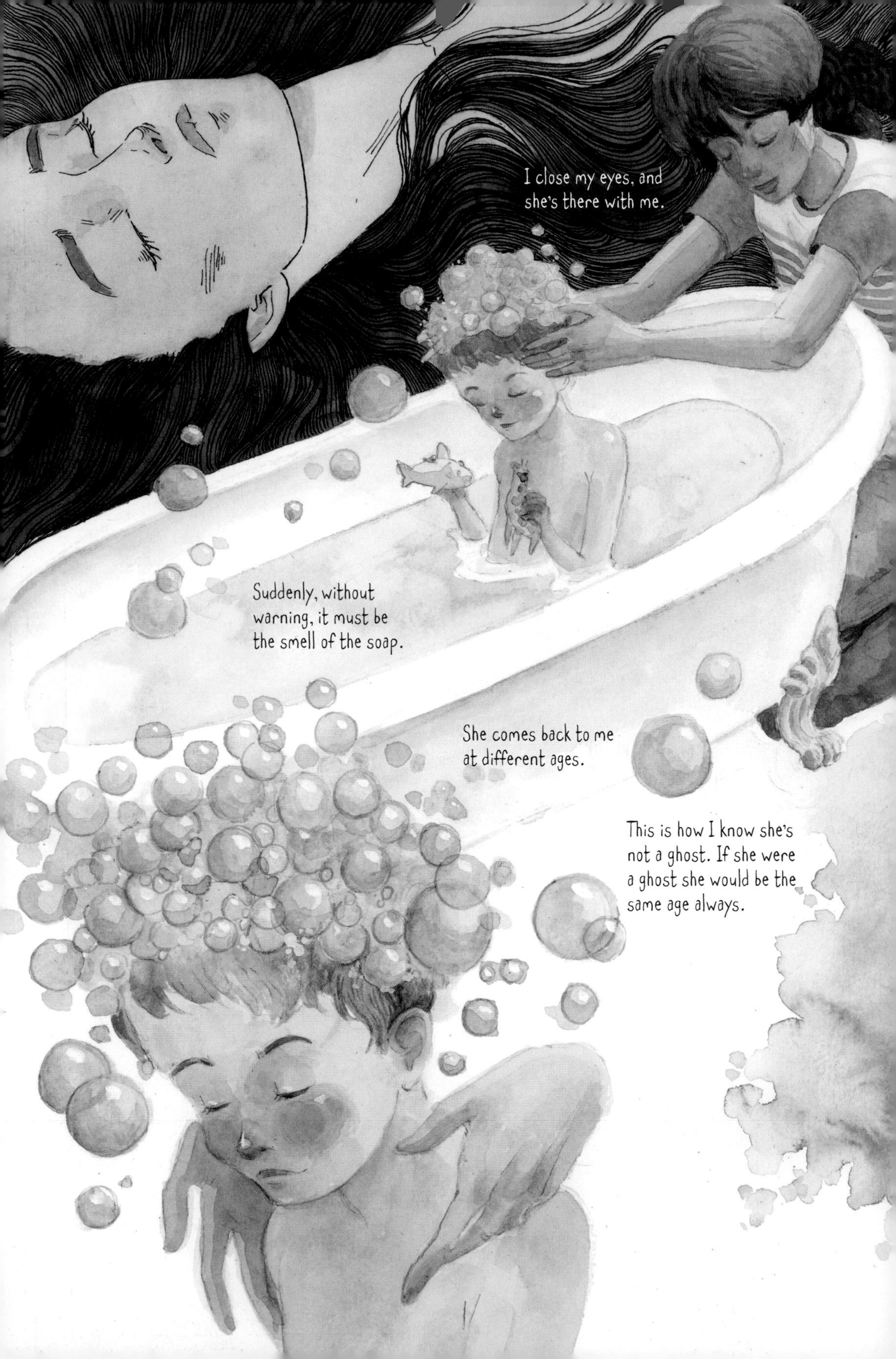
I close my eyes, and she's there with me.
Suddenly, without warning, it must be the smell of the soap.
She comes back to me at different ages.
This is how I know she's not a ghost. If she were a ghost she would be the same age always.

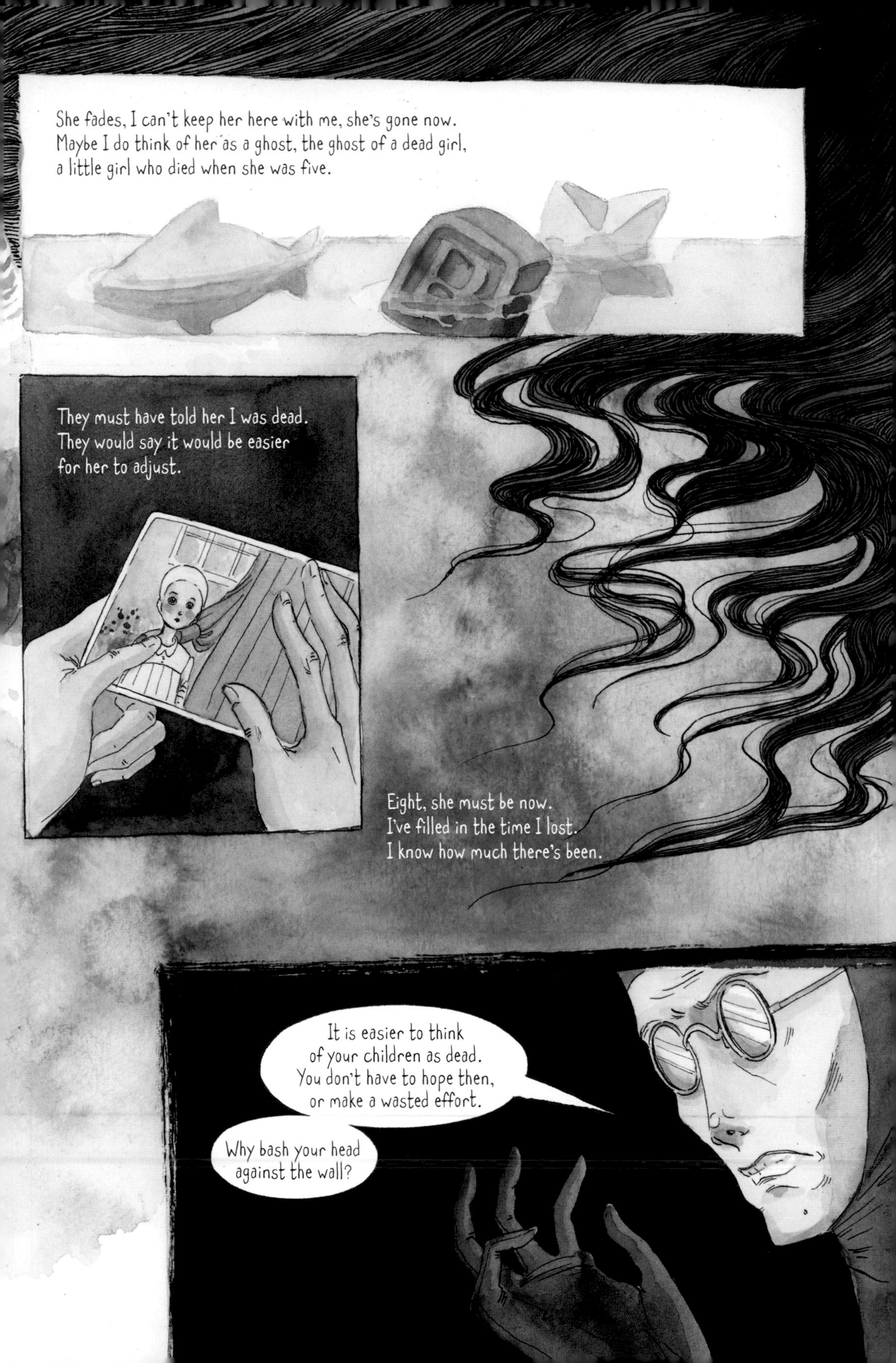
She fades, I can't keep her here with me, she's gone now. Maybe I do think of her as a ghost, the ghost of a dead girl, a little girl who died when she was five.
They must have told her I was dead. They would say it would be easier for her to adjust.
Eight, she must be now. I've filled in the time I lost. I know how much there's been.
It is easier to think of your children as dead. You don't have to hope then, or make a wasted effort.
Why bash your head against the wall?

I'm not hungry tonight.

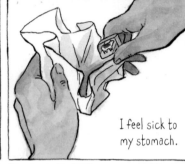

I feel sick to my stomach.

I will use the butter later.
It would not do, this evening,
to smell of butter.

V
—

NAP

I wait,

washed,

brushed,

fed,

like a prize pig.

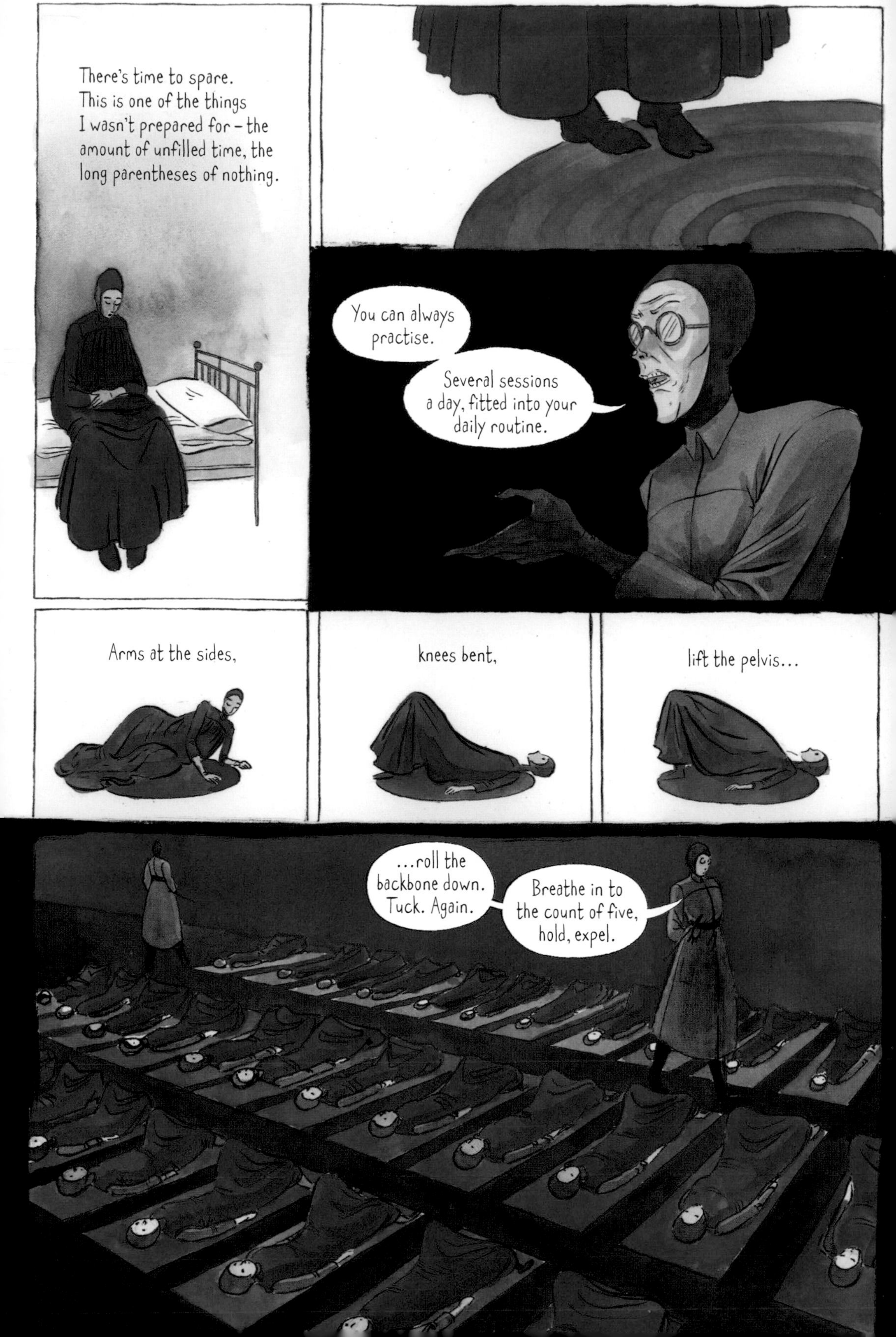
There's time to spare.
This is one of the things
I wasn't prepared for – the
amount of unfilled time, the
long parentheses of nothing.
You can always practise.
Several sessions a day, fitted into your daily routine.
Arms at the sides,
knees bent,
lift the pelvis...
...roll the backbone down. Tuck. Again.
Breathe in to the count of five, hold, expel.

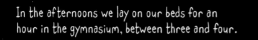

In the afternoons we lay on our beds for an
hour in the gymnasium, between three and four.

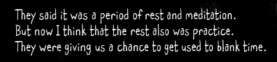

They said it was a period of rest and meditation.
But now I think that the rest also was practice.
They were giving us a chance to get used to blank time.

The strange thing is we needed the rest. Many of us went to sleep.
We were tired there, a lot of the time. We were on some kind of pill
or drug I think, they put it in the food, to keep us calm. But maybe not.
Maybe it was the place itself. After the first shock, after you'd come to
terms, it was better to be lethargic. You could tell yourself you were
saving up your strength.

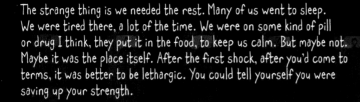

I must have been there three
weeks when Moira came.

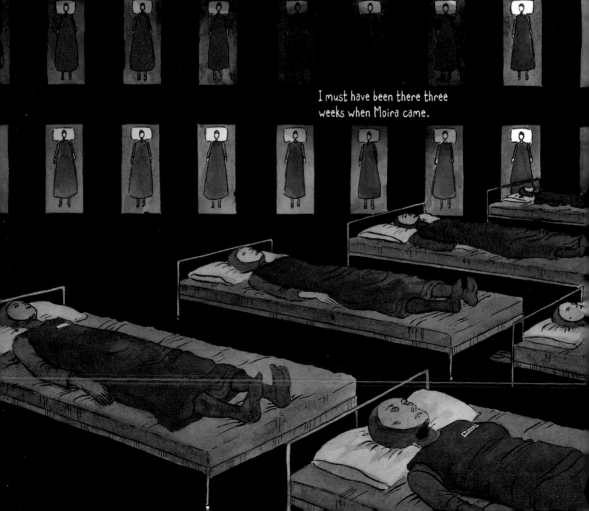

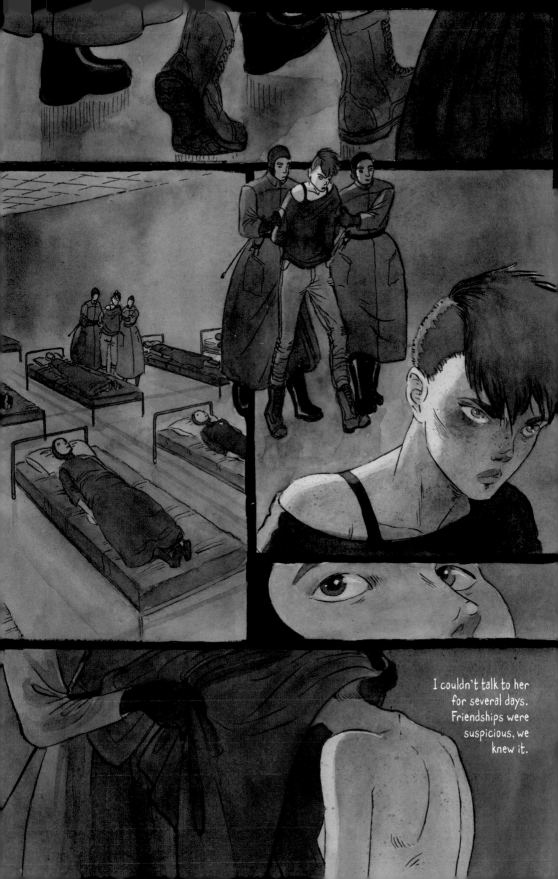

I couldn't talk to her for several days. Friendships were suspicious, we knew it.

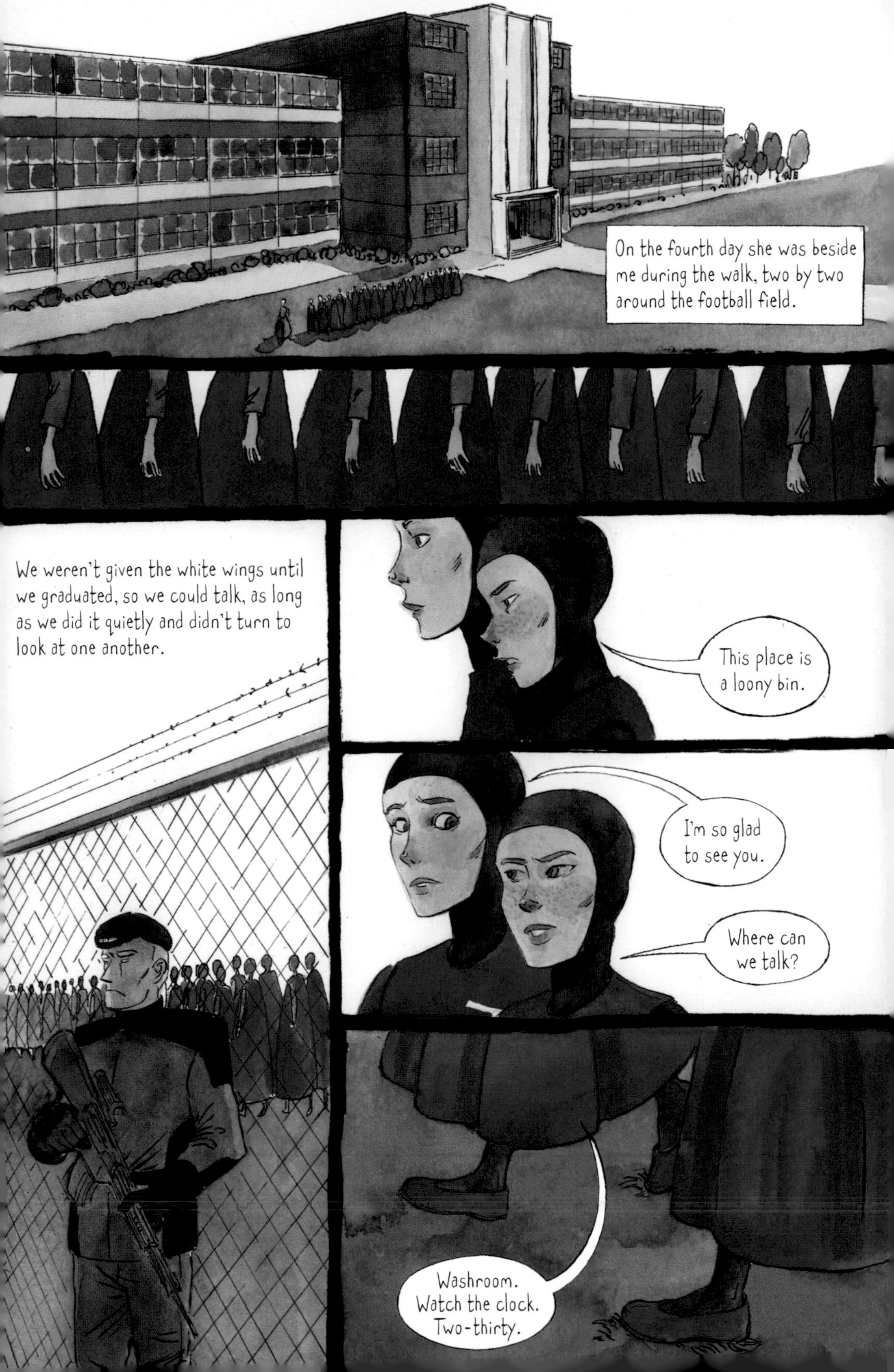
On the fourth day she was beside me during the walk, two by two around the football field.
We weren't given the white wings until we graduated, so we could talk, as long as we did it quietly and didn't turn to look at one another.
This place is a loony bin.
I'm so glad to see you.
Where can we talk?
Washroom. Watch the clock. Two-thirty.

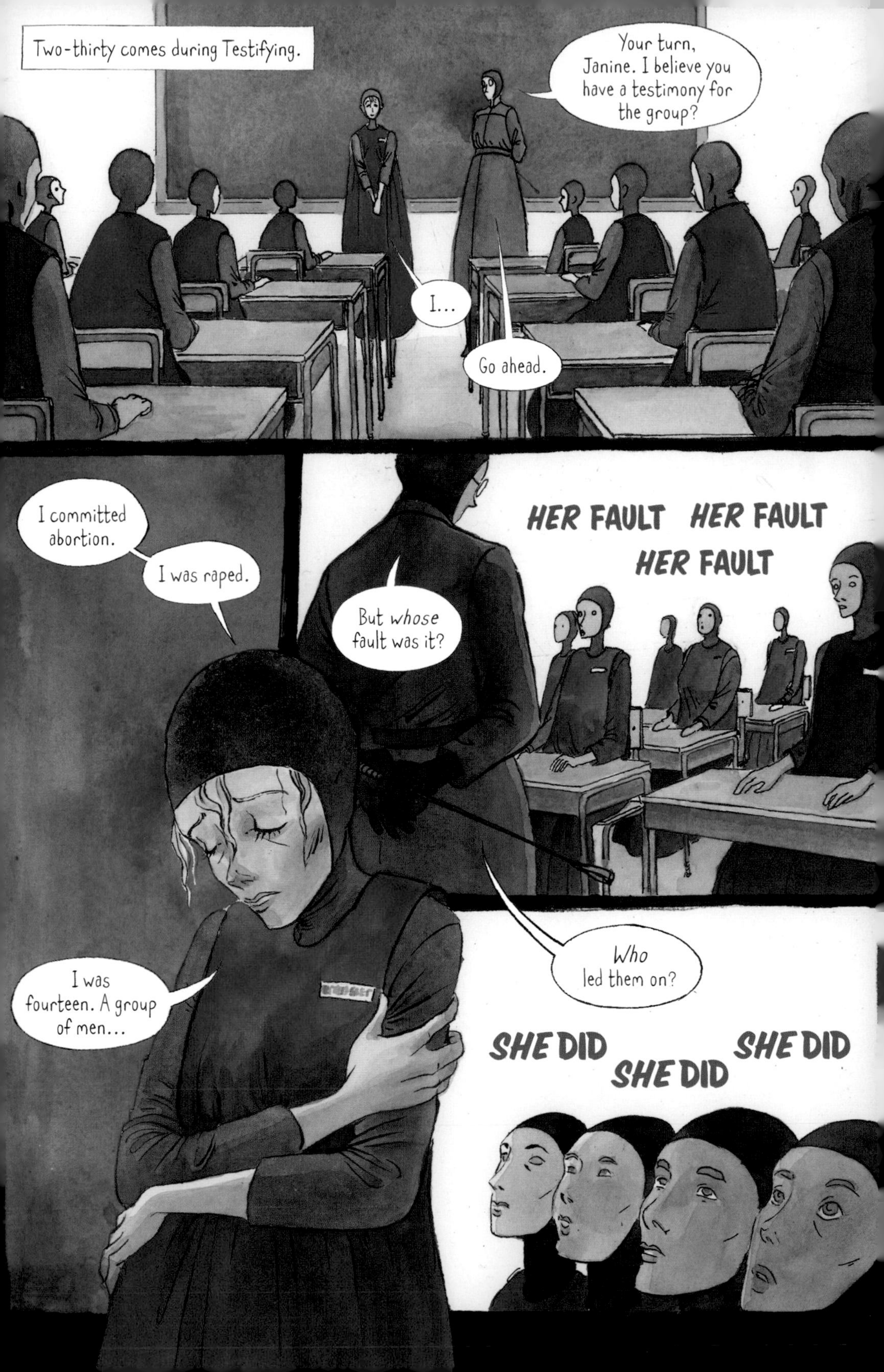
Two-thirty comes during Testifying.
Your turn, Janine. I believe you have a testimony for the group?
I...
Go ahead.
I committed abortion.
I was raped.
But *whose* fault was it?
HER FAULT HER FAULT HER FAULT
I was fourteen. A group of men...
Who led them on?
SHE DID SHE DID SHE DID

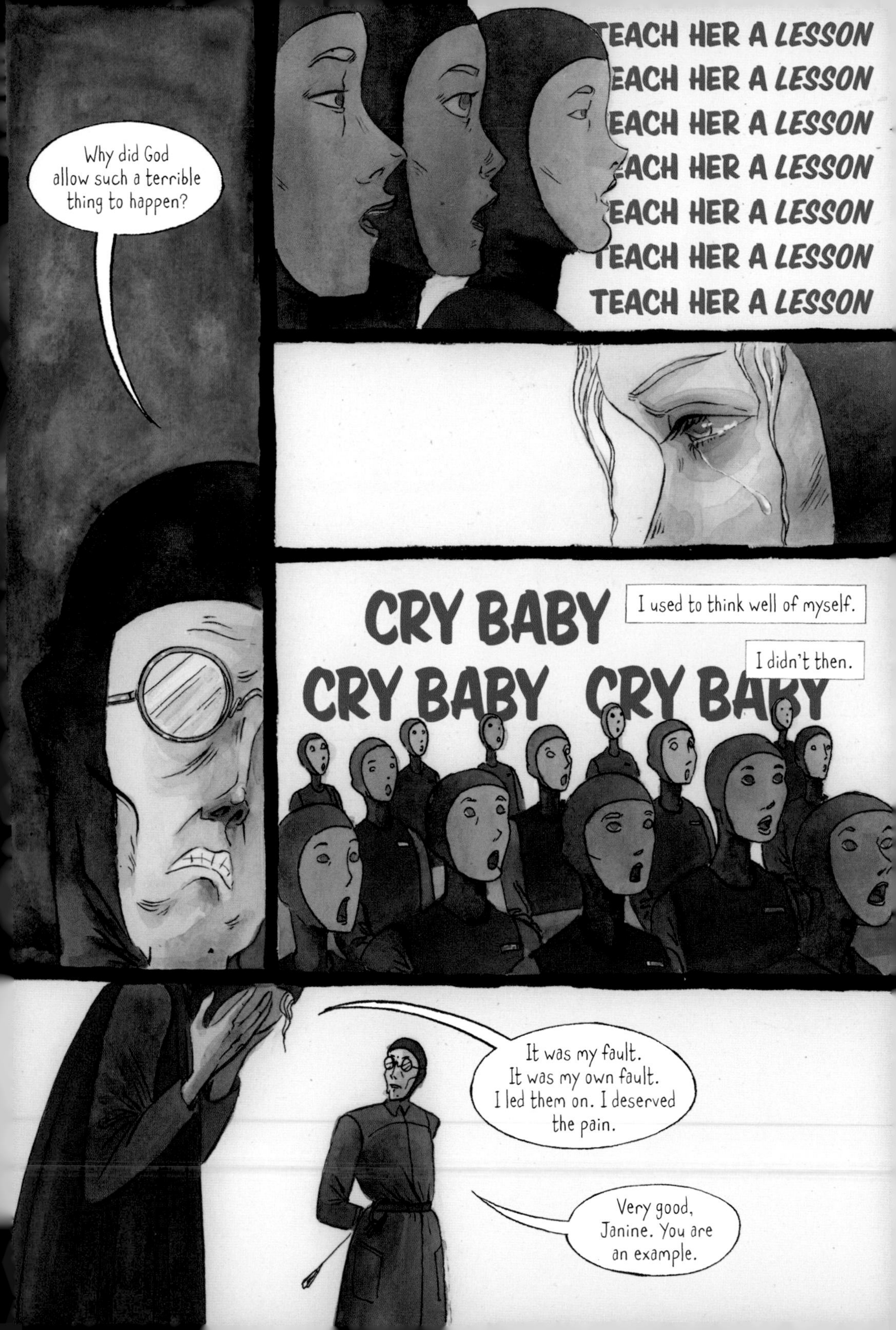
Why did God allow such a terrible thing to happen?
TEACH HER A LESSON
TEACH HER A LESSON
TEACH HER A LESSON
TEACH HER A LESSON
TEACH HER A LESSON
TEACH HER A LESSON
TEACH HER A LESSON
CRY BABY
I used to think well of myself.
I didn't then.
CRY BABY CRY BABY
It was my fault. It was my own fault. I led them on. I deserved the pain.
Very good, Janine. You are an example.

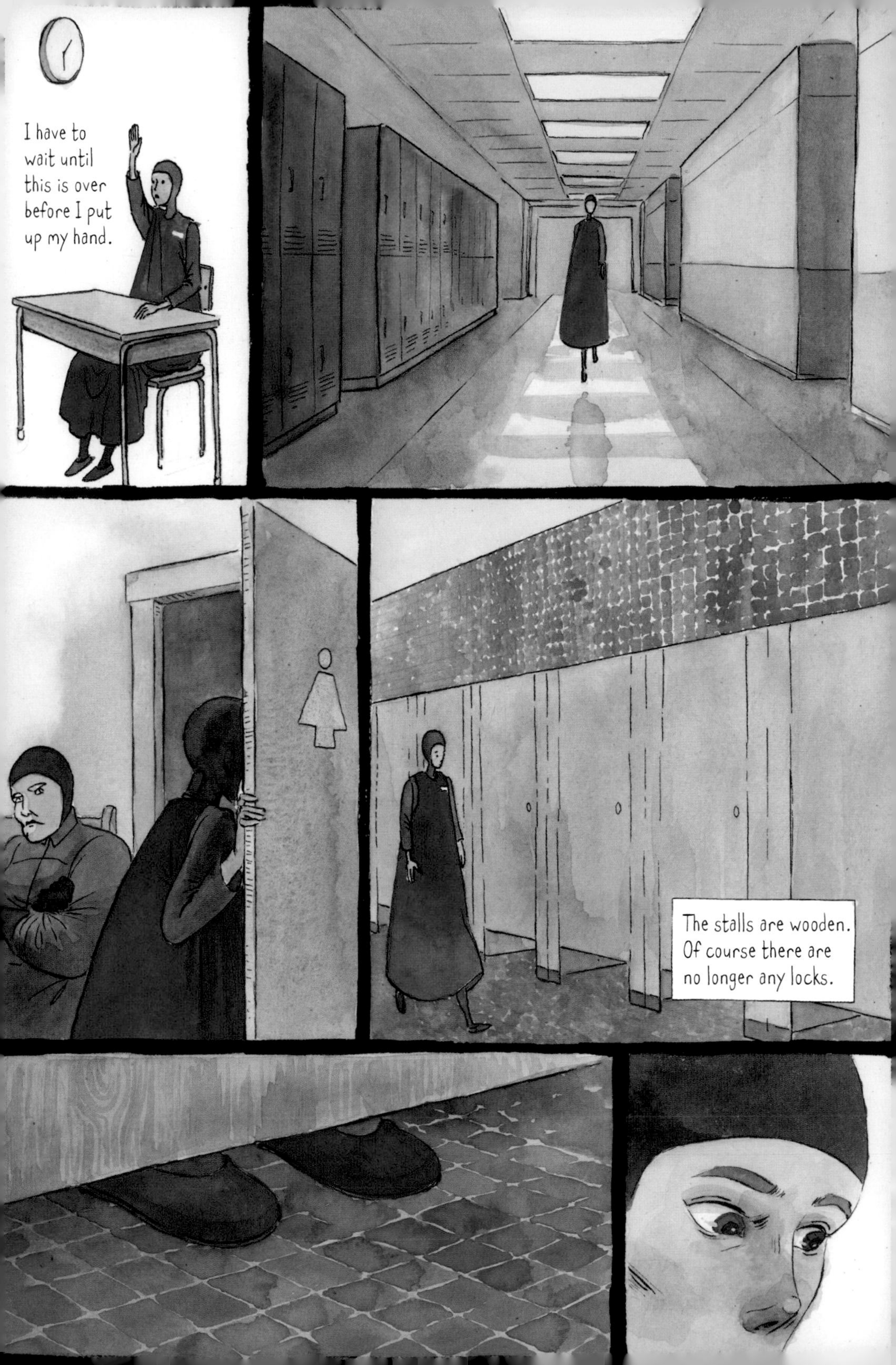
I have to wait until this is over before I put up my hand.
The stalls are wooden. Of course there are no longer any locks.

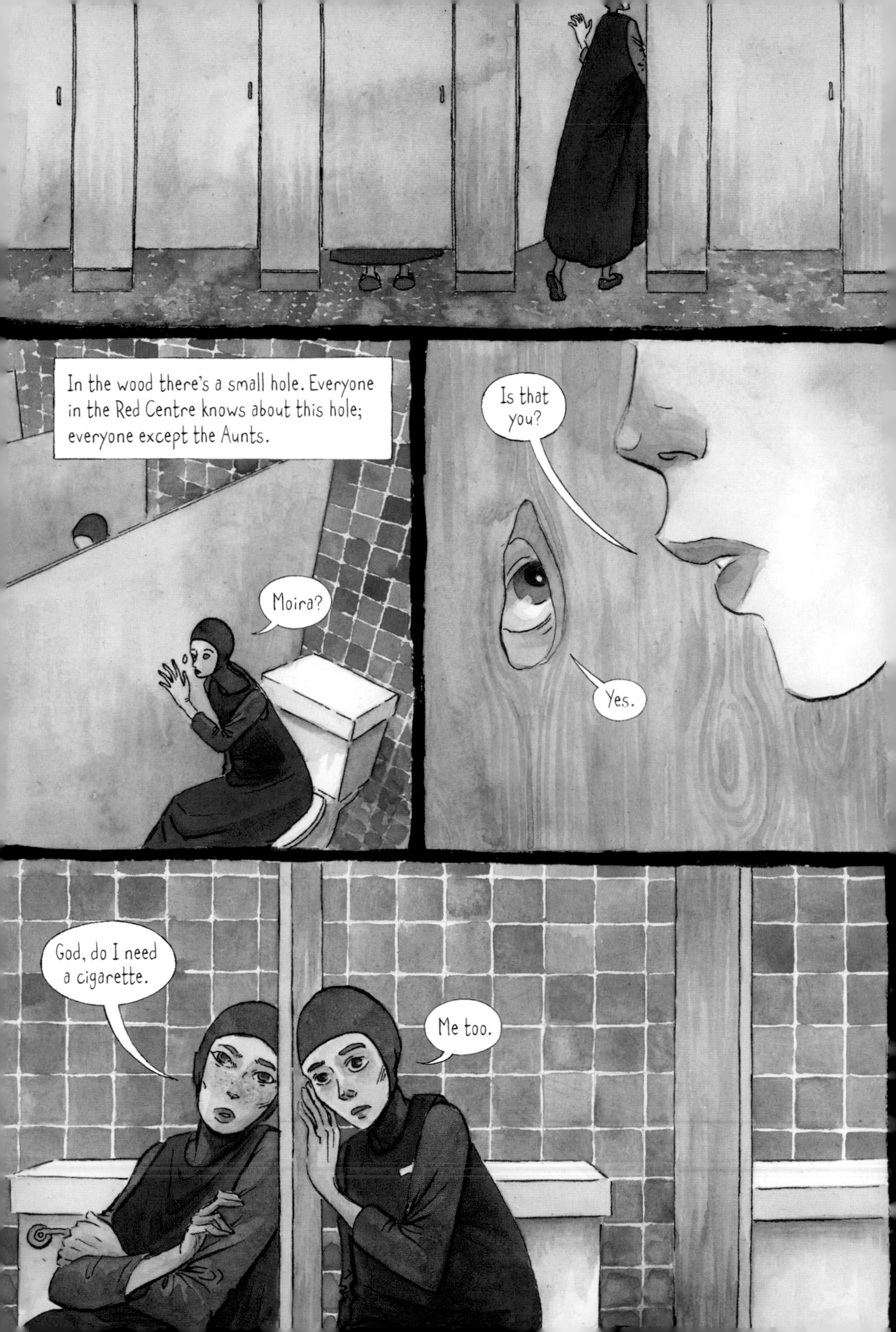
In the wood there's a small hole. Everyone in the Red Centre knows about this hole; everyone except the Aunts.
Moira?
Is that you?
Yes.
God, do I need a cigarette.
Me too.

VI

HOUSEHOLD

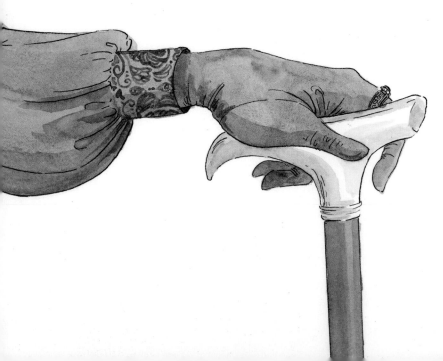

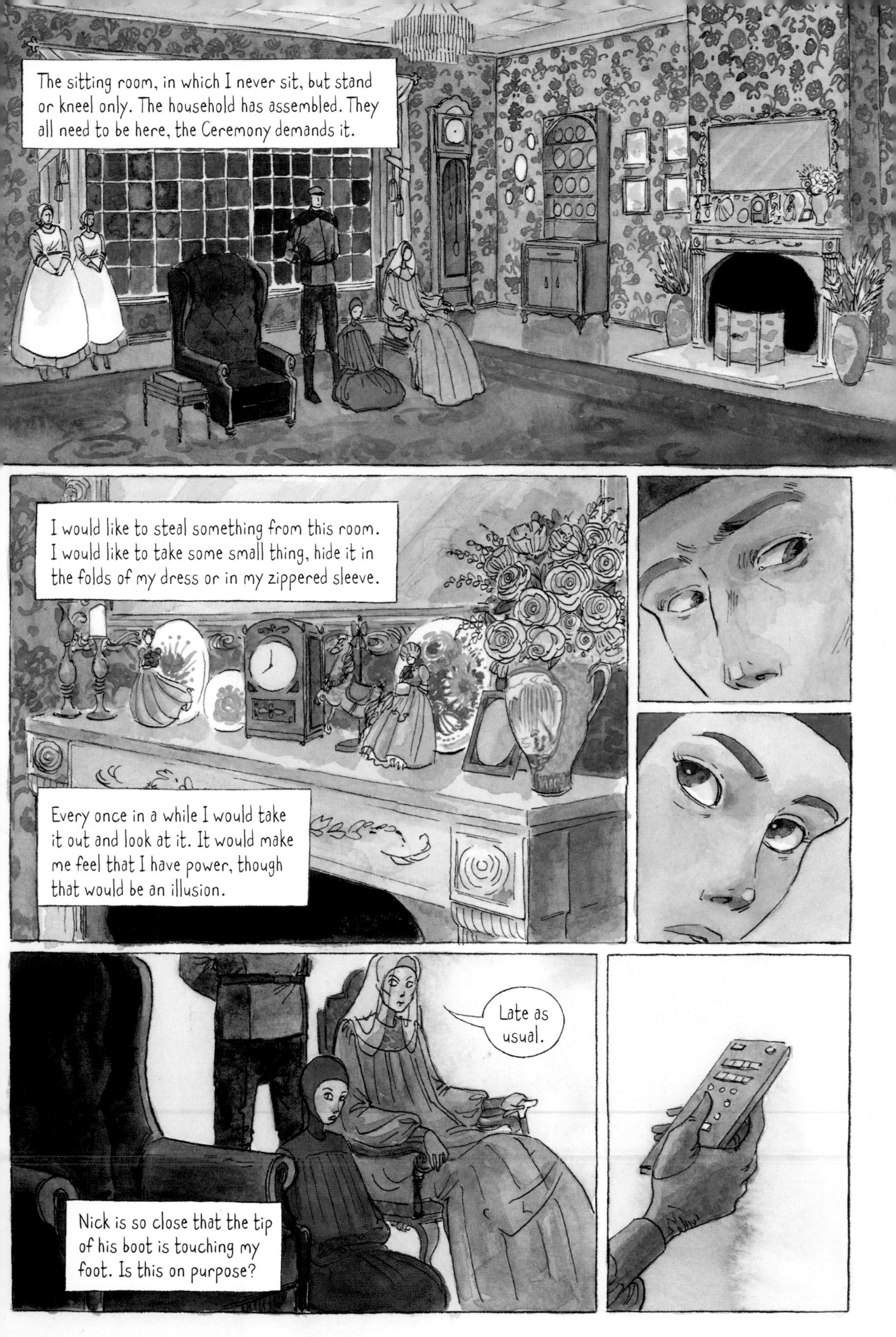
The sitting room, in which I never sit, but stand or kneel only. The household has assembled. They all need to be here, the Ceremony demands it.
I would like to steal something from this room. I would like to take some small thing, hide it in the folds of my dress or in my zippered sleeve.
Every once in a while I would take it out and look at it. It would make me feel that I have power, though that would be an illusion.
Late as usual.
Nick is so close that the tip of his boot is touching my foot. Is this on purpose?

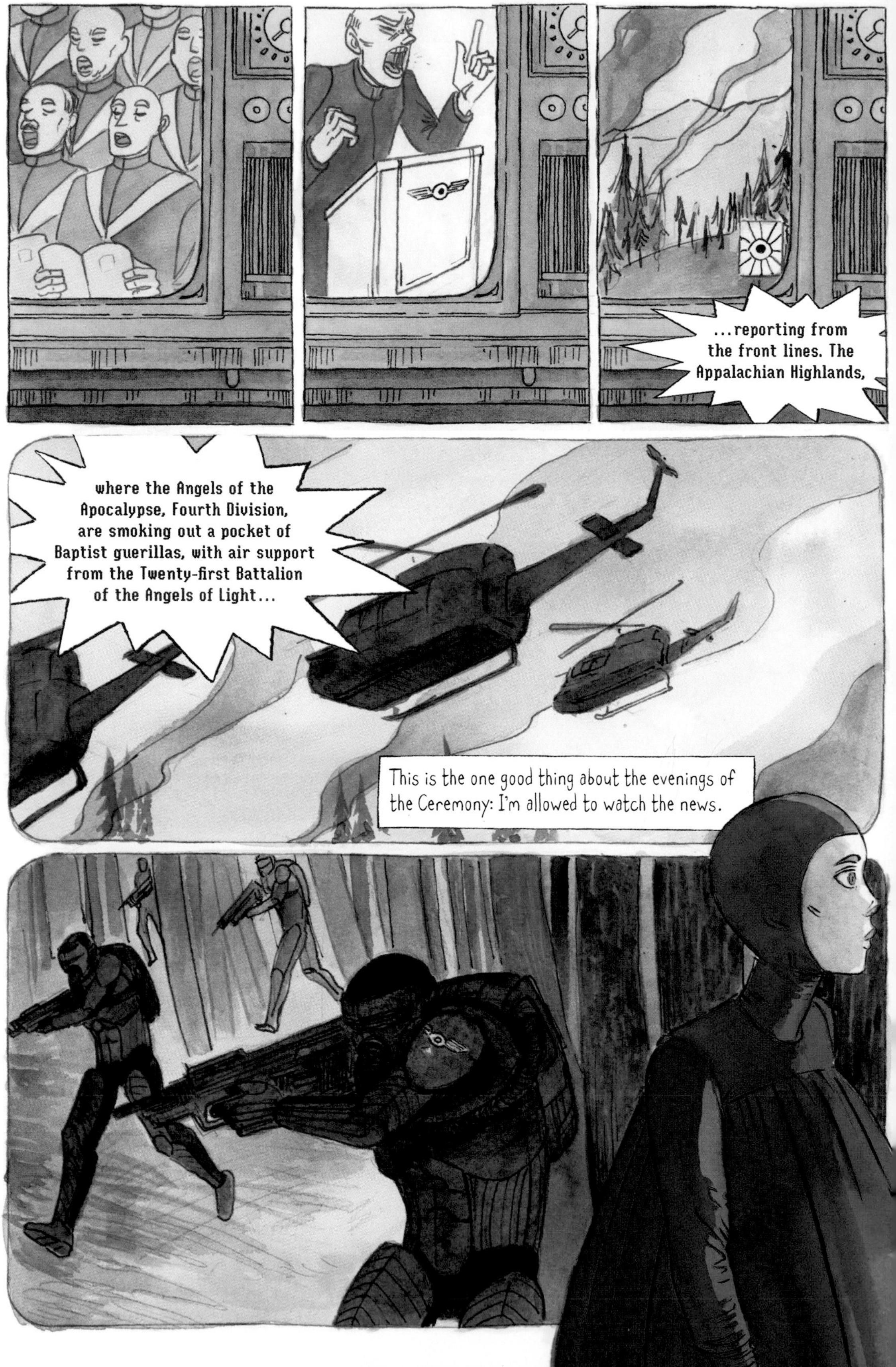
...reporting from the front lines. The Appalachian Highlands,
where the Angels of the Apocalypse, Fourth Division, are smoking out a pocket of Baptist guerillas, with air support from the Twenty-first Battalion of the Angels of Light...
This is the one good thing about the evenings of the Ceremony: I'm allowed to watch the news.

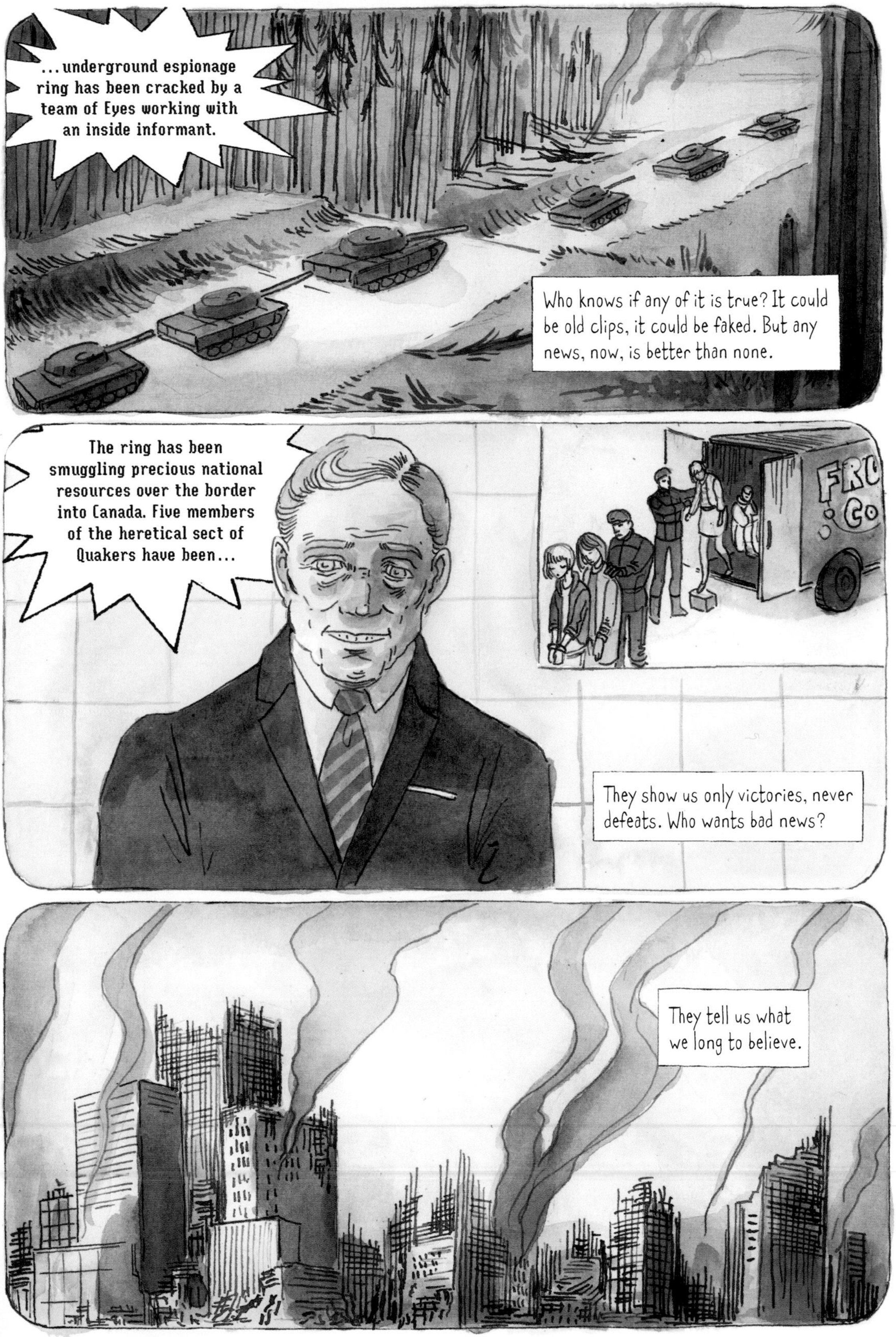
...underground espionage ring has been cracked by a team of Eyes working with an inside informant.
Who knows if any of it is true? It could be old clips, it could be faked. But any news, now, is better than none.
The ring has been smuggling precious national resources over the border into Canada. Five members of the heretical sect of Quakers have been...
They show us only victories, never defeats. Who wants bad news?
They tell us what we long to believe.

The Commander.

If he were to falter, fail, or die,
what would become of us?

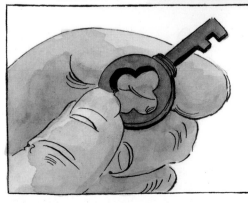

The Bible is kept locked up, the way people once kept
tea locked up, so the servants wouldn't steal it. It is
an incendiary device: who knows what we'd make of it,
if we ever got our hands on it? We can be read to
from it, by him, but we cannot read.

Our heads turn towards him, we are expectant,
here comes our bedtime story.

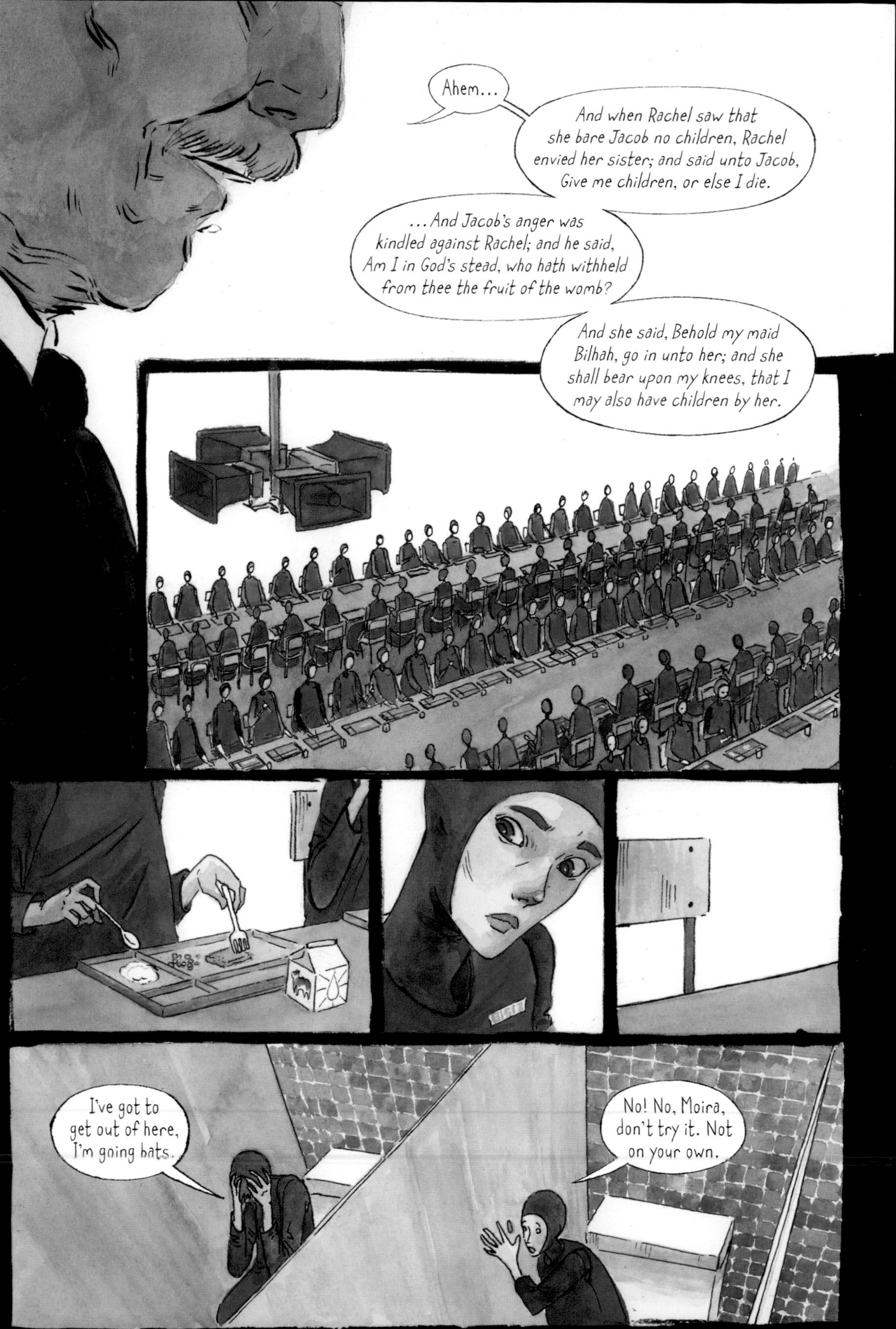
Ahem...
And when Rachel saw that she bare Jacob no children, Rachel envied her sister; and said unto Jacob, Give me children, or else I die.
...And Jacob's anger was kindled against Rachel; and he said, Am I in God's stead, who hath withheld from thee the fruit of the womb?
And she said, Behold my maid Bilhah, go in unto her; and she shall bear upon my knees, that I may also have children by her.
I've got to get out of here, I'm going bats.
No! No, Moira, don't try it. Not on your own.

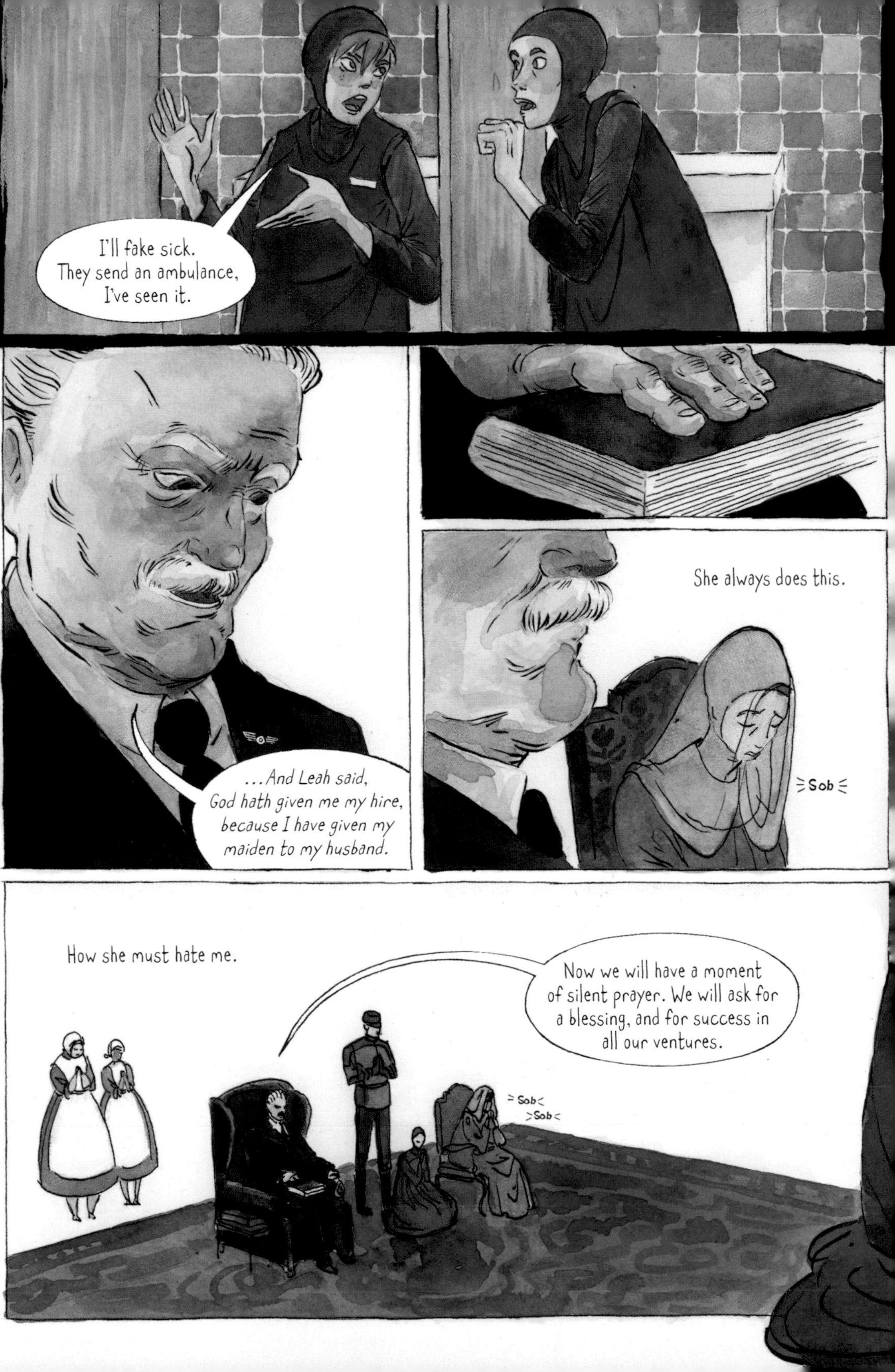
I'll fake sick. They send an ambulance, I've seen it.
...And Leah said, God hath given me my hire, because I have given my maiden to my husband.
She always does this.
Sob
How she must hate me.
Now we will have a moment of silent prayer. We will ask for a blessing, and for success in all our ventures.
Sob
Sob

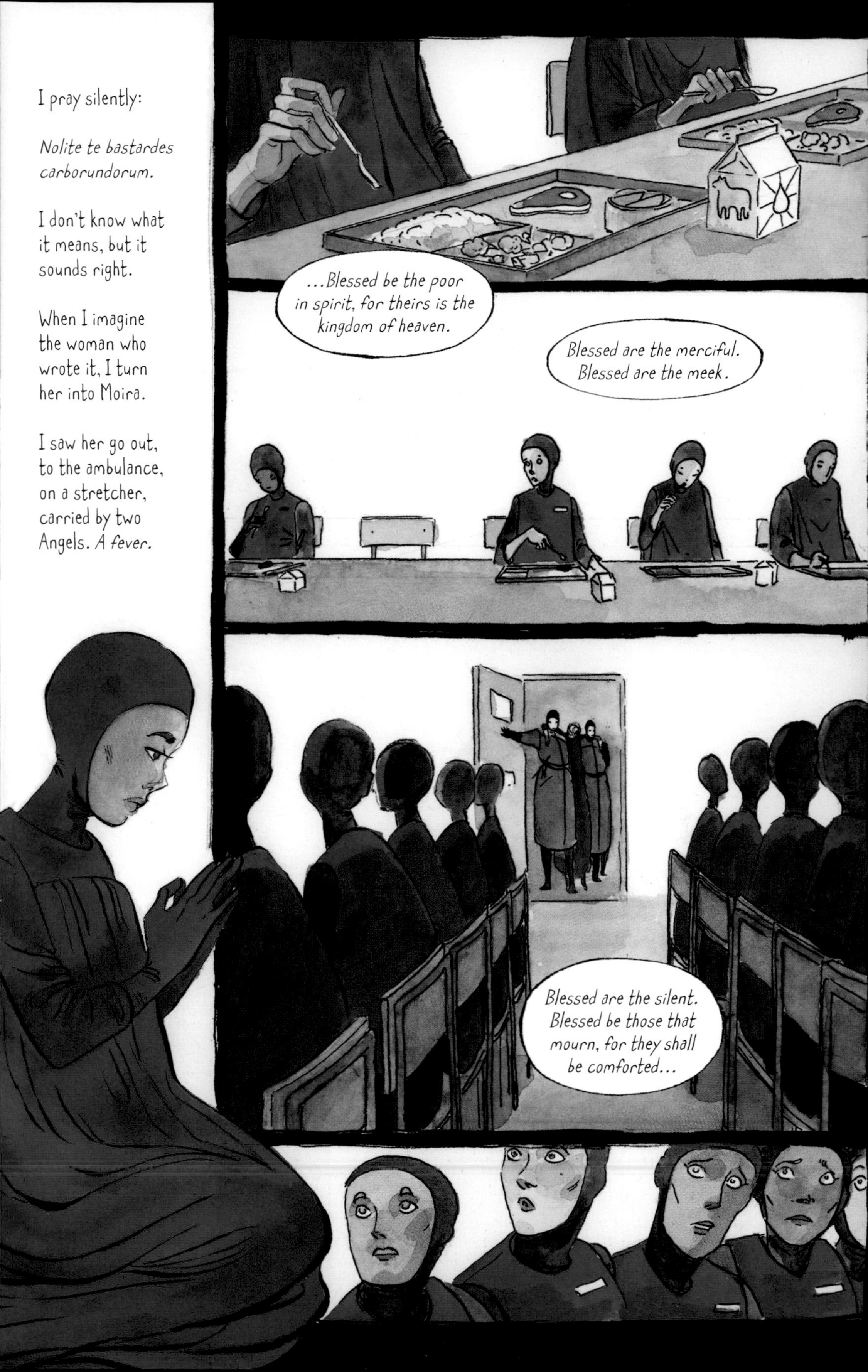
I pray silently:
Nolite te bastardes carborundorum.
I don't know what it means, but it sounds right.
When I imagine the woman who wrote it, I turn her into Moira.
I saw her go out, to the ambulance, on a stretcher, carried by two Angels. *A fever.*
...Blessed be the poor in spirit, for theirs is the kingdom of heaven.
Blessed are the merciful. Blessed are the meek.
Blessed are the silent. Blessed be those that mourn, for they shall be comforted...

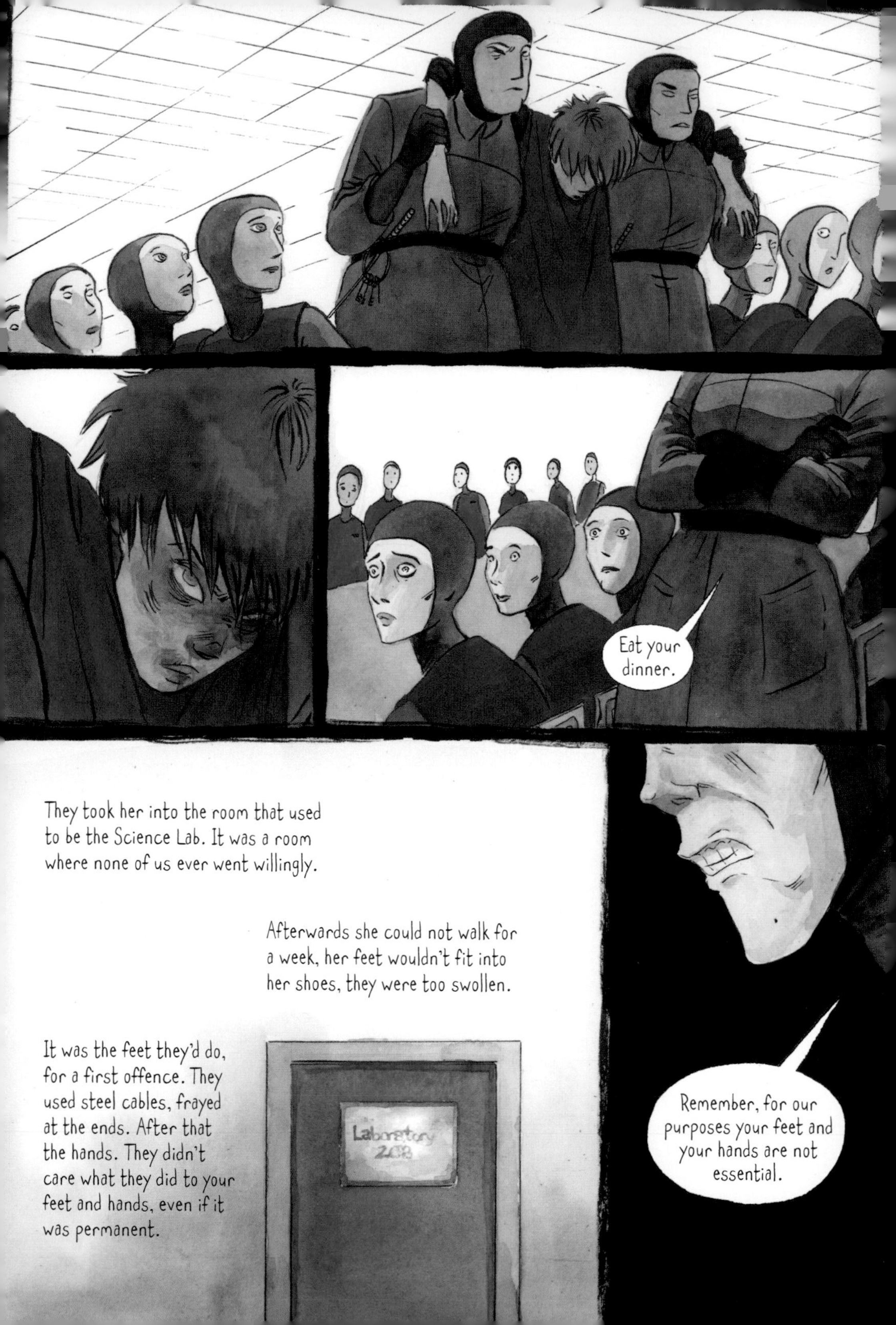
Eat your dinner.
They took her into the room that used to be the Science Lab. It was a room where none of us ever went willingly.
Afterwards she could not walk for a week, her feet wouldn't fit into her shoes, they were too swollen.
It was the feet they'd do, for a first offence. They used steel cables, frayed at the ends. After that the hands. They didn't care what they did to your feet and hands, even if it was permanent.
Laboratory
Remember, for our purposes your feet and your hands are not essential.

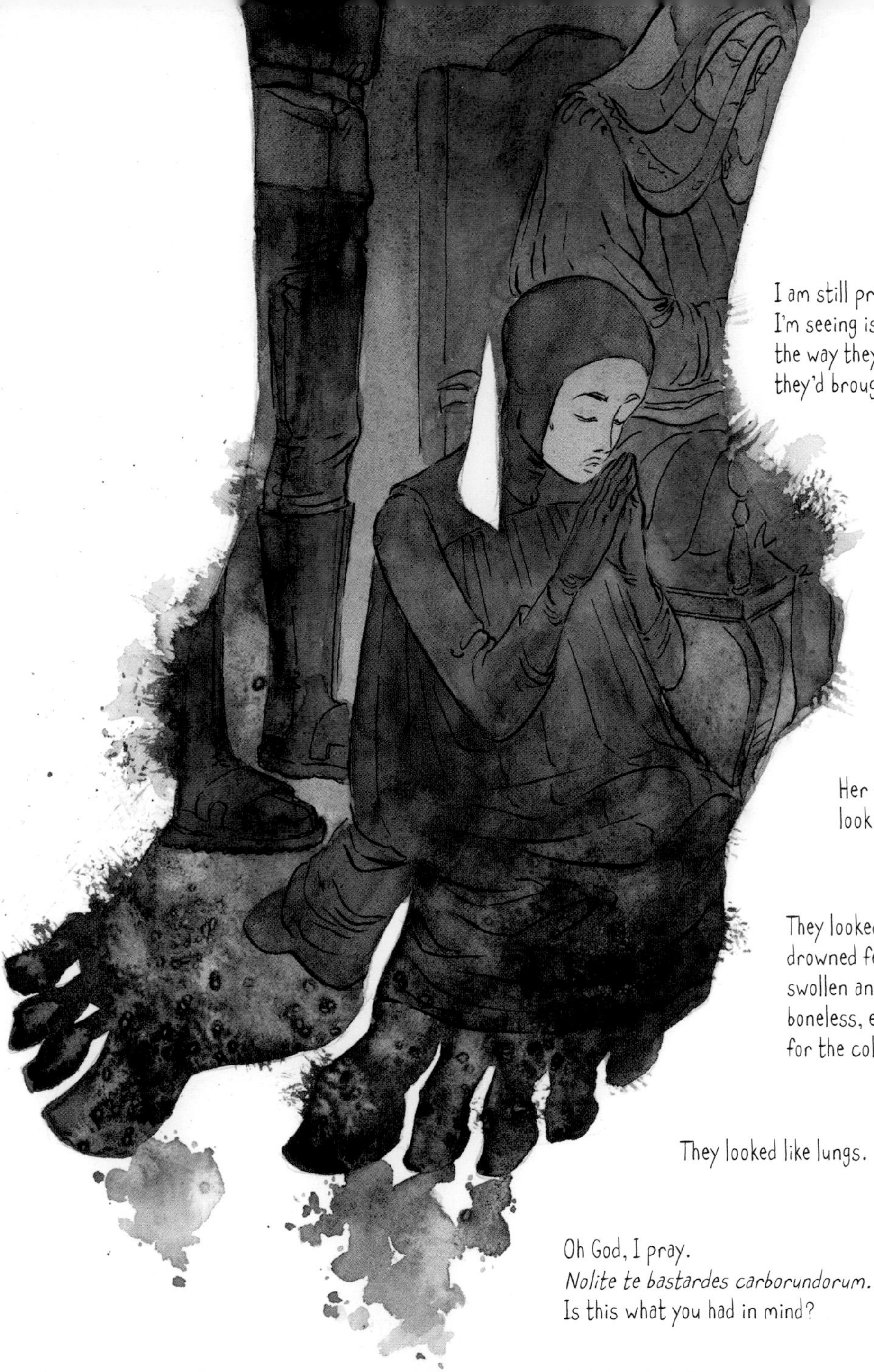
I am still praying but what I'm seeing is Moira's feet, the way they looked after they'd brought her back.
Her feet did not look like feet at all.
They looked like drowned feet, swollen and boneless, except for the colour.
They looked like lungs.
Oh God, I pray.
Nolite te bastardes carborundorum.
Is this what you had in mind?

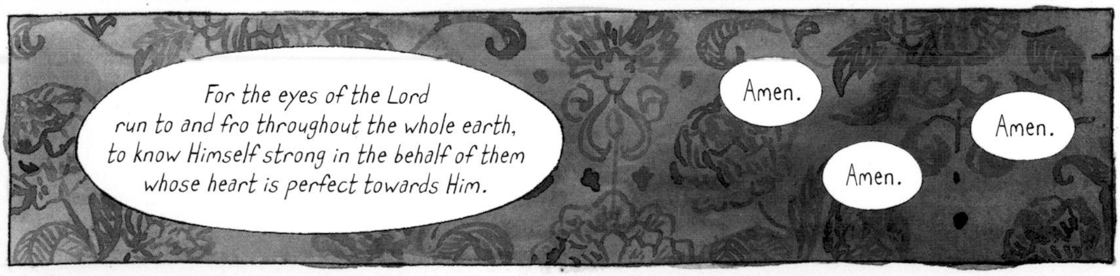
For the eyes of the Lord run to and fro throughout the whole earth, to know Himself strong in the behalf of them whose heart is perfect towards Him.
Amen.
Amen.
Amen.

The Ceremony goes as usual.

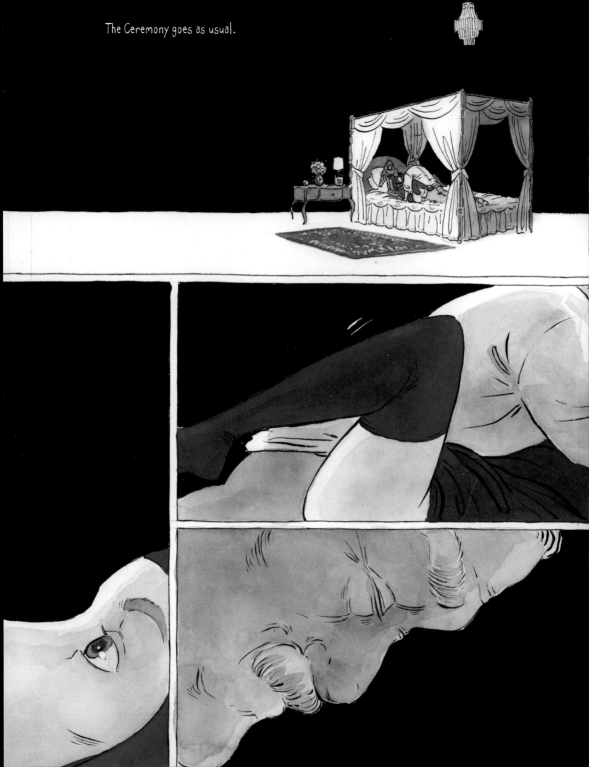

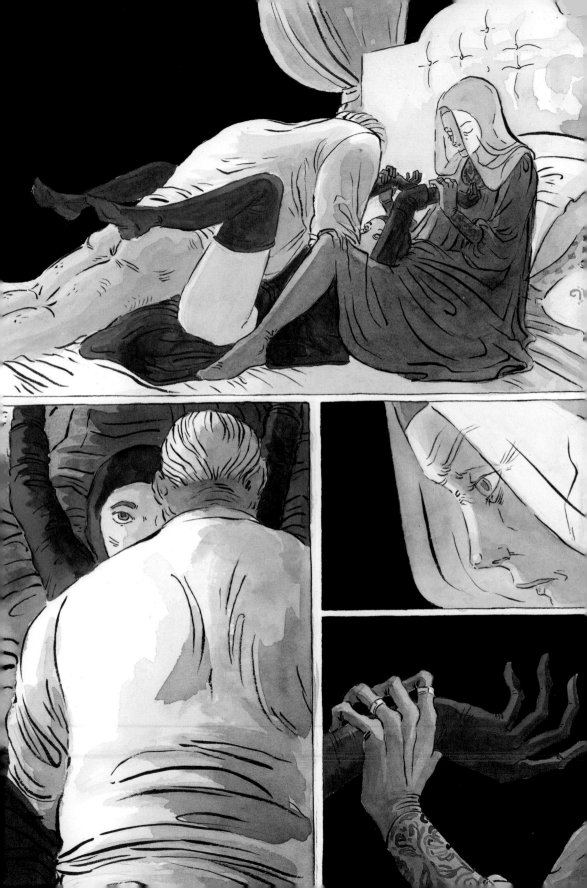

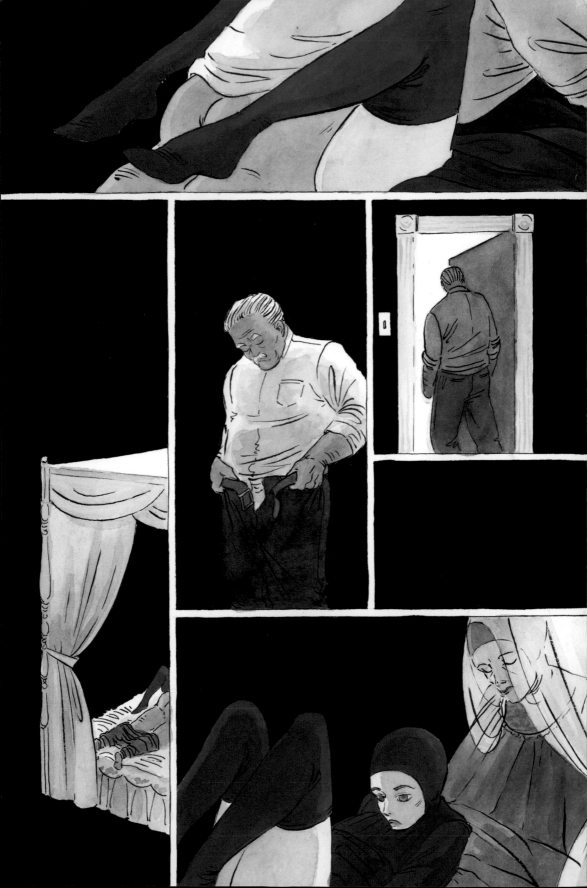

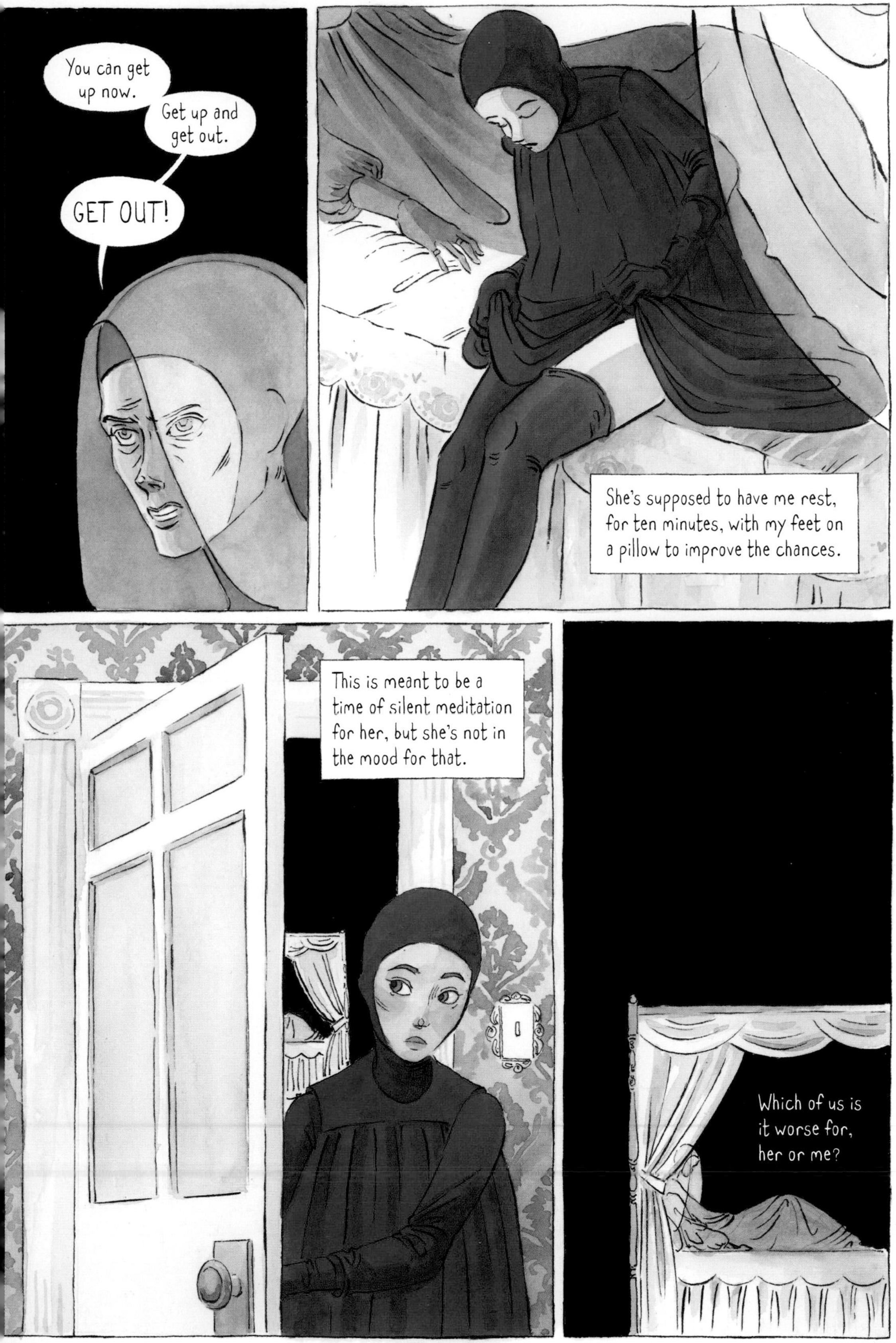
You can get up now.
Get up and get out.
GET OUT!
She's supposed to have me rest, for ten minutes, with my feet on a pillow to improve the chances.
This is meant to be a time of silent meditation for her, but she's not in the mood for that.
Which of us is it worse for, her or me?

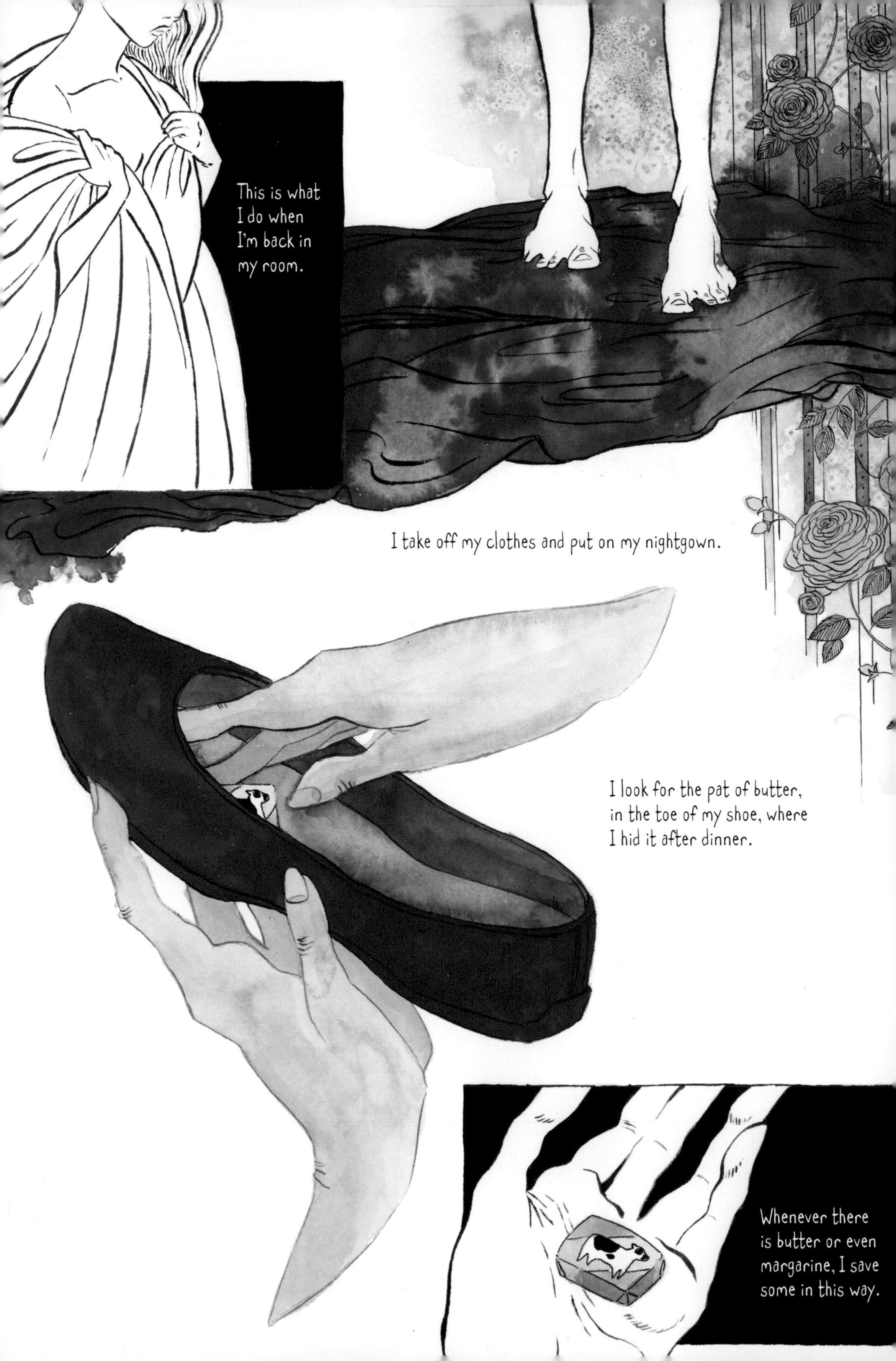
This is what I do when I'm back in my room.
I take off my clothes and put on my nightgown.
I look for the pat of butter, in the toe of my shoe, where I hid it after dinner.
Whenever there is butter or even margarine, I save some in this way.

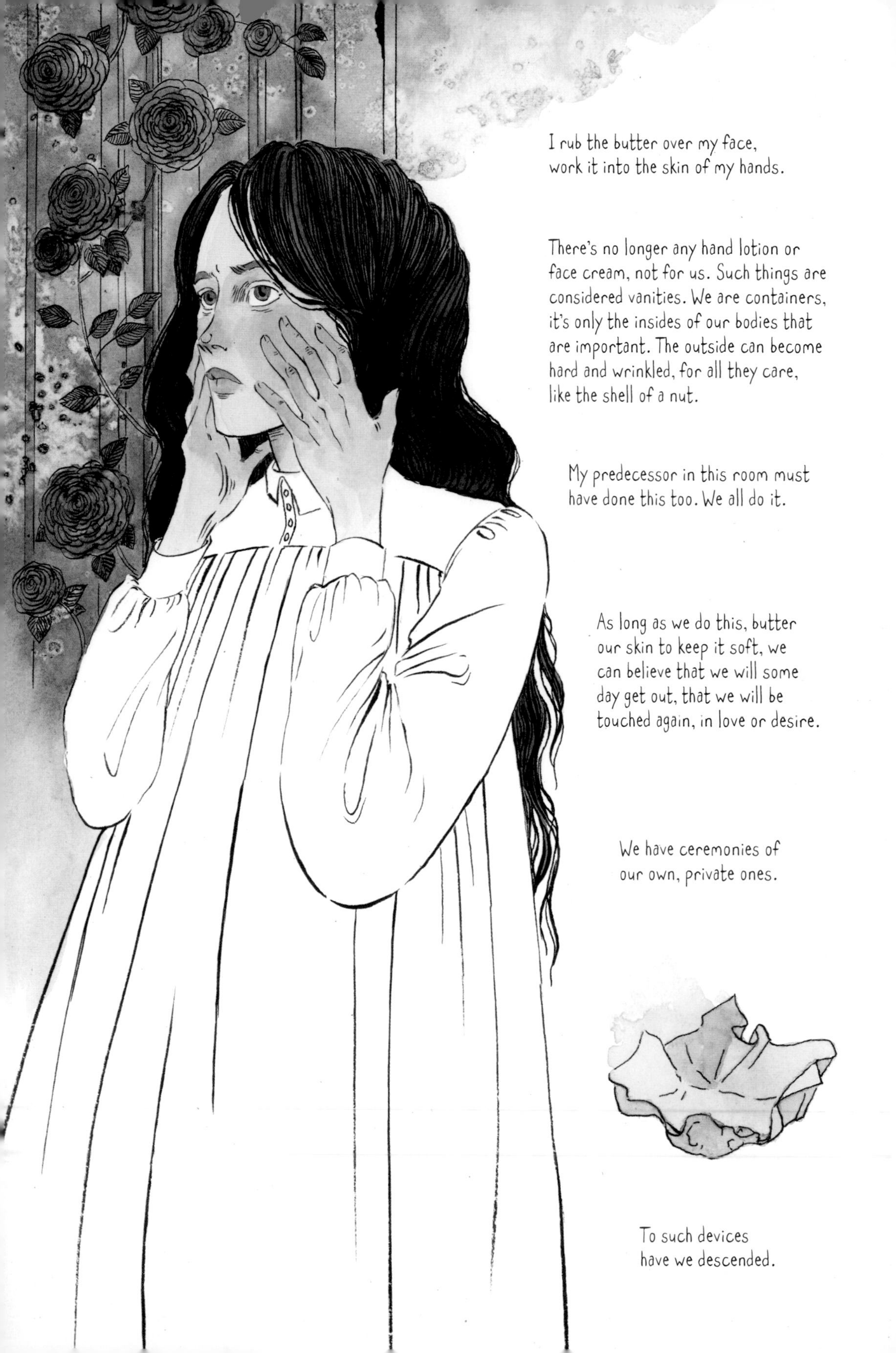
I rub the butter over my face,
work it into the skin of my hands.
There's no longer any hand lotion or face cream, not for us. Such things are considered vanities. We are containers, it's only the insides of our bodies that are important. The outside can become hard and wrinkled, for all they care, like the shell of a nut.
My predecessor in this room must have done this too. We all do it.
As long as we do this, butter our skin to keep it soft, we can believe that we will some day get out, that we will be touched again, in love or desire.
We have ceremonies of our own, private ones.
To such devices have we descended.

VII

NIGHT

Buttered, I lie on my bed, flat, like a piece of toast.

I can't sleep.

In the semi-dark I stare up at the blind plaster eye in the middle of the ceiling, which stares back down at me, even though it can't see.

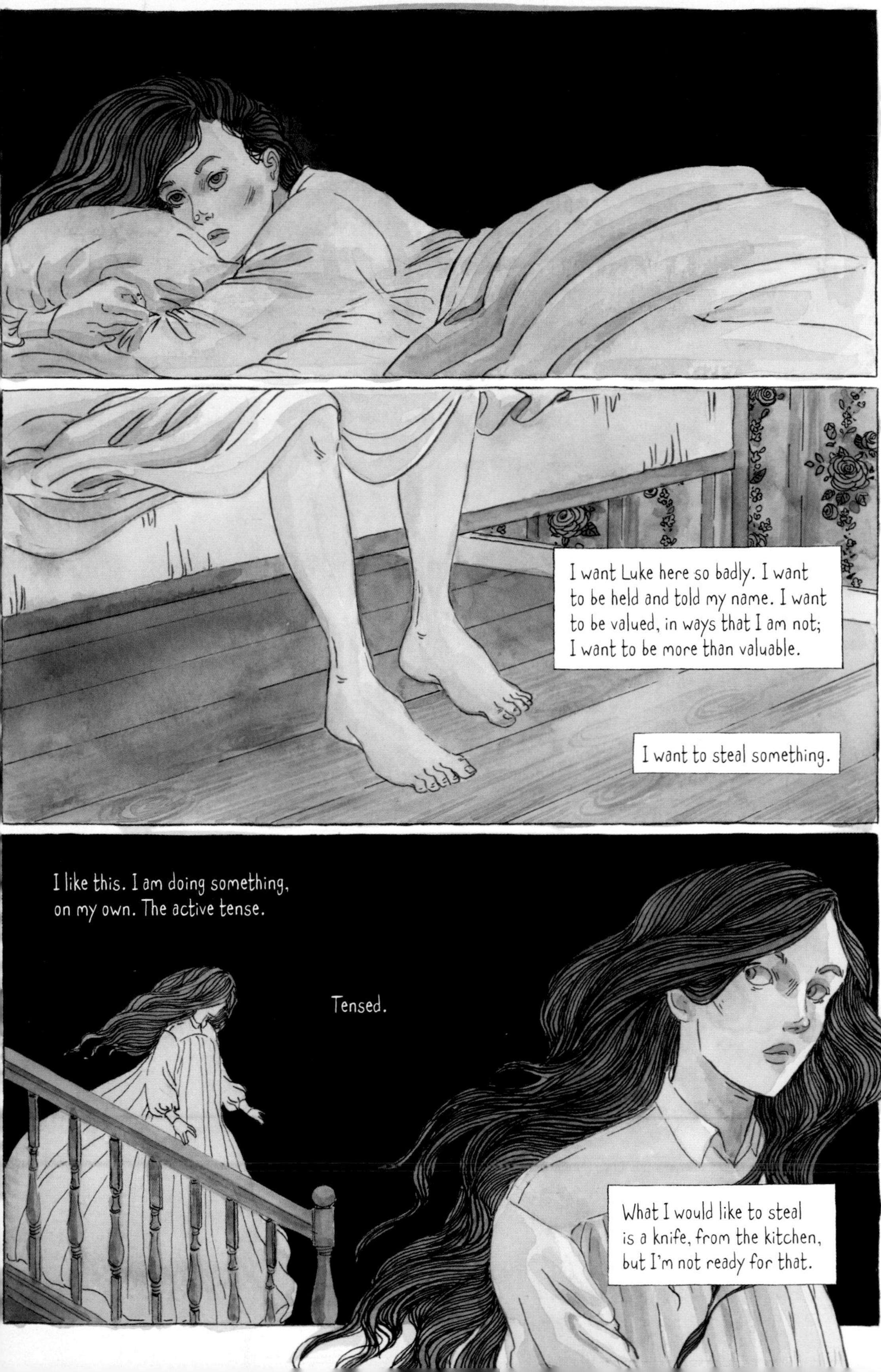

I want Luke here so badly. I want to be held and told my name. I want to be valued, in ways that I am not; I want to be more than valuable.
I want to steal something.
I like this. I am doing something, on my own. The active tense.
Tensed.
What I would like to steal is a knife, from the kitchen, but I'm not ready for that.

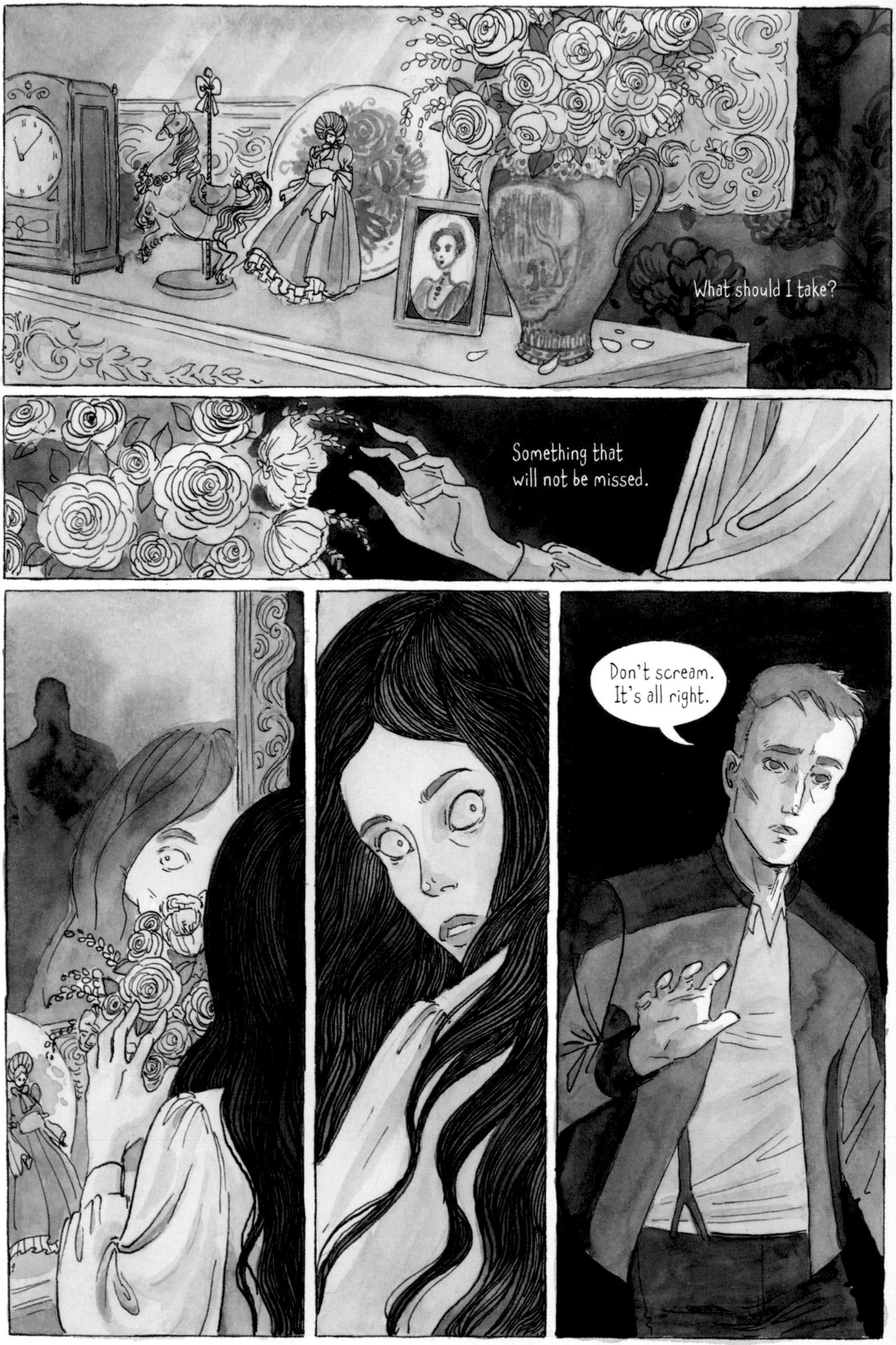
What should I take?
Something that will not be missed.
Don't scream. It's all right.

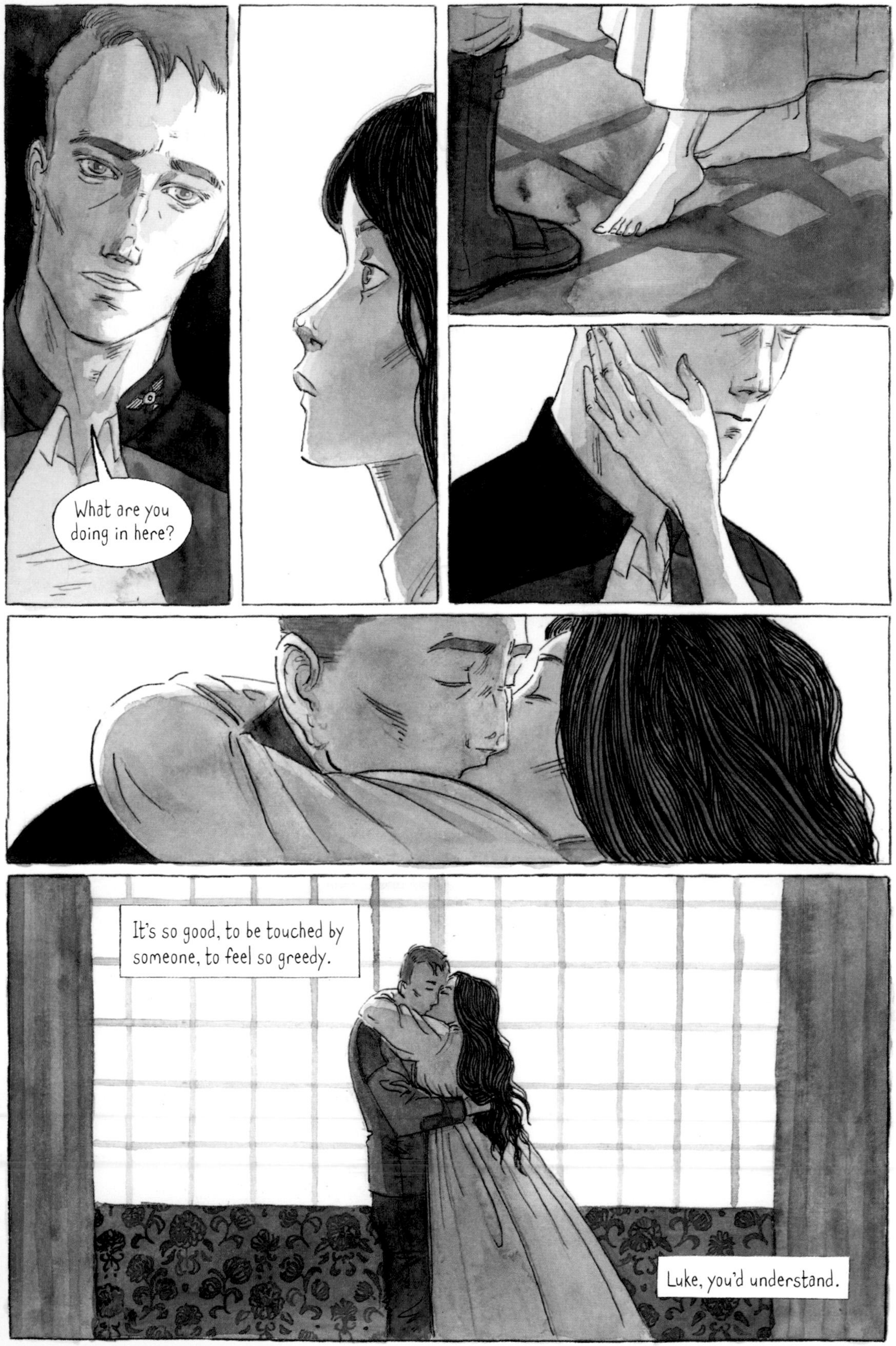
What are you doing in here?
It's so good, to be touched by someone, to feel so greedy.
Luke, you'd understand.

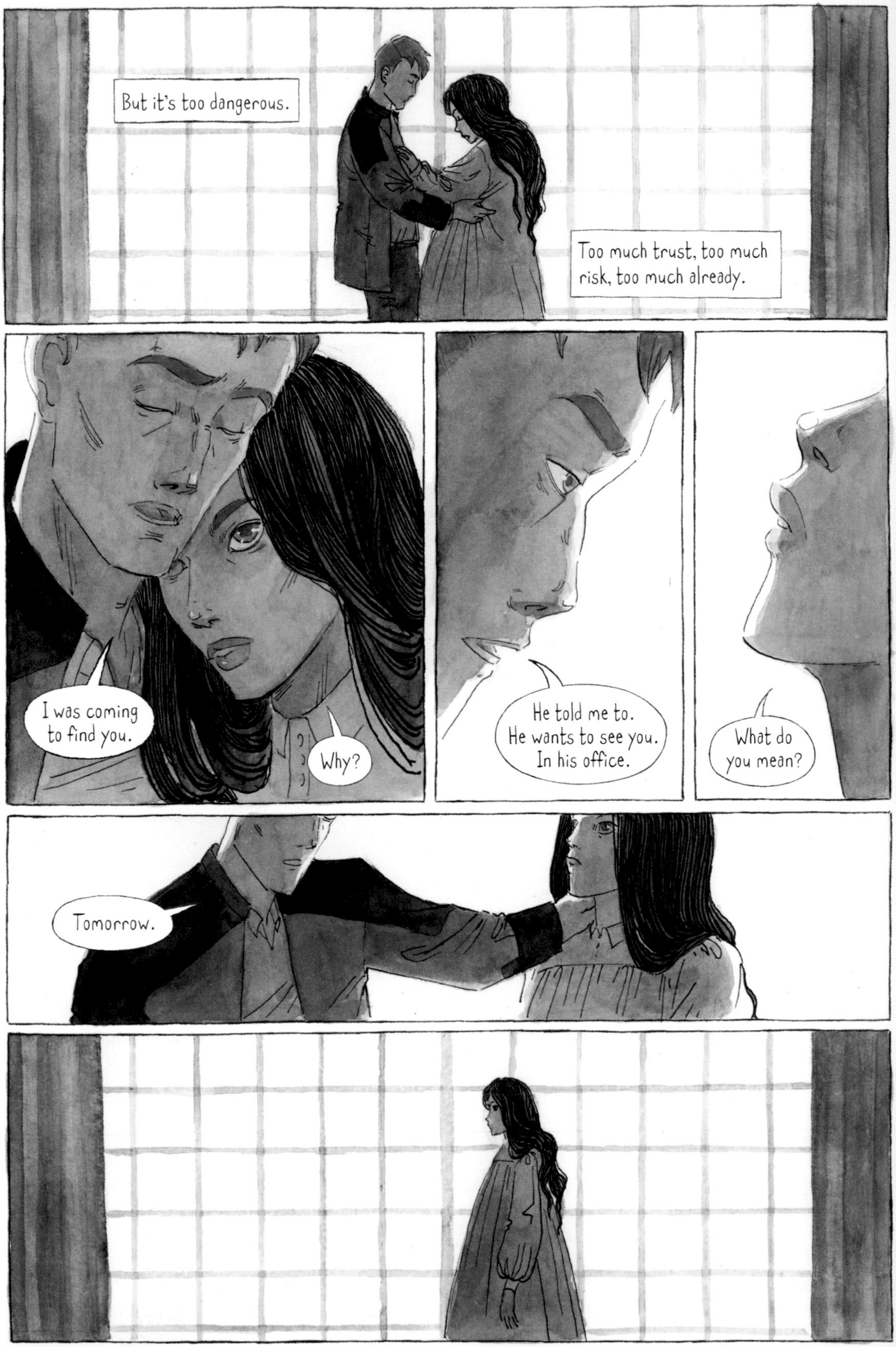
But it's too dangerous.
Too much trust, too much risk, too much already.
I was coming to find you.
Why?
He told me to. He wants to see you. In his office.
What do you mean?
Tomorrow.

VIII

BIRTH DAY

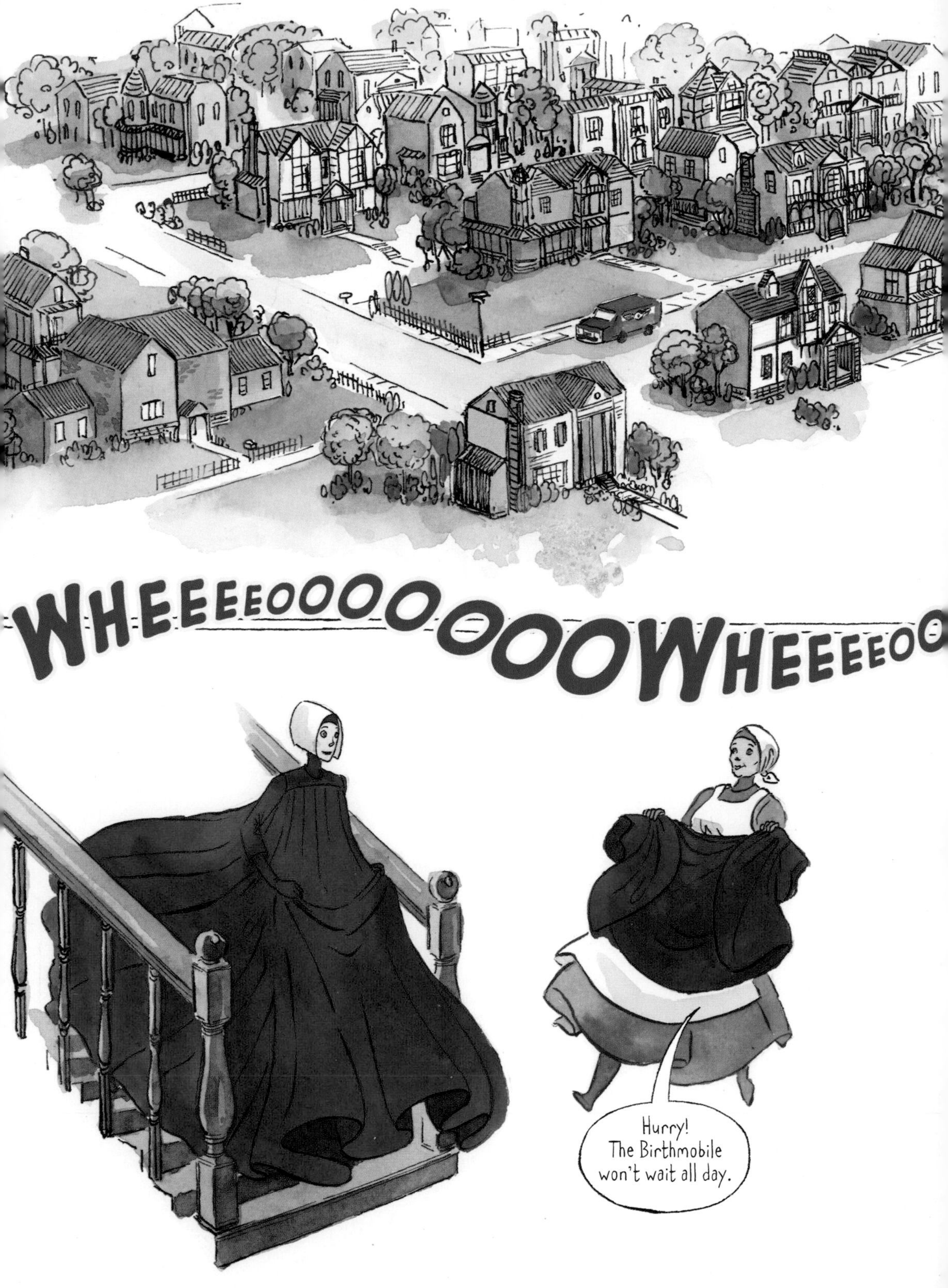
WHEEEEOOOOOOOOWHEEEEEO
Hurry! The Birthmobile won't wait all day.

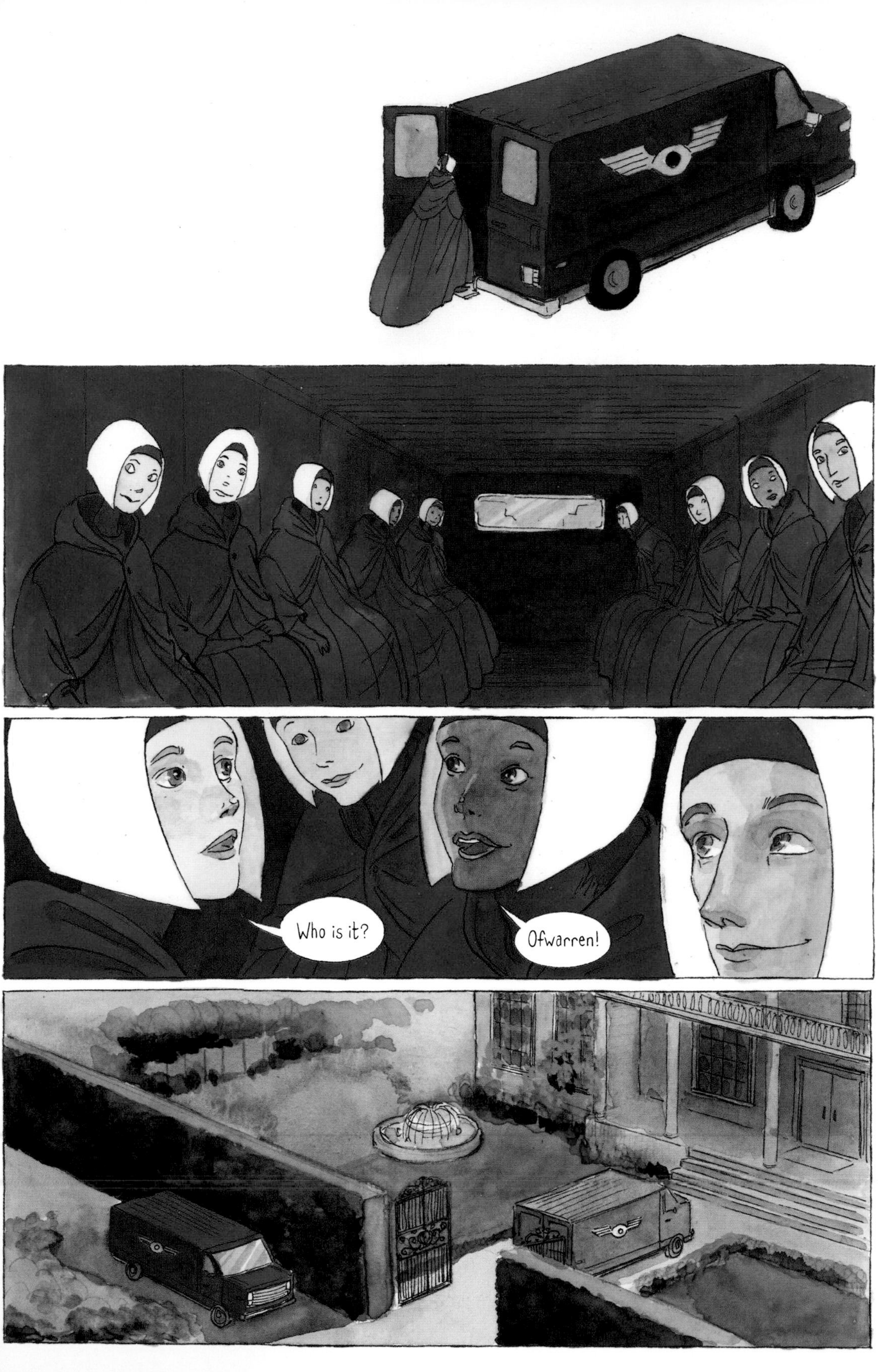
Who is it?
Ofwarren!

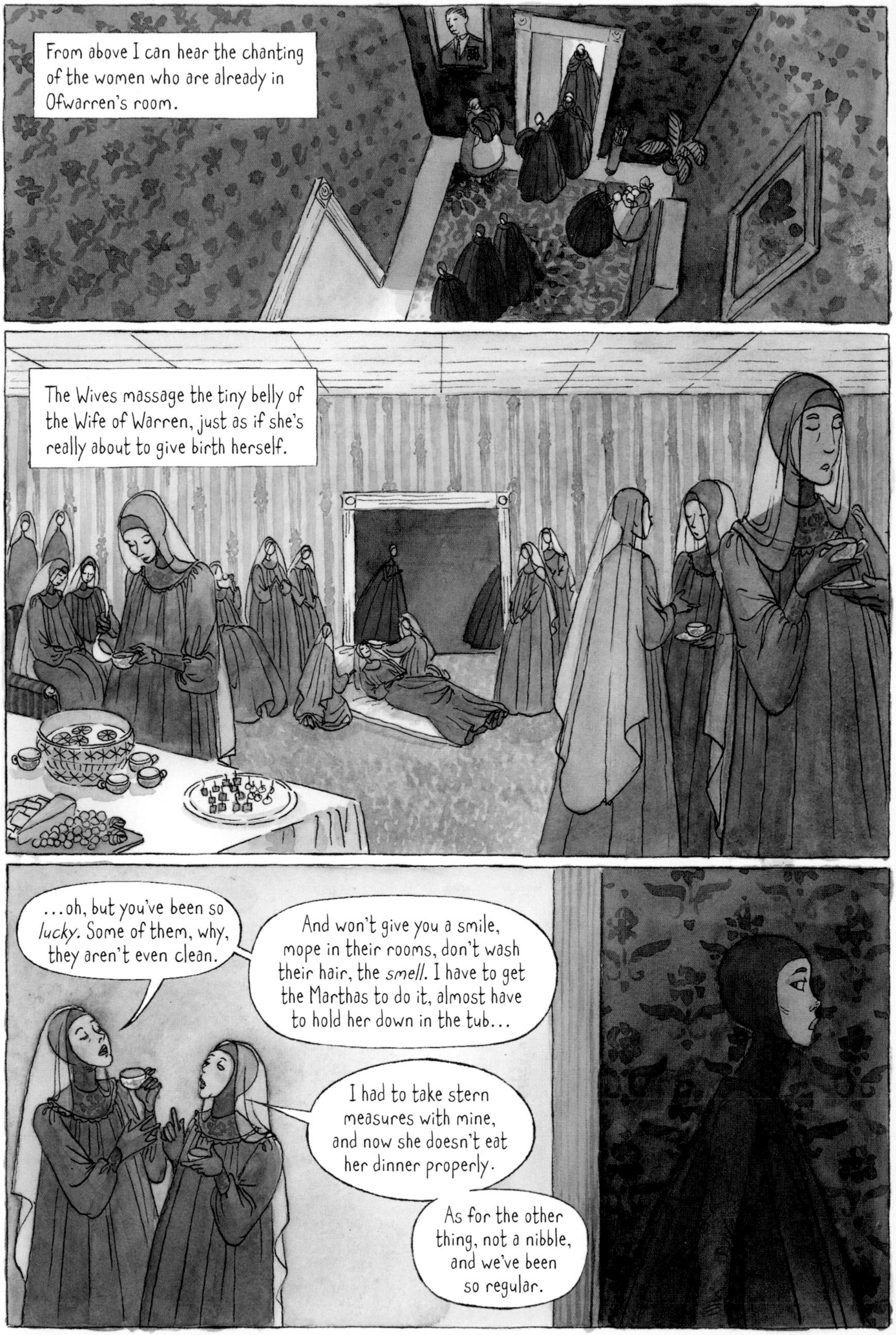
From above I can hear the chanting of the women who are already in Ofwarren's room.
The Wives massage the tiny belly of the Wife of Warren, just as if she's really about to give birth herself.
...oh, but you've been so *lucky*. Some of them, why, they aren't even clean.
And won't give you a smile, mope in their rooms, don't wash their hair, the *smell*. I have to get the Marthas to do it, almost have to hold her down in the tub...
I had to take stern measures with mine, and now she doesn't eat her dinner properly.
As for the other thing, not a nibble, and we've been so regular.

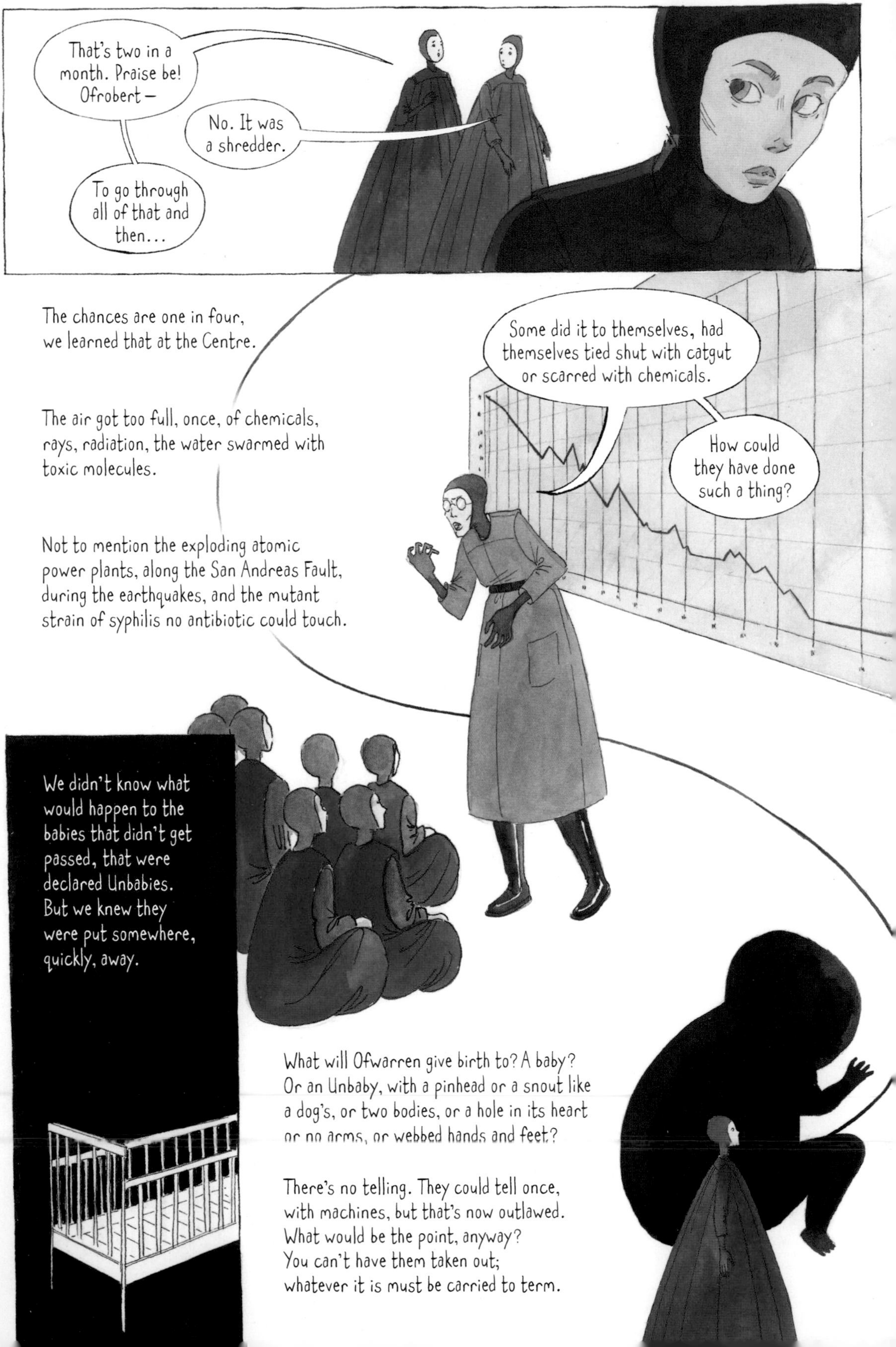
That's two in a month. Praise be! Ofrobert –
No. It was a shredder.
To go through all of that and then...
The chances are one in four, we learned that at the Centre.
The air got too full, once, of chemicals, rays, radiation, the water swarmed with toxic molecules.
Not to mention the exploding atomic power plants, along the San Andreas Fault, during the earthquakes, and the mutant strain of syphilis no antibiotic could touch.
Some did it to themselves, had themselves tied shut with catgut or scarred with chemicals.
How could they have done such a thing?
We didn't know what would happen to the babies that didn't get passed, that were declared Unbabies. But we knew they were put somewhere, quickly, away.
What will Ofwarren give birth to? A baby? Or an Unbaby, with a pinhead or a snout like a dog's, or two bodies, or a hole in its heart or no arms, or webbed hands and feet?
There's no telling. They could tell once, with machines, but that's now outlawed. What would be the point, anyway? You can't have them taken out; whatever it is must be carried to term.

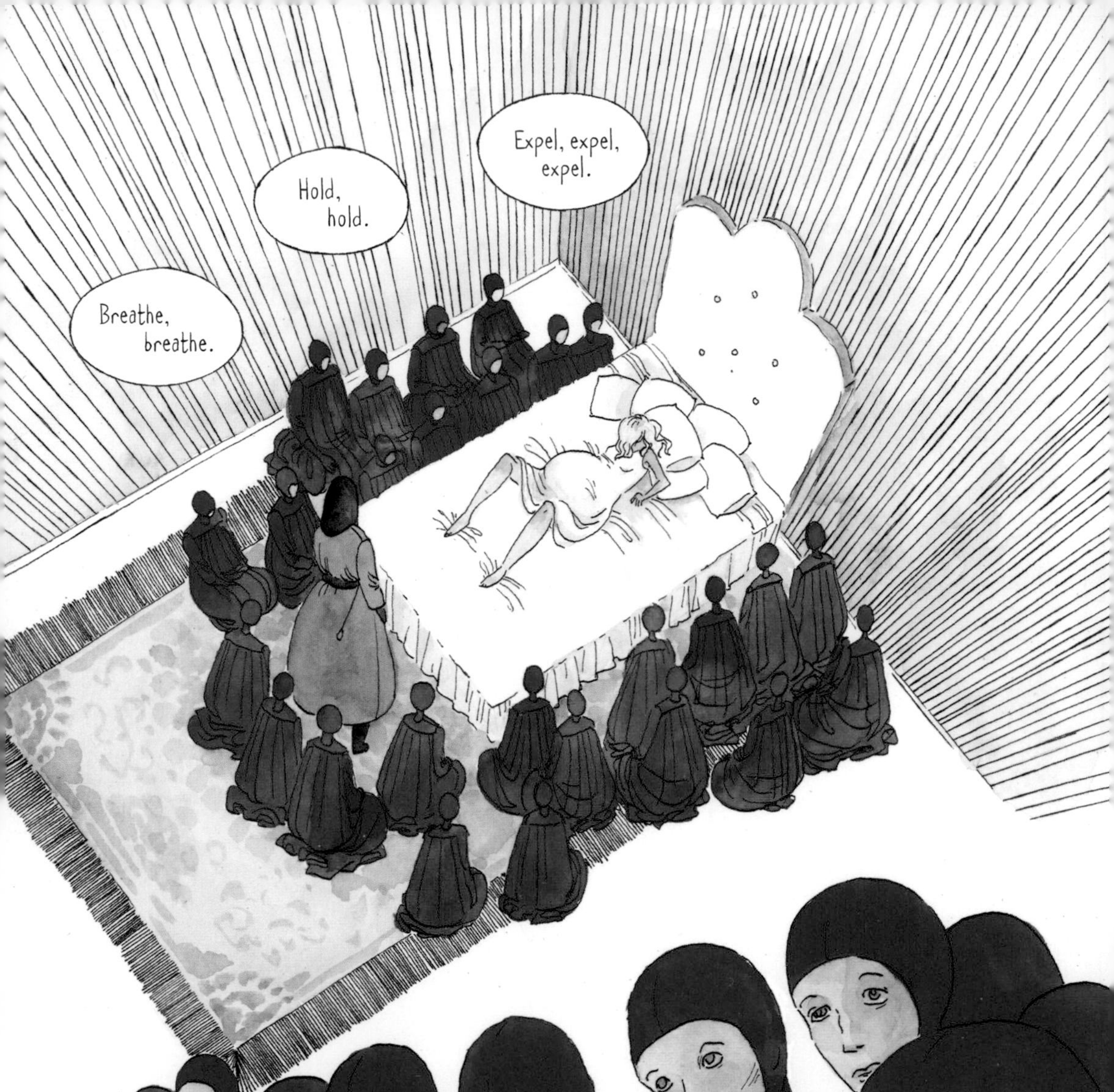
Breathe,
breathe.
Hold,
hold.
Expel, expel,
expel.
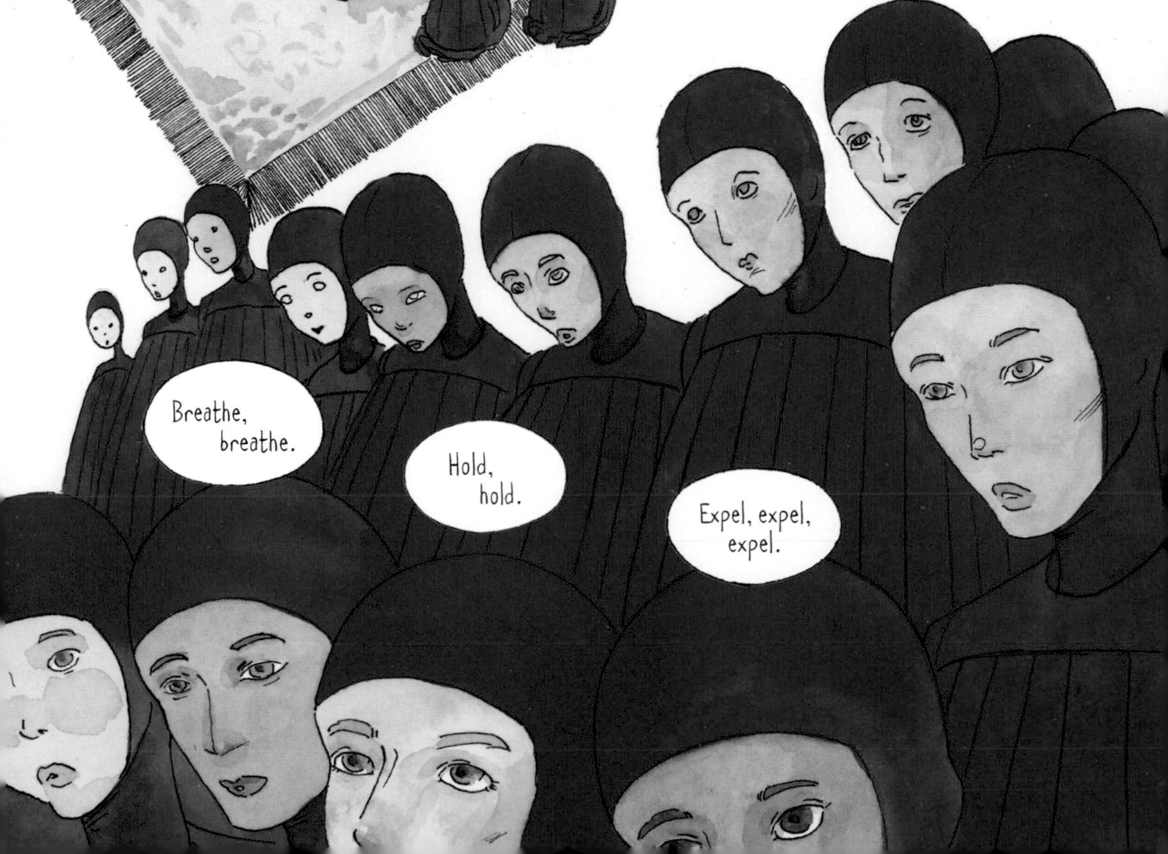
Breathe,
breathe.
Hold,
hold.
Expel, expel,
expel.

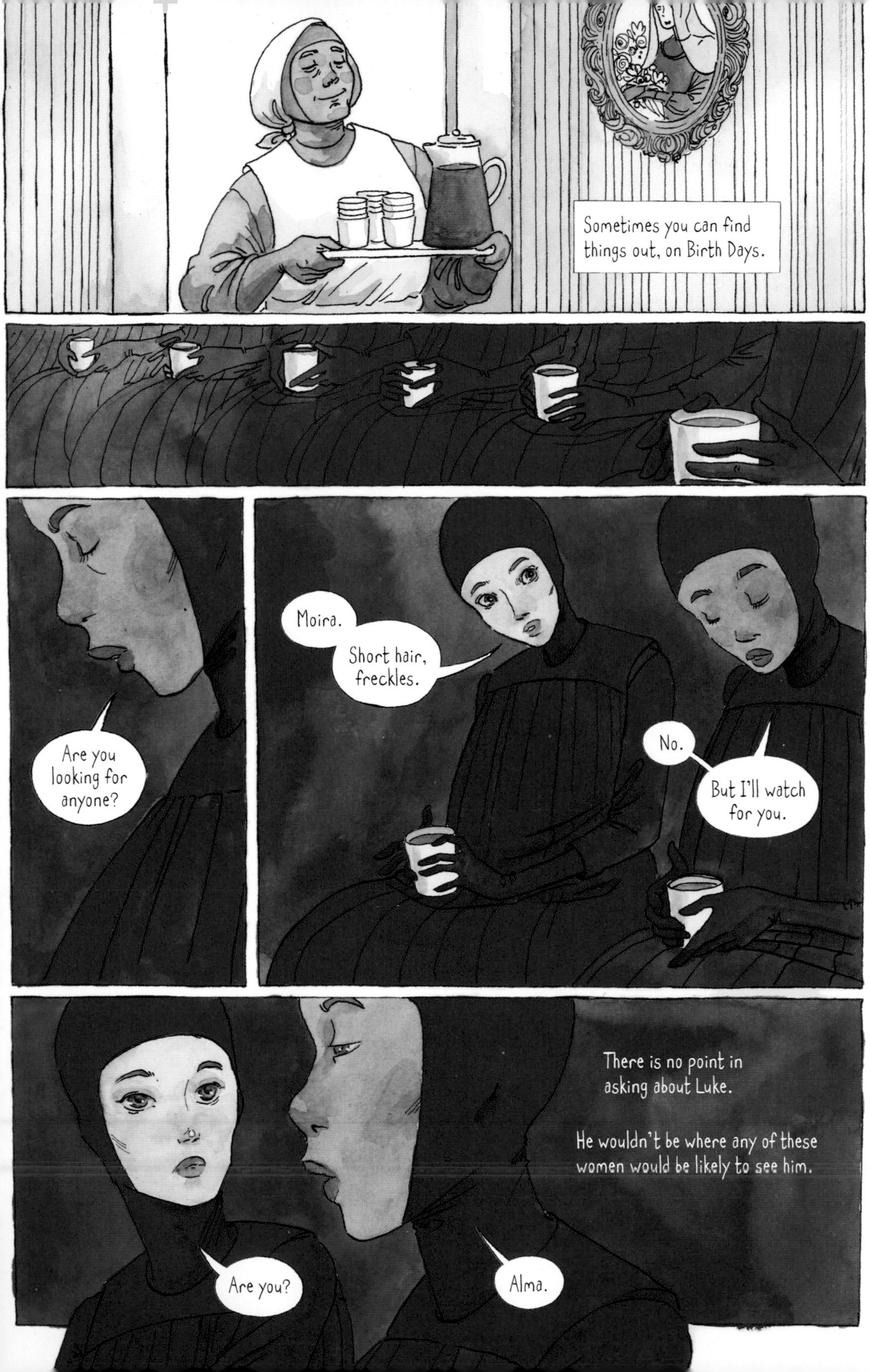
Sometimes you can find things out, on Birth Days.
Are you looking for anyone?
Moira.
Short hair, freckles.
No.
But I'll watch for you.
Are you?
Alma.
There is no point in asking about Luke.
He wouldn't be where any of these women would be likely to see him.

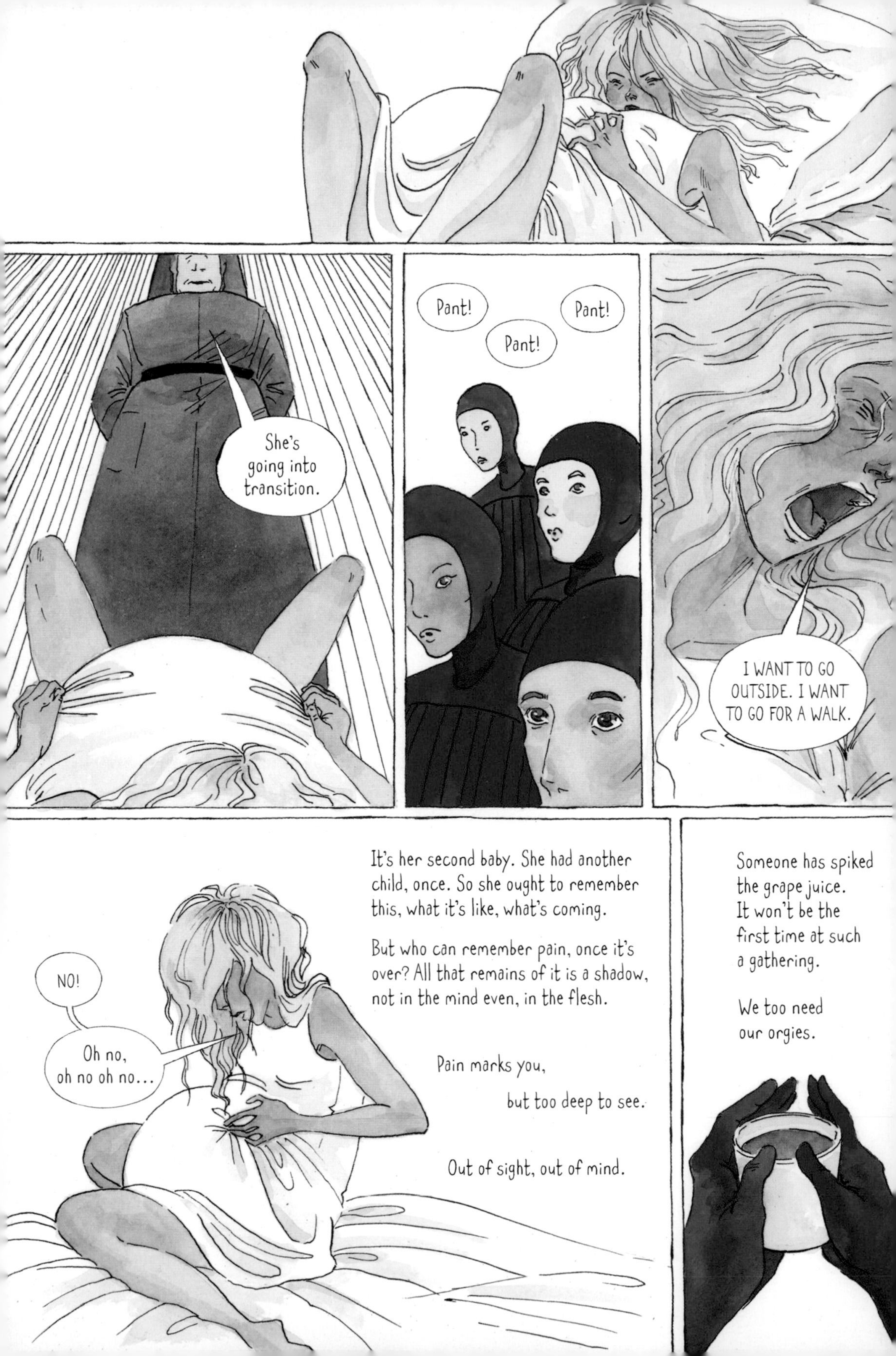
She's going into transition.
Pant!
Pant!
Pant!
I WANT TO GO OUTSIDE. I WANT TO GO FOR A WALK.
It's her second baby. She had another child, once. So she ought to remember this, what it's like, what's coming.
But who can remember pain, once it's over? All that remains of it is a shadow, not in the mind even, in the flesh.
NO!
Oh no, oh no oh no...
Pain marks you,
but too deep to see.
Out of sight, out of mind.
Someone has spiked the grape juice. It won't be the first time at such a gathering.
We too need our orgies.

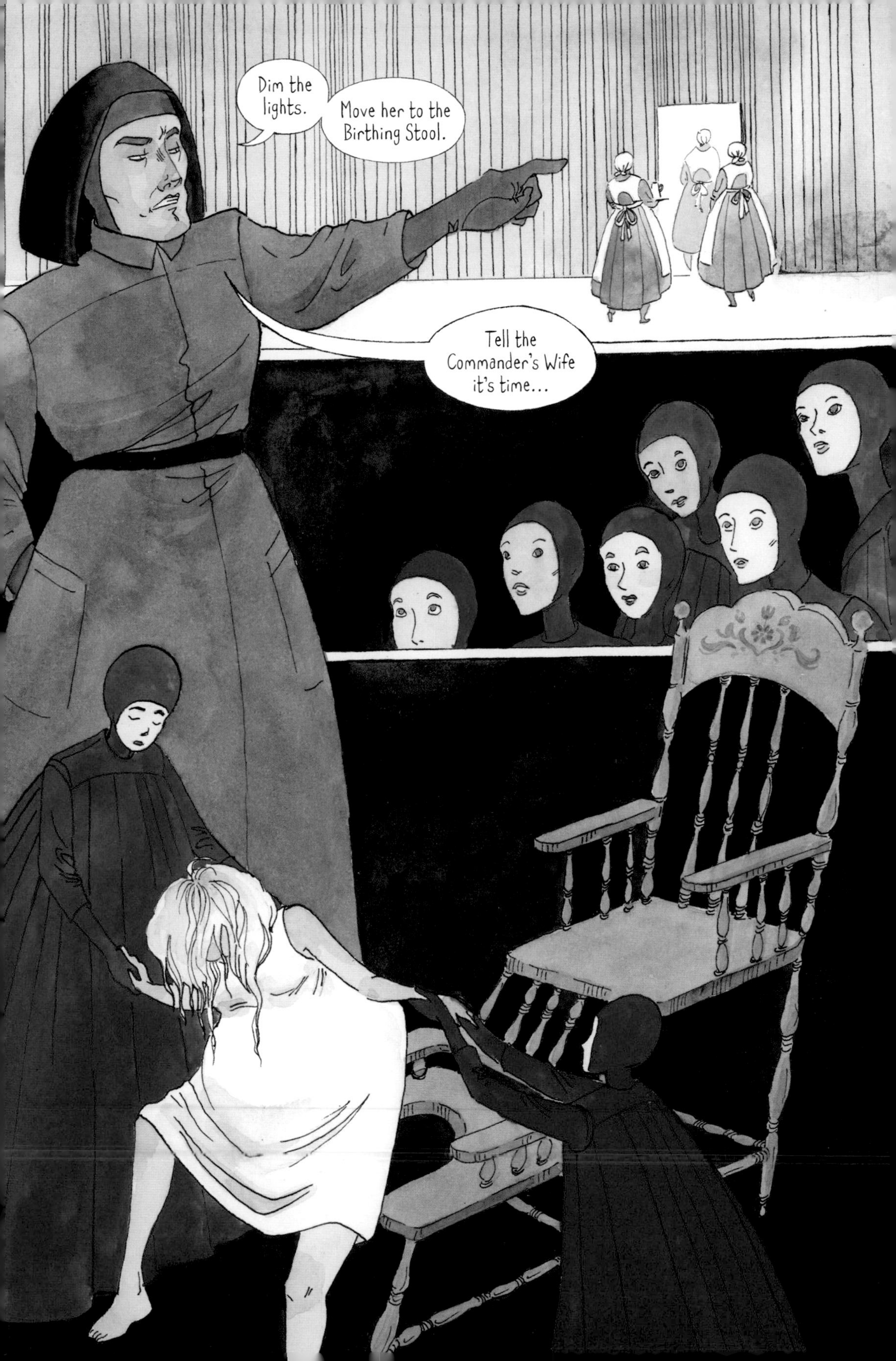
Dim the lights.
Move her to the Birthing Stool.
Tell the Commander's Wife it's time...

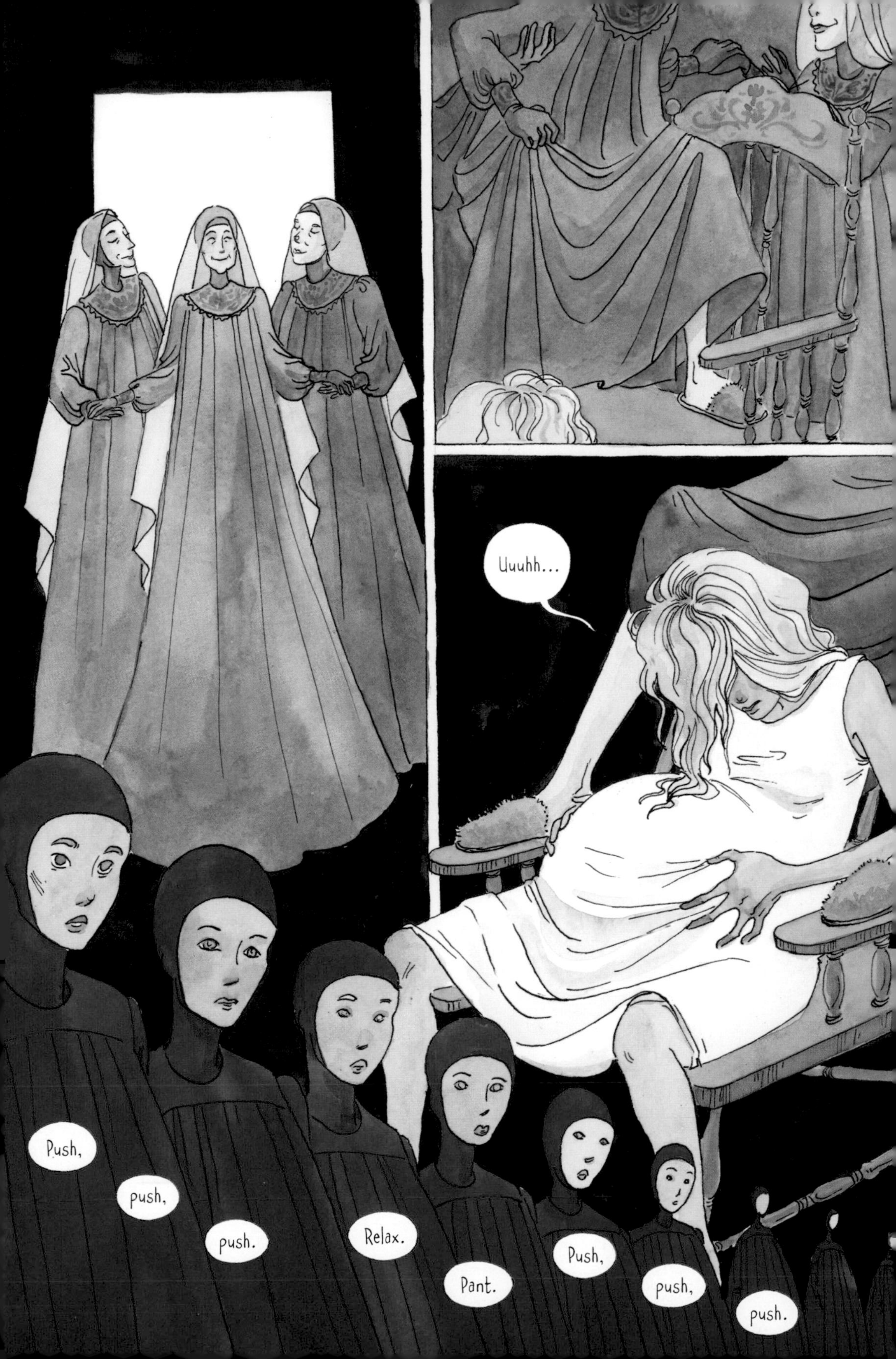
Uuuhh...
Push,
push,
push.
Relax.
Pant.
Push,
push,
push.

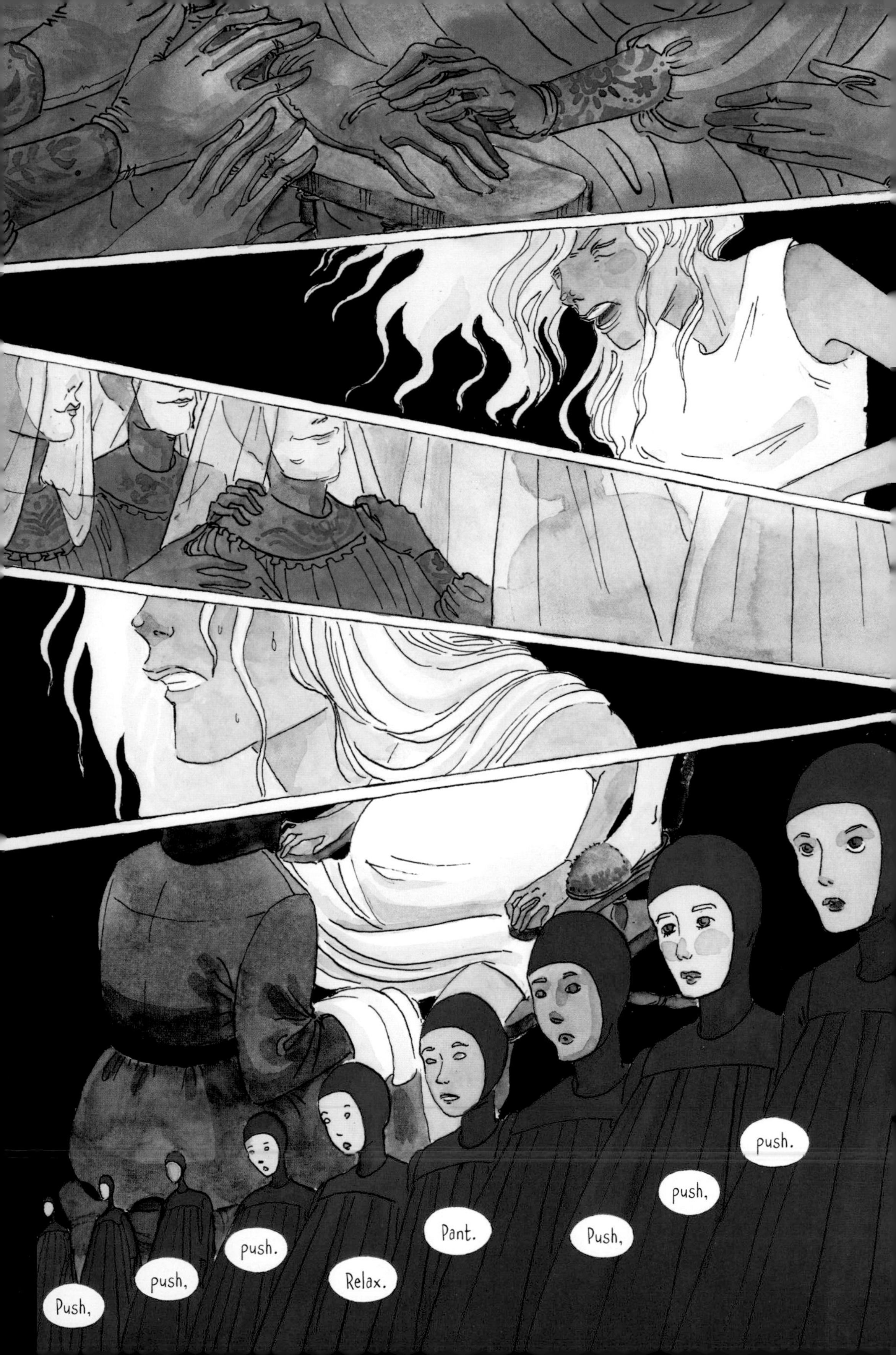
Push,
push,
push.
Relax.
Pant.
Push,
push,
push.

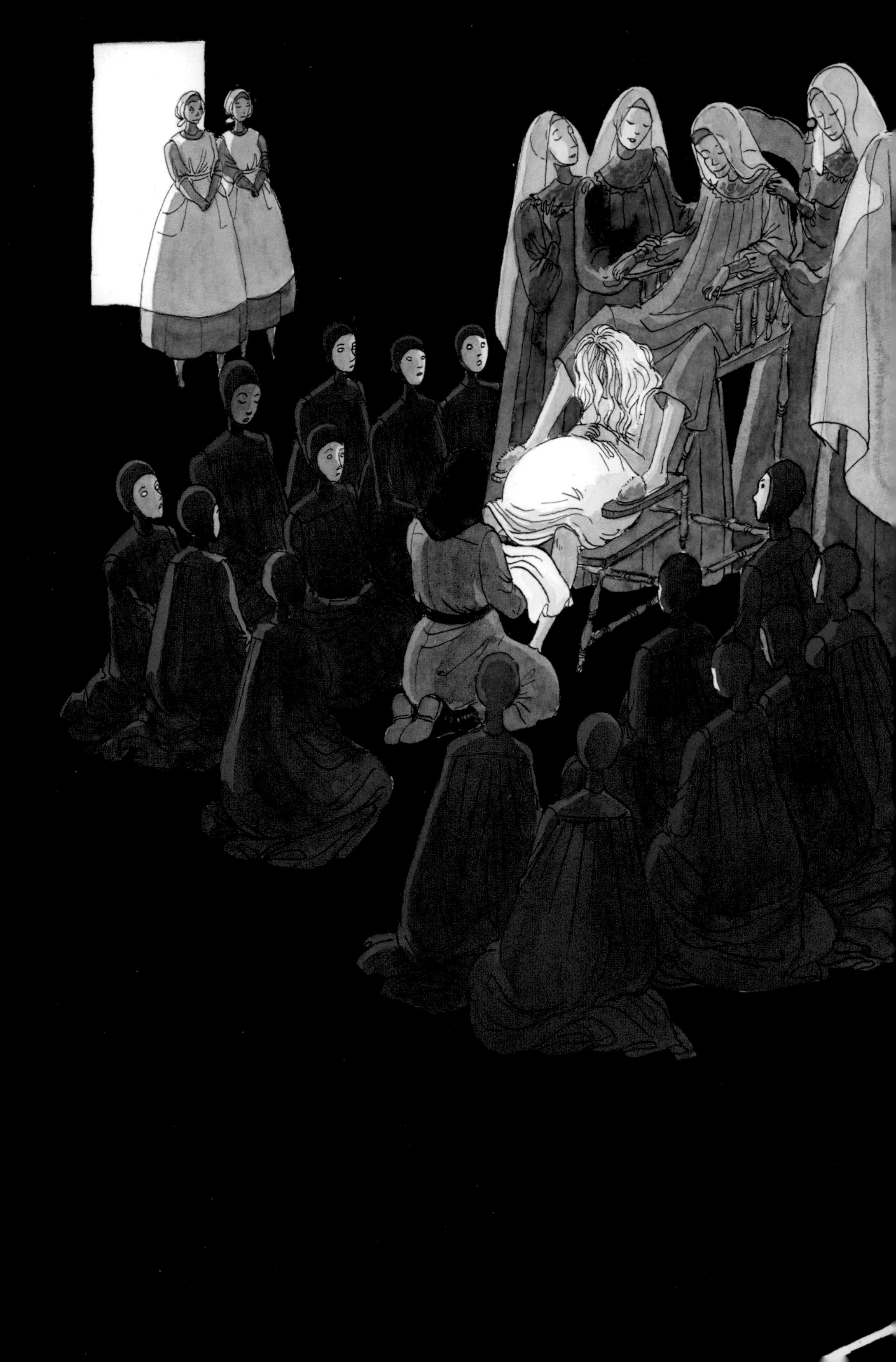

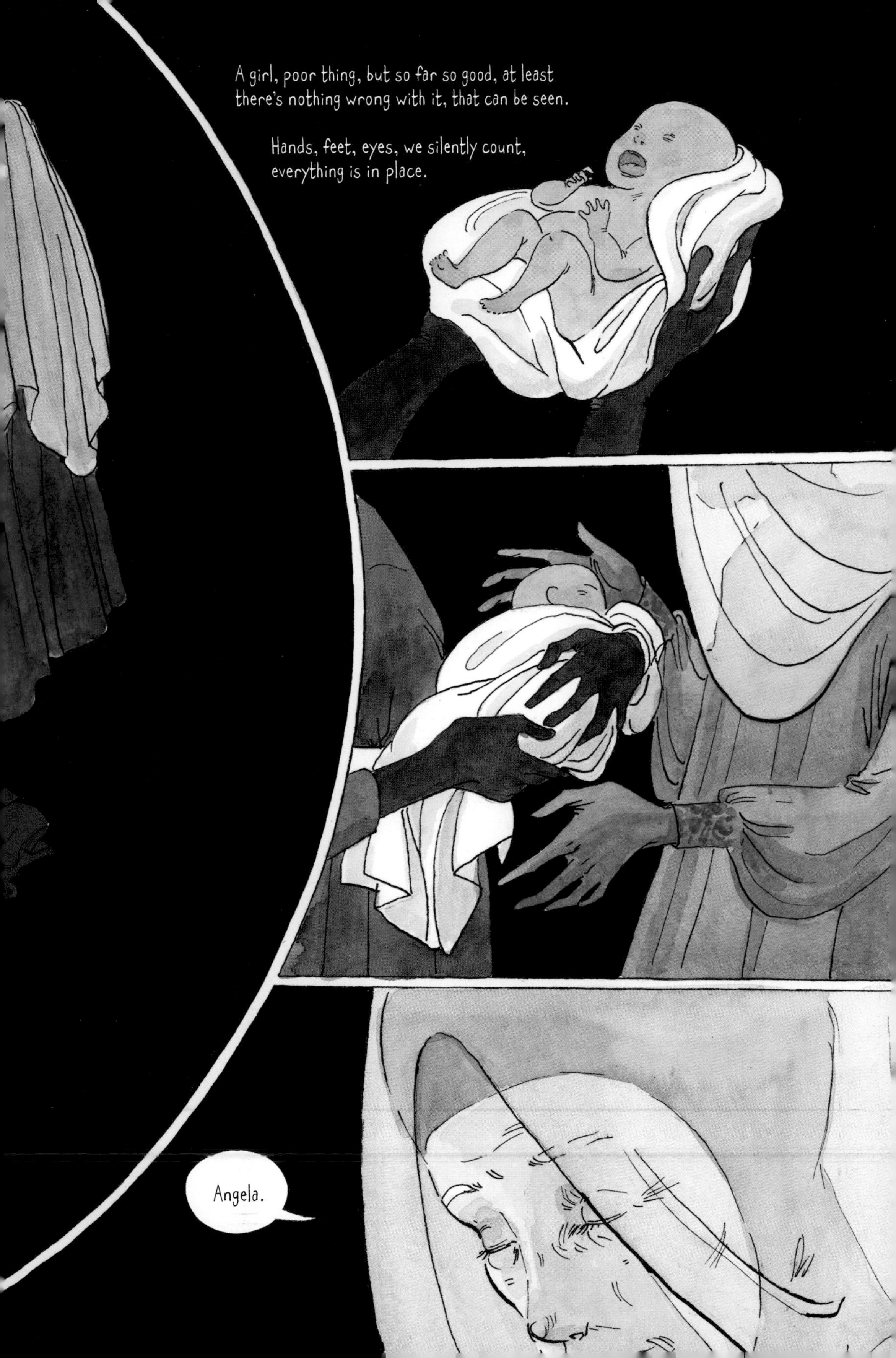
A girl, poor thing, but so far so good, at least there's nothing wrong with it, that can be seen.
Hands, feet, eyes, we silently count, everything is in place.
Angela.

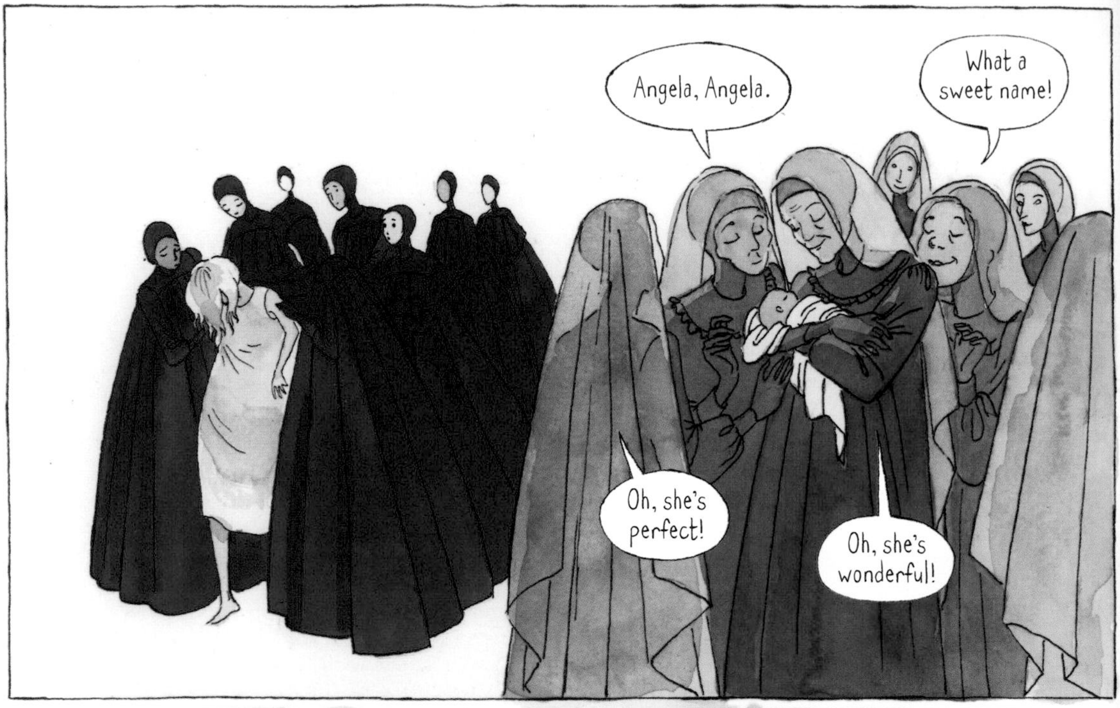
Angela, Angela.
What a sweet name!
Oh, she's perfect!
Oh, she's wonderful!

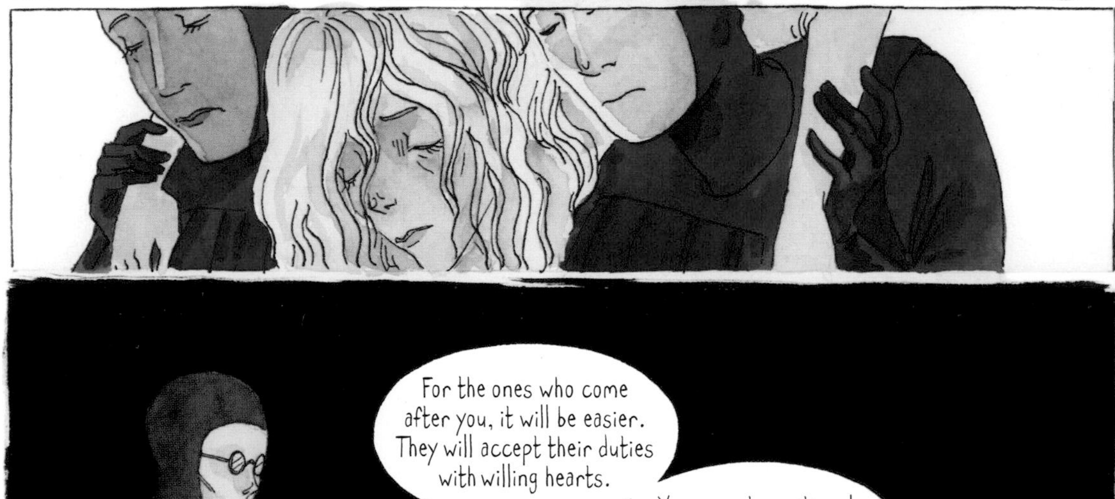

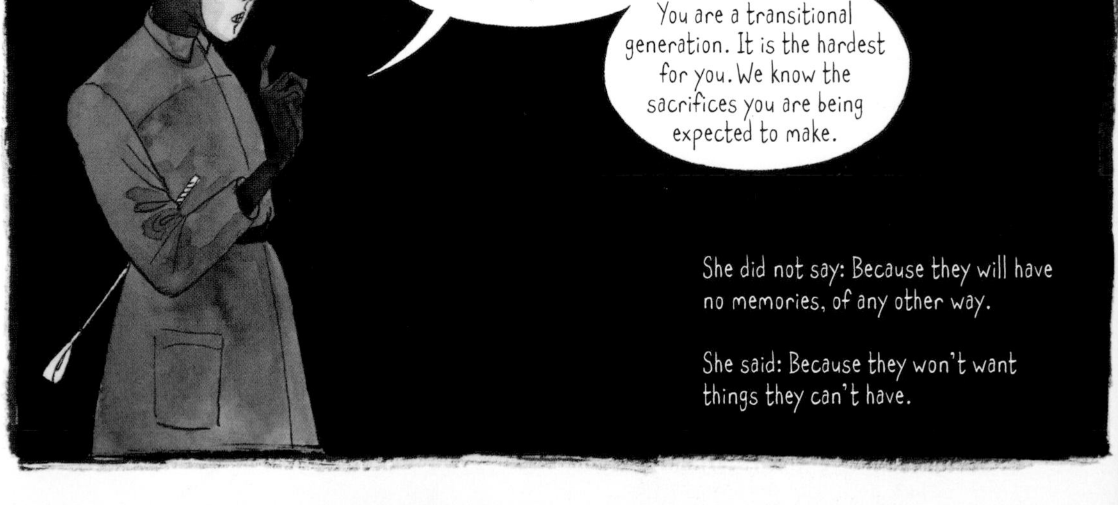
For the ones who come after you, it will be easier. They will accept their duties with willing hearts.
You are a transitional generation. It is the hardest for you. We know the sacrifices you are being expected to make.
She did not say: Because they will have no memories, of any other way.
She said: Because they won't want things they can't have.

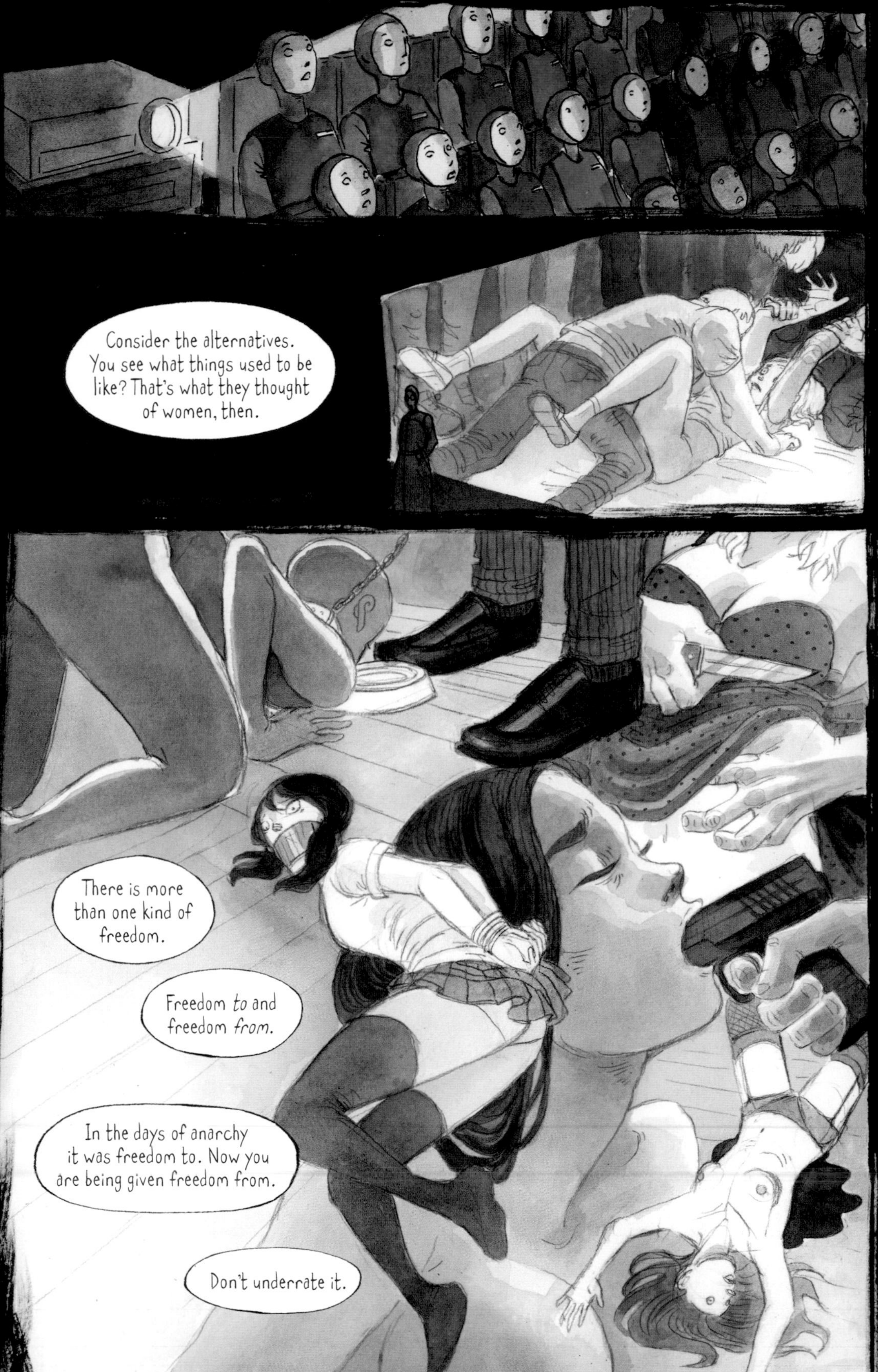
Consider the alternatives. You see what things used to be like? That's what they thought of women, then.
There is more than one kind of freedom.
Freedom *to* and freedom *from*.
In the days of anarchy it was freedom to. Now you are being given freedom from.
Don't underrate it.

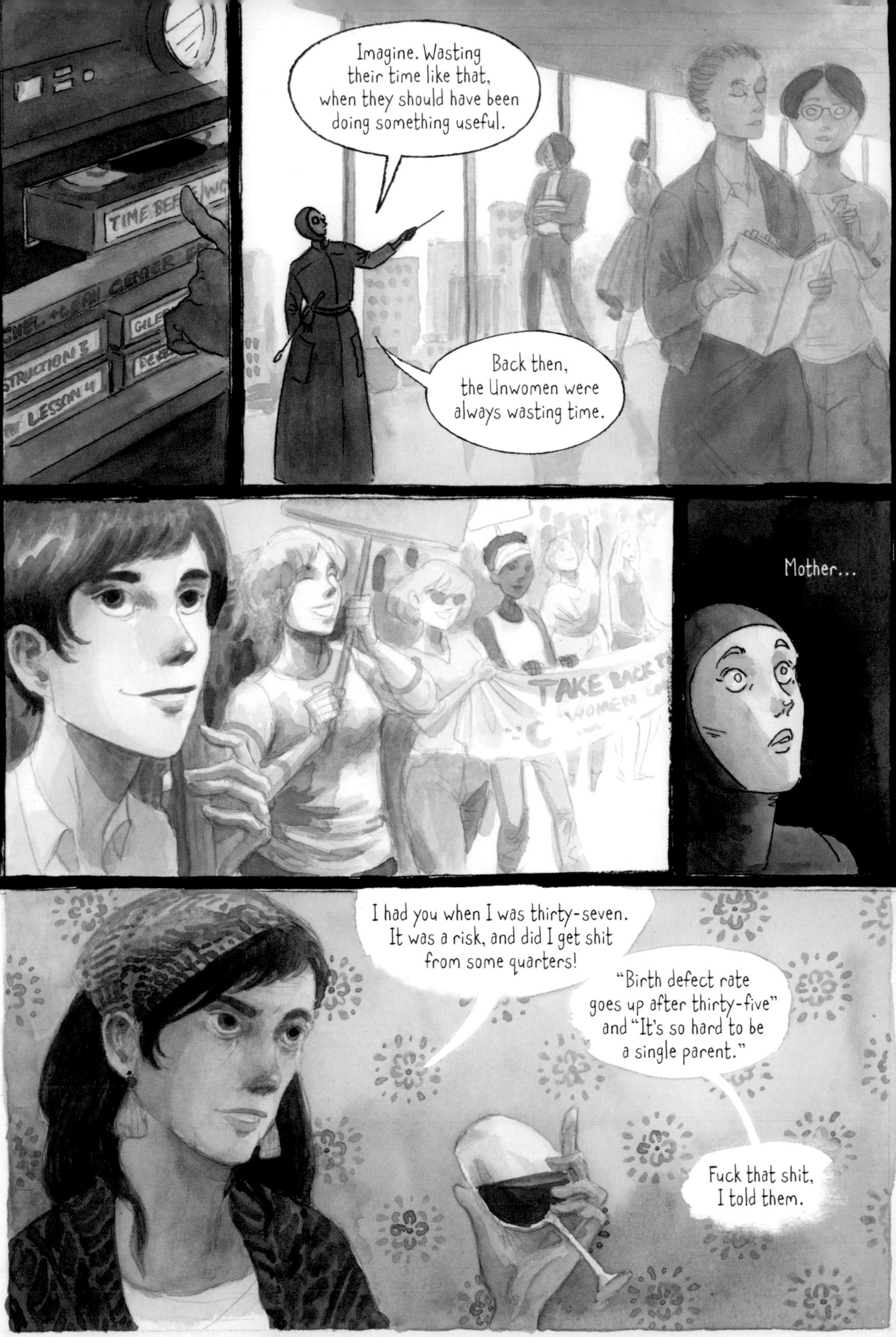
Imagine. Wasting their time like that, when they should have been doing something useful.
Back then, the Unwomen were always wasting time.
Mother...
I had you when I was thirty-seven. It was a risk, and did I get shit from some quarters!
"Birth defect rate goes up after thirty-five" and "It's so hard to be a single parent."
Fuck that shit, I told them.

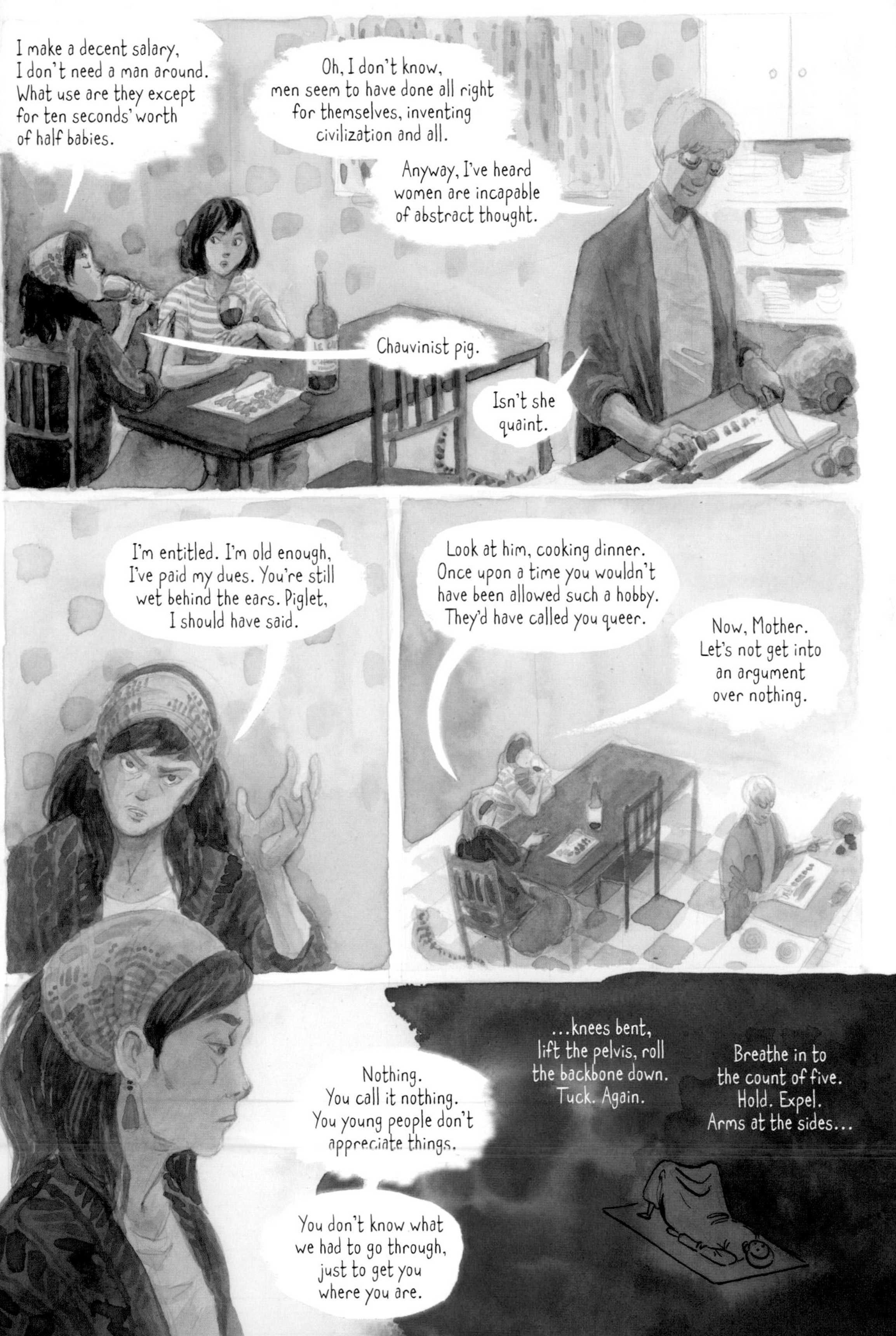
I make a decent salary, I don't need a man around. What use are they except for ten seconds' worth of half babies.
Oh, I don't know, men seem to have done all right for themselves, inventing civilization and all.
Anyway, I've heard women are incapable of abstract thought.
Chauvinist pig.
Isn't she quaint.
I'm entitled. I'm old enough, I've paid my dues. You're still wet behind the ears. Piglet, I should have said.
Look at him, cooking dinner. Once upon a time you wouldn't have been allowed such a hobby. They'd have called you queer.
Now, Mother. Let's not get into an argument over nothing.
Nothing. You call it nothing. You young people don't appreciate things.
You don't know what we had to go through, just to get you where you are.
...knees bent, lift the pelvis, roll the backbone down. Tuck. Again.
Breathe in to the count of five. Hold. Expel. Arms at the sides...

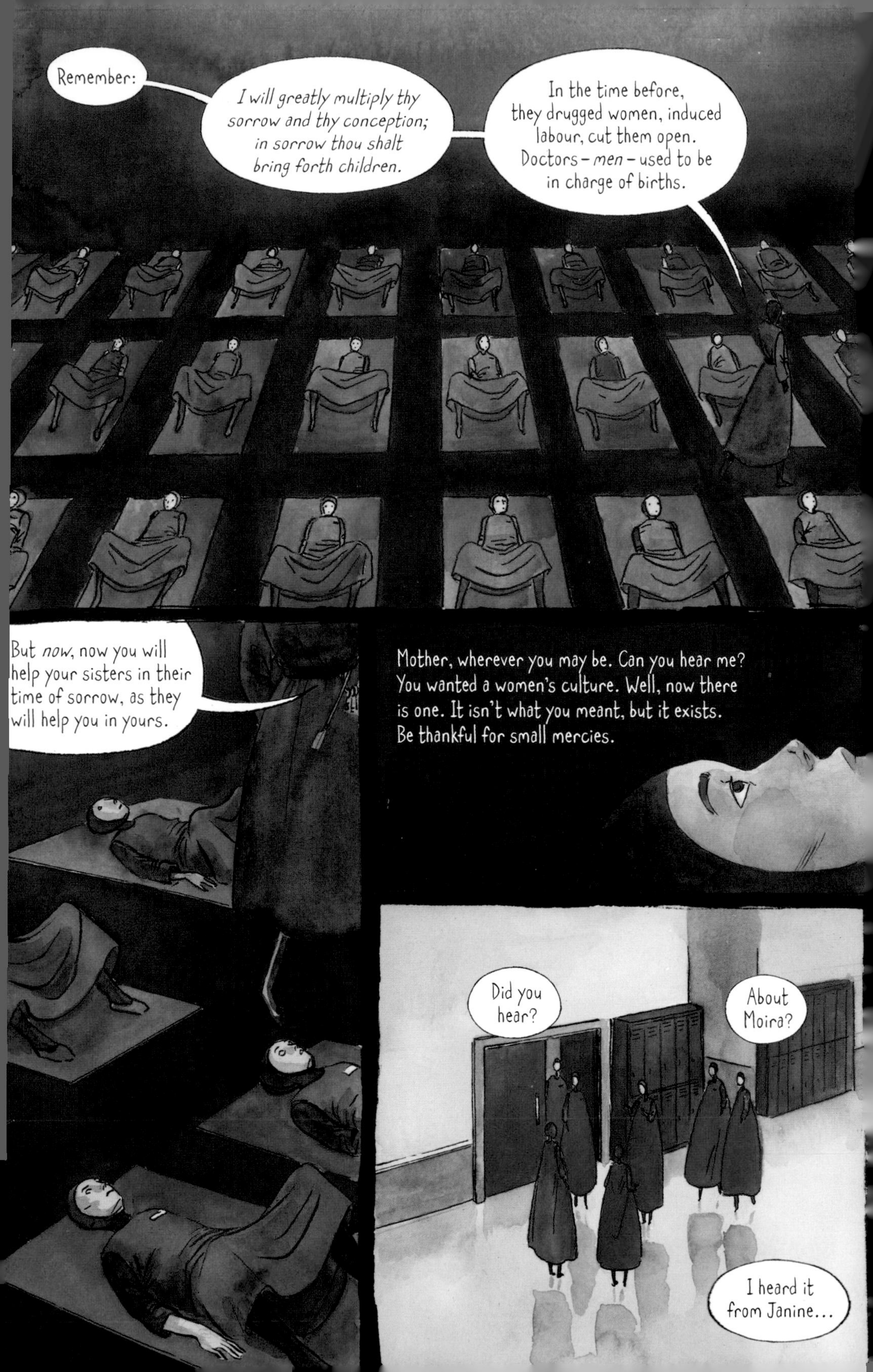
Remember:
I will greatly multiply thy sorrow and thy conception; in sorrow thou shalt bring forth children.
In the time before, they drugged women, induced labour, cut them open. Doctors – *men* – used to be in charge of births.
But *now*, now you will help your sisters in their time of sorrow, as they will help you in yours.
Mother, wherever you may be. Can you hear me? You wanted a women's culture. Well, now there is one. It isn't what you meant, but it exists. Be thankful for small mercies.
Did you hear?
About Moira?
I heard it from Janine...

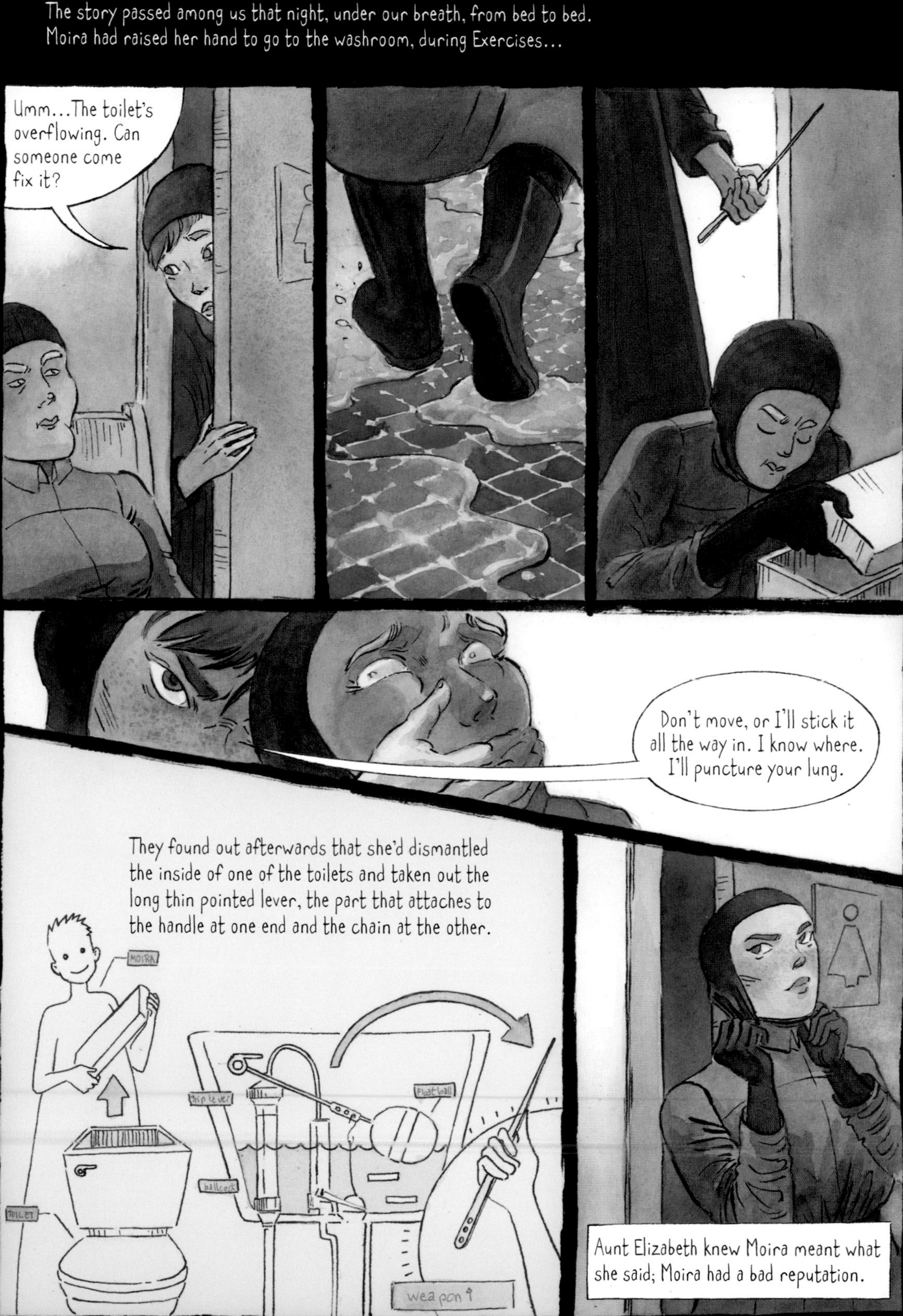
The story passed among us that night, under our breath, from bed to bed.
Moira had raised her hand to go to the washroom, during Exercises...
Umm...The toilet's overflowing. Can someone come fix it?
Don't move, or I'll stick it all the way in. I know where. I'll puncture your lung.
They found out afterwards that she'd dismantled the inside of one of the toilets and taken out the long thin pointed lever, the part that attaches to the handle at one end and the chain at the other.
MOIRA
trip lever
float ball
ballcock
TOILET
weapon
Aunt Elizabeth knew Moira meant what she said; Moira had a bad reputation.

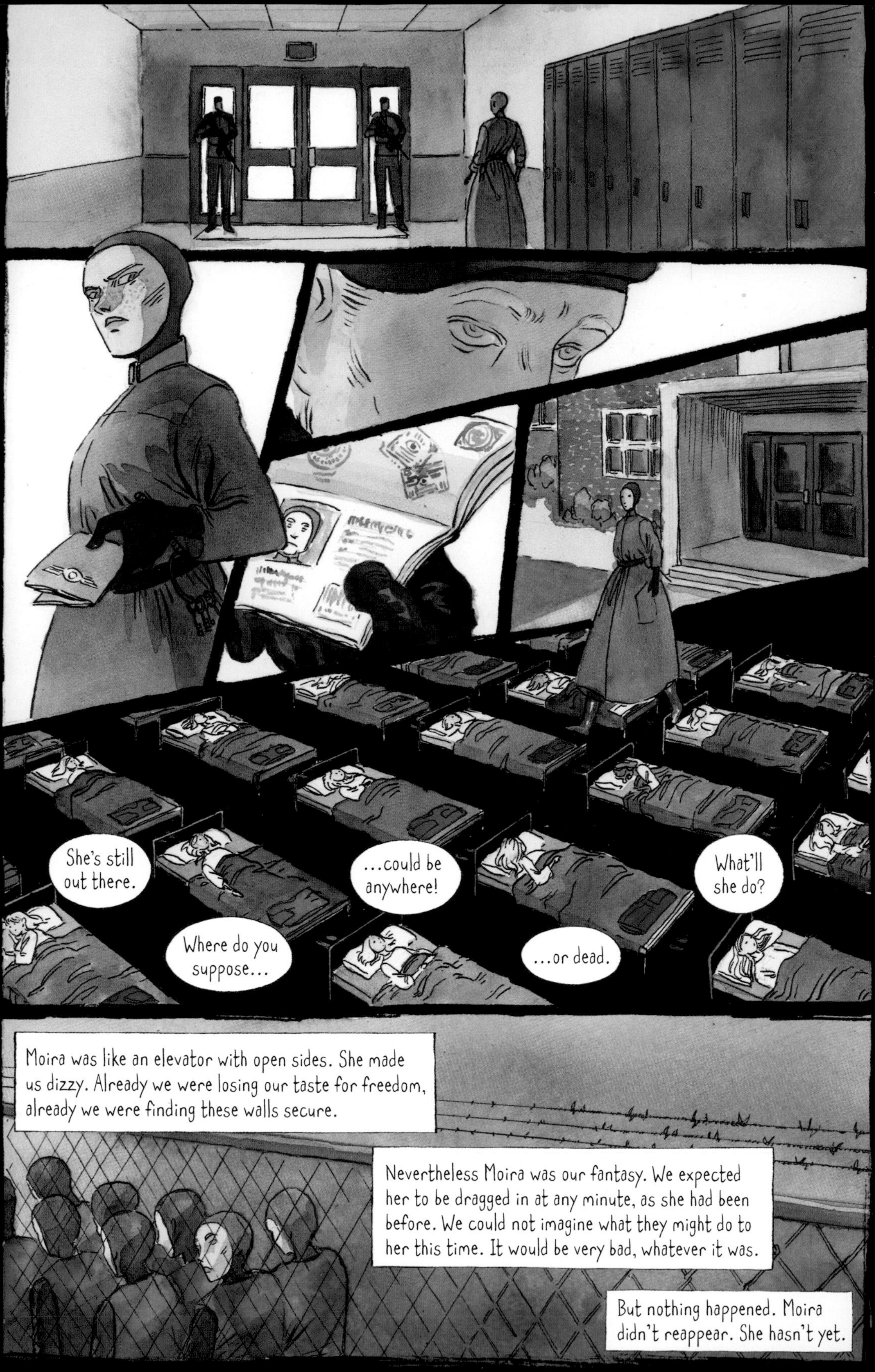
She's still out there.
Where do you suppose...
...could be anywhere!
...or dead.
What'll she do?
Moira was like an elevator with open sides. She made us dizzy. Already we were losing our taste for freedom, already we were finding these walls secure.
Nevertheless Moira was our fantasy. We expected her to be dragged in at any minute, as she had been before. We could not imagine what they might do to her this time. It would be very bad, whatever it was.
But nothing happened. Moira didn't reappear. She hasn't yet.

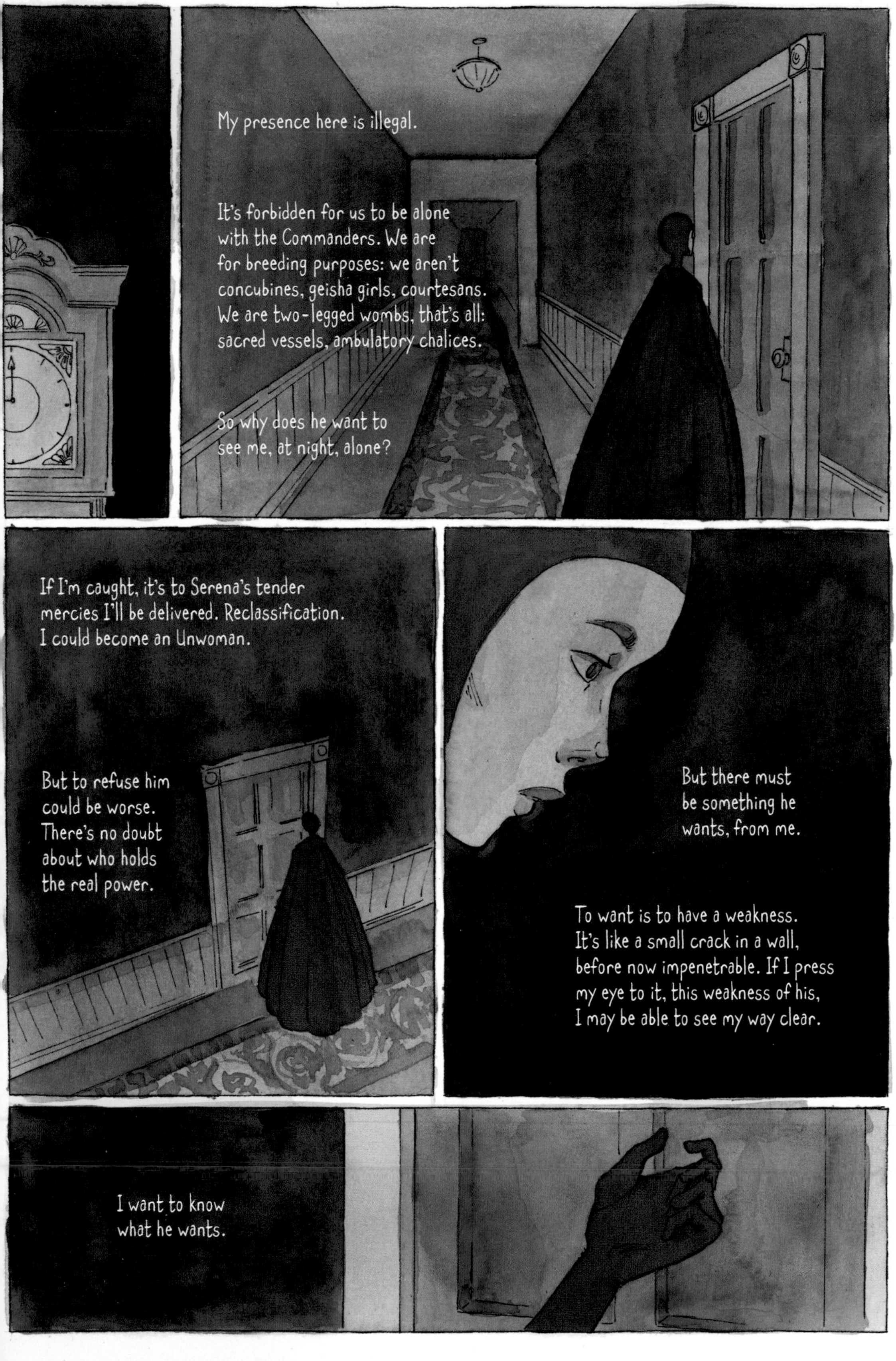
My presence here is illegal.
It's forbidden for us to be alone with the Commanders. We are for breeding purposes: we aren't concubines, geisha girls, courtesans. We are two-legged wombs, that's all: sacred vessels, ambulatory chalices.
So why does he want to see me, at night, alone?
If I'm caught, it's to Serena's tender mercies I'll be delivered. Reclassification. I could become an Unwoman.
But to refuse him could be worse. There's no doubt about who holds the real power.
But there must be something he wants, from me.
To want is to have a weakness. It's like a small crack in a wall, before now impenetrable. If I press my eye to it, this weakness of his, I may be able to see my way clear.
I want to know what he wants.

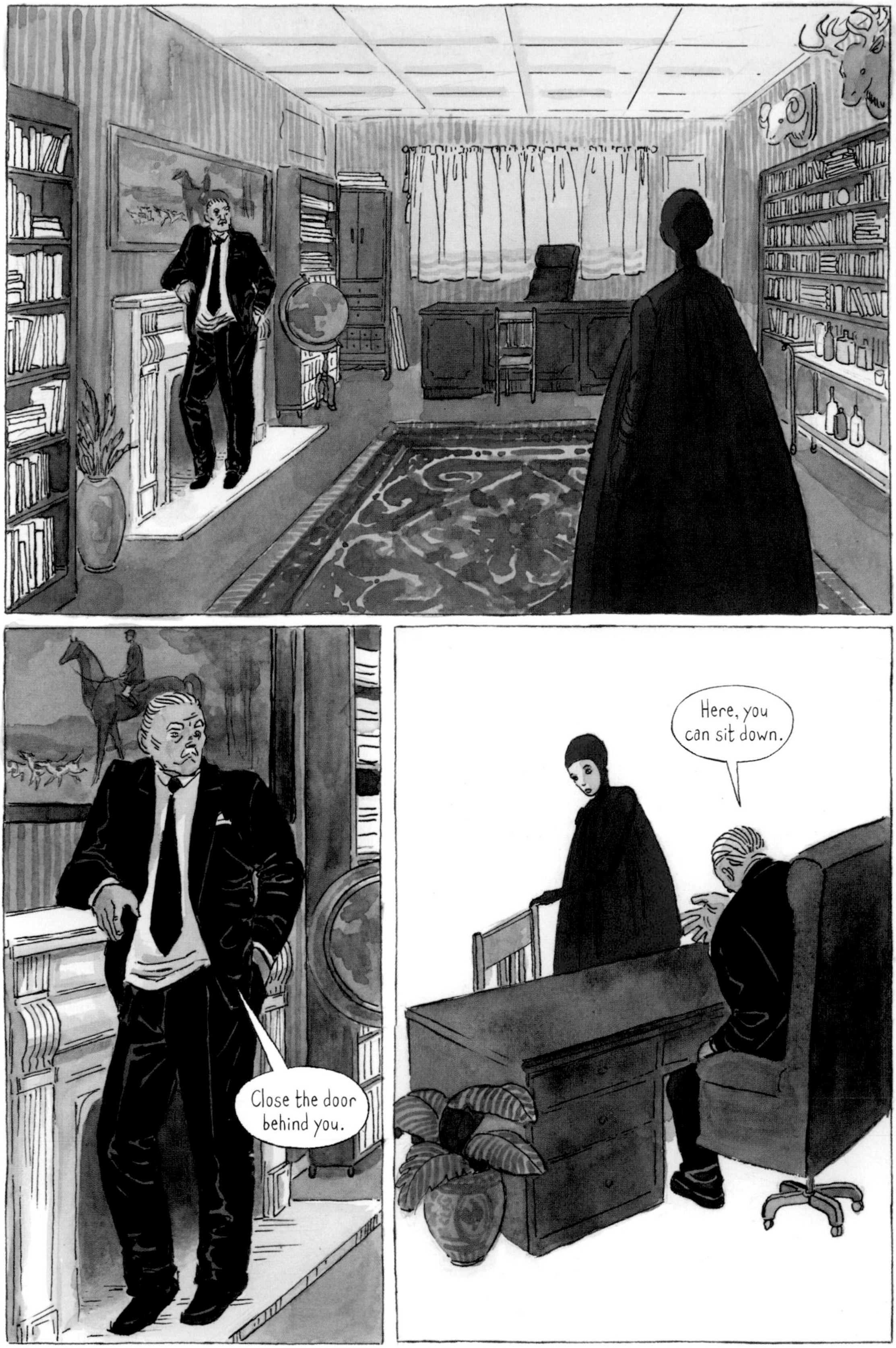
Close the door behind you.
Here, you can sit down.

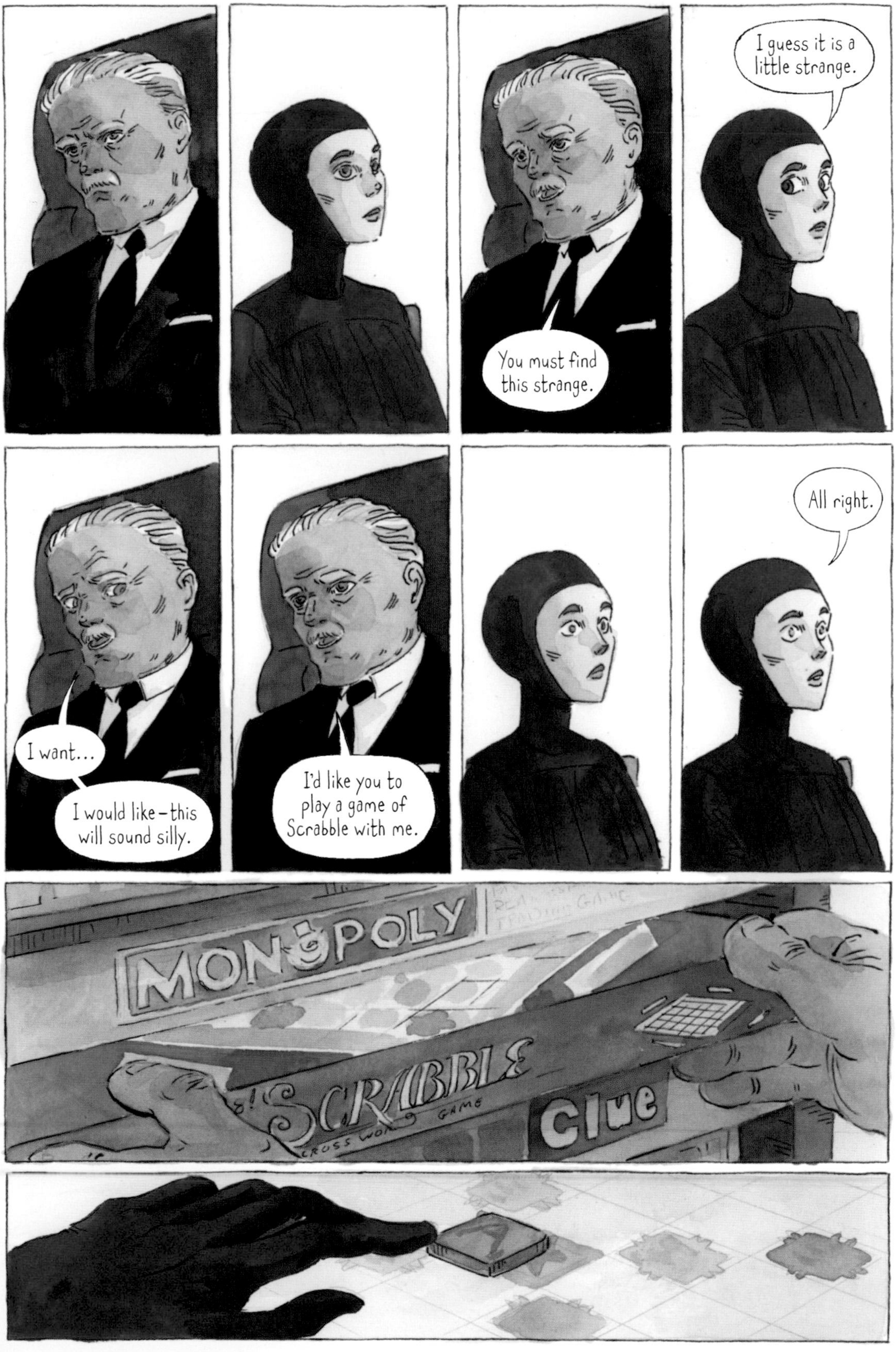
You must find this strange.
I guess it is a little strange.
I want...
I would like – this will sound silly.
I'd like you to play a game of Scrabble with me.
All right.
MONOPOLY
SCRABBLE
CROSSWORD GAME
Clue

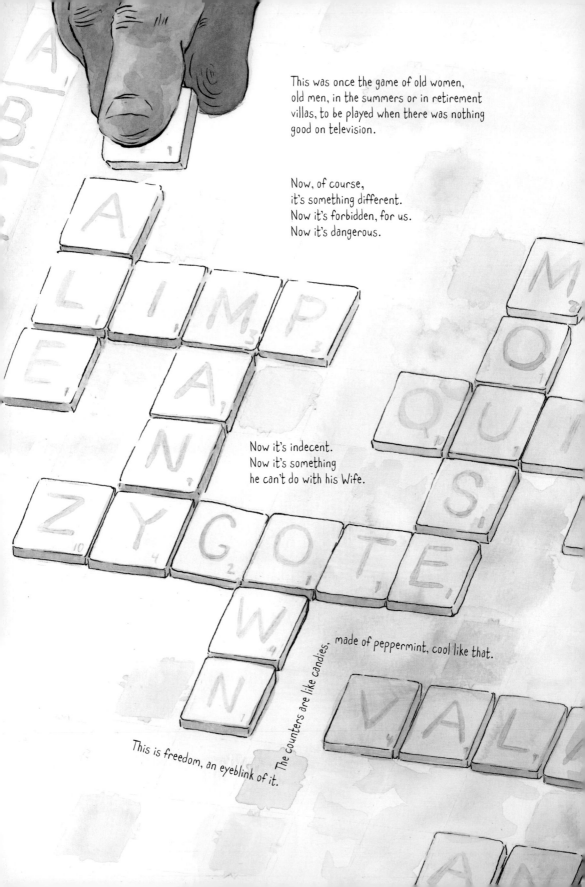

This was once the game of old women, old men, in the summers or in retirement villas, to be played when there was nothing good on television.

Now, of course, it's something different. Now it's forbidden, for us. Now it's dangerous.

Now it's indecent. Now it's something he can't do with his Wife.

The counters are like candies, made of peppermint, cool like that.

This is freedom, an eyeblink of it.

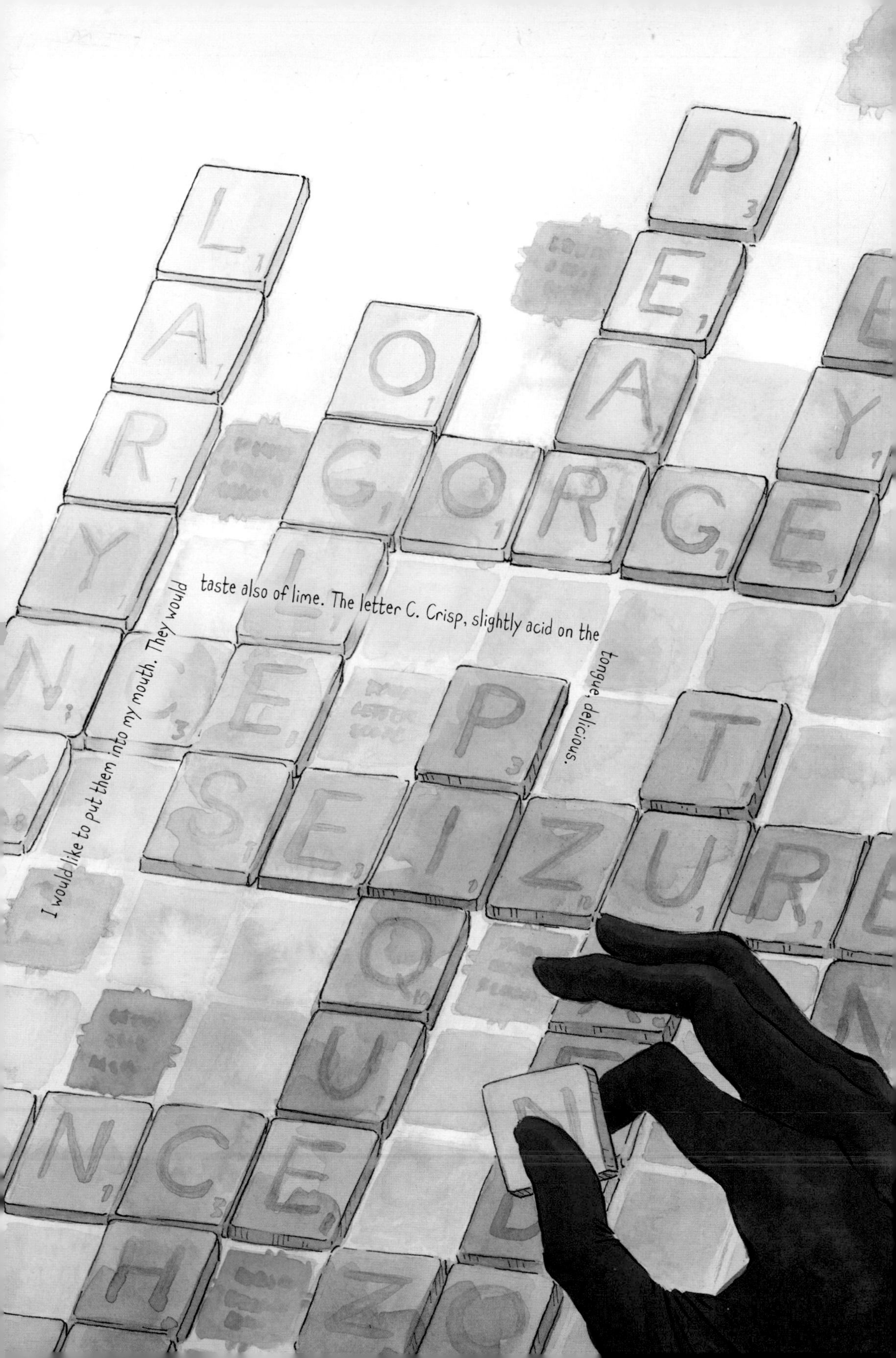
I would like to put them into my mouth. They would
taste also of lime. The letter C. Crisp, slightly acid on the
tongue, delicious.

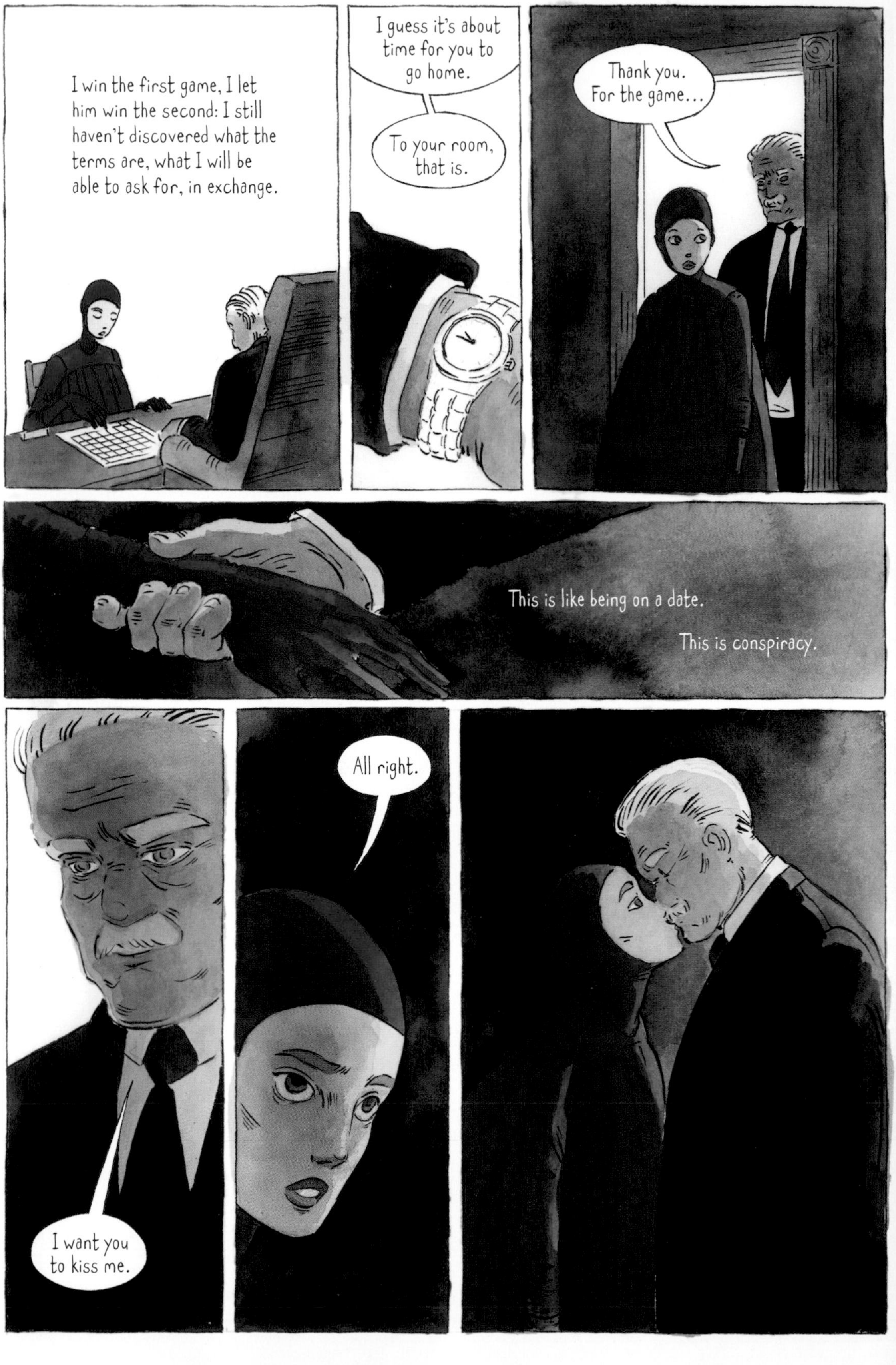
I win the first game, I let him win the second: I still haven't discovered what the terms are, what I will be able to ask for, in exchange.
I guess it's about time for you to go home.
To your room, that is.
Thank you. For the game...
This is like being on a date.
This is conspiracy.
I want you to kiss me.
All right.

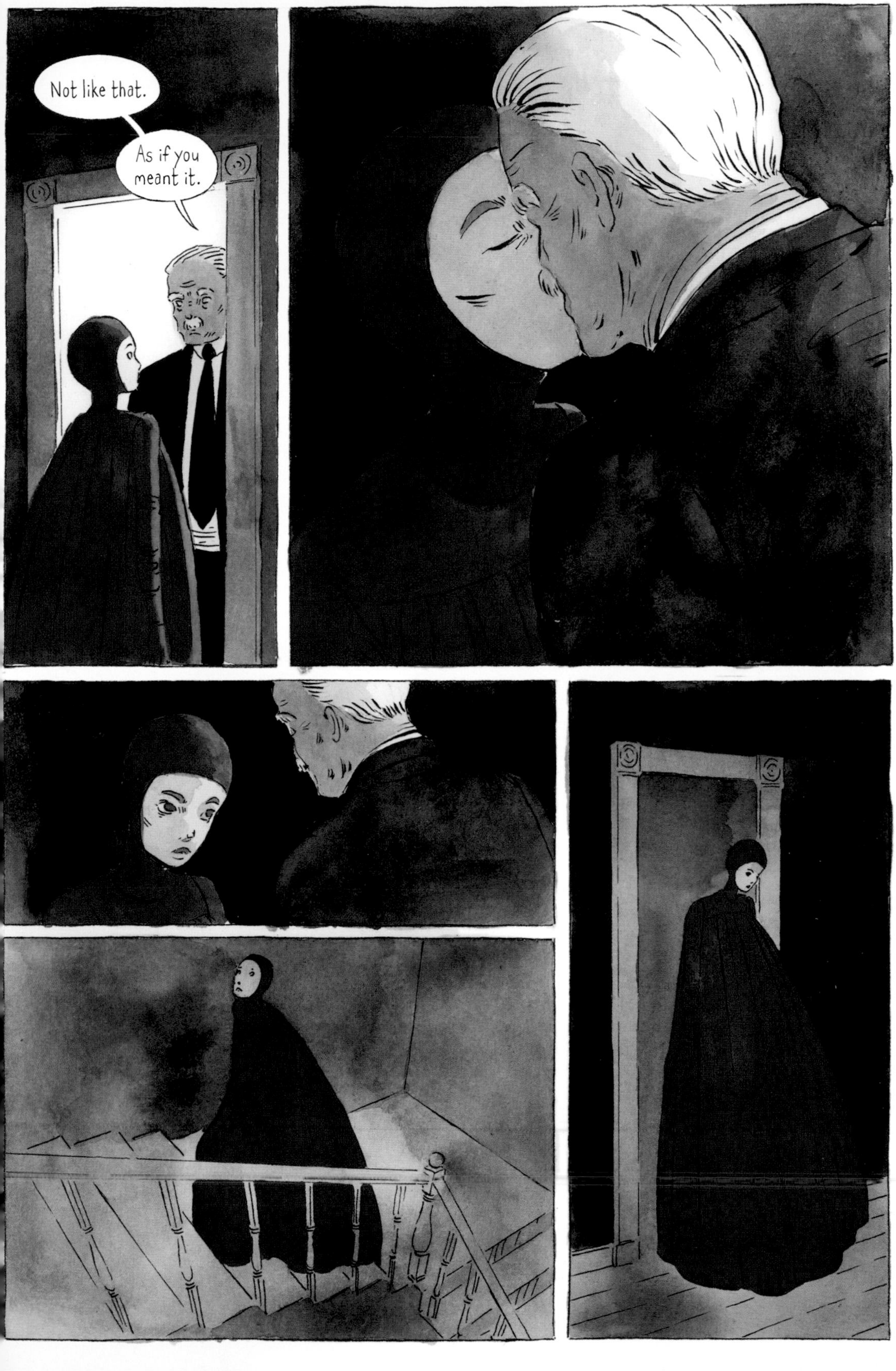
Not like that.
As if you meant it.

IX

NIGHT

Something has changed.
Circumstances have altered.

I need to take it seriously, this desire of his.
It could be important, it could be a passport,
it could be my downfall.

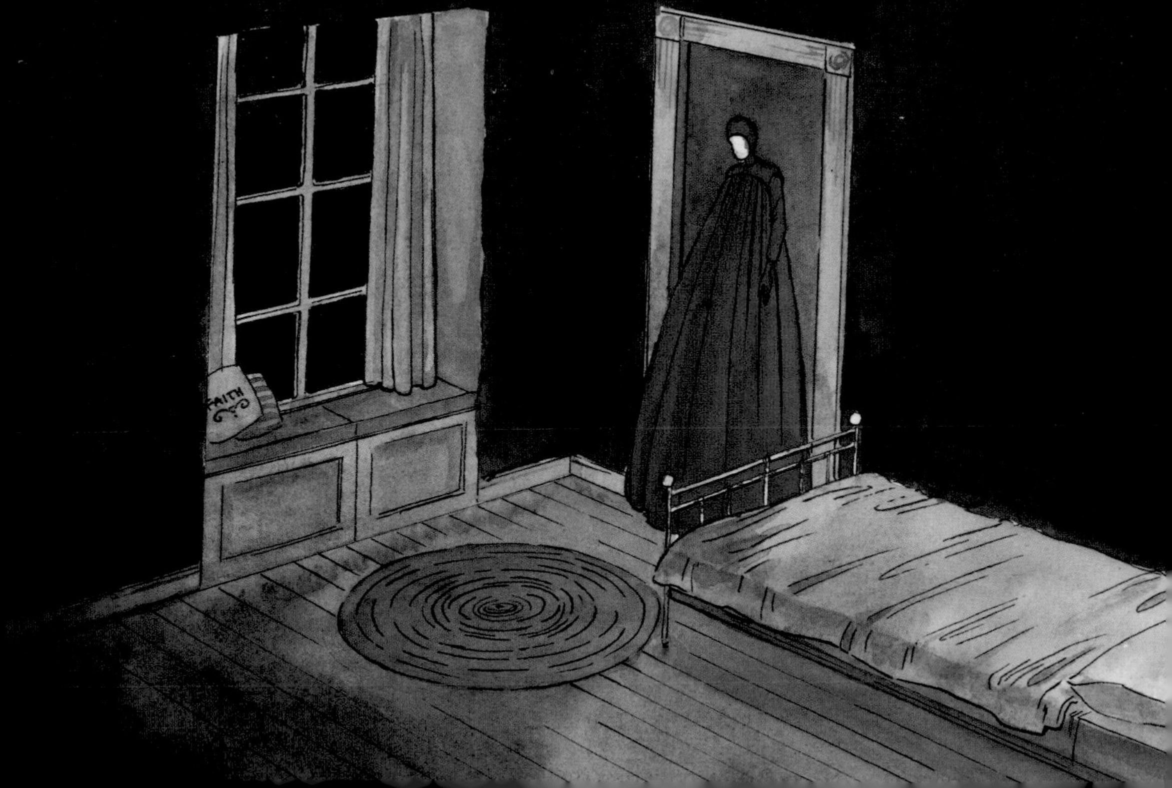
FAITH

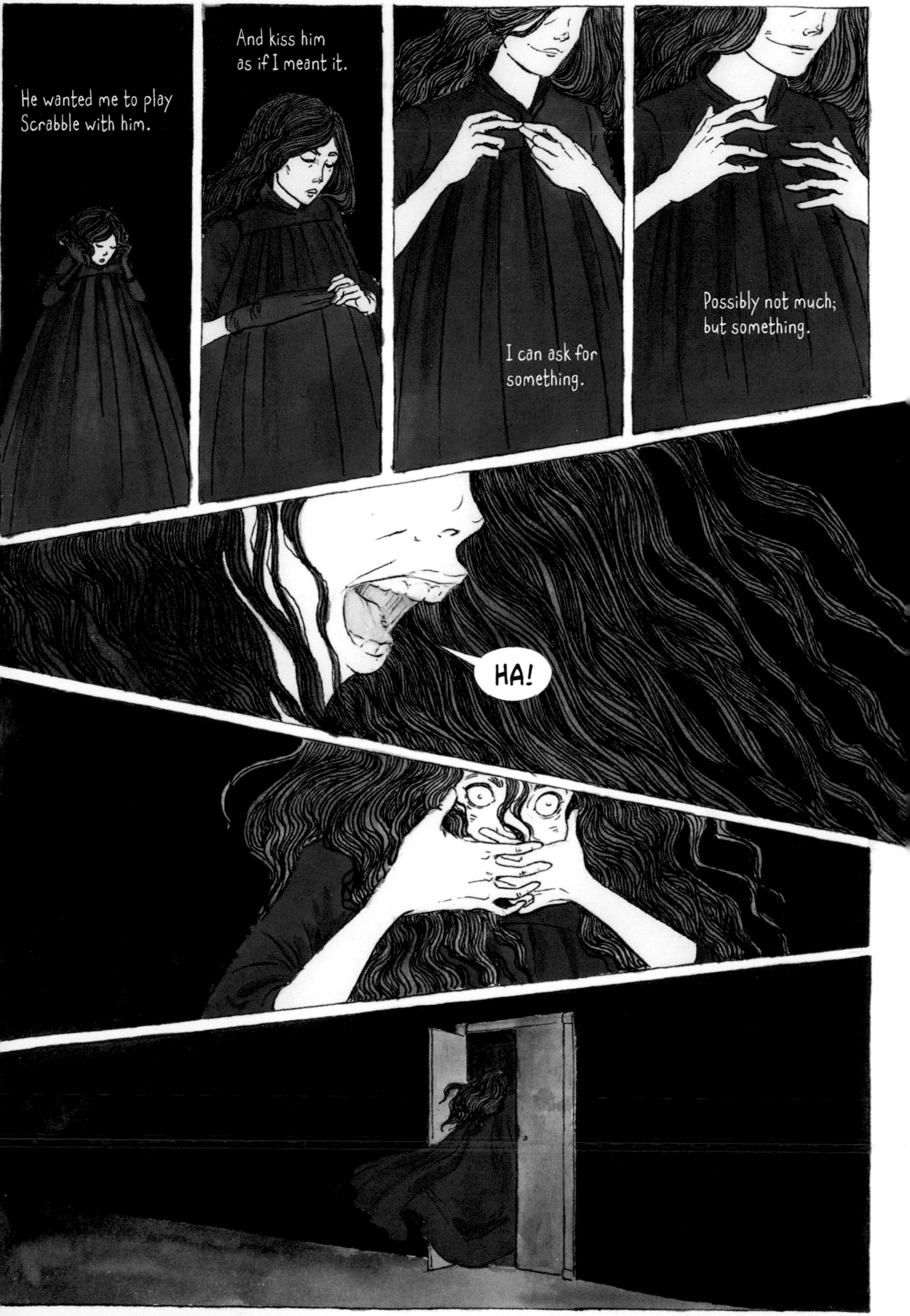
He wanted me to play
Scrabble with him.
And kiss him
as if I meant it.
I can ask for
something.
Possibly not much;
but something.
HA!

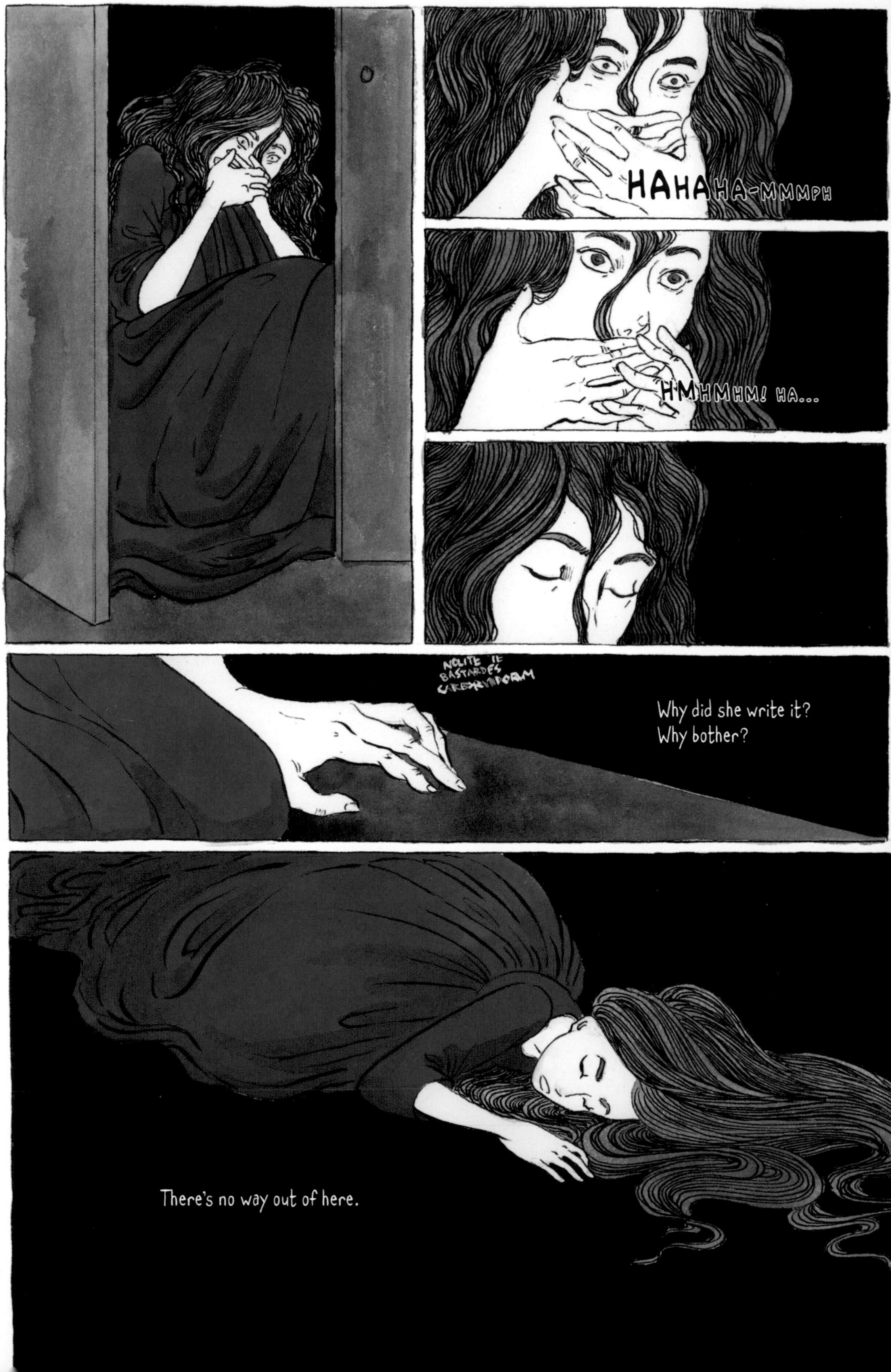
HAHAHA-MMMPH
HMHMHM! HA...
NOLITE TE
BASTARDES
Why did she write it?
Why bother?
There's no way out of here.

X

SOUL SCROLLS

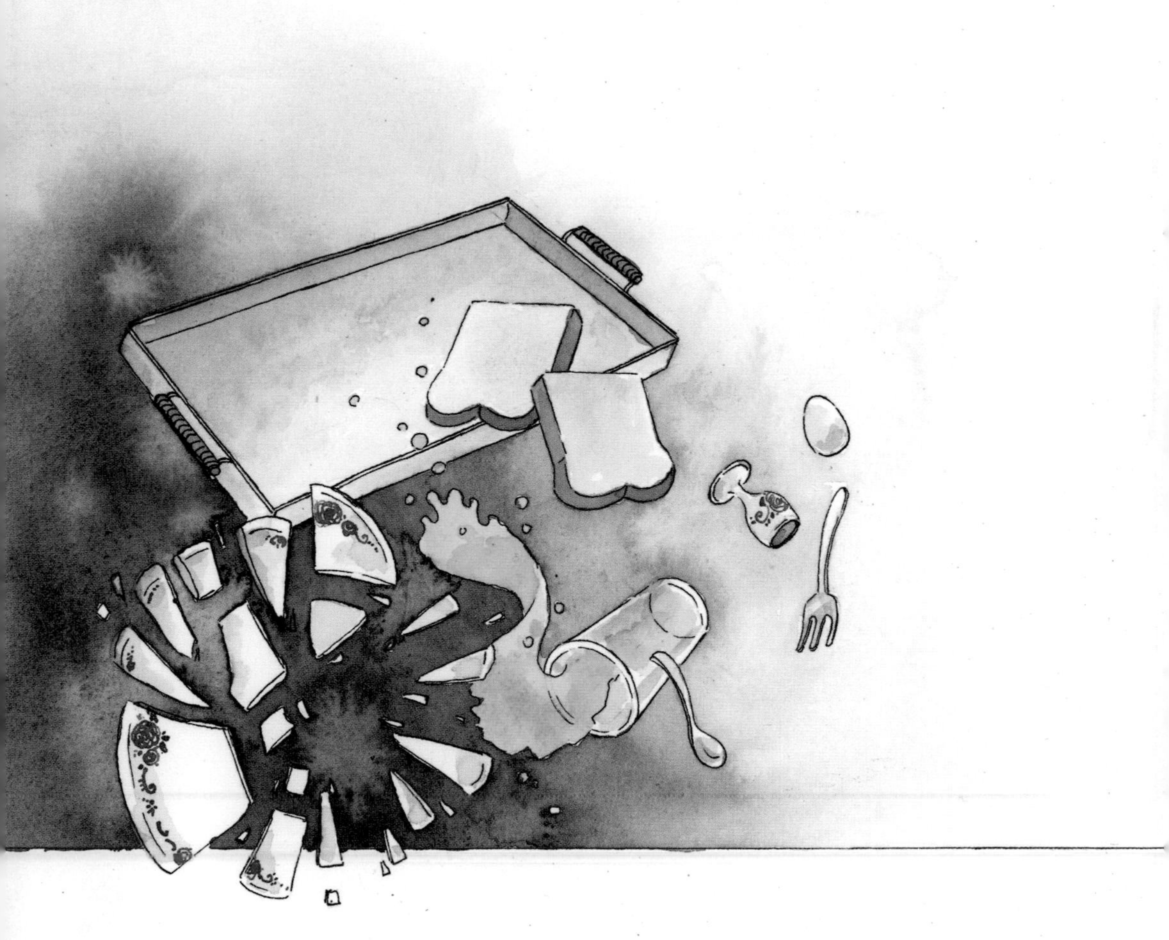

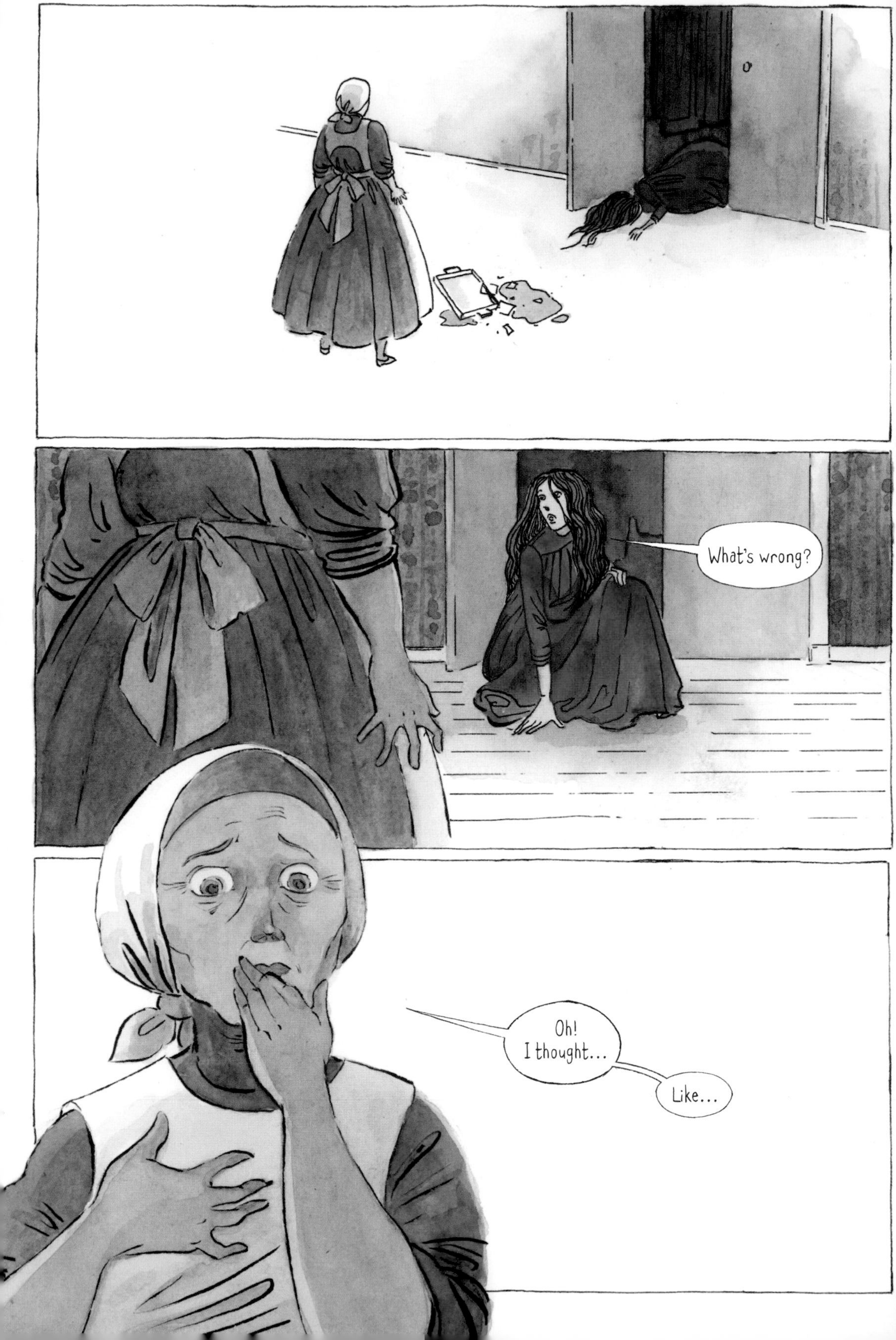
What's wrong?
Oh!
I thought...
Like...

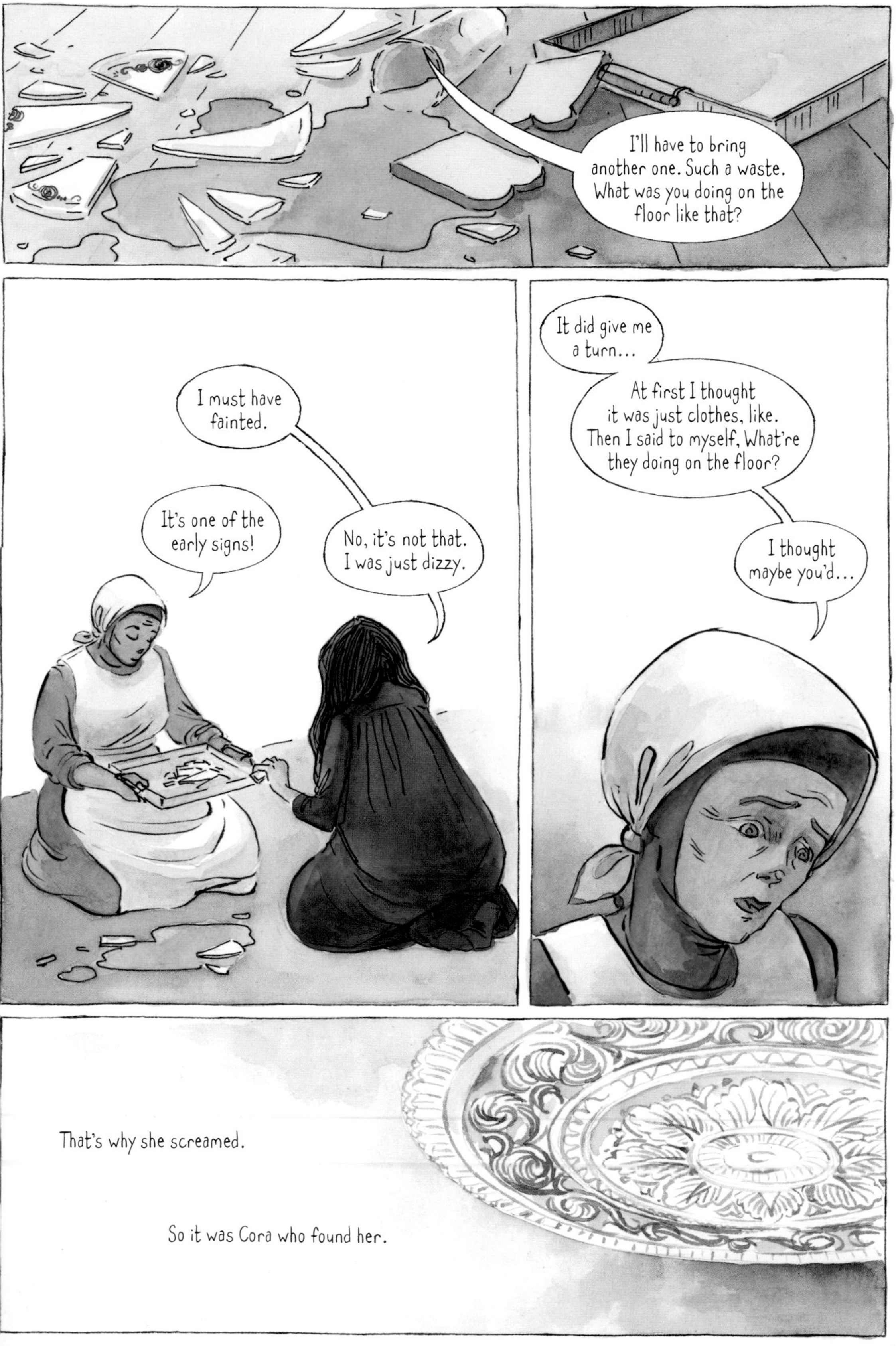
I'll have to bring another one. Such a waste. What was you doing on the floor like that?
I must have fainted.
It's one of the early signs!
No, it's not that. I was just dizzy.
It did give me a turn...
At first I thought it was just clothes, like. Then I said to myself, What're they doing on the floor?
I thought maybe you'd...
That's why she screamed.
So it was Cora who found her.

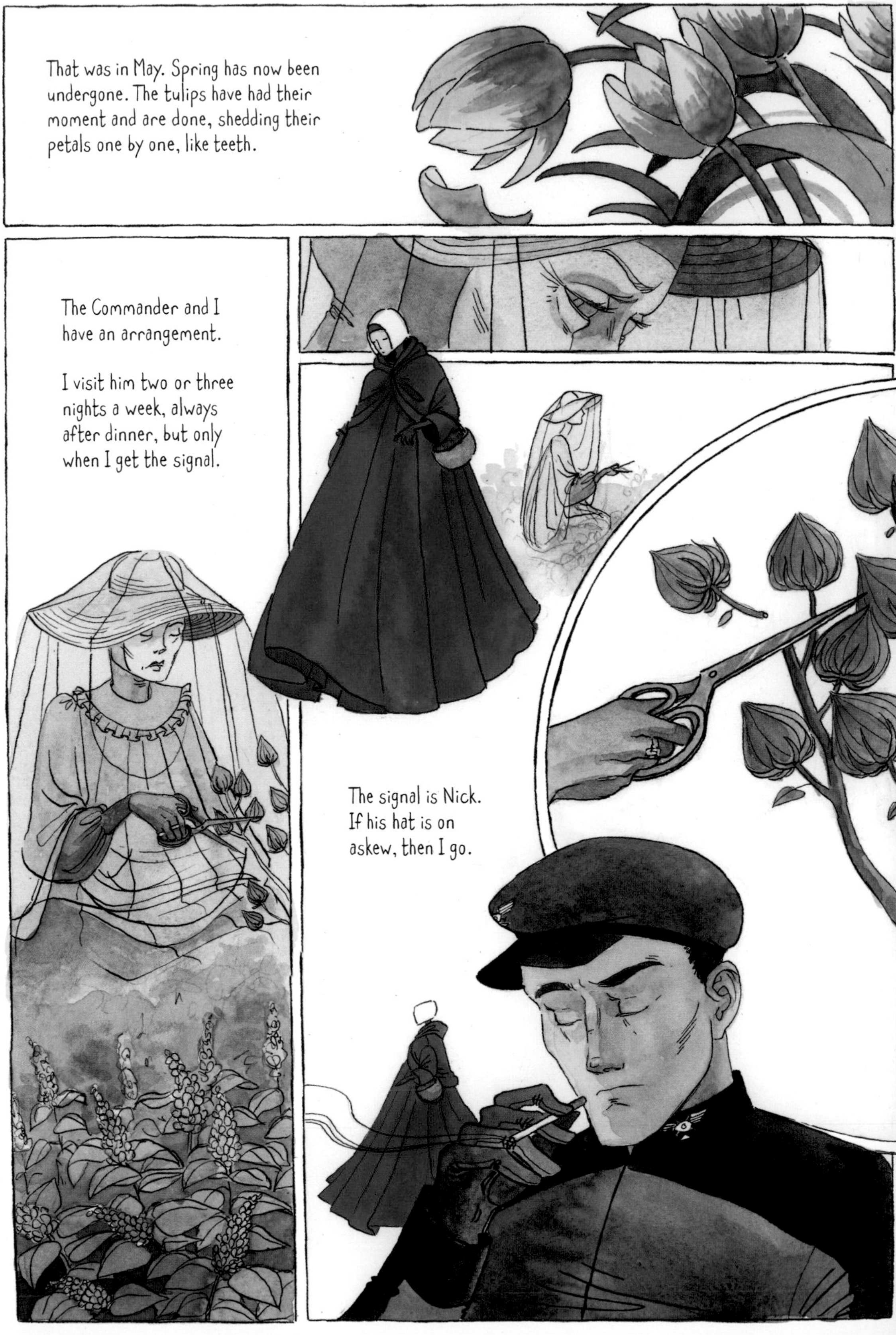

That was in May. Spring has now been undergone. The tulips have had their moment and are done, shedding their petals one by one, like teeth.
The Commander and I have an arrangement.
I visit him two or three nights a week, always after dinner, but only when I get the signal.
The signal is Nick. If his hat is on askew, then I go.

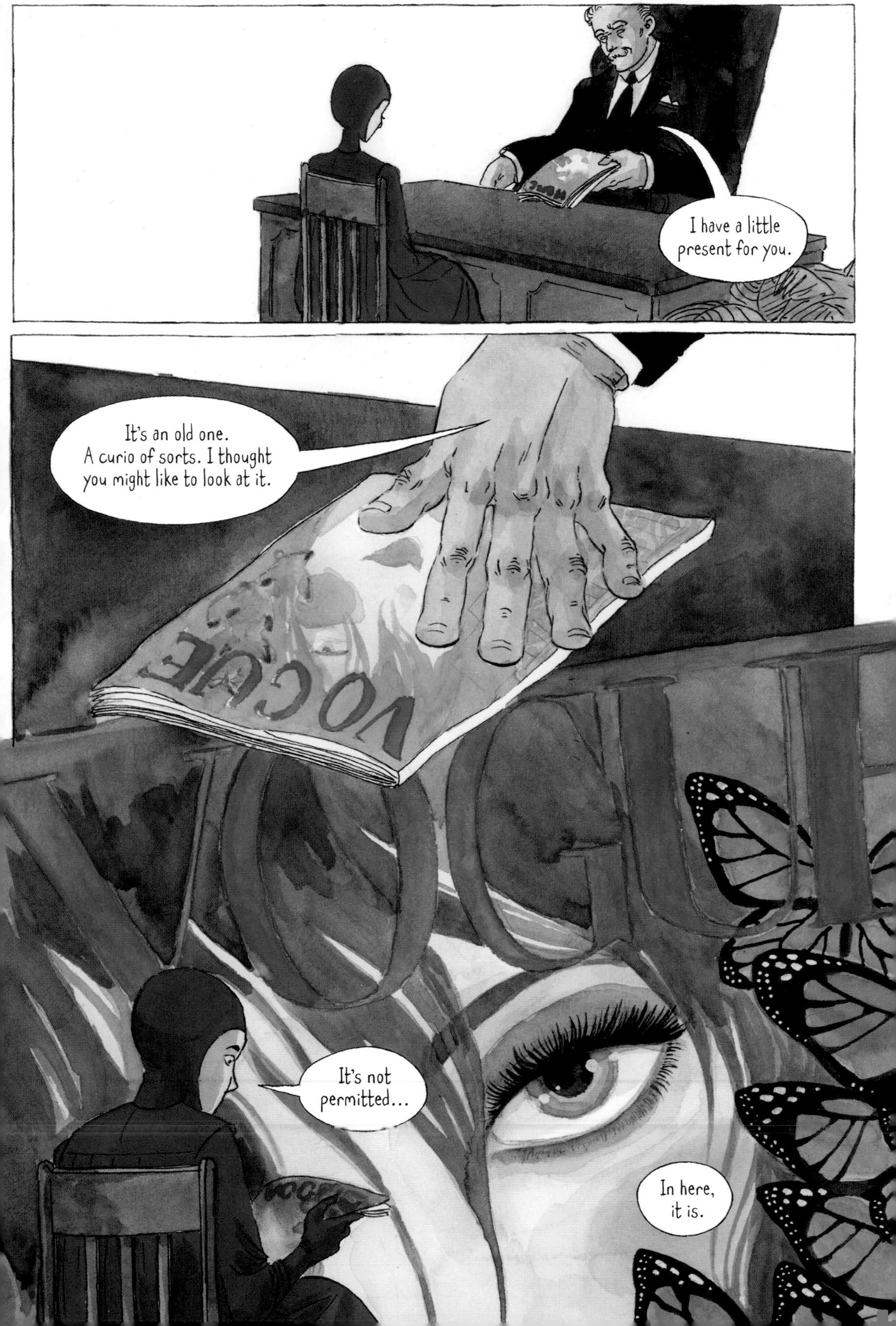
I have a little present for you.
It's an old one. A curio of sorts. I thought you might like to look at it.
VOGUE
It's not permitted...
In here, it is.

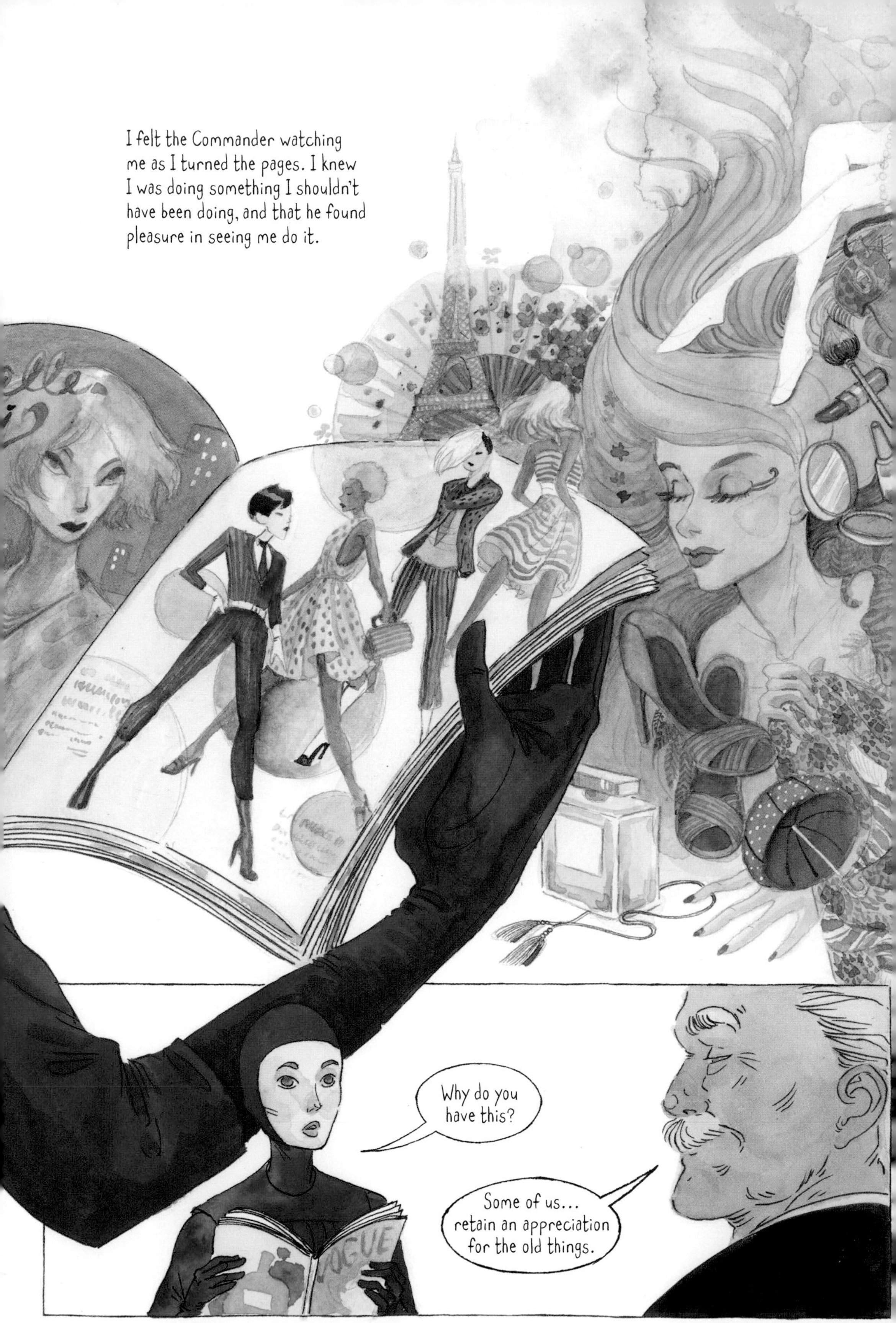
I felt the Commander watching me as I turned the pages. I knew I was doing something I shouldn't have been doing, and that he found pleasure in seeing me do it.
Why do you have this?
Some of us... retain an appreciation for the old things.
VOGUE

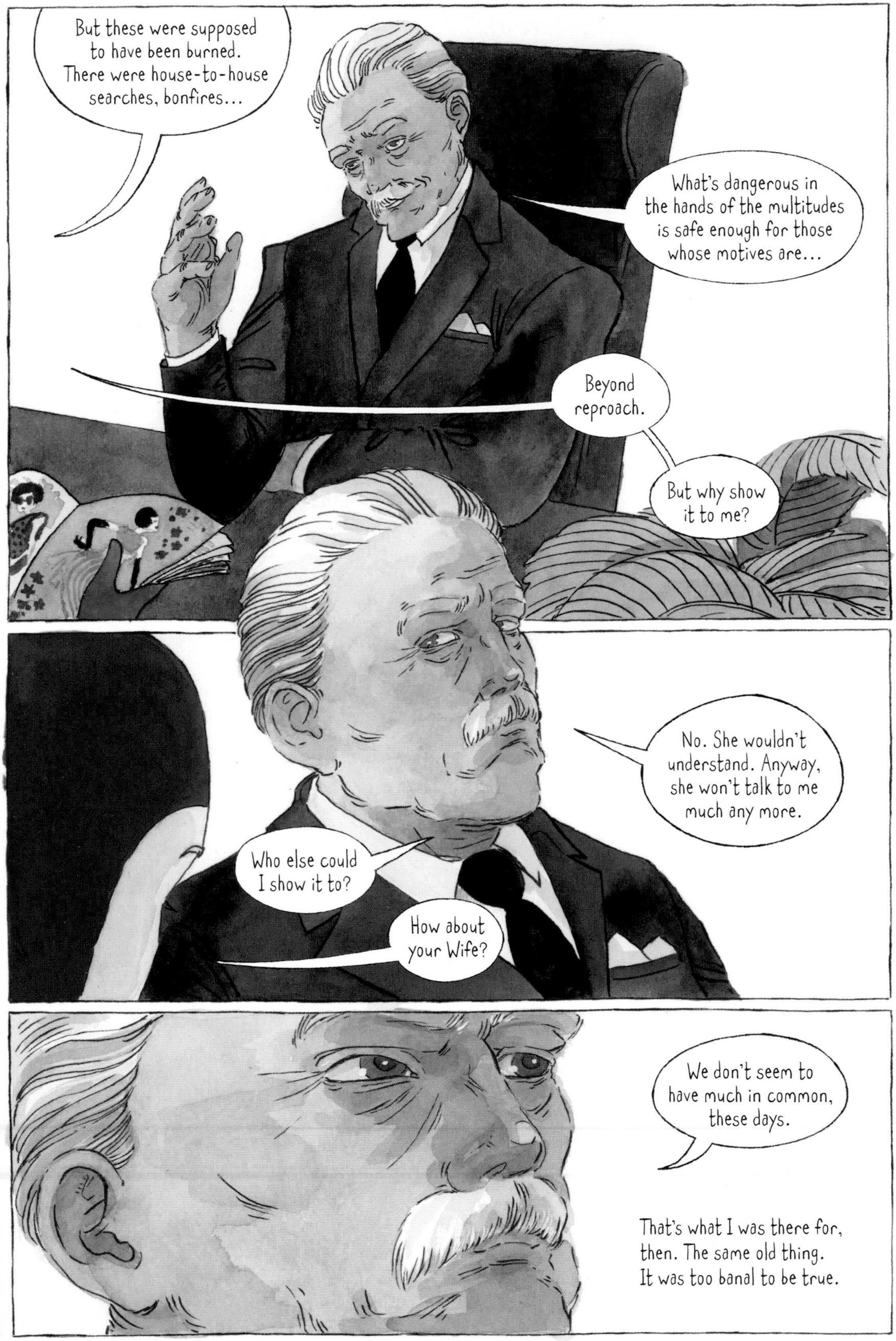
But these were supposed to have been burned. There were house-to-house searches, bonfires...
What's dangerous in the hands of the multitudes is safe enough for those whose motives are...
Beyond reproach.
But why show it to me?
Who else could I show it to?
How about your Wife?
No. She wouldn't understand. Anyway, she won't talk to me much any more.
We don't seem to have much in common, these days.
That's what I was there for, then. The same old thing. It was too banal to be true.

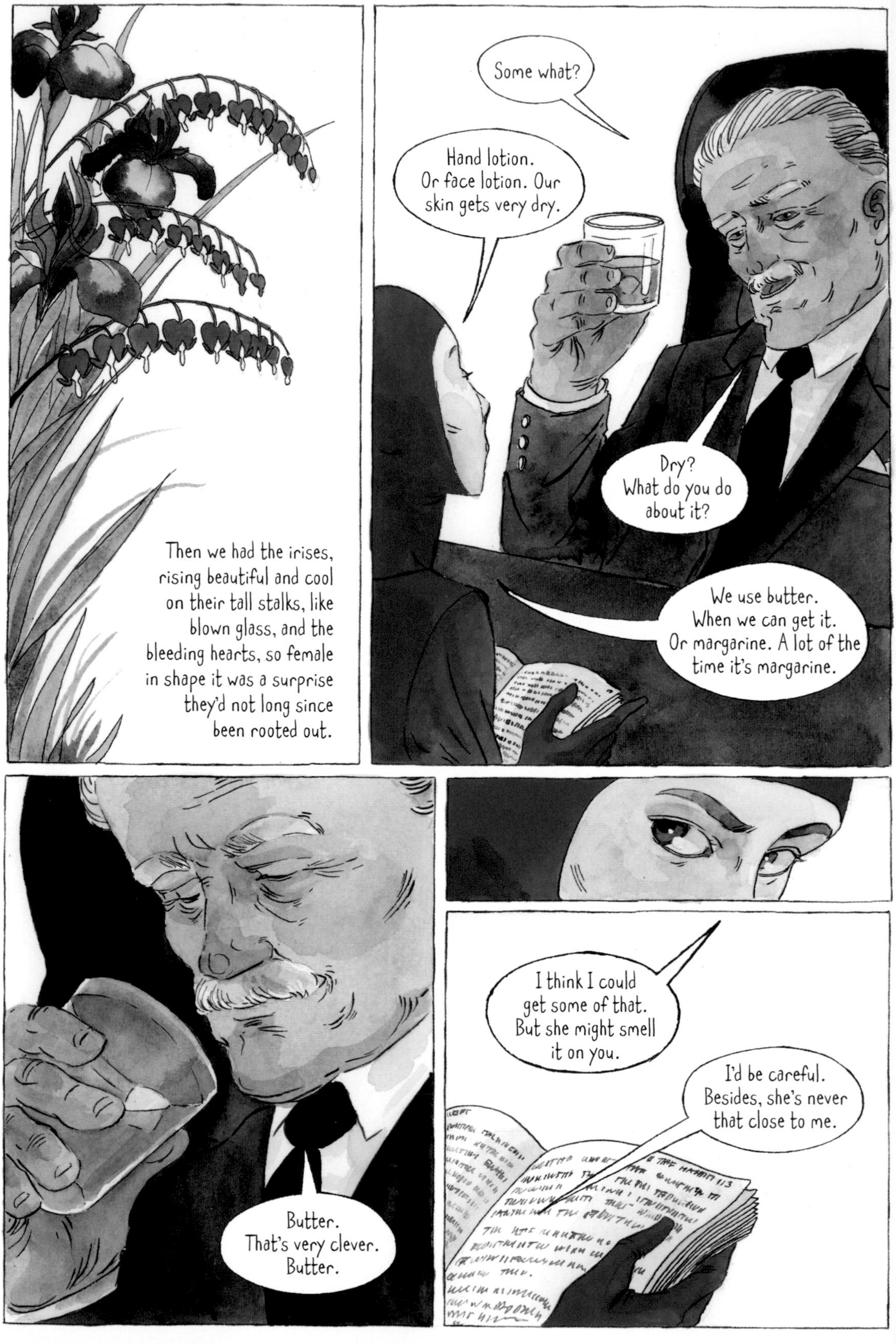
Then we had the irises, rising beautiful and cool on their tall stalks, like blown glass, and the bleeding hearts, so female in shape it was a surprise they'd not long since been rooted out.
Some what?
Hand lotion. Or face lotion. Our skin gets very dry.
Dry? What do you do about it?
We use butter. When we can get it. Or margarine. A lot of the time it's margarine.
Butter. That's very clever. Butter.
I think I could get some of that. But she might smell it on you.
I'd be careful. Besides, she's never that close to me.

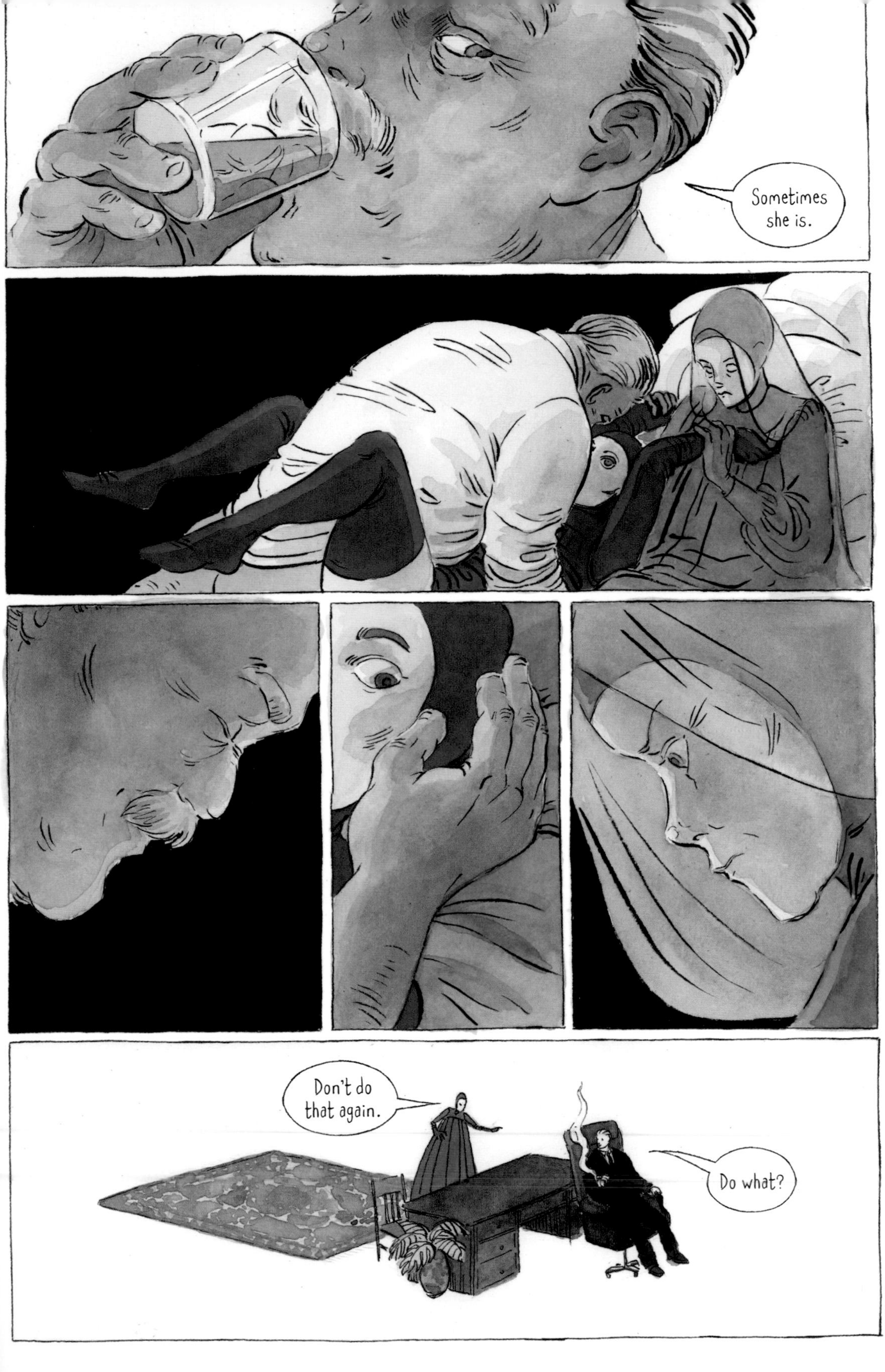
Sometimes she is.
Don't do that again.
Do what?

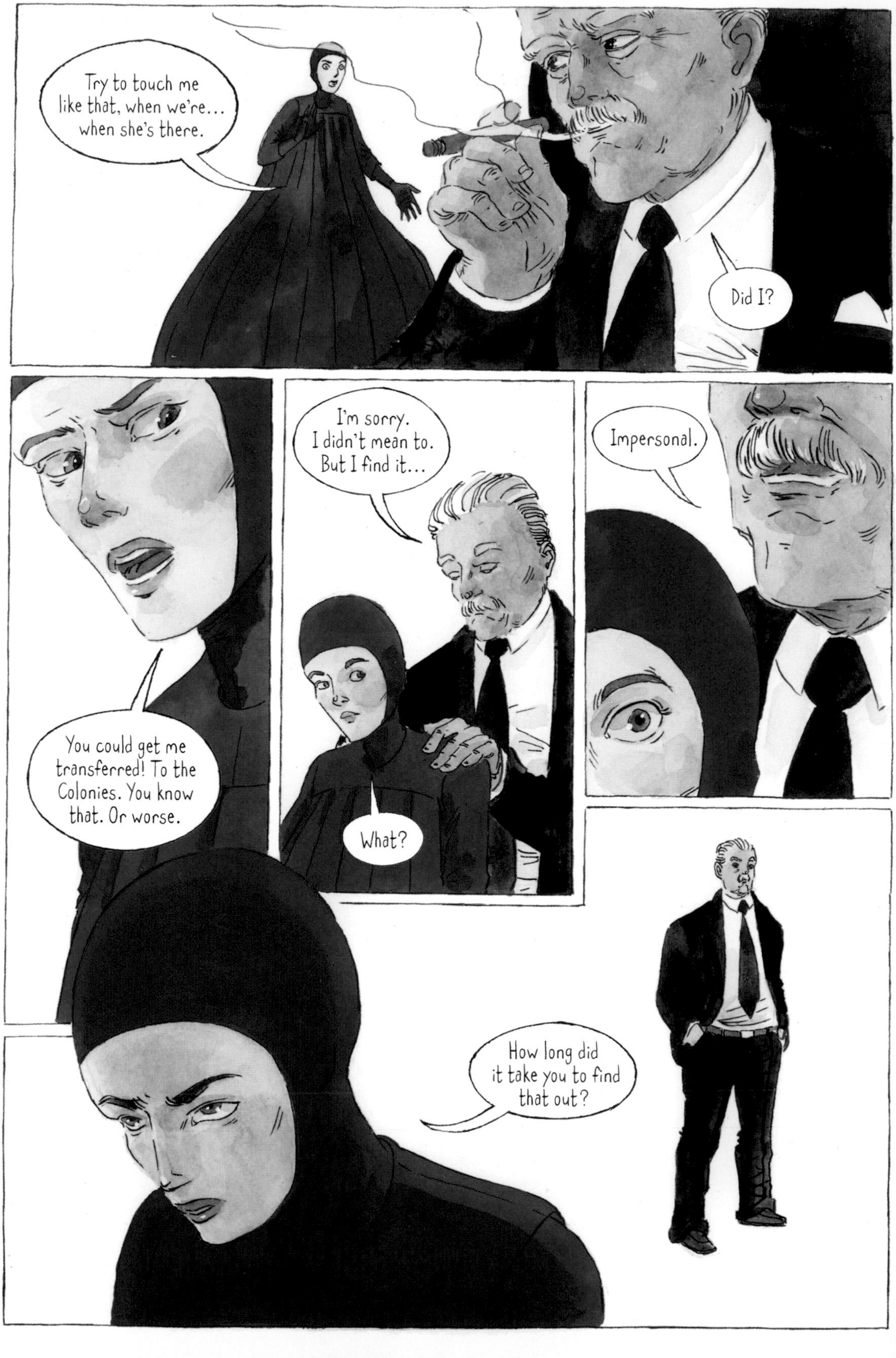
Try to touch me like that, when we're... when she's there.
Did I?
You could get me transferred! To the Colonies. You know that. Or worse.
I'm sorry. I didn't mean to. But I find it...
What?
Impersonal.
How long did it take you to find that out?

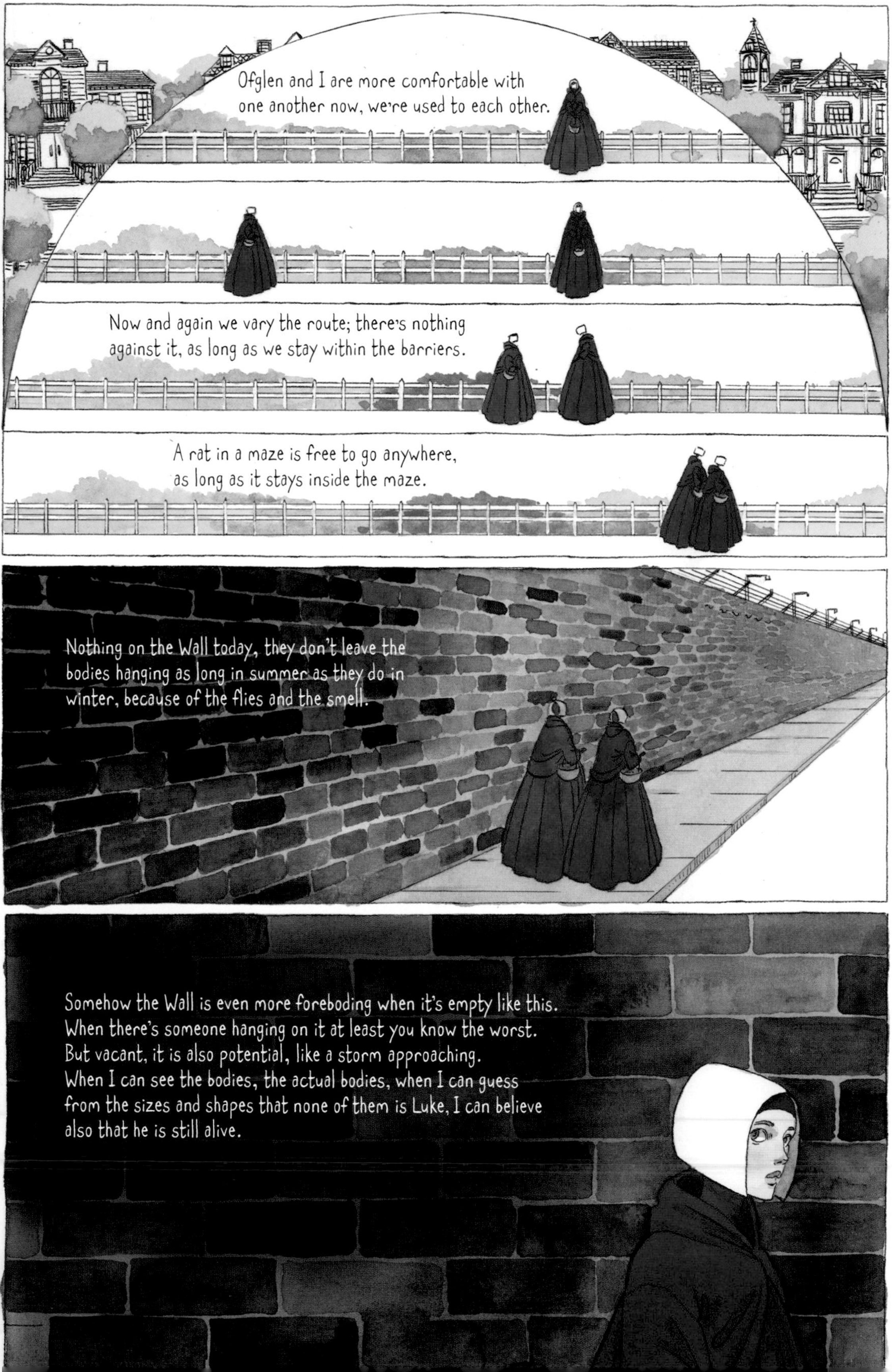
Ofglen and I are more comfortable with one another now, we're used to each other.
Now and again we vary the route; there's nothing against it, as long as we stay within the barriers.
A rat in a maze is free to go anywhere, as long as it stays inside the maze.
Nothing on the Wall today, they don't leave the bodies hanging as long in summer as they do in winter, because of the flies and the smell.
Somehow the Wall is even more foreboding when it's empty like this. When there's someone hanging on it at least you know the worst. But vacant, it is also potential, like a storm approaching. When I can see the bodies, the actual bodies, when I can guess from the sizes and shapes that none of them is Luke, I can believe also that he is still alive.

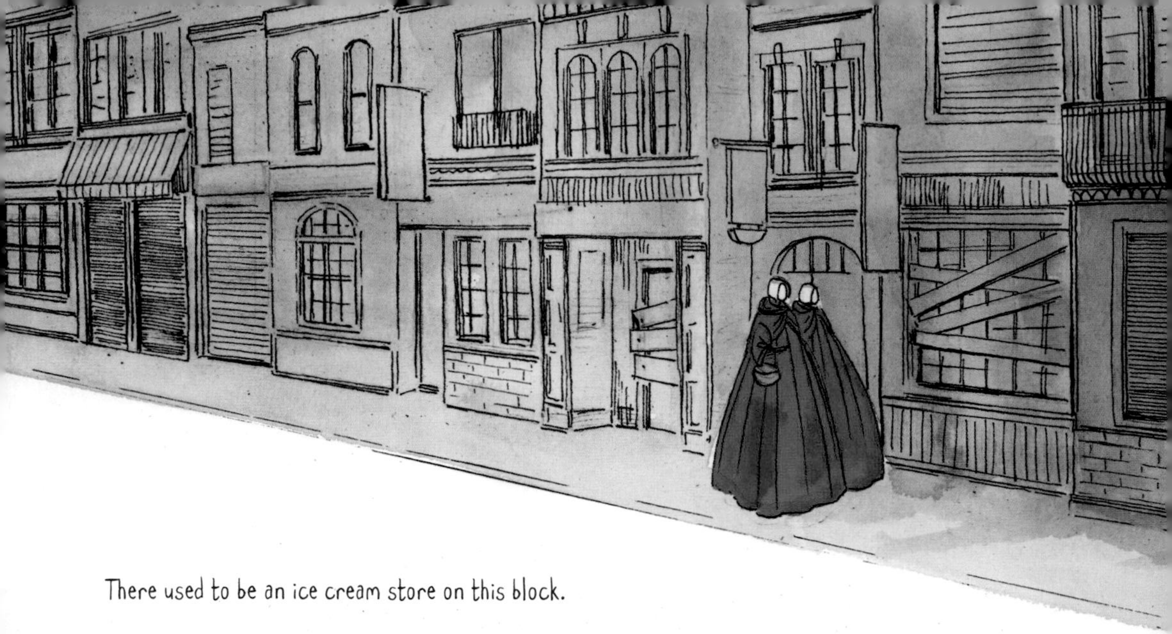

There used to be an ice cream store on this block.

You could get double scoops. If you wanted they would put chocolate sprinkles on top.

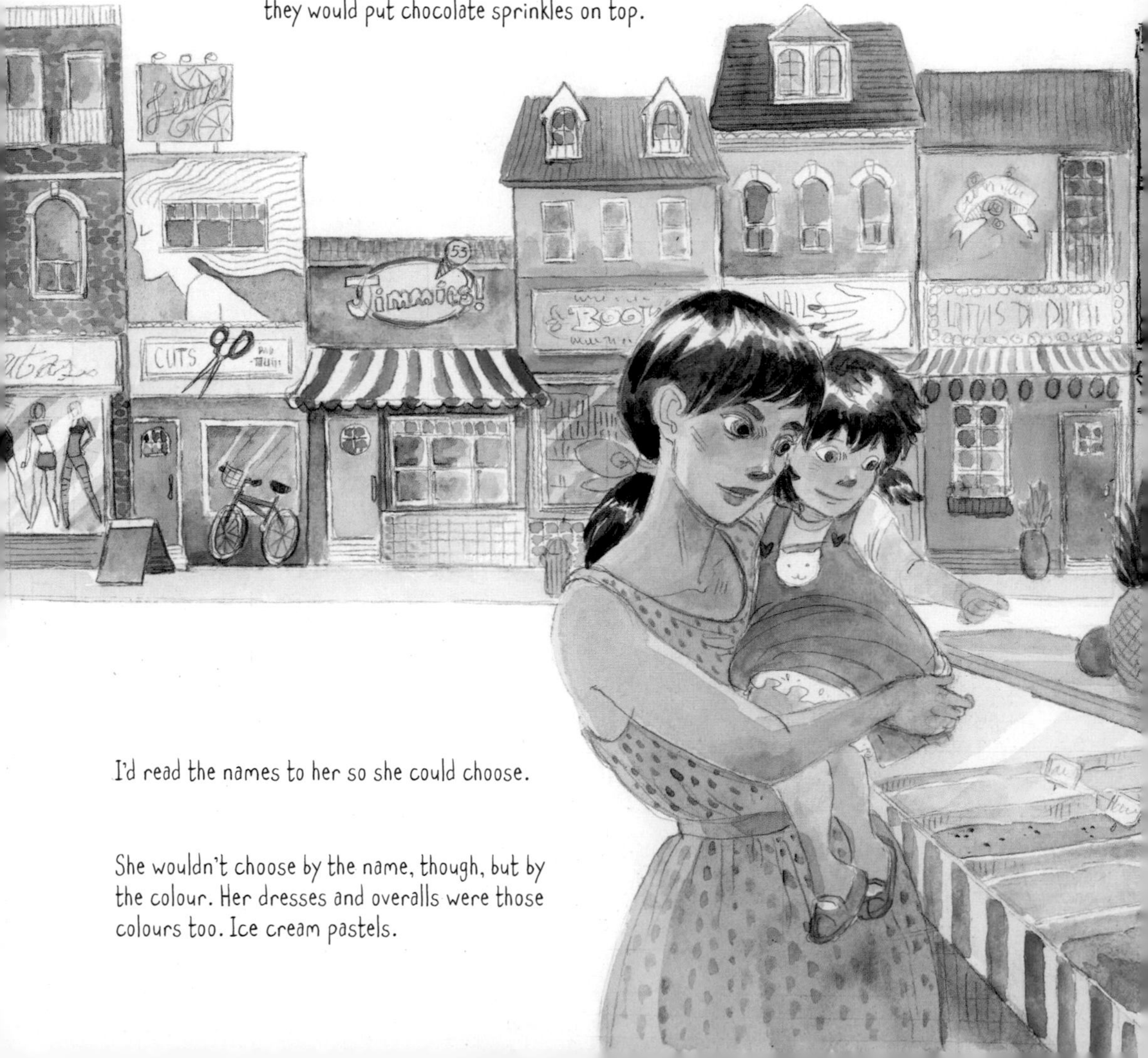

53
Jimmies!
CUTS
NAILS

I'd read the names to her so she could choose.

She wouldn't choose by the name, though, but by the colour. Her dresses and overalls were those colours too. Ice cream pastels.

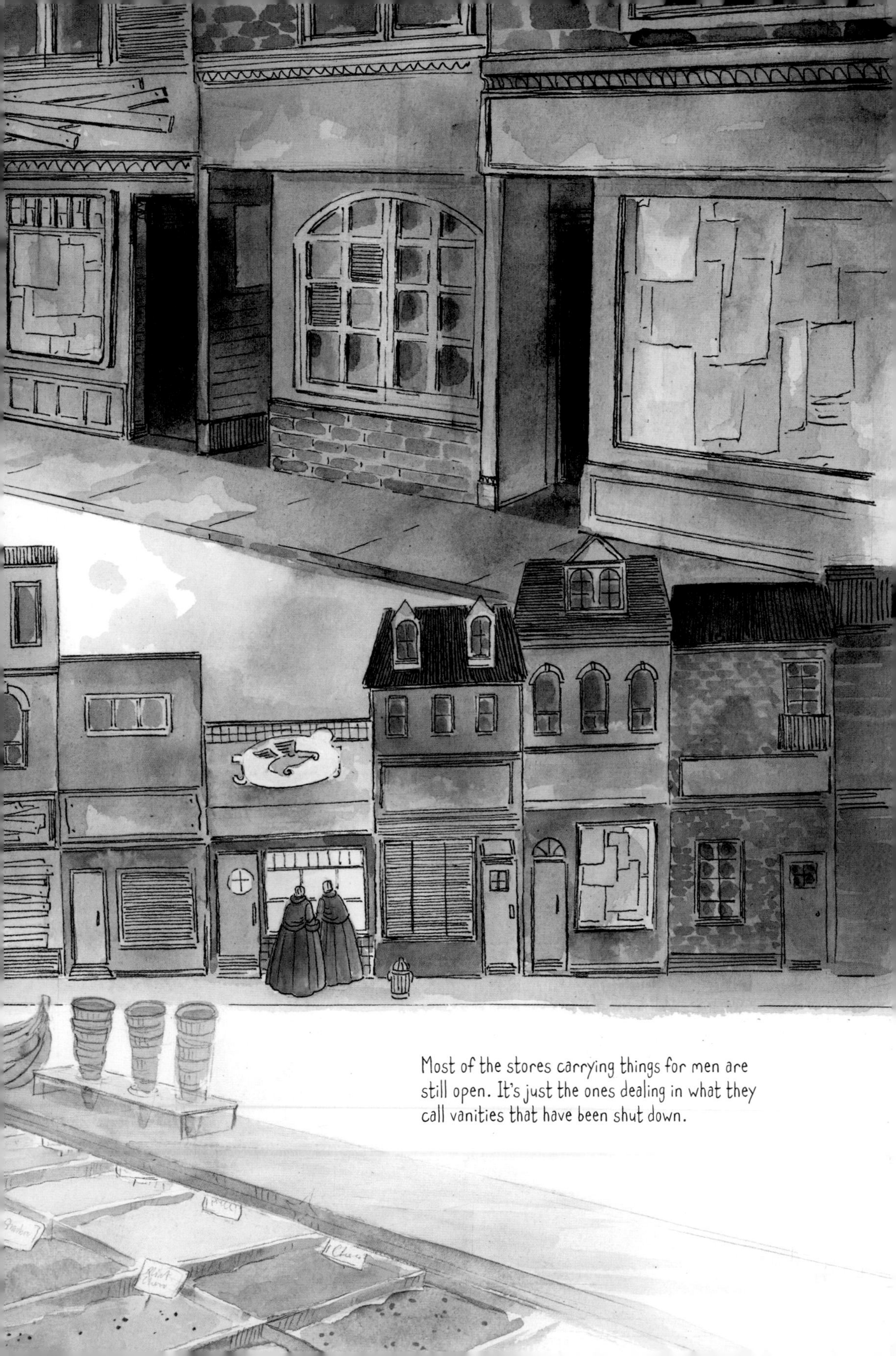
Most of the stores carrying things for men are still open. It's just the ones dealing in what they call vanities that have been shut down.

Soul Scrolls.

It's a franchise:
there are Soul Scrolls
in every city centre,
in every suburb, or
so they say. It must
make a lot of profit.

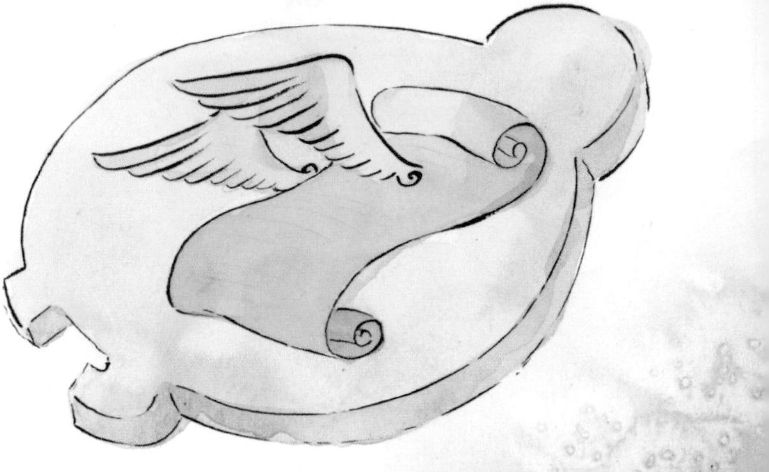

What the machines print is prayers:
for health, wealth, a death, a birth, a sin.

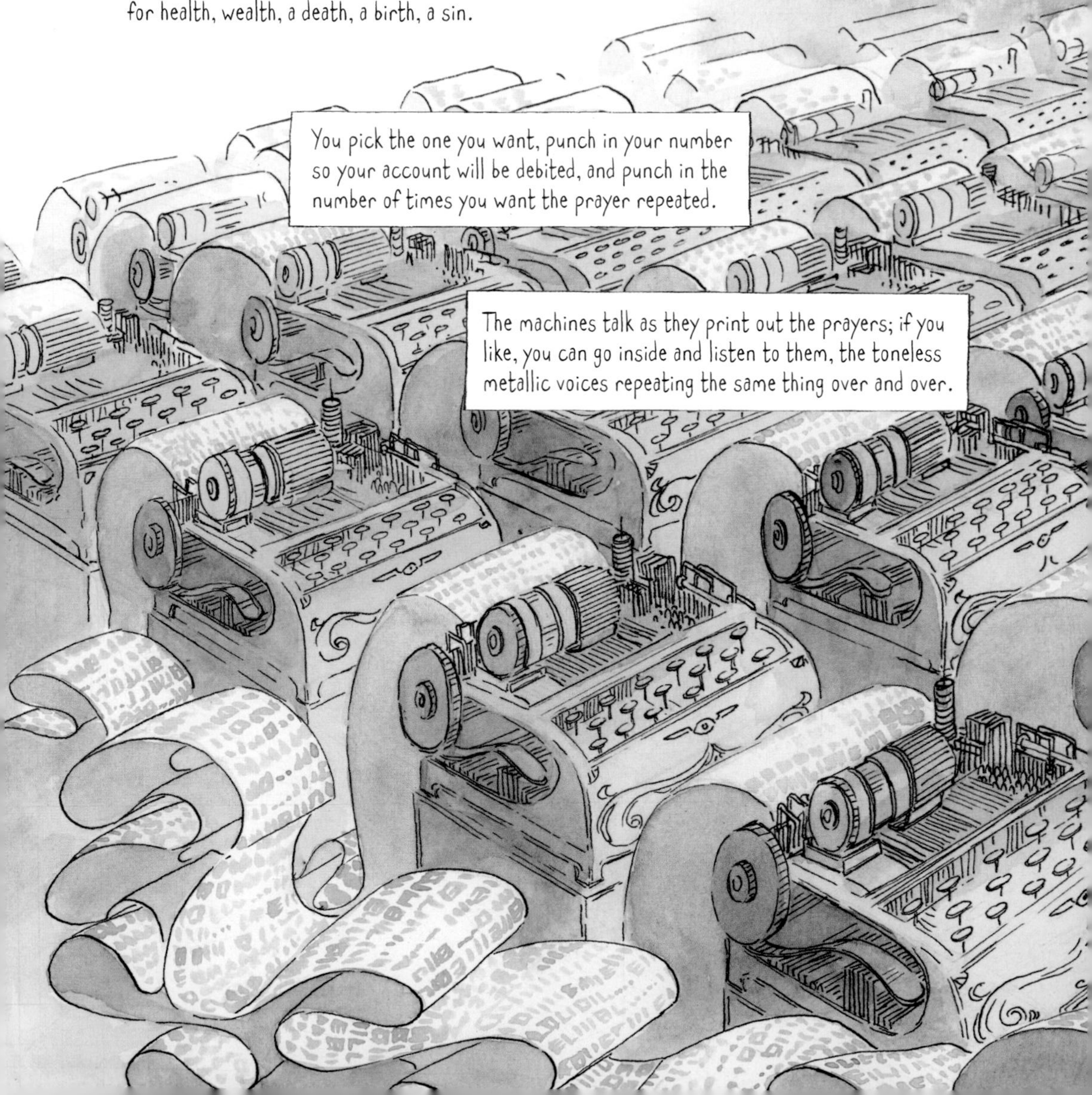
You pick the one you want, punch in your number so your account will be debited, and punch in the number of times you want the prayer repeated.
The machines talk as they print out the prayers; if you like, you can go inside and listen to them, the toneless metallic voices repeating the same thing over and over.

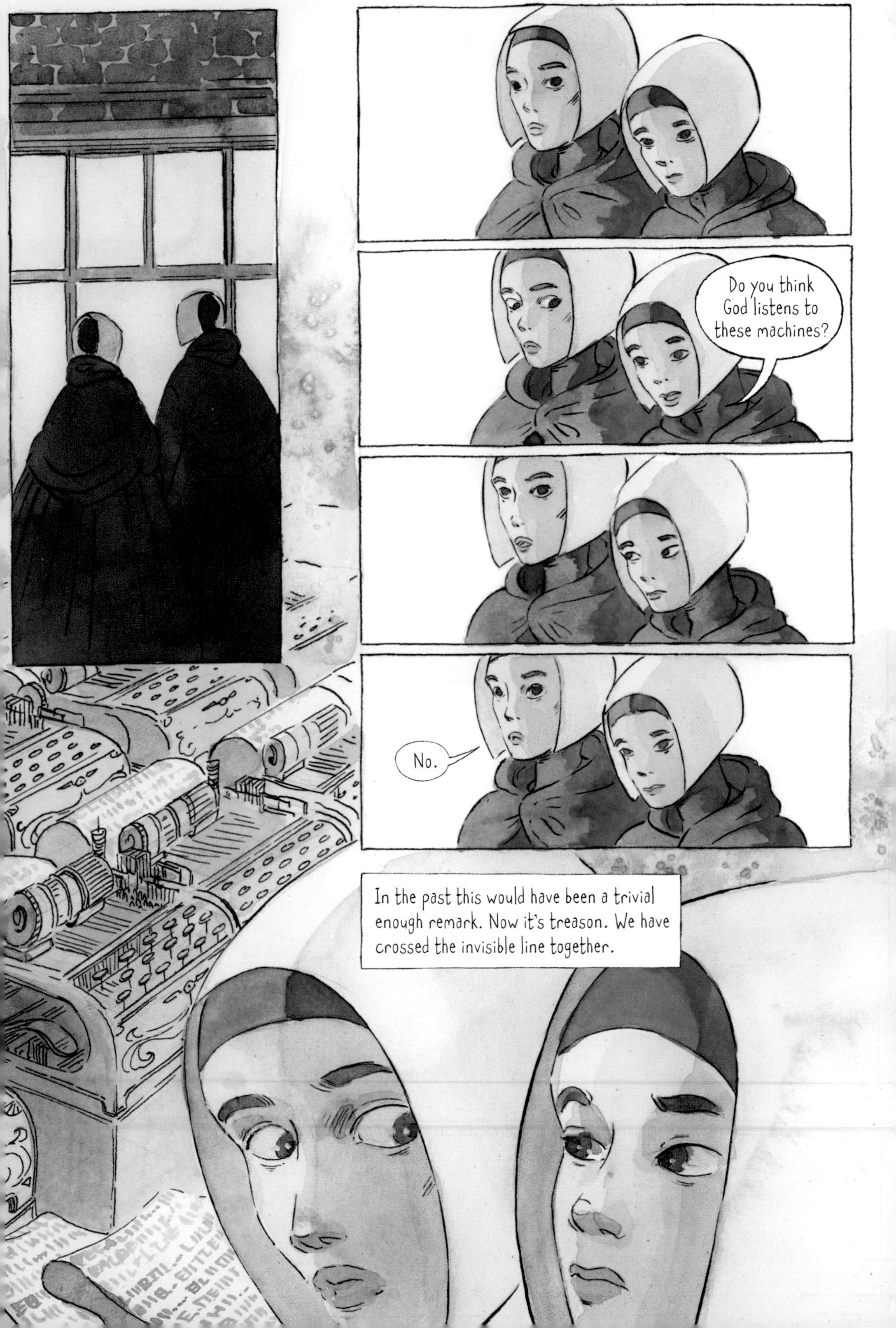
Do you think God listens to these machines?
No.
In the past this would have been a trivial enough remark. Now it's treason. We have crossed the invisible line together.

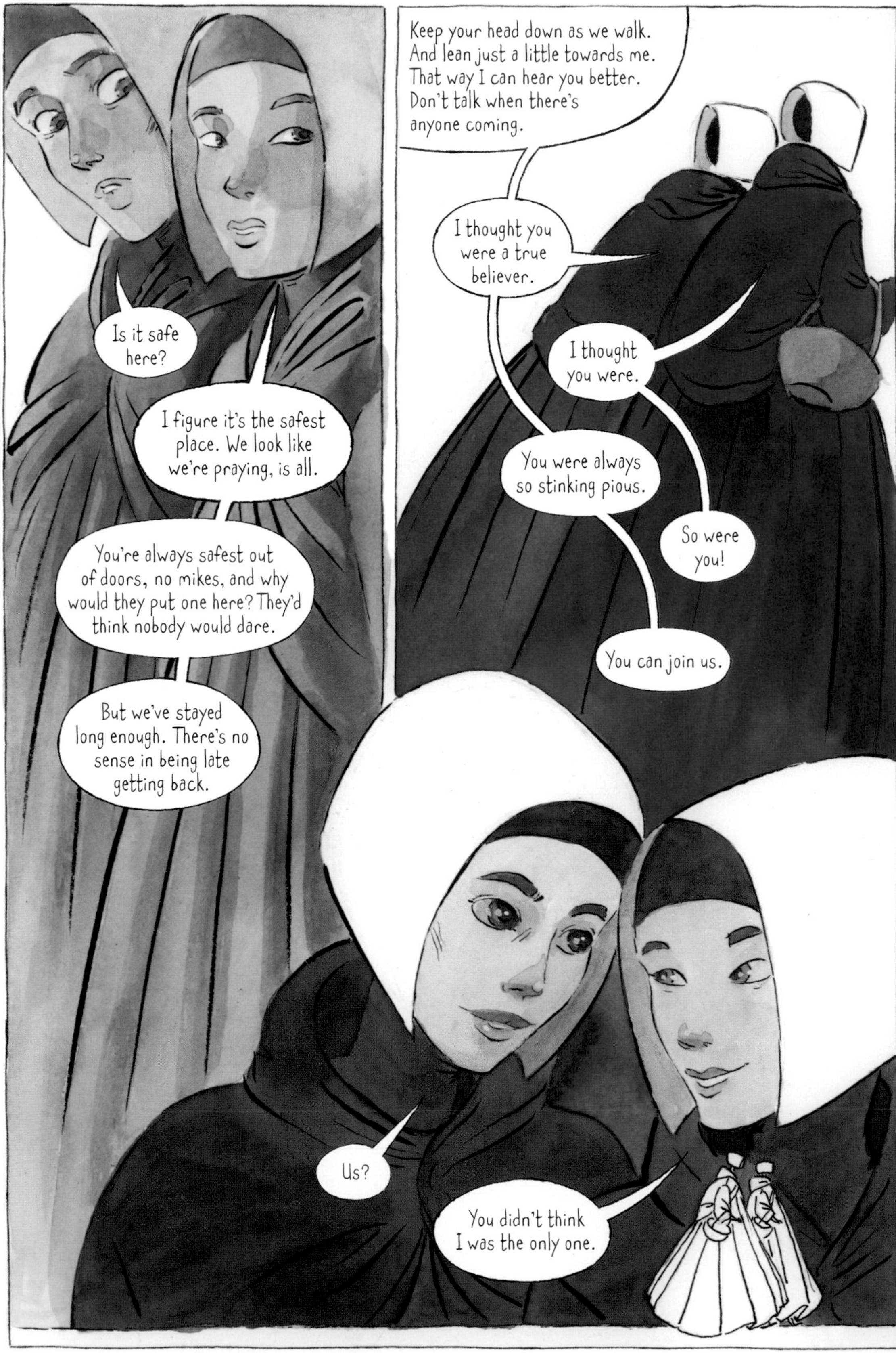
Is it safe here?
I figure it's the safest place. We look like we're praying, is all.
You're always safest out of doors, no mikes, and why would they put one here? They'd think nobody would dare.
But we've stayed long enough. There's no sense in being late getting back.
Keep your head down as we walk. And lean just a little towards me. That way I can hear you better. Don't talk when there's anyone coming.
I thought you were a true believer.
I thought you were.
You were always so stinking pious.
So were you!
You can join us.
Us?
You didn't think I was the only one.

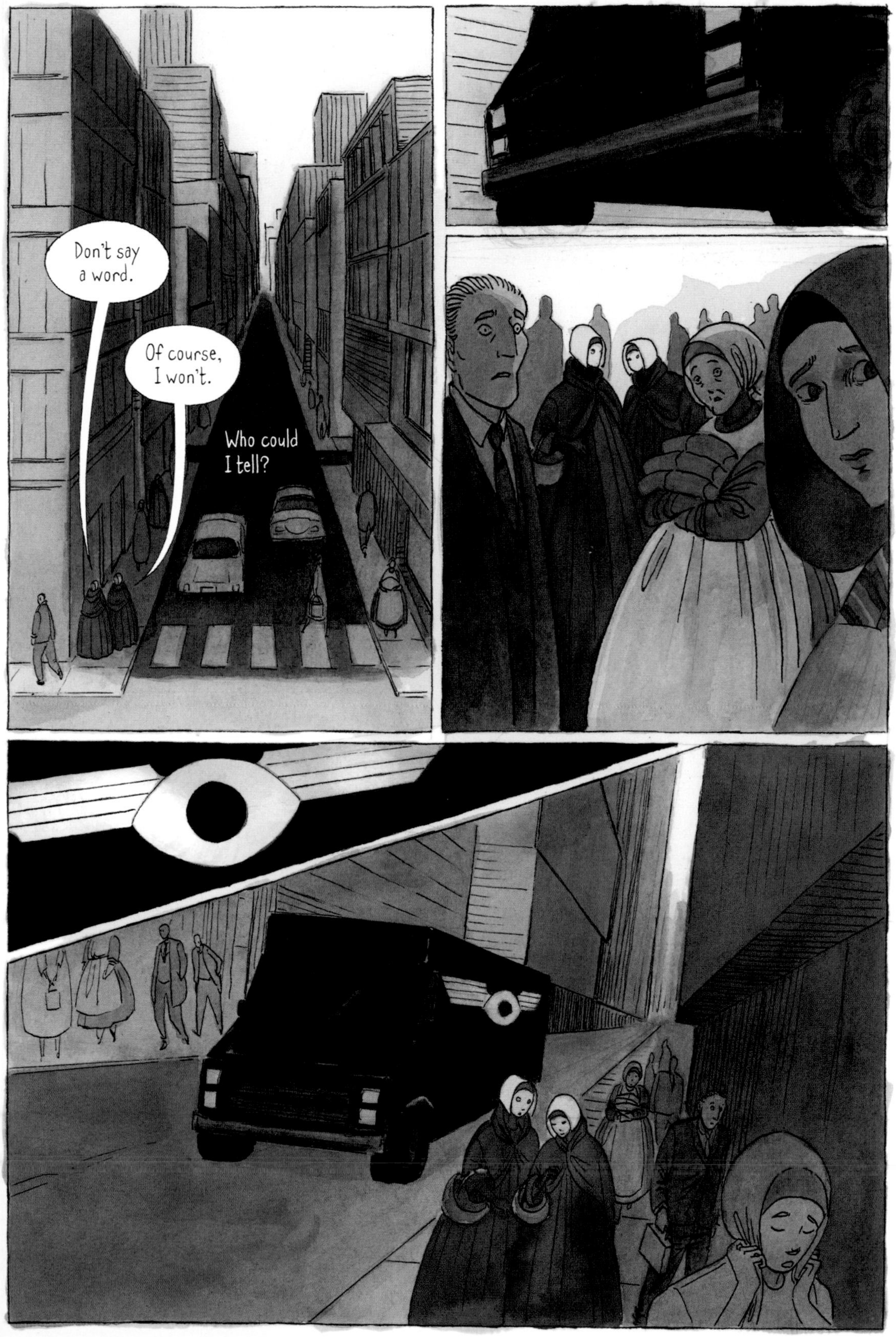
Don't say a word.
Of course, I won't.
Who could I tell?

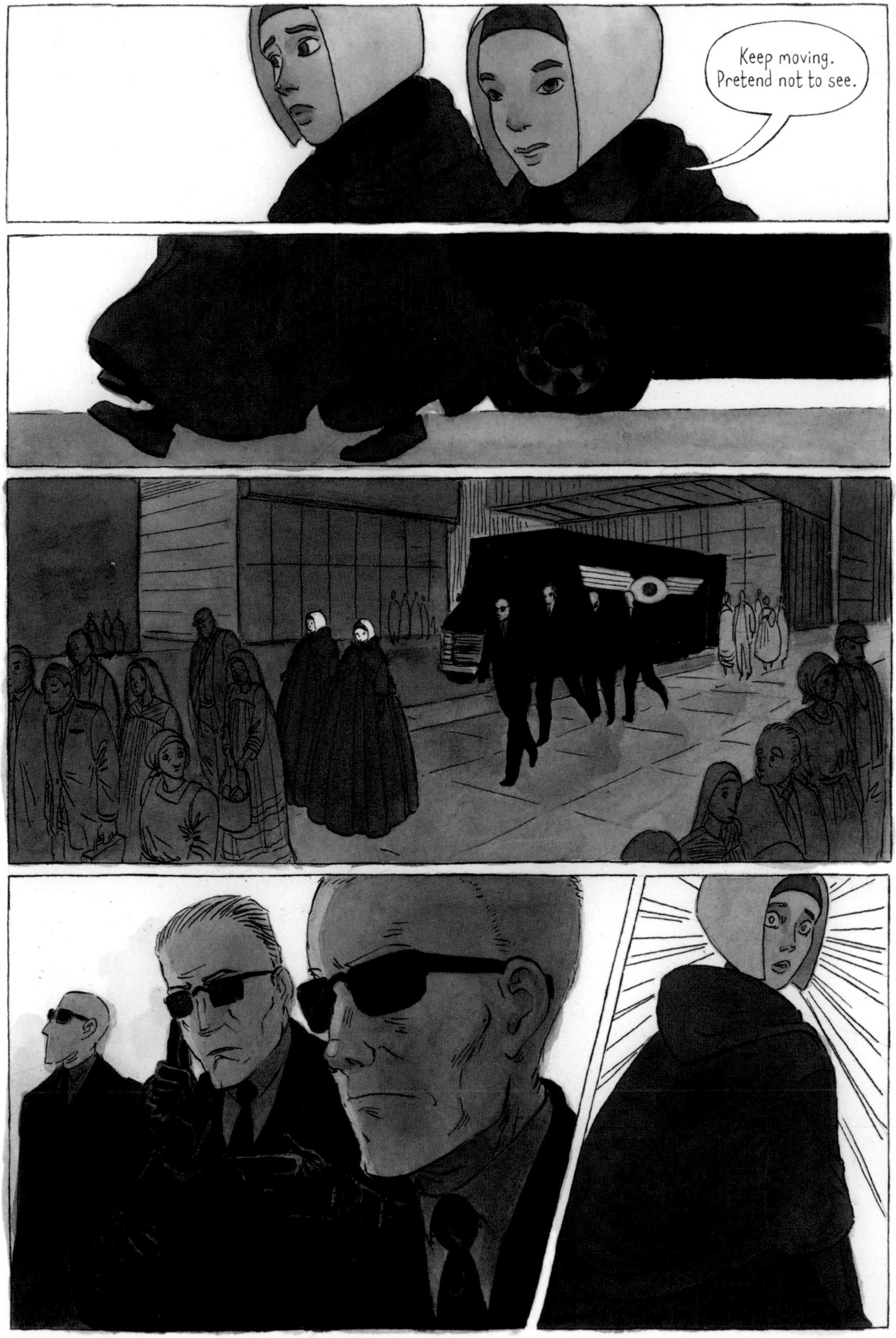
Keep moving.
Pretend not to see.

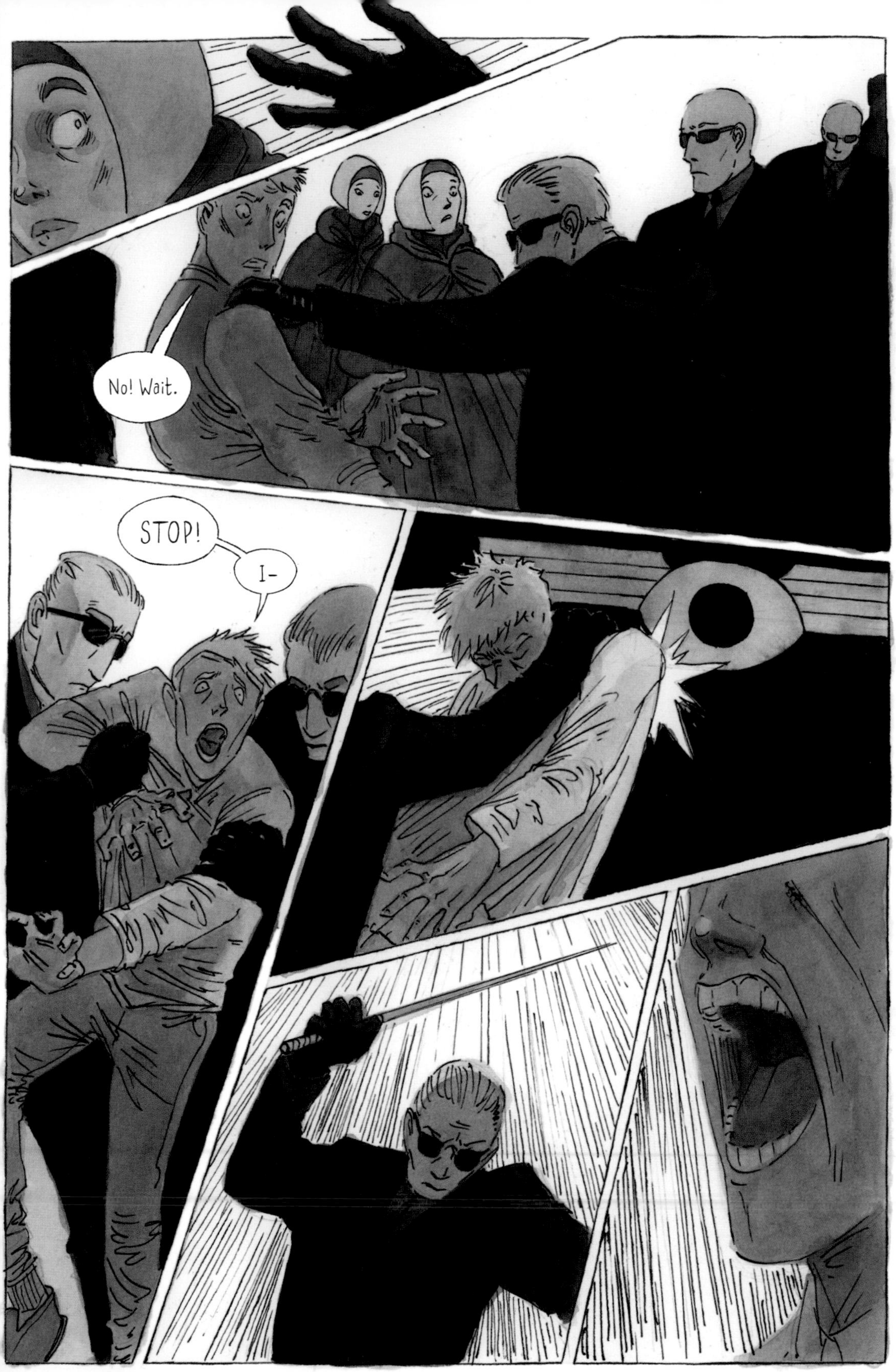
No! Wait.
STOP!
I-

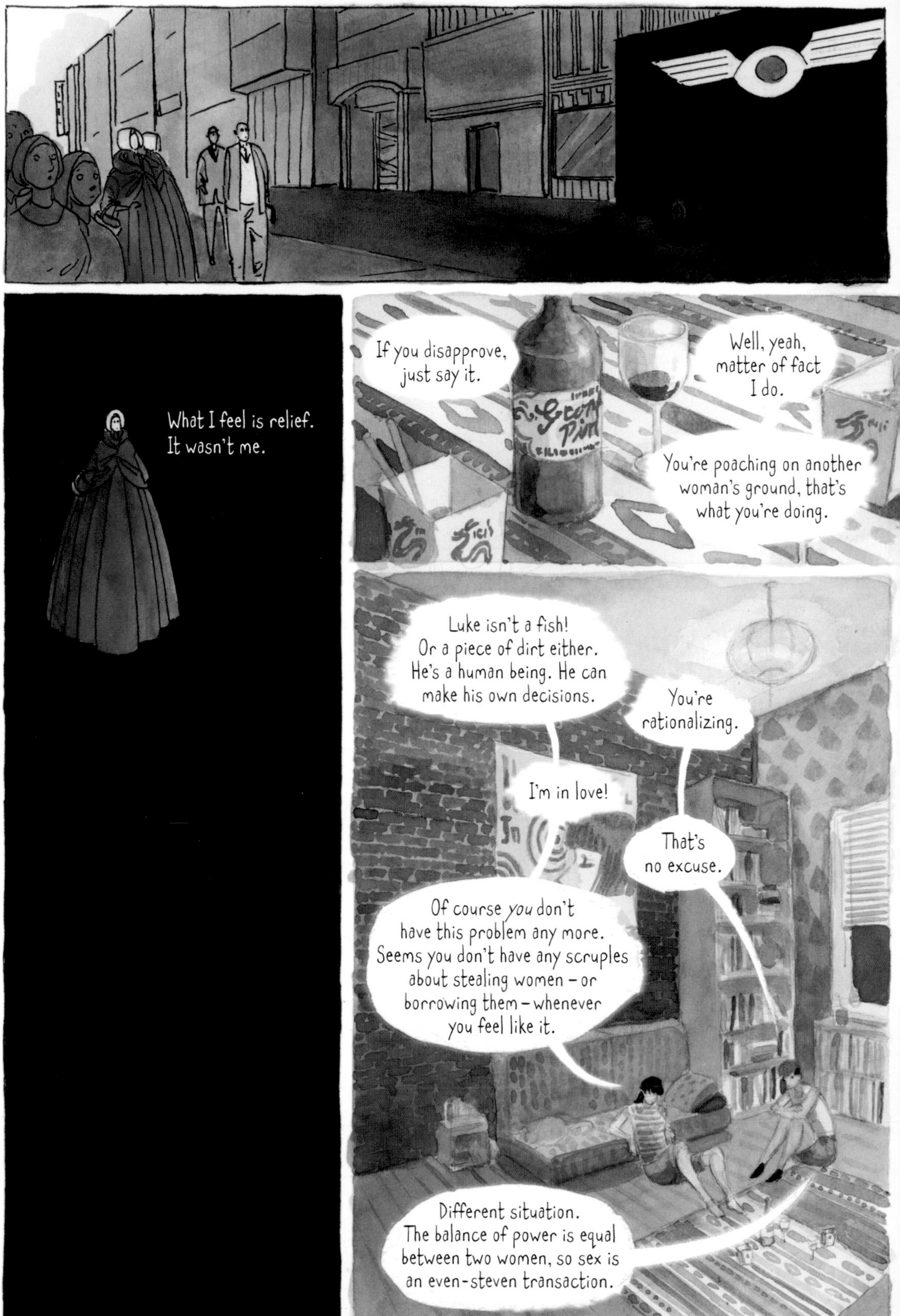
What I feel is relief. It wasn't me.
If you disapprove, just say it.
Well, yeah, matter of fact I do.
You're poaching on another woman's ground, that's what you're doing.
Luke isn't a fish! Or a piece of dirt either. He's a human being. He can make his own decisions.
You're rationalizing.
I'm in love!
That's no excuse.
Of course *you* don't have this problem any more. Seems you don't have any scruples about stealing women – or borrowing them – whenever you feel like it.
Different situation. The balance of power is equal between two women, so sex is an even-steven transaction.

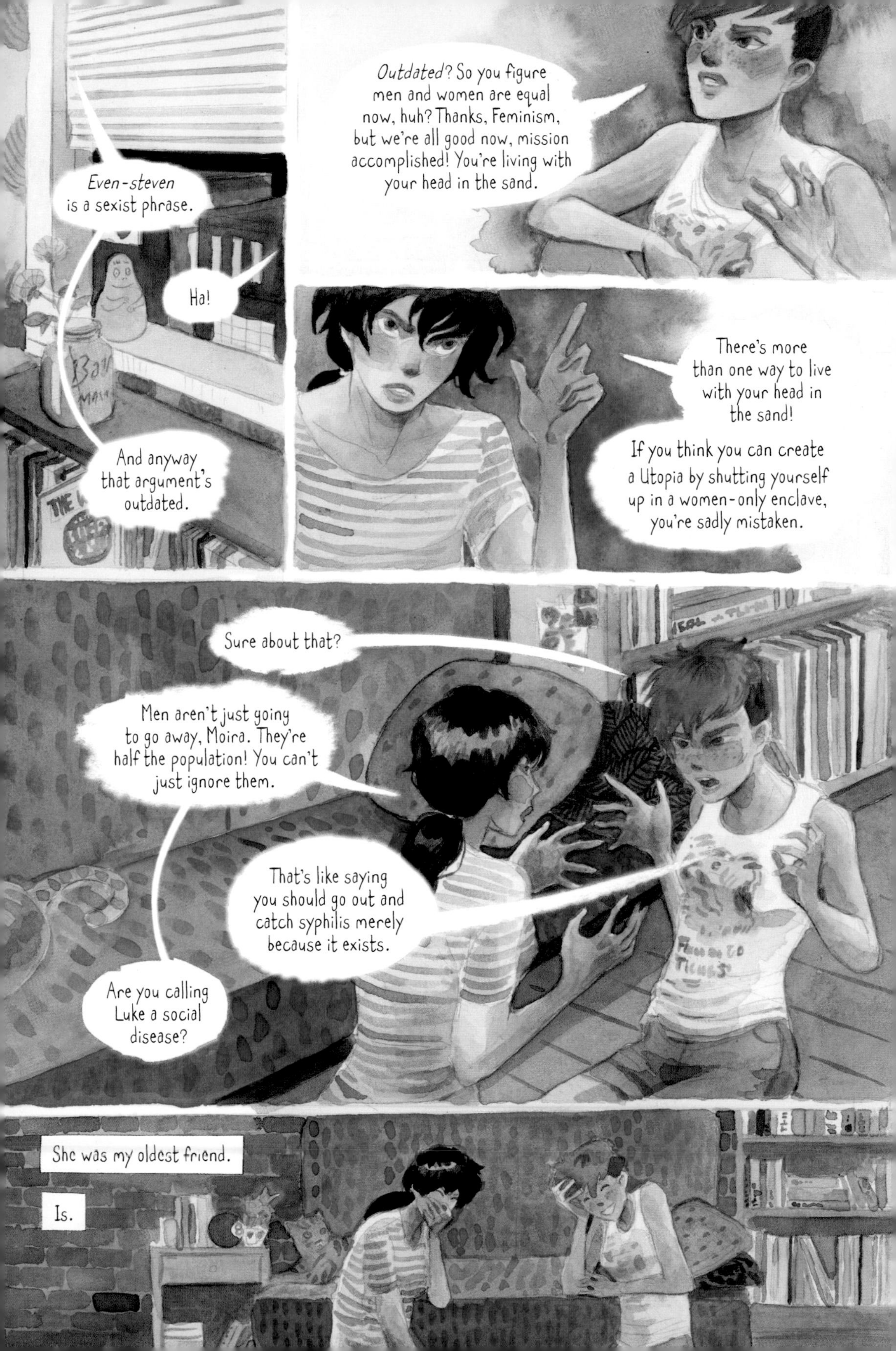

Even-steven is a sexist phrase.
Outdated? So you figure men and women are equal now, huh? Thanks, Feminism, but we're all good now, mission accomplished! You're living with your head in the sand.
Ha!
And anyway that argument's outdated.
There's more than one way to live with your head in the sand!
If you think you can create a Utopia by shutting yourself up in a women-only enclave, you're sadly mistaken.
Sure about that?
Men aren't just going to go away, Moira. They're half the population! You can't just ignore them.
That's like saying you should go out and catch syphilis merely because it exists.
Are you calling Luke a social disease?
She was my oldest friend.
Is.

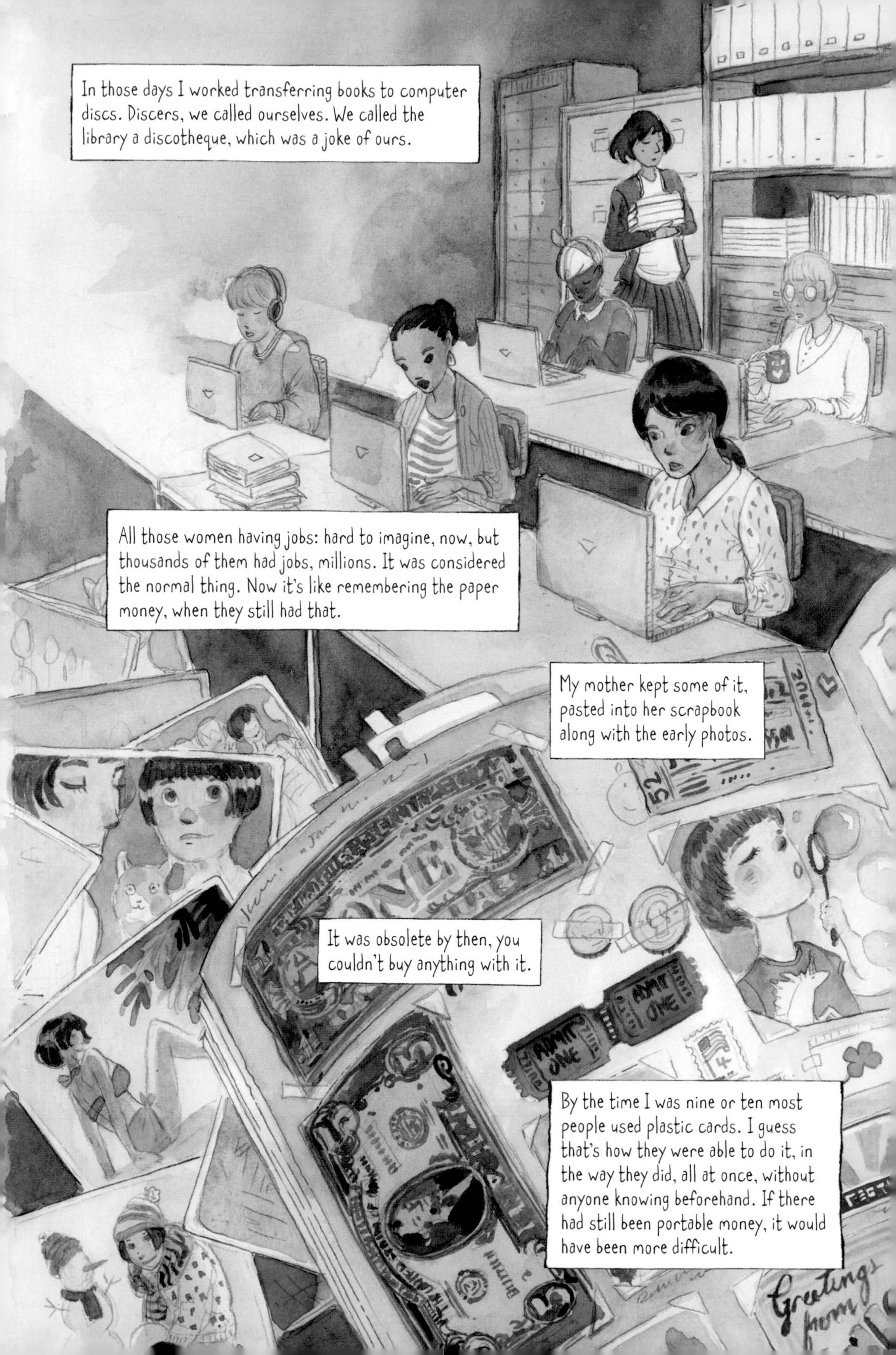
In those days I worked transferring books to computer discs. Discers, we called ourselves. We called the library a discotheque, which was a joke of ours.
All those women having jobs: hard to imagine, now, but thousands of them had jobs, millions. It was considered the normal thing. Now it's like remembering the paper money, when they still had that.
My mother kept some of it, pasted into her scrapbook along with the early photos.
It was obsolete by then, you couldn't buy anything with it.
ADMIT ONE
ADMIT ONE
By the time I was nine or ten most people used plastic cards. I guess that's how they were able to do it, in the way they did, all at once, without anyone knowing beforehand. If there had still been portable money, it would have been more difficult.
Greetings from

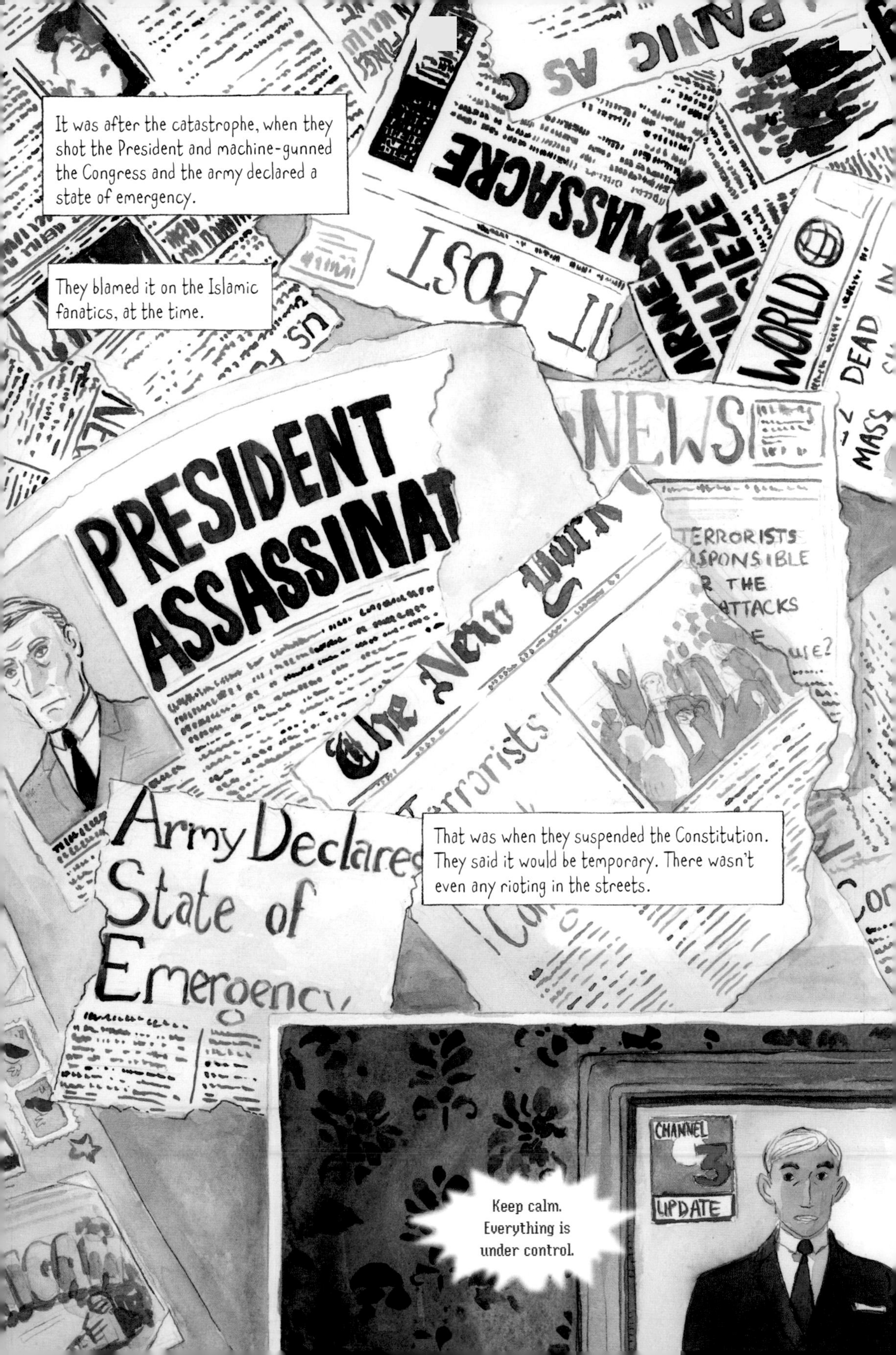

It was after the catastrophe, when they shot the President and machine-gunned the Congress and the army declared a state of emergency.
They blamed it on the Islamic fanatics, at the time.
MASSACRE
WORLD
NEWS
PRESIDENT ASSASSINAT
Army Declares State of Emergency
TERRORISTS
That was when they suspended the Constitution. They said it would be temporary. There wasn't even any rioting in the streets.
CHANNEL 3 UPDATE
Keep calm. Everything is under control.

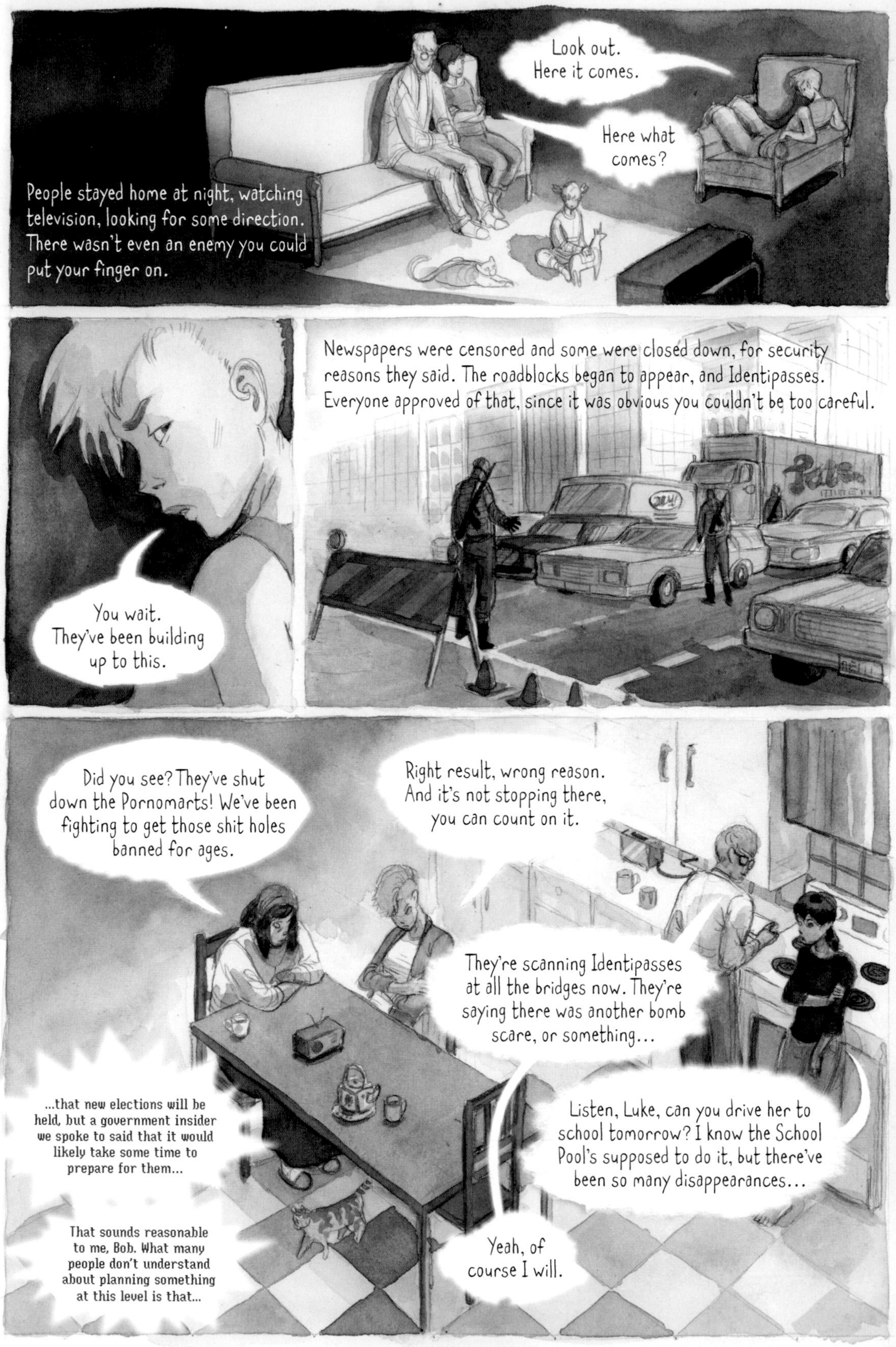
People stayed home at night, watching television, looking for some direction. There wasn't even an enemy you could put your finger on.
Look out. Here it comes.
Here what comes?
You wait. They've been building up to this.
Newspapers were censored and some were closed down, for security reasons they said. The roadblocks began to appear, and Identipasses. Everyone approved of that, since it was obvious you couldn't be too careful.
Did you see? They've shut down the Pornomarts! We've been fighting to get those shit holes banned for ages.
Right result, wrong reason. And it's not stopping there, you can count on it.
They're scanning Identipasses at all the bridges now. They're saying there was another bomb scare, or something...
...that new elections will be held, but a government insider we spoke to said that it would likely take some time to prepare for them...
That sounds reasonable to me, Bob. What many people don't understand about planning something at this level is that...
Listen, Luke, can you drive her to school tomorrow? I know the School Pool's supposed to do it, but there've been so many disappearances...
Yeah, of course I will.

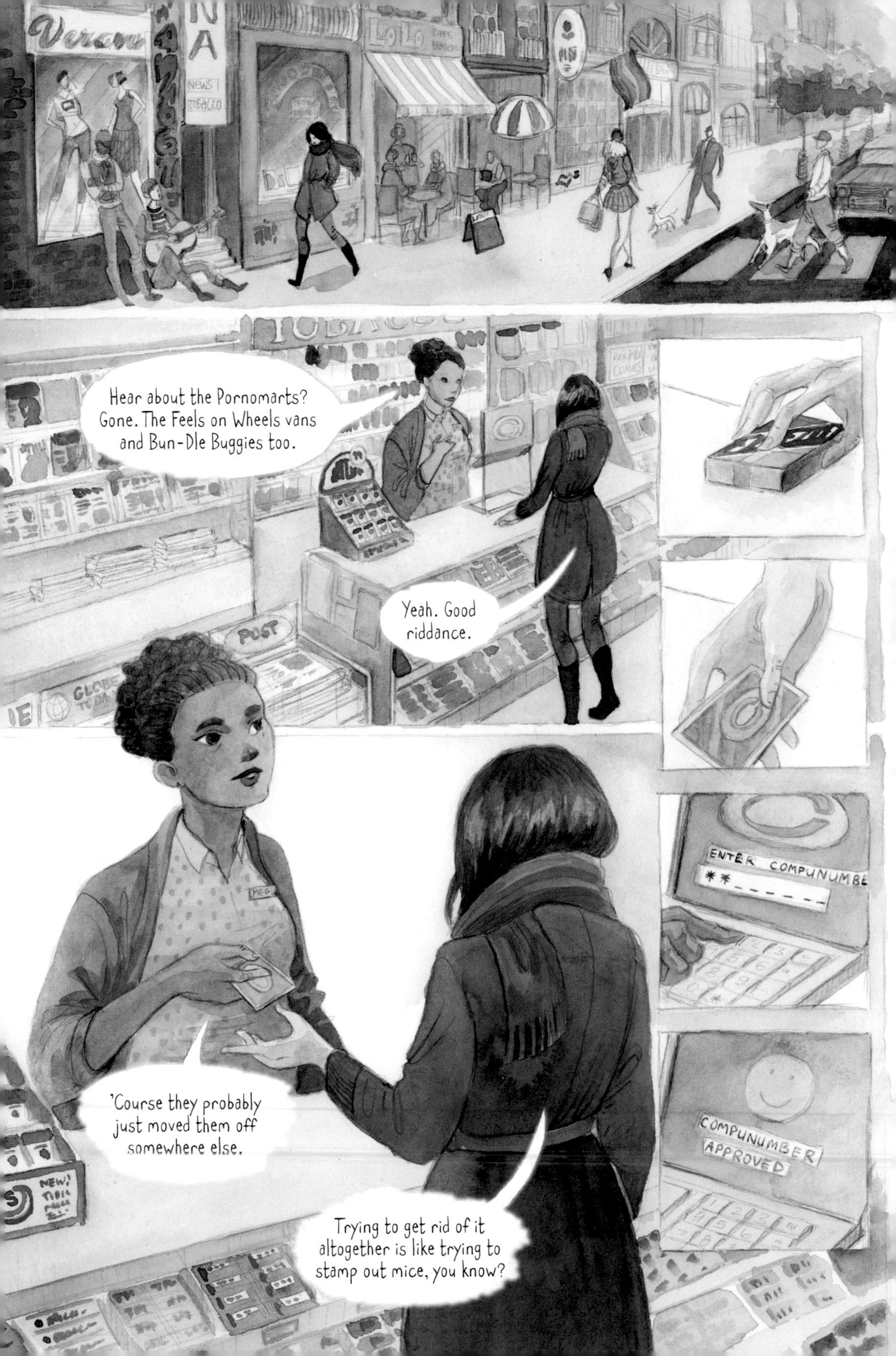
NEWS
TOBACCO
Hear about the Pornomarts? Gone. The Feels on Wheels vans and Bun-Dle Buggies too.
POST
Yeah. Good riddance.
ENTER COMPUNUMBE
'Course they probably just moved them off somewhere else.
COMPUNUMBER APPROVED
Trying to get rid of it altogether is like trying to stamp out mice, you know?

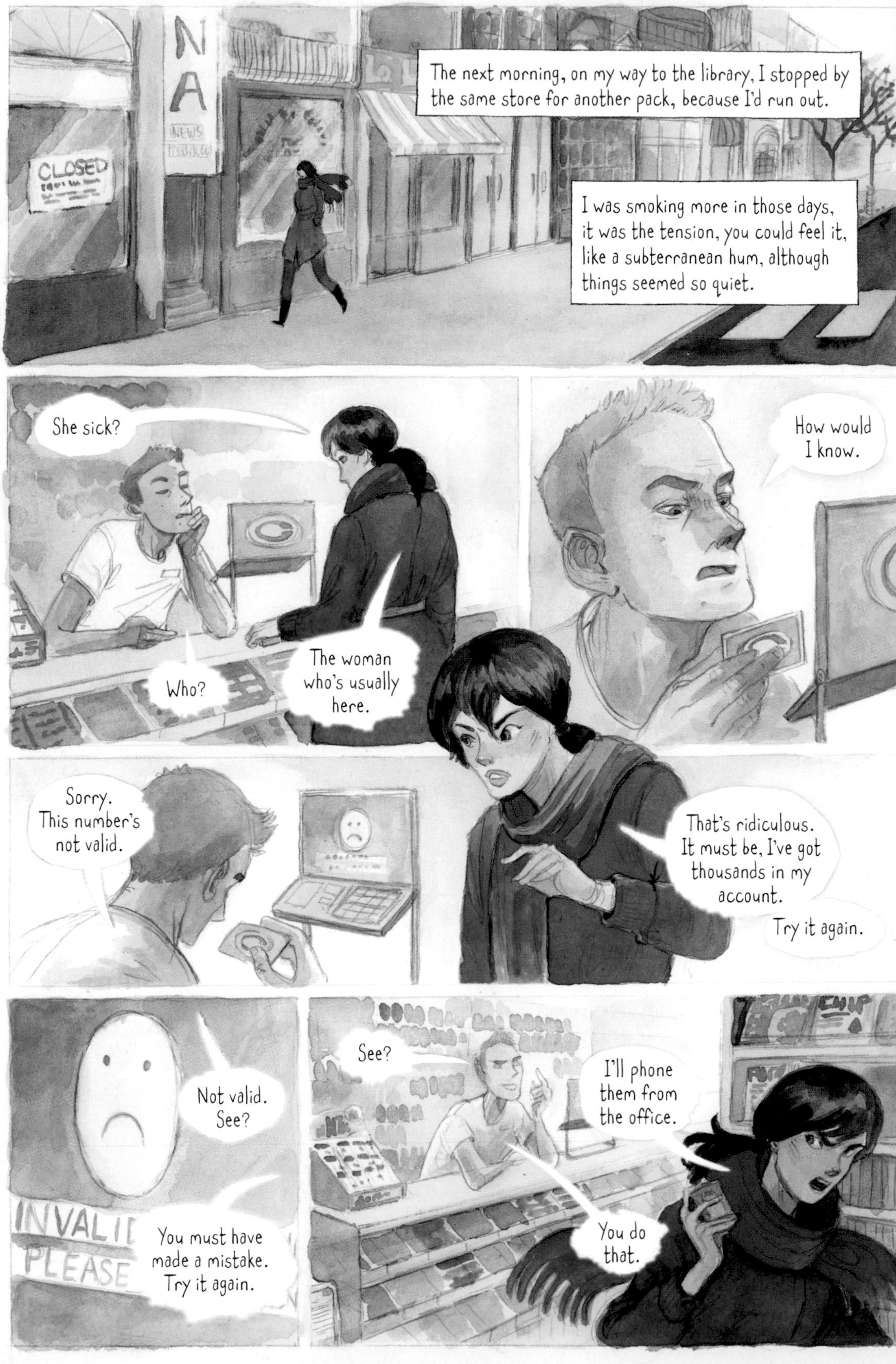

The next morning, on my way to the library, I stopped by the same store for another pack, because I'd run out.
I was smoking more in those days, it was the tension, you could feel it, like a subterranean hum, although things seemed so quiet.
CLOSED
NA
NEWS TOBACCO
She sick?
Who?
The woman who's usually here.
How would I know.
Sorry. This number's not valid.
That's ridiculous. It must be, I've got thousands in my account.
Try it again.
Not valid. See?
INVALI
PLEASE
You must have made a mistake. Try it again.
See?
I'll phone them from the office.
You do that.

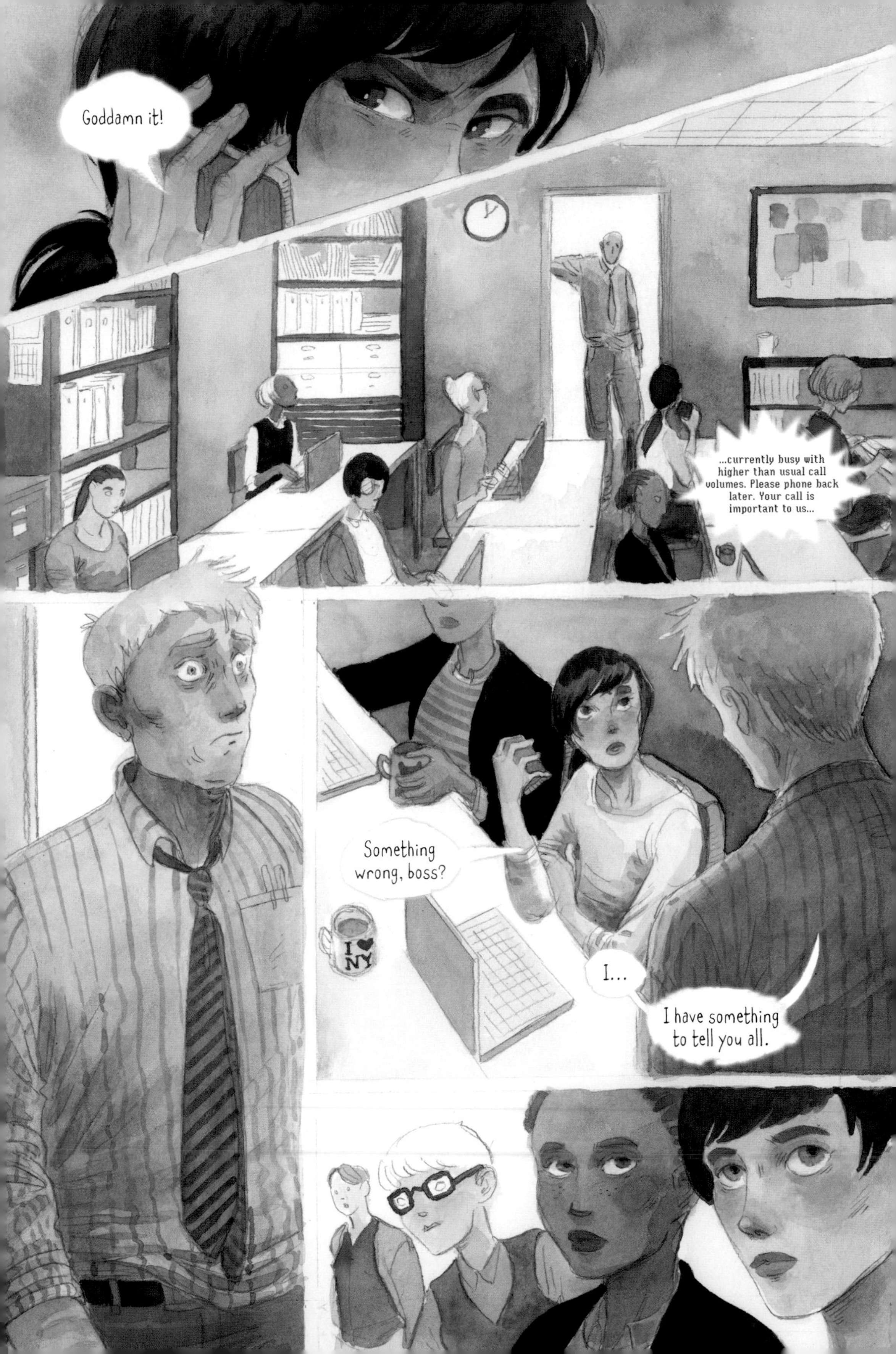
Goddamn it!
...currently busy with higher than usual call volumes. Please phone back later. Your call is important to us...
Something wrong, boss?
I ♥ NY
I...
I have something to tell you all.

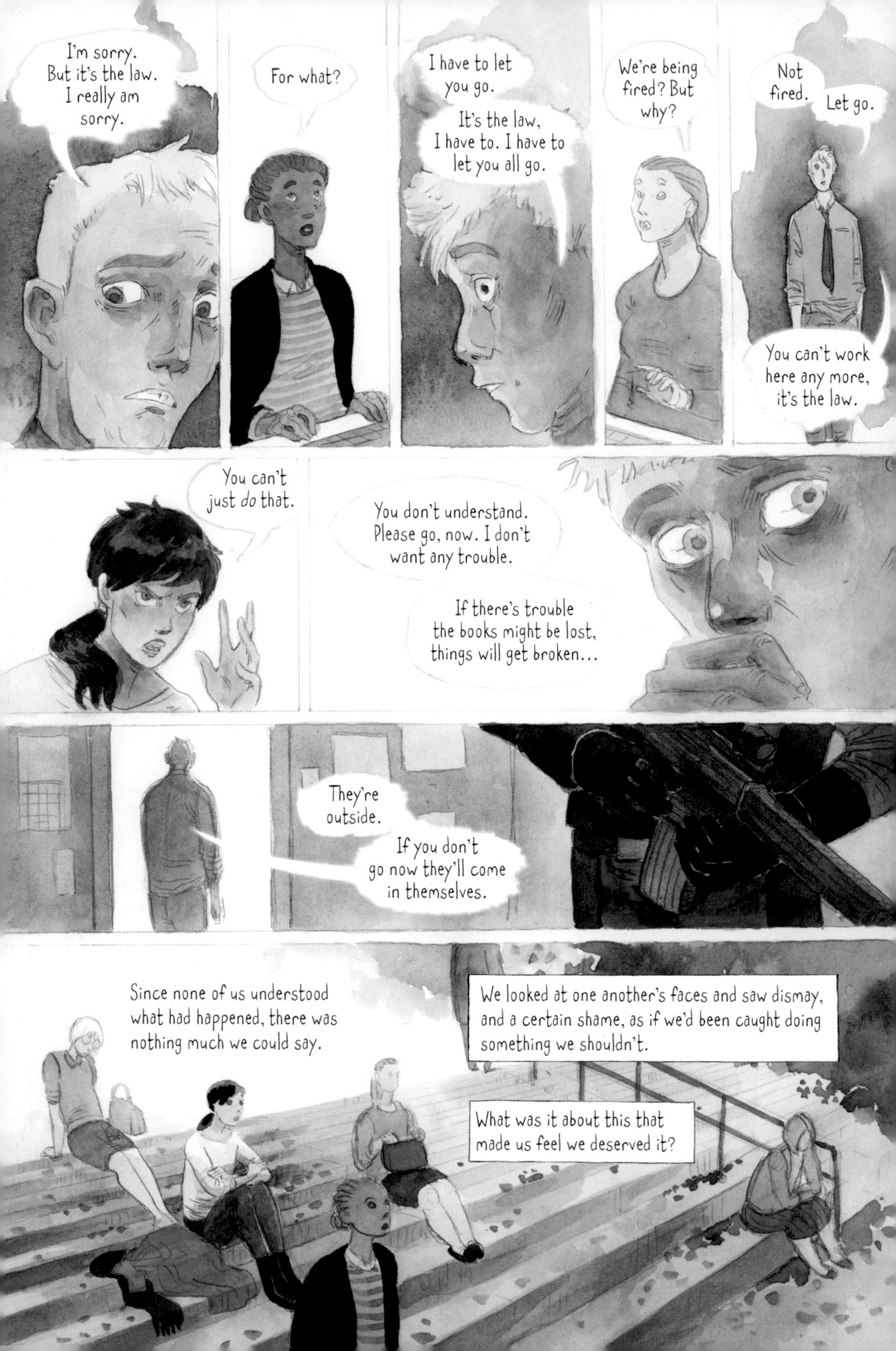
I'm sorry. But it's the law. I really am sorry.
For what?
I have to let you go.
It's the law, I have to. I have to let you all go.
We're being fired? But why?
Not fired.
Let go.
You can't work here any more, it's the law.
You can't just *do* that.
You don't understand. Please go, now. I don't want any trouble.
If there's trouble the books might be lost, things will get broken...
They're outside.
If you don't go now they'll come in themselves.
Since none of us understood what had happened, there was nothing much we could say.
We looked at one another's faces and saw dismay, and a certain shame, as if we'd been caught doing something we shouldn't.
What was it about this that made us feel we deserved it?

Tried getting anything on your Compucard today?

They've frozen them. Mine too. Any account with an F on it instead of an M. All they needed to do was push a few buttons. We're cut off.

But I've got over two thousand dollars in the bank!

Women can't hold property any more. It's a new law. Turned on the TV today?

Luke can use your Compucount for you. They'll transfer your number to him, or that's what they say.

Husband or male next of kin.

But what about you?

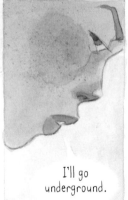

I'll go underground.

But...why?

Why did they?

They had to do it that way. The Compucounts and the jobs both at once. Can you picture the airports, otherwise?

They don't want us going anywhere, you can bet on that.

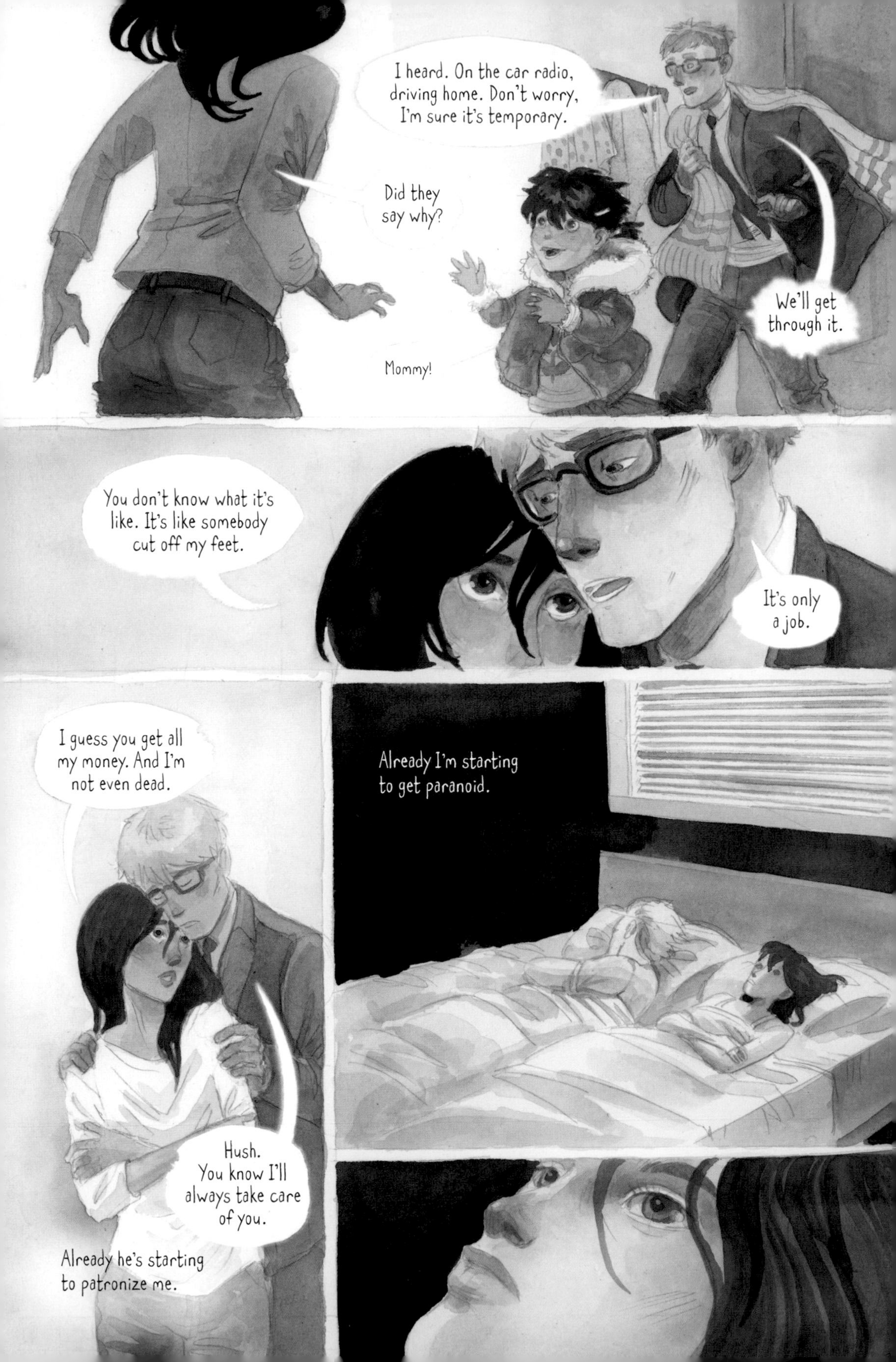

I heard. On the car radio, driving home. Don't worry, I'm sure it's temporary.
Did they say why?
Mommy!
We'll get through it.
You don't know what it's like. It's like somebody cut off my feet.
It's only a job.
I guess you get all my money. And I'm not even dead.
Hush. You know I'll always take care of you.
Already he's starting to patronize me.
Already I'm starting to get paranoid.

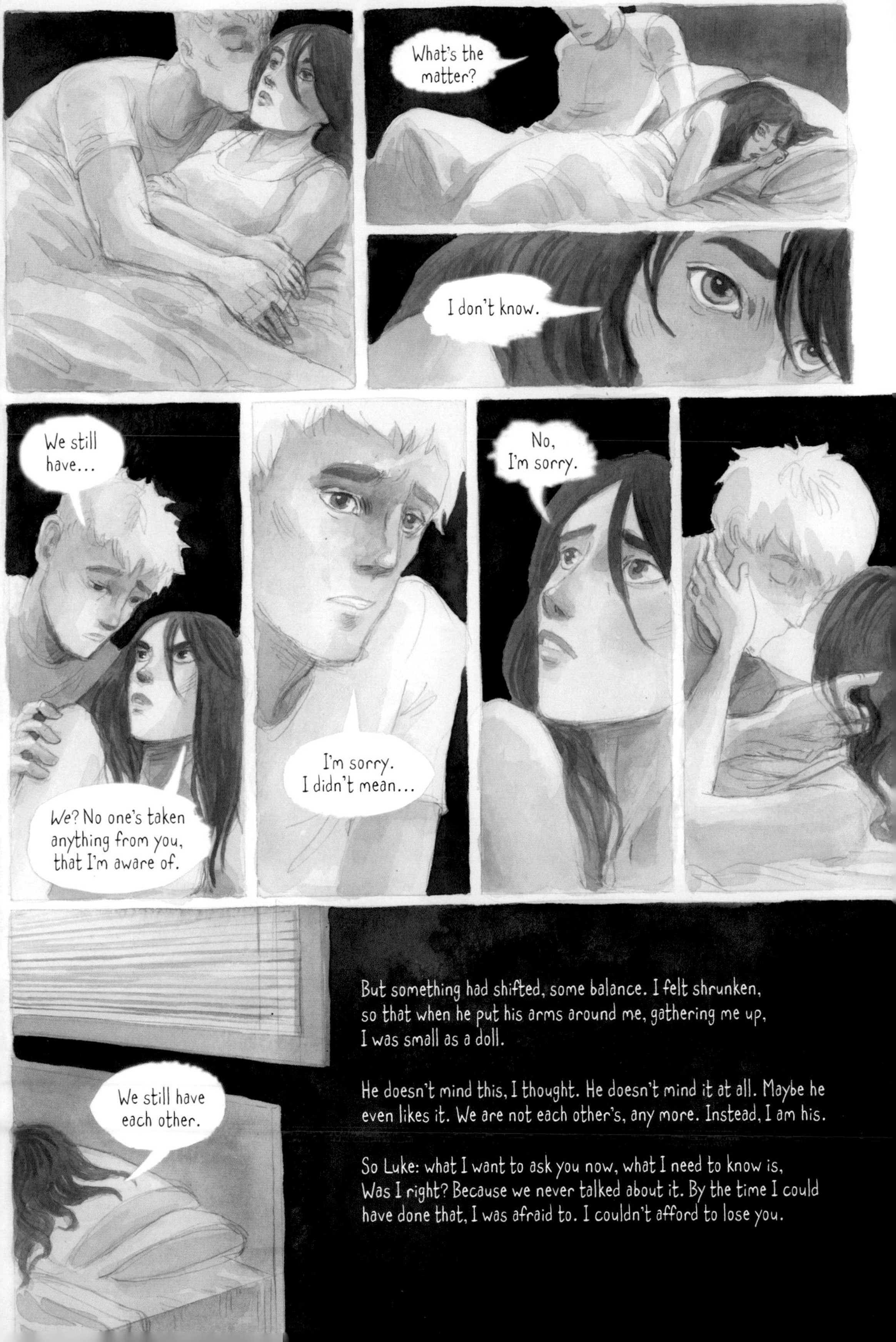
What's the matter?
I don't know.
We still have…
We? No one's taken anything from you, that I'm aware of.
I'm sorry. I didn't mean…
No, I'm sorry.
We still have each other.
But something had shifted, some balance. I felt shrunken, so that when he put his arms around me, gathering me up, I was small as a doll.
He doesn't mind this, I thought. He doesn't mind it at all. Maybe he even likes it. We are not each other's, any more. Instead, I am his.
So Luke: what I want to ask you now, what I need to know is, Was I right? Because we never talked about it. By the time I could have done that, I was afraid to. I couldn't afford to lose you.

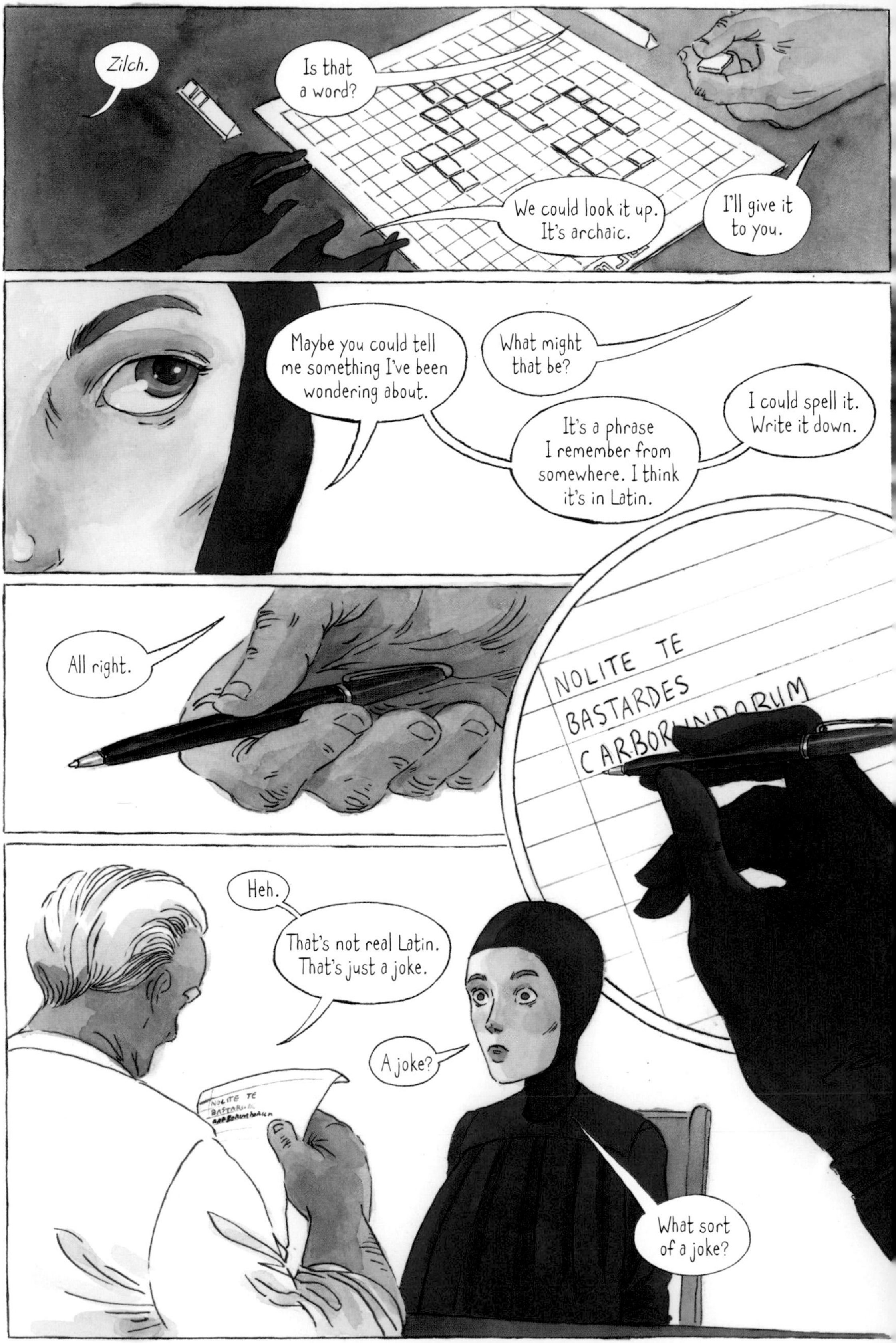
Zilch.
Is that a word?
We could look it up. It's archaic.
I'll give it to you.
Maybe you could tell me something I've been wondering about.
What might that be?
It's a phrase I remember from somewhere. I think it's in Latin.
I could spell it. Write it down.
All right.
NOLITE TE BASTARDES CARBORUNDORUM
Heh.
That's not real Latin. That's just a joke.
A joke?
What sort of a joke?

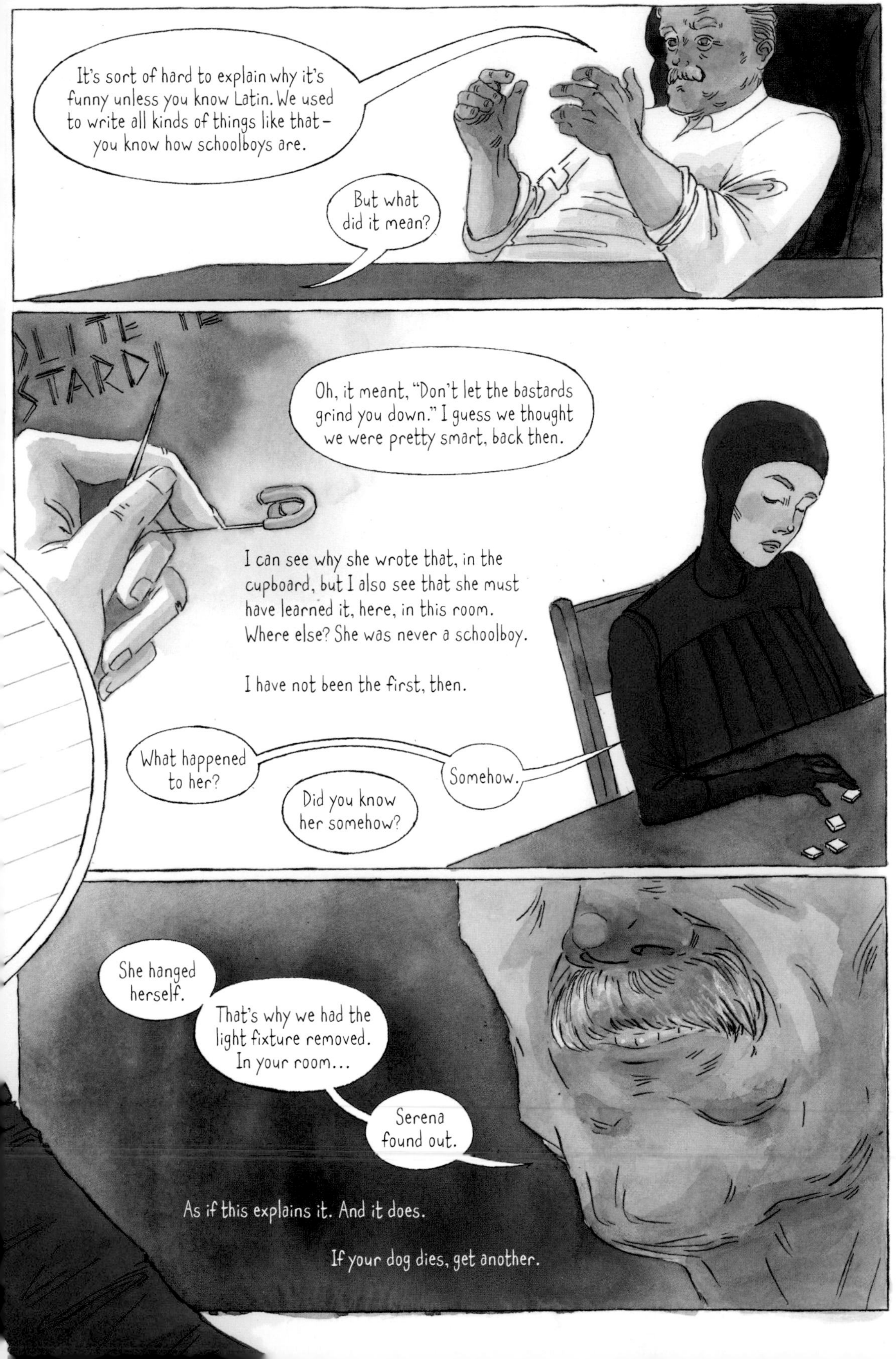
It's sort of hard to explain why it's funny unless you know Latin. We used to write all kinds of things like that – you know how schoolboys are.
But what did it mean?
Oh, it meant, "Don't let the bastards grind you down." I guess we thought we were pretty smart, back then.
I can see why she wrote that, in the cupboard, but I also see that she must have learned it, here, in this room. Where else? She was never a schoolboy.
I have not been the first, then.
What happened to her?
Did you know her somehow?
Somehow.
She hanged herself.
That's why we had the light fixture removed. In your room...
Serena found out.
As if this explains it. And it does.
If your dog dies, get another.

XI

NIGHT

That's where she was swinging,

just lightly, like a pendulum;

the way you could swing as a child,

hanging by your hands from a branch.

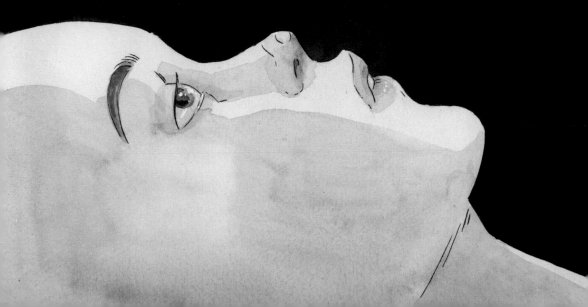

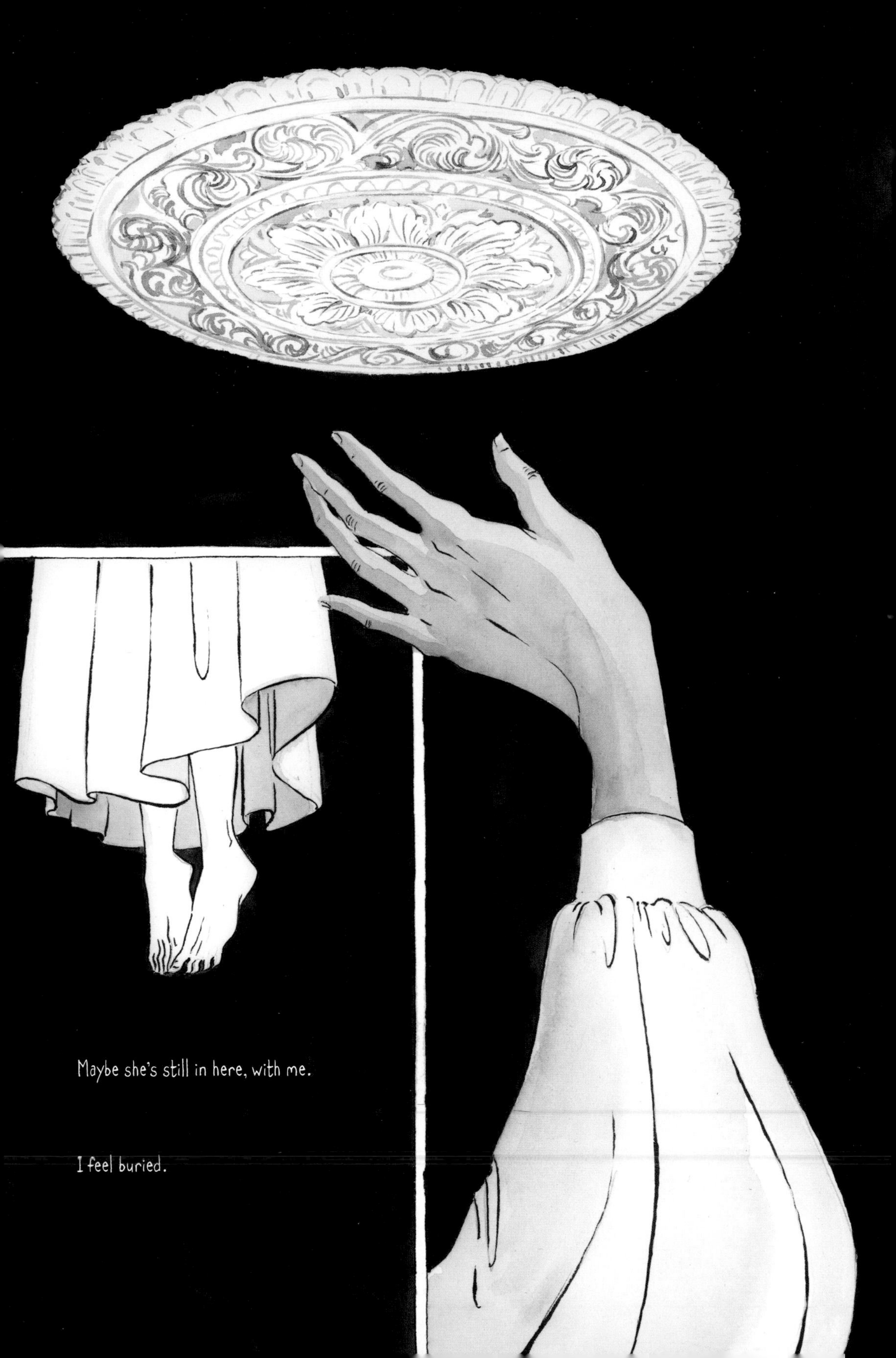
Maybe she's still in here, with me.
I feel buried.

XII

JEZEBEL'S

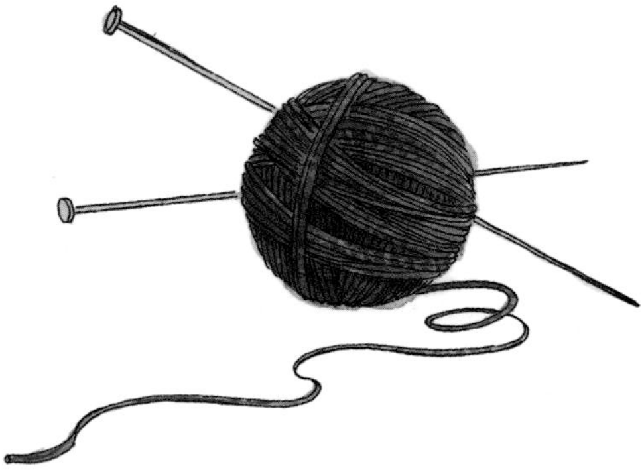

Every night when I go to bed I think, In the morning I will wake up in my own house and things will be back the way they were.

It hasn't happened this morning, either.

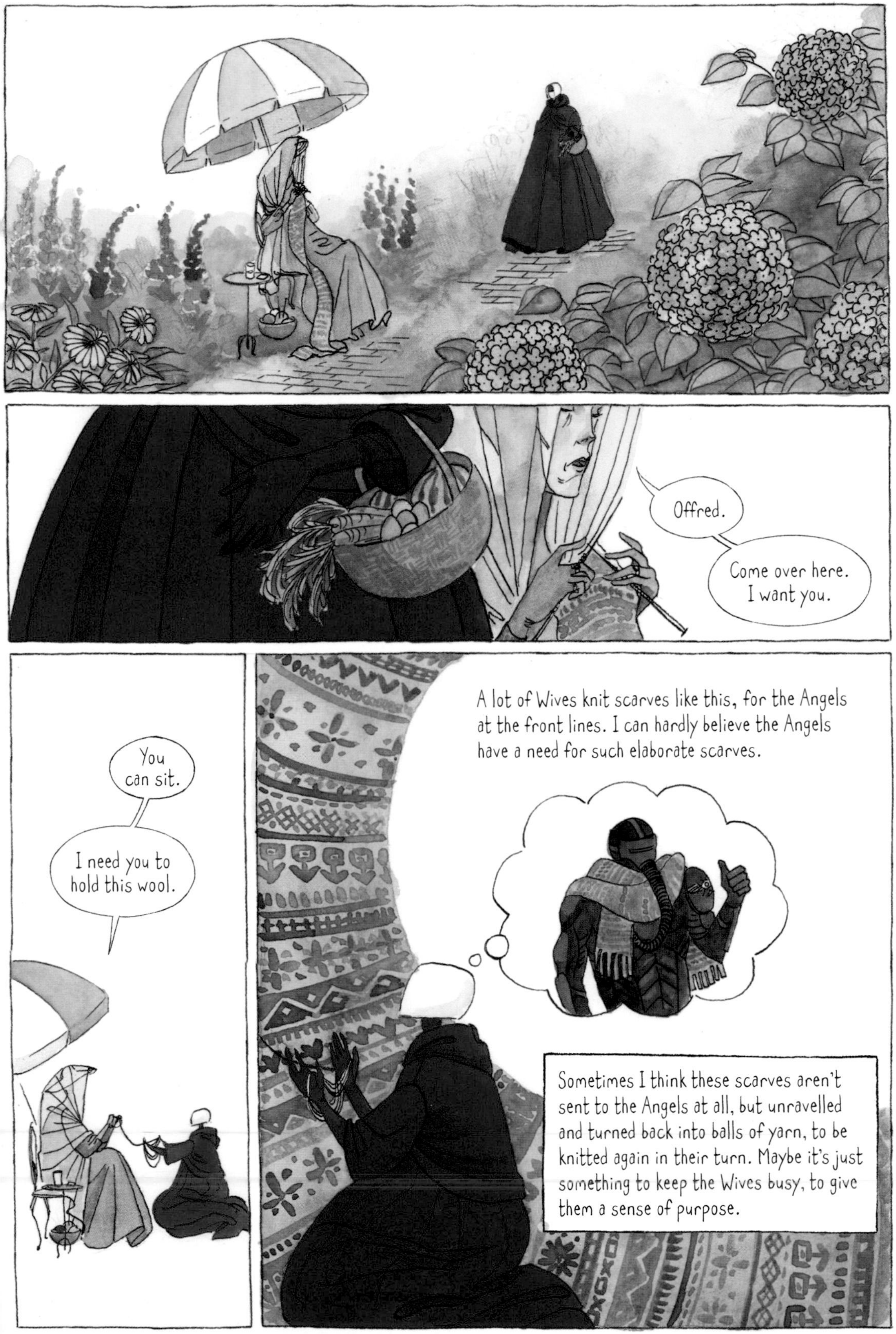
Offred.
Come over here. I want you.
You can sit.
I need you to hold this wool.
A lot of Wives knit scarves like this, for the Angels at the front lines. I can hardly believe the Angels have a need for such elaborate scarves.
Sometimes I think these scarves aren't sent to the Angels at all, but unravelled and turned back into balls of yarn, to be knitted again in their turn. Maybe it's just something to keep the Wives busy, to give them a sense of purpose.

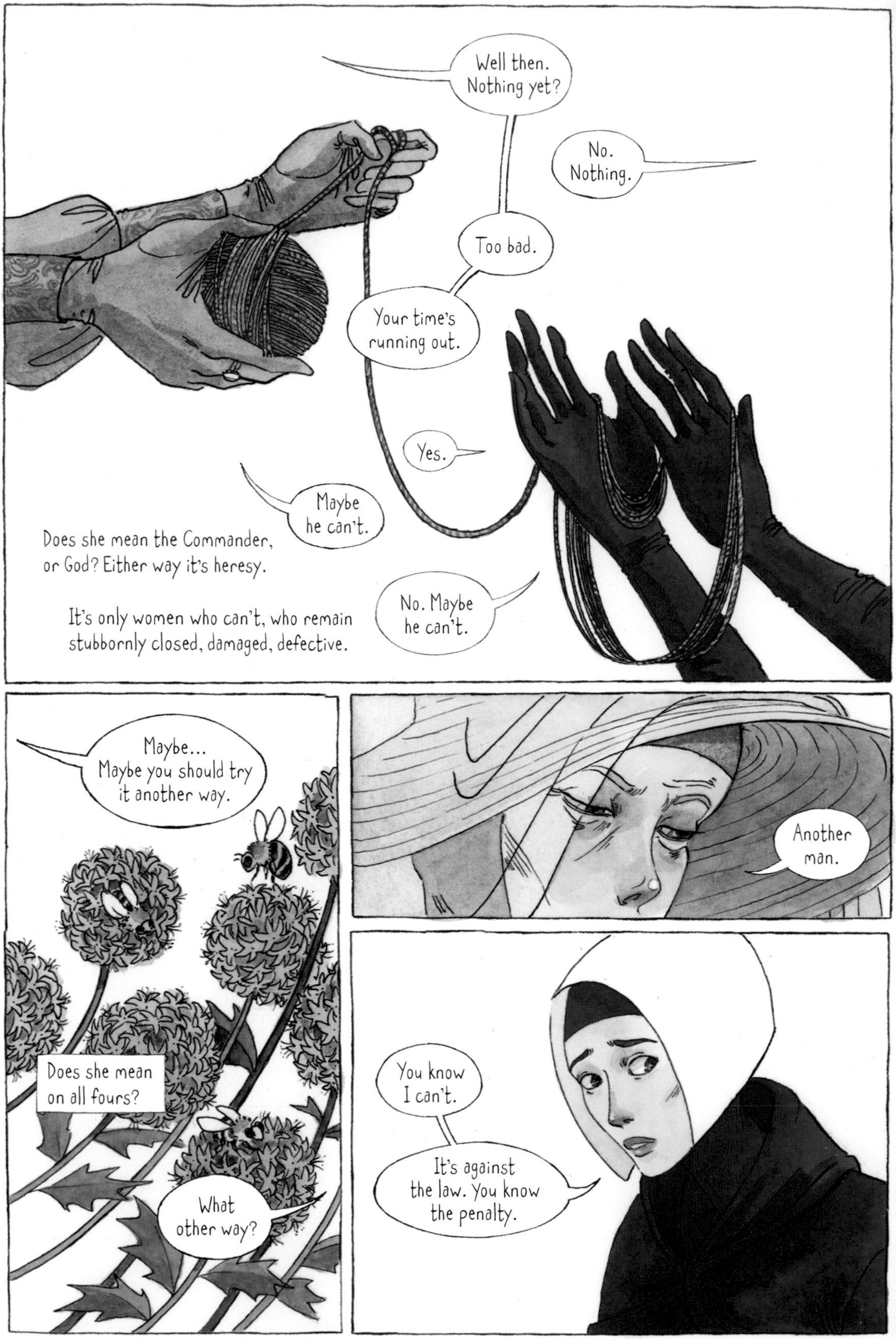
Well then. Nothing yet?
No. Nothing.
Too bad.
Your time's running out.
Yes.
Maybe he can't.
Does she mean the Commander, or God? Either way it's heresy.
No. Maybe he can't.
It's only women who can't, who remain stubbornly closed, damaged, defective.
Maybe... Maybe you should try it another way.
Another man.
Does she mean on all fours?
What other way?
You know I can't.
It's against the law. You know the penalty.

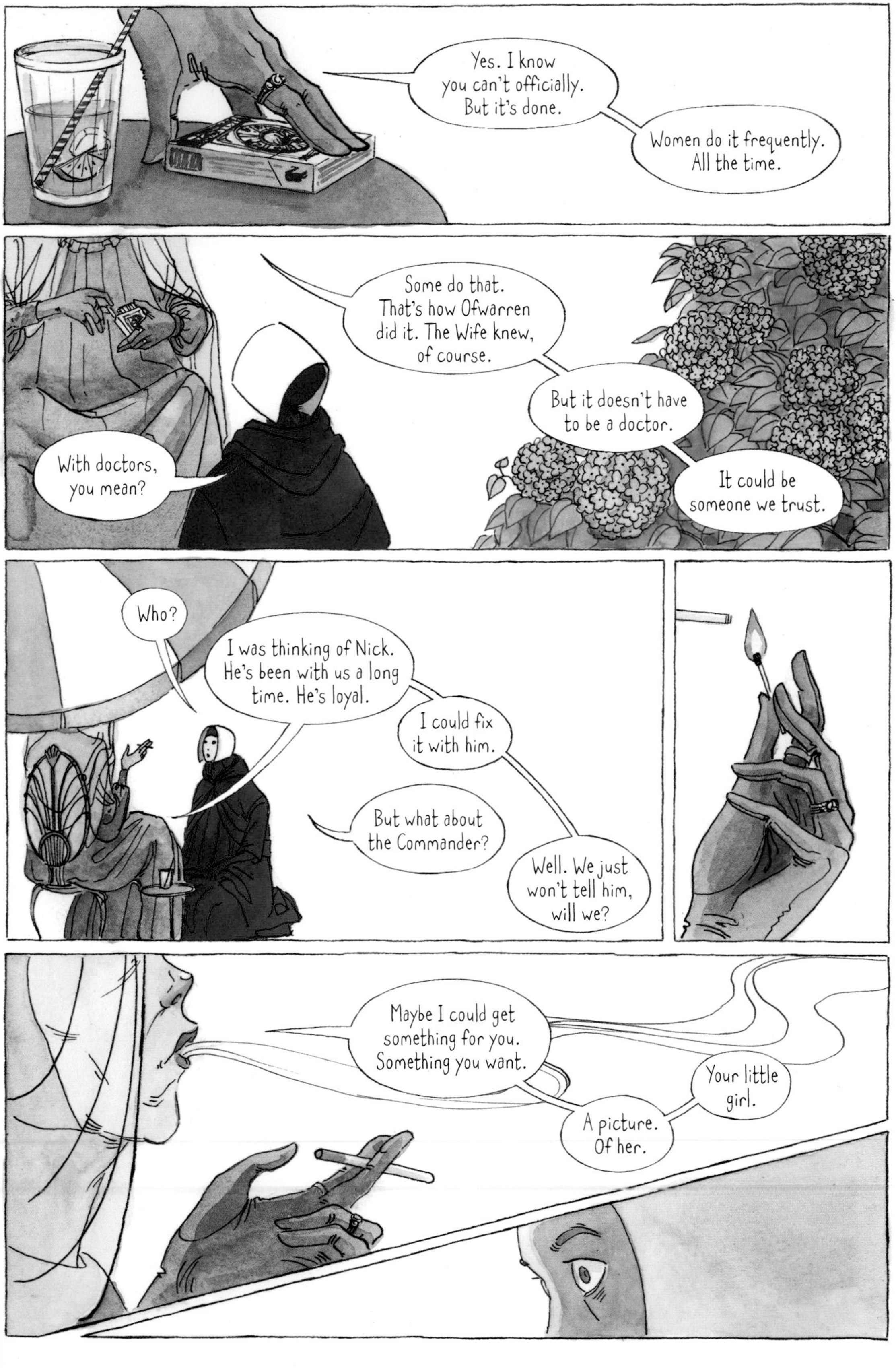
Yes. I know you can't officially. But it's done.
Women do it frequently. All the time.
Some do that. That's how Ofwarren did it. The Wife knew, of course.
But it doesn't have to be a doctor.
With doctors, you mean?
It could be someone we trust.
Who?
I was thinking of Nick. He's been with us a long time. He's loyal.
I could fix it with him.
But what about the Commander?
Well. We just won't tell him, will we?
Maybe I could get something for you. Something you want.
A picture. Of her.
Your little girl.

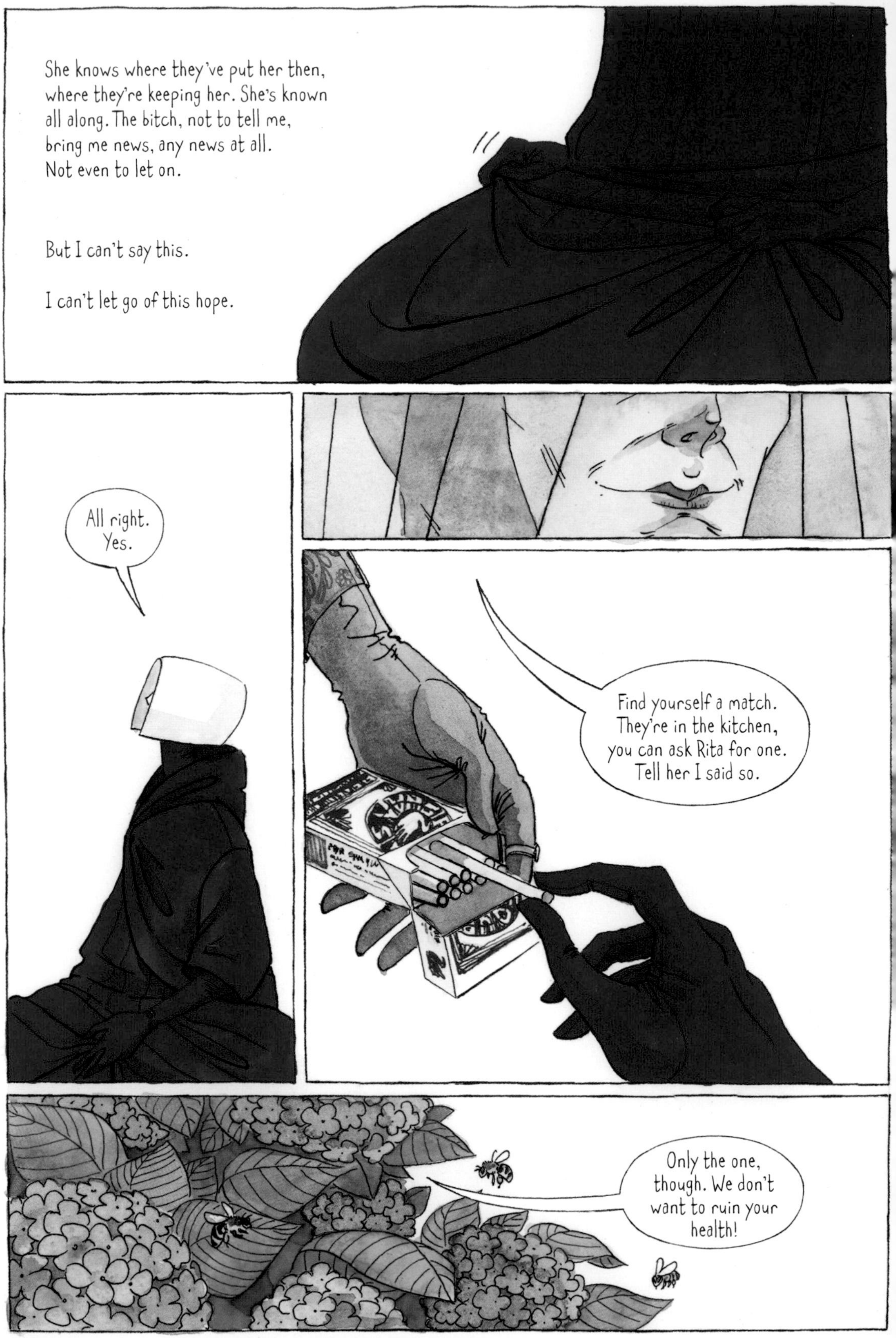
She knows where they've put her then, where they're keeping her. She's known all along. The bitch, not to tell me, bring me news, any news at all. Not even to let on.
But I can't say this.
I can't let go of this hope.
All right. Yes.
Find yourself a match. They're in the kitchen, you can ask Rita for one. Tell her I said so.
Only the one, though. We don't want to ruin your health!

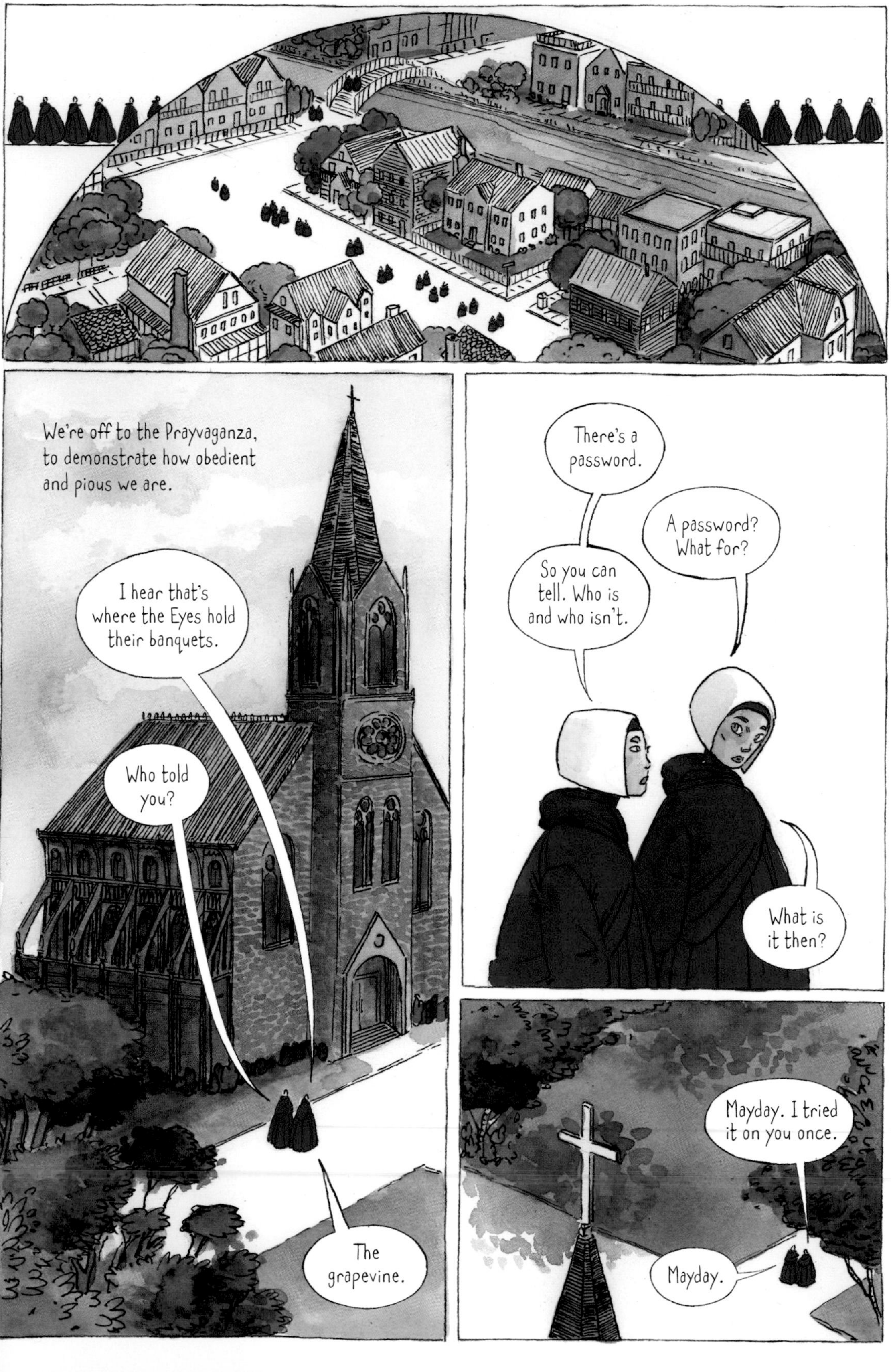
We're off to the Prayvaganza, to demonstrate how obedient and pious we are.
I hear that's where the Eyes hold their banquets.
Who told you?
The grapevine.
There's a password.
A password? What for?
So you can tell. Who is and who isn't.
What is it then?
Mayday. I tried it on you once.
Mayday.

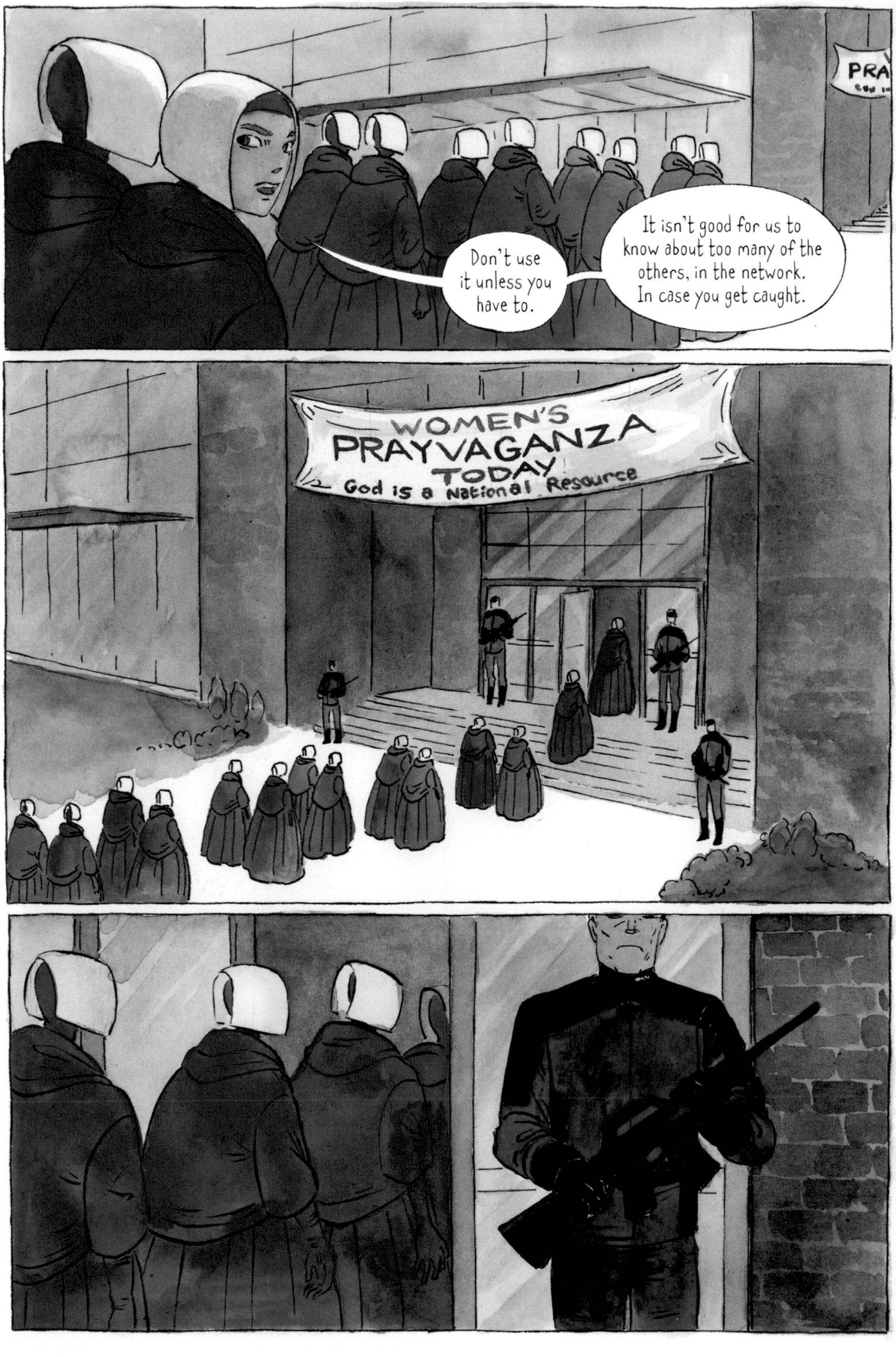

Don't use it unless you have to.
It isn't good for us to know about too many of the others, in the network. In case you get caught.
WOMEN'S PRAYVAGANZA TODAY
God is a National Resource

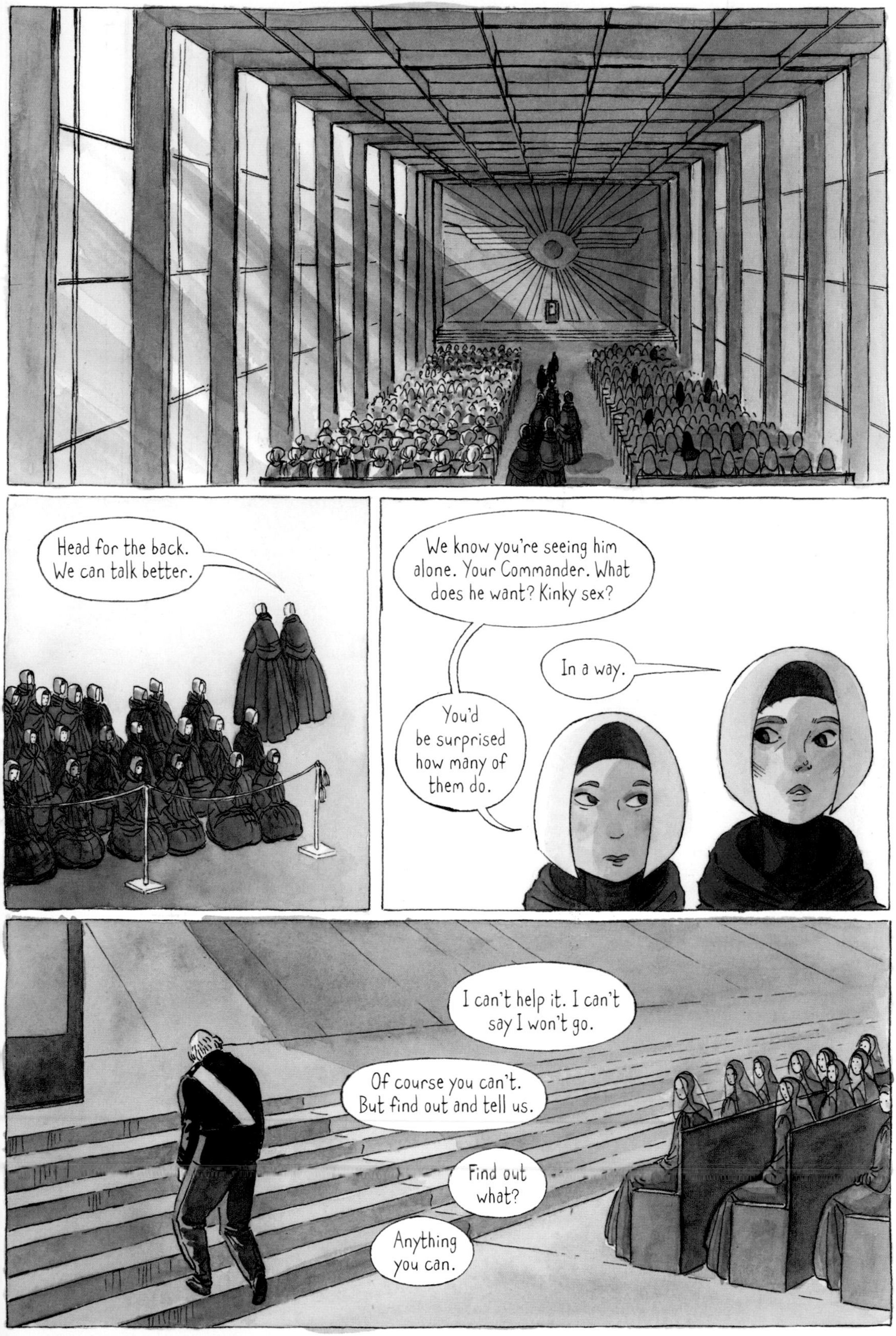
Head for the back. We can talk better.
We know you're seeing him alone. Your Commander. What does he want? Kinky sex?
In a way.
You'd be surprised how many of them do.
I can't help it. I can't say I won't go.
Of course you can't. But find out and tell us.
Find out what?
Anything you can.

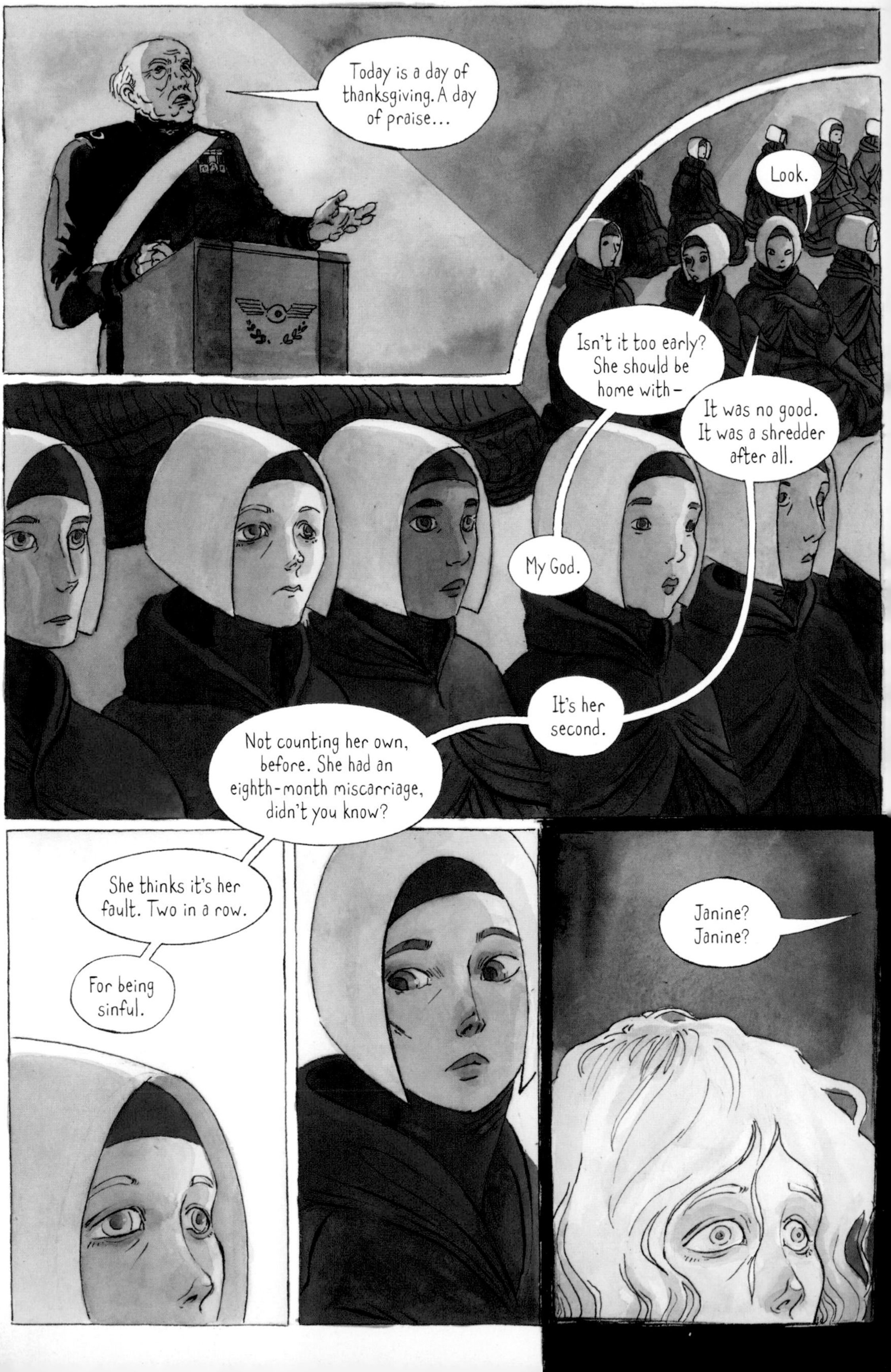
Today is a day of thanksgiving. A day of praise...
Look.
Isn't it too early? She should be home with—
It was no good. It was a shredder after all.
My God.
It's her second.
Not counting her own, before. She had an eighth-month miscarriage, didn't you know?
She thinks it's her fault. Two in a row.
For being sinful.
Janine? Janine?

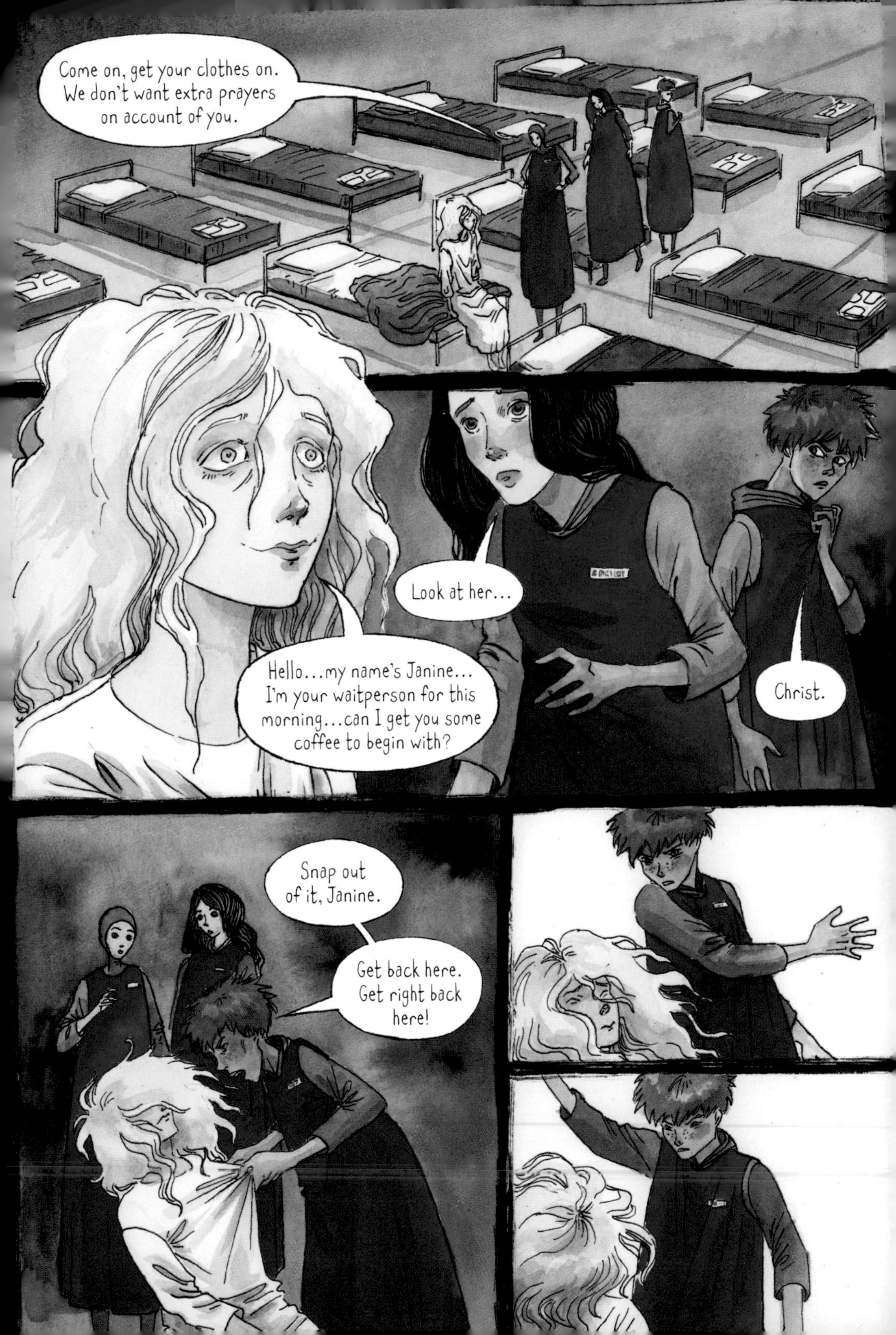
Come on, get your clothes on. We don't want extra prayers on account of you.
Look at her...
Hello...my name's Janine... I'm your waitperson for this morning...can I get you some coffee to begin with?
Christ.
Snap out of it, Janine.
Get back here. Get right back here!

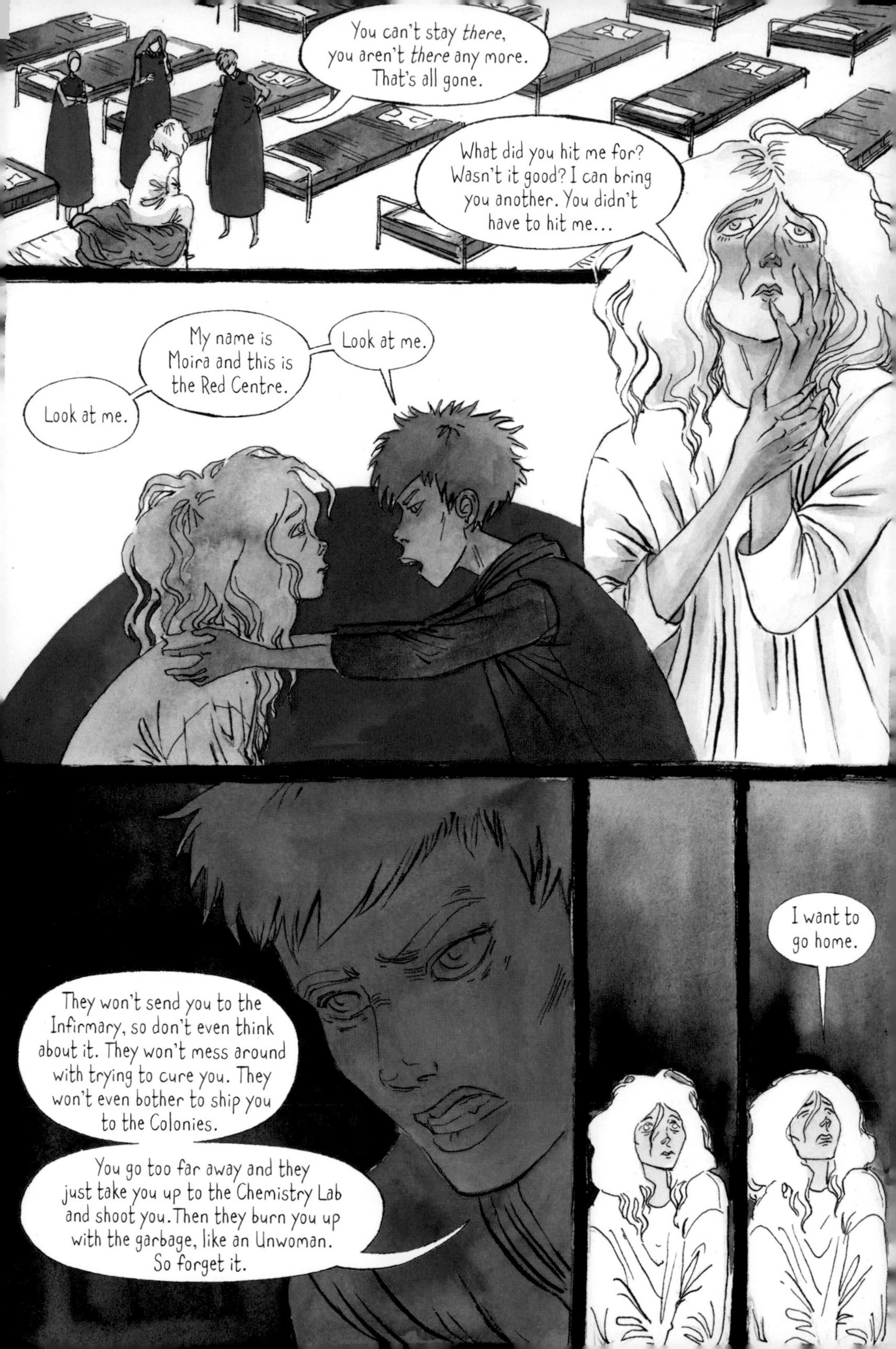
You can't stay *there*, you aren't *there* any more. That's all gone.
What did you hit me for? Wasn't it good? I can bring you another. You didn't have to hit me...
Look at me.
My name is Moira and this is the Red Centre.
Look at me.
They won't send you to the Infirmary, so don't even think about it. They won't mess around with trying to cure you. They won't even bother to ship you to the Colonies.
You go too far away and they just take you up to the Chemistry Lab and shoot you. Then they burn you up with the garbage, like an Unwoman. So forget it.
I want to go home.

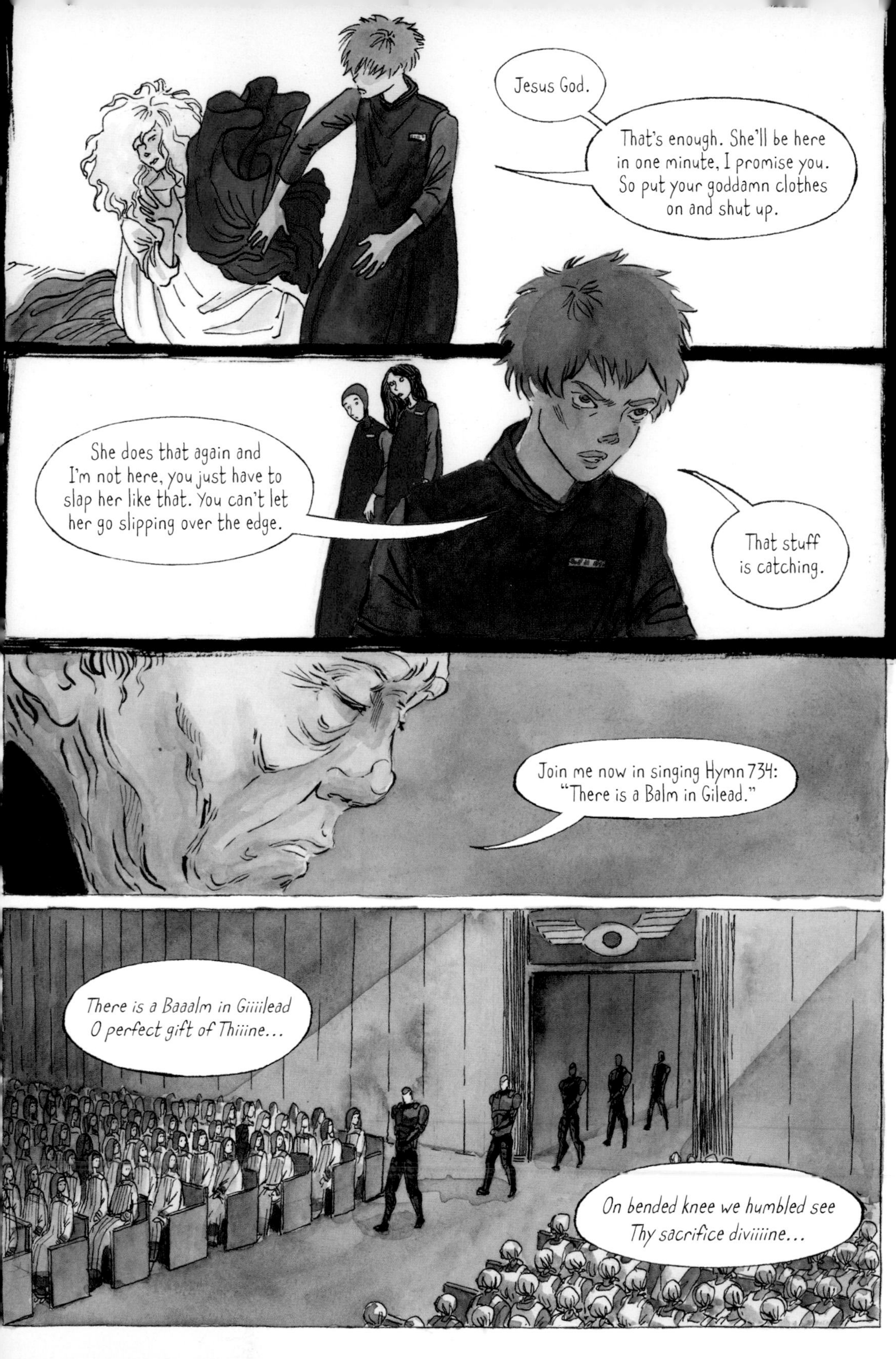
Jesus God.
That's enough. She'll be here in one minute, I promise you. So put your goddamn clothes on and shut up.
She does that again and I'm not here, you just have to slap her like that. You can't let her go slipping over the edge.
That stuff is catching.
Join me now in singing Hymn 734: "There is a Balm in Gilead."
There is a Baaalm in Giiiilead O perfect gift of Thiiine...
On bended knee we humbled see Thy sacrifice diviiiine...

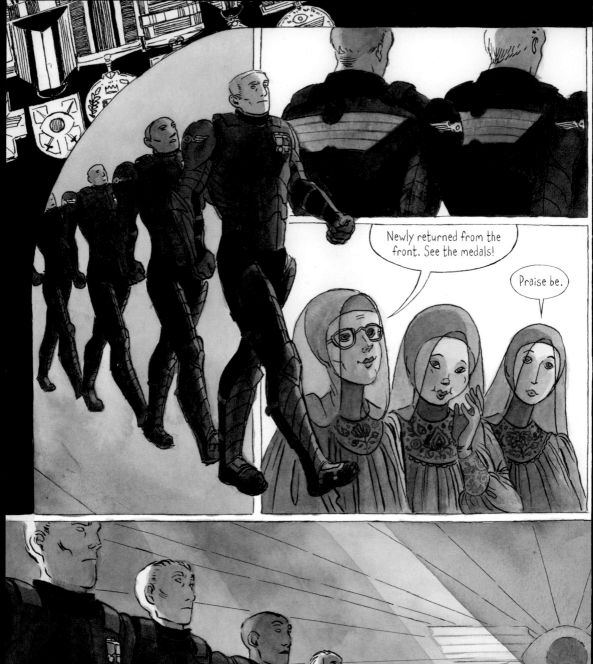

Newly returned from the front. See the medals!

Praise be.

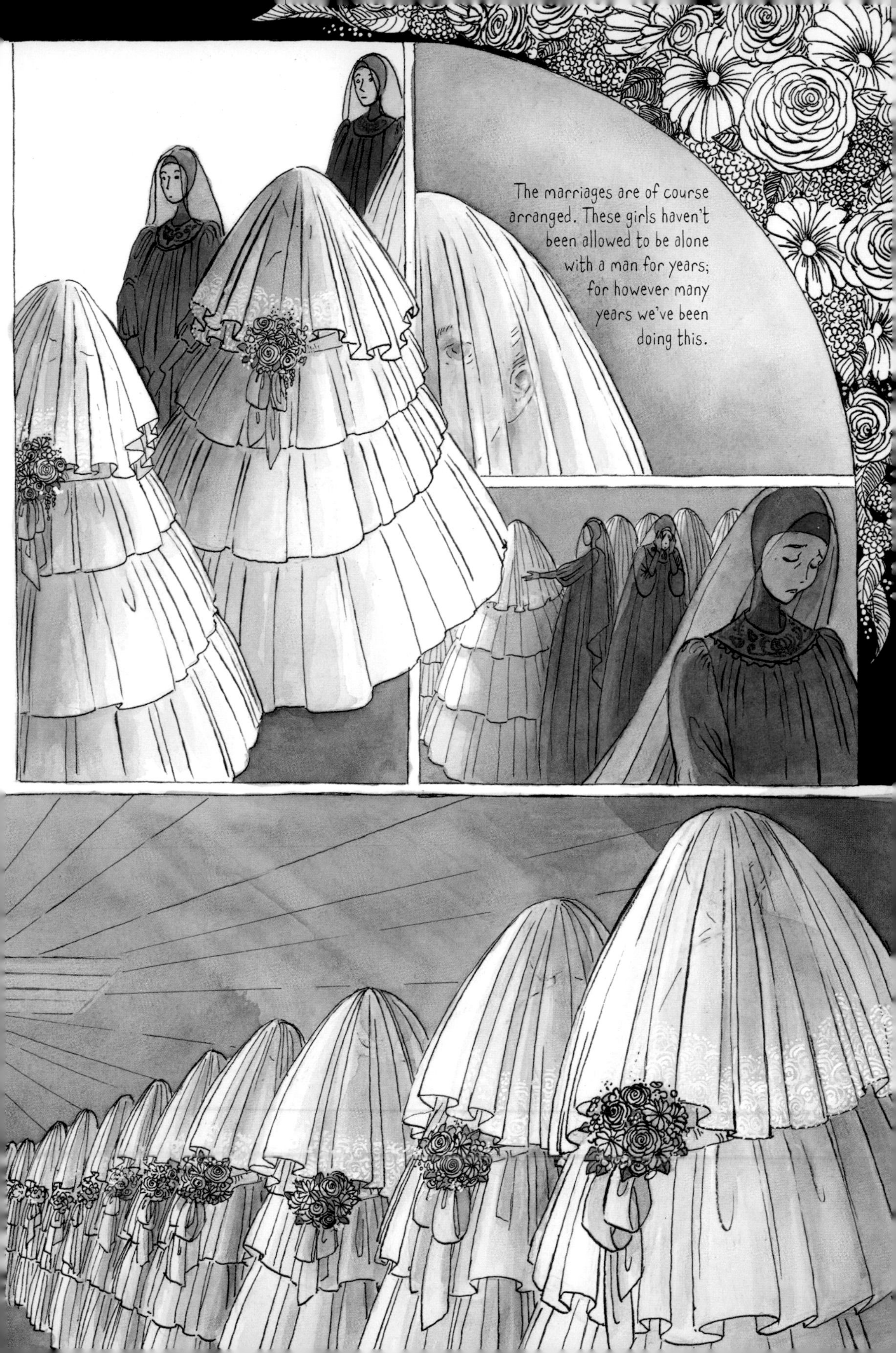
The marriages are of course arranged. These girls haven't been allowed to be alone with a man for years; for however many years we've been doing this.

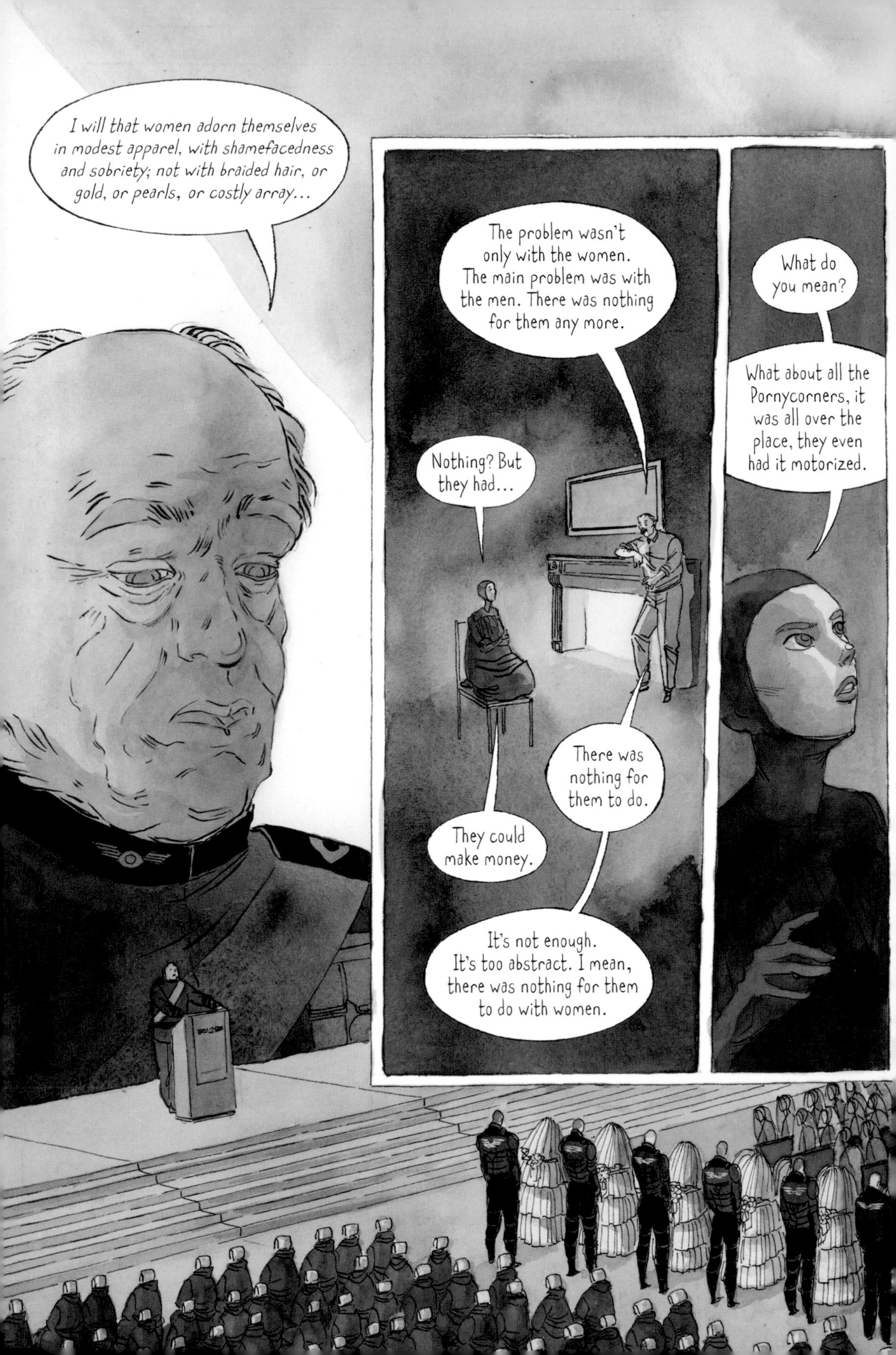
I will that women adorn themselves in modest apparel, with shamefacedness and sobriety; not with braided hair, or gold, or pearls, or costly array...
The problem wasn't only with the women. The main problem was with the men. There was nothing for them any more.
Nothing? But they had...
There was nothing for them to do.
They could make money.
It's not enough. It's too abstract. I mean, there was nothing for them to do with women.
What do you mean?
What about all the Pornycorners, it was all over the place, they even had it motorized.

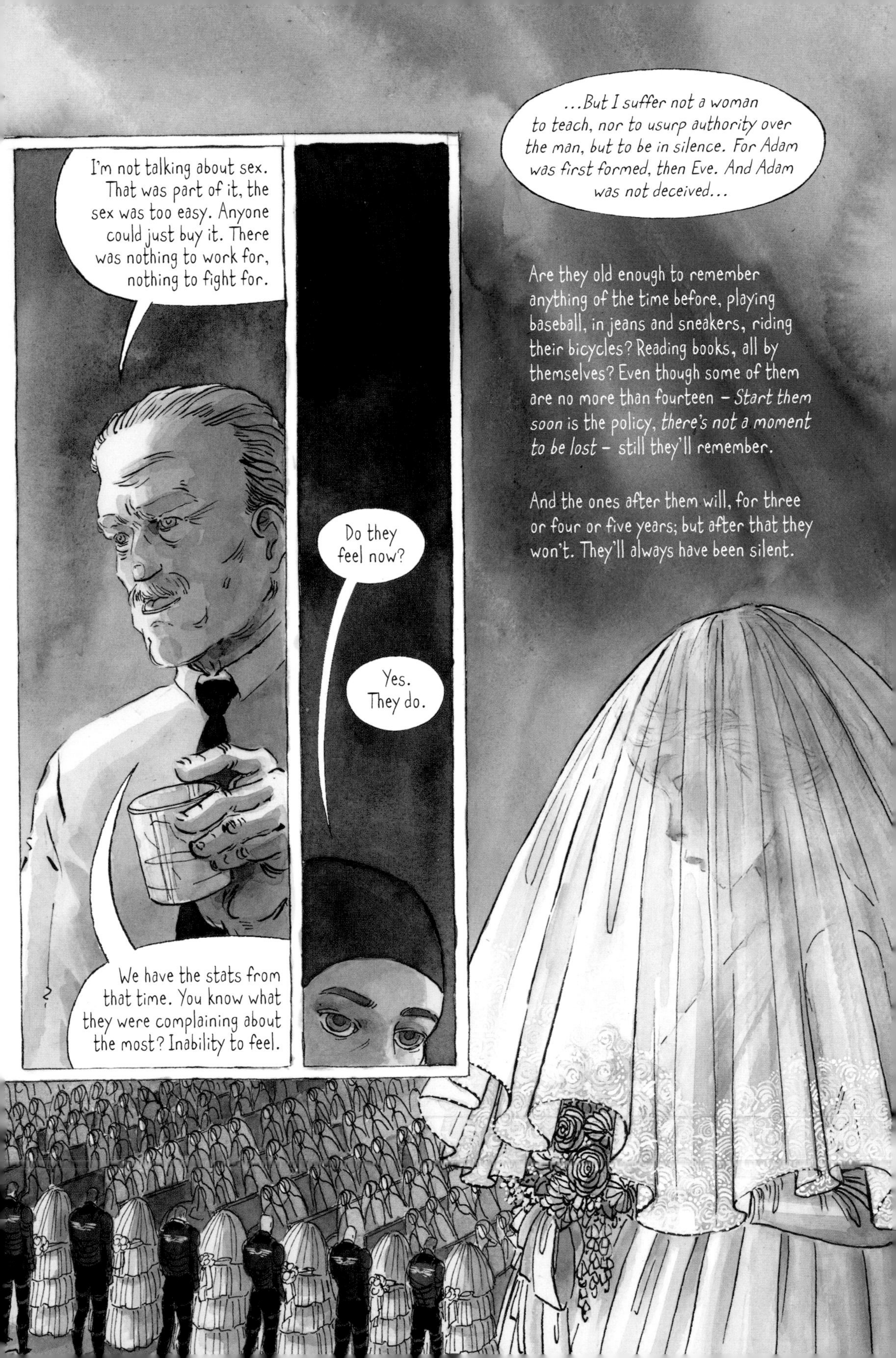
...But I suffer not a woman to teach, nor to usurp authority over the man, but to be in silence. For Adam was first formed, then Eve. And Adam was not deceived...
I'm not talking about sex. That was part of it, the sex was too easy. Anyone could just buy it. There was nothing to work for, nothing to fight for.
We have the stats from that time. You know what they were complaining about the most? Inability to feel.
Do they feel now?
Yes. They do.
Are they old enough to remember anything of the time before, playing baseball, in jeans and sneakers, riding their bicycles? Reading books, all by themselves? Even though some of them are no more than fourteen – *Start them soon* is the policy, *there's not a moment to be lost* – still they'll remember.
And the ones after them will, for three or four or five years; but after that they won't. They'll always have been silent.

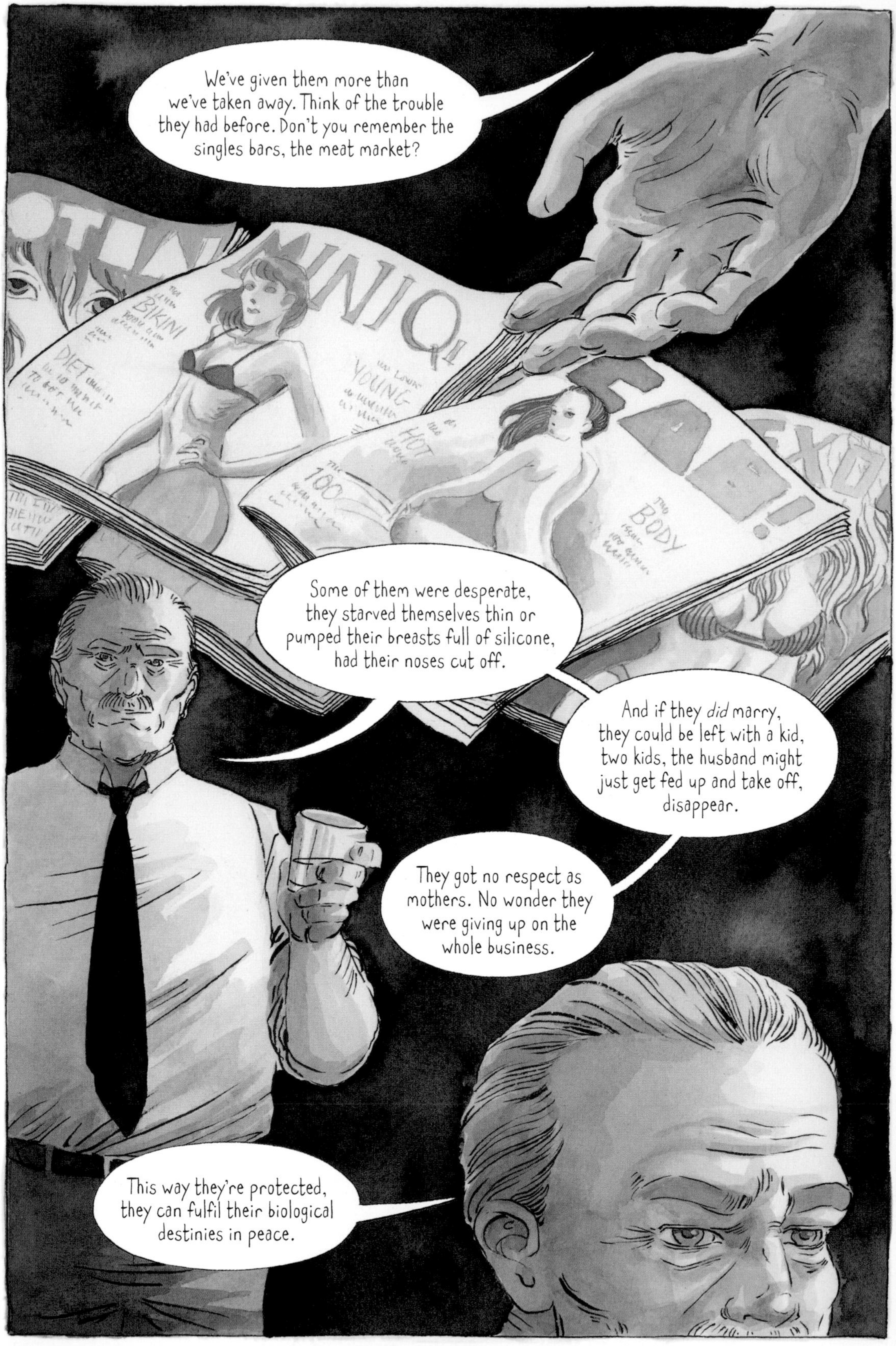
We've given them more than we've taken away. Think of the trouble they had before. Don't you remember the singles bars, the meat market?
Some of them were desperate, they starved themselves thin or pumped their breasts full of silicone, had their noses cut off.
And if they *did* marry, they could be left with a kid, two kids, the husband might just get fed up and take off, disappear.
They got no respect as mothers. No wonder they were giving up on the whole business.
This way they're protected, they can fulfil their biological destinies in peace.

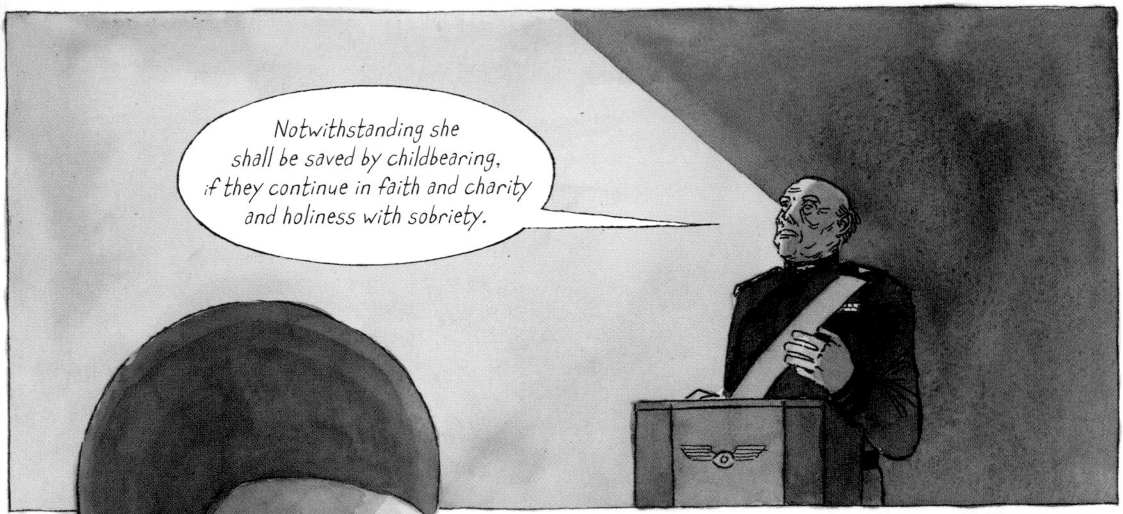
Notwithstanding she shall be saved by childbearing, if they continue in faith and charity and holiness with sobriety.

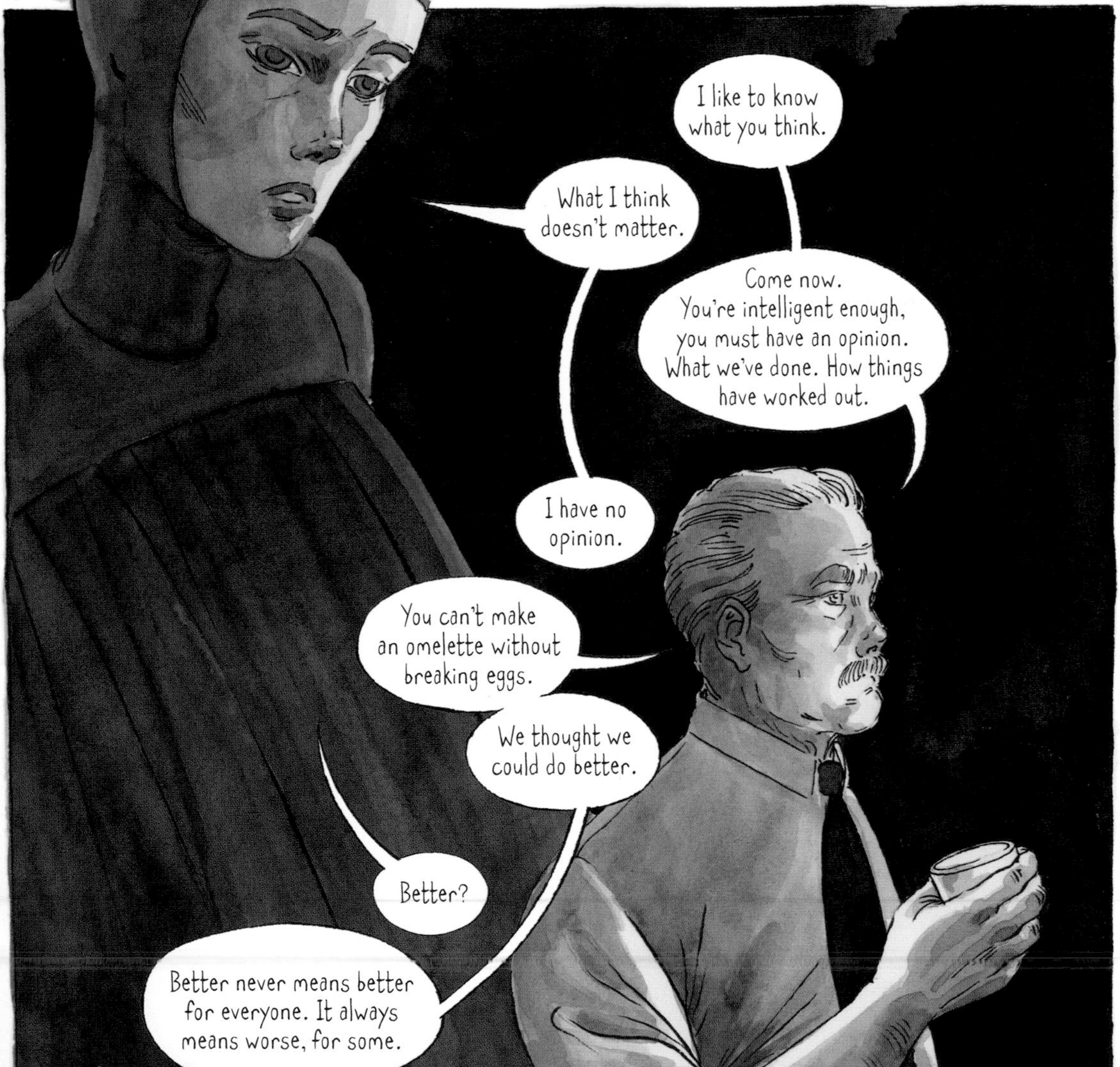
I like to know what you think.
What I think doesn't matter.
Come now. You're intelligent enough, you must have an opinion. What we've done. How things have worked out.
I have no opinion.
You can't make an omelette without breaking eggs.
We thought we could do better.
Better?
Better never means better for everyone. It always means worse, for some.

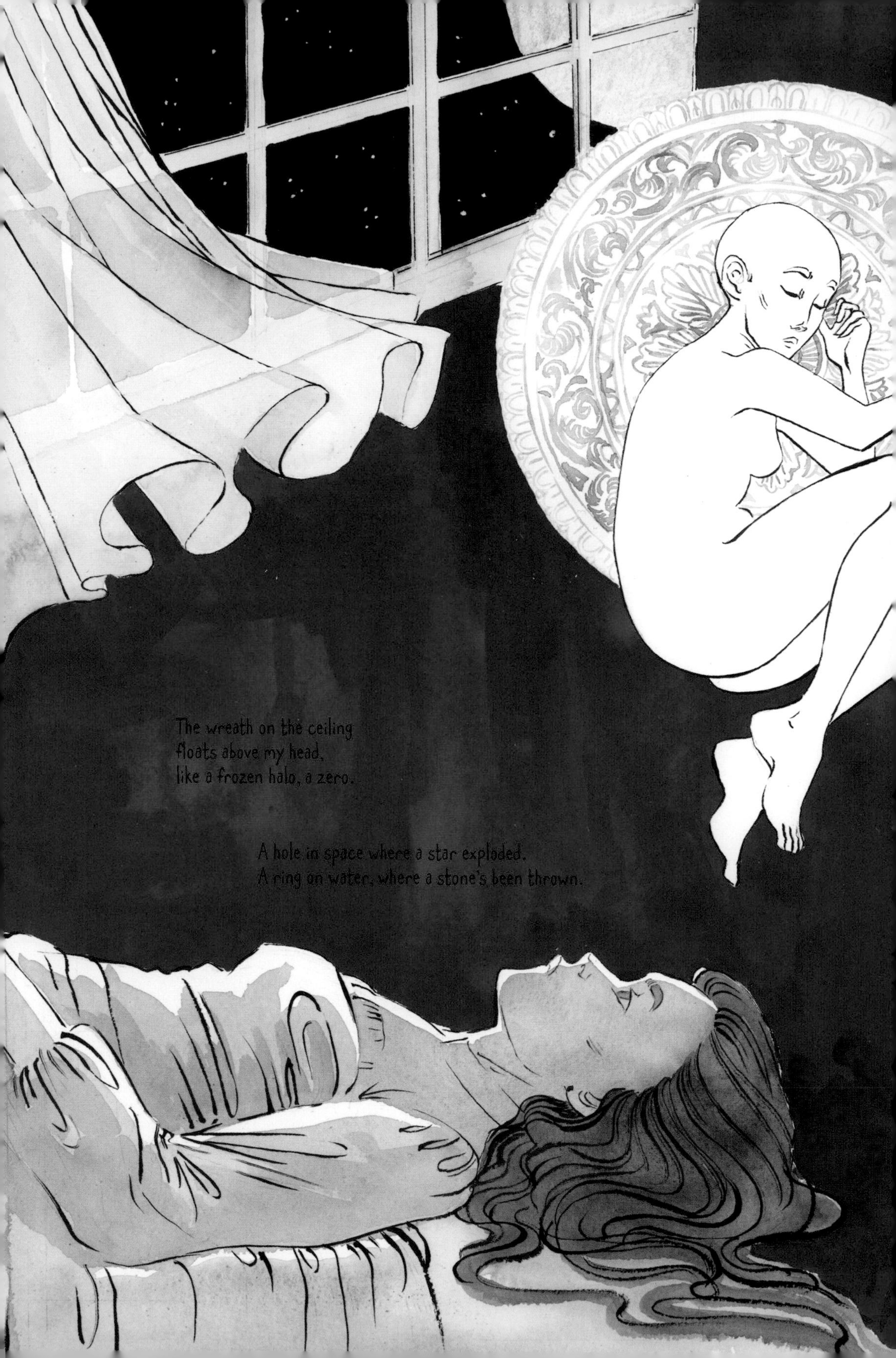

The wreath on the ceiling
floats above my head,
like a frozen halo, a zero.
A hole in space where a star exploded.
A ring on water, where a stone's been thrown.

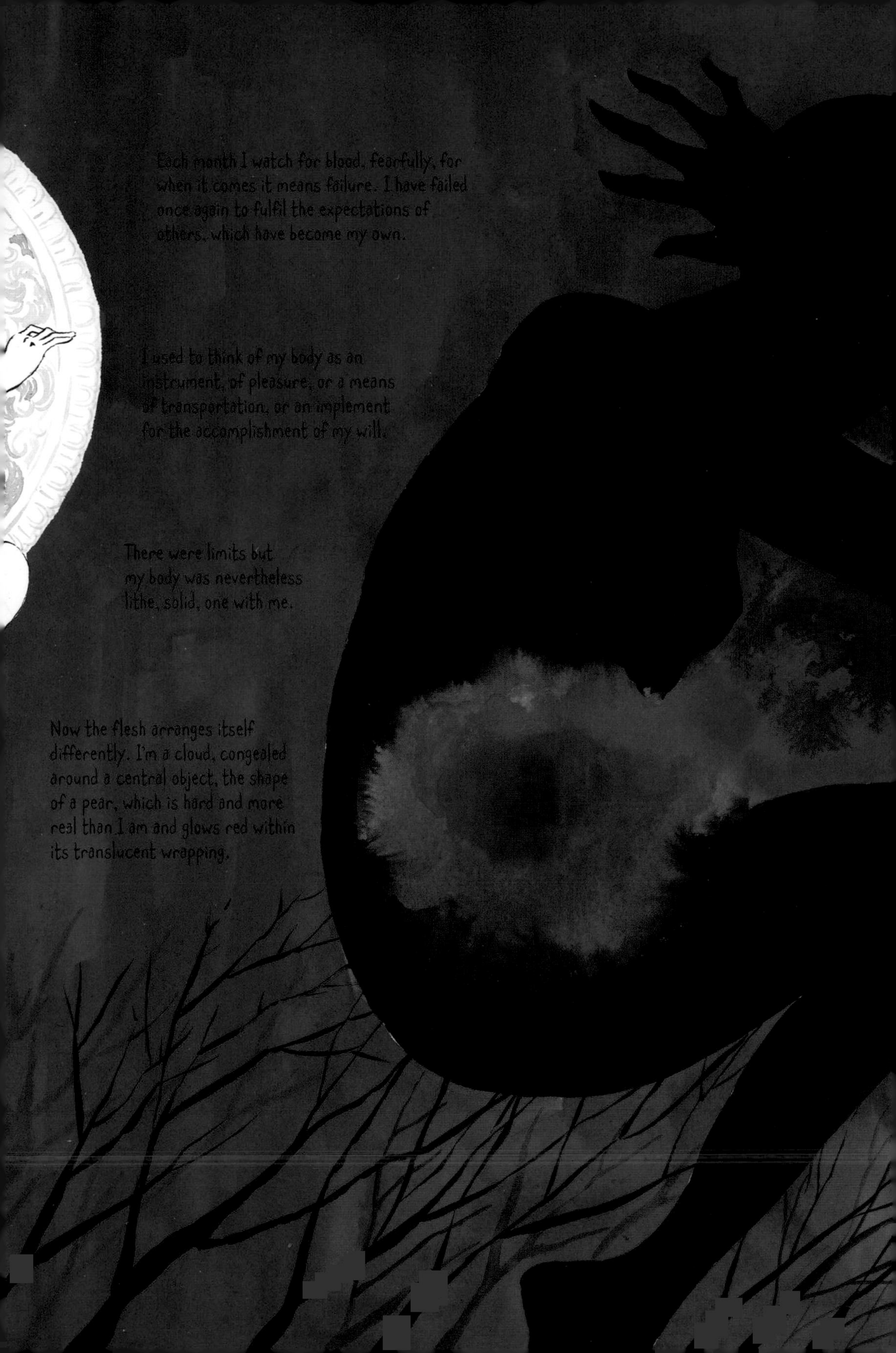

Each month I watch for blood, fearfully, for when it comes it means failure. I have failed once again to fulfil the expectations of others, which have become my own.
I used to think of my body as an instrument, of pleasure, or a means of transportation, or an implement for the accomplishment of my will.
There were limits but my body was nevertheless lithe, solid, one with me.
Now the flesh arranges itself differently. I'm a cloud, congealed around a central object, the shape of a pear, which is hard and more real than I am and glows red within its translucent wrapping.

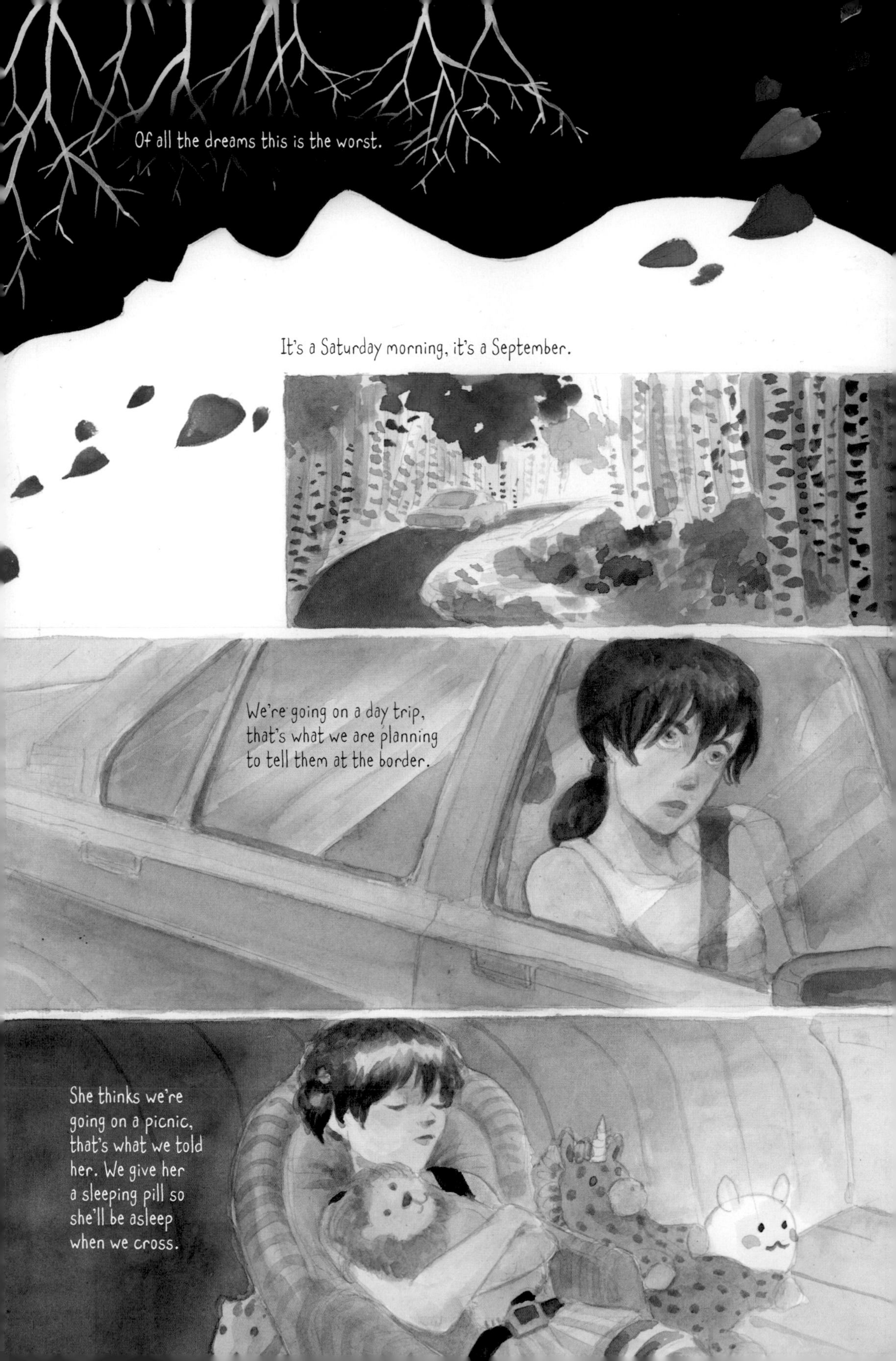
Of all the dreams this is the worst.
It's a Saturday morning, it's a September.
We're going on a day trip, that's what we are planning to tell them at the border.
She thinks we're going on a picnic, that's what we told her. We give her a sleeping pill so she'll be asleep when we cross.

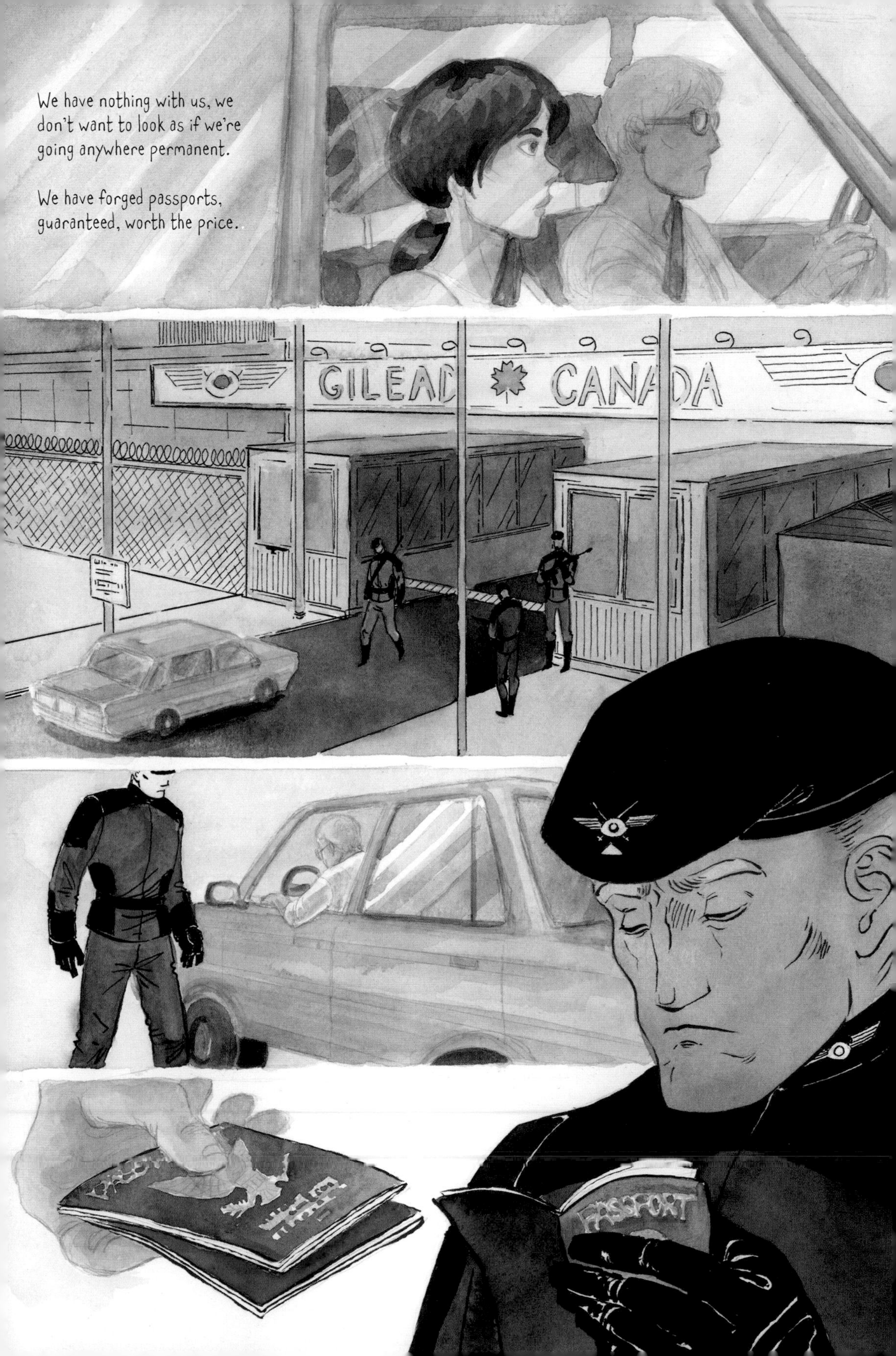
We have nothing with us, we don't want to look as if we're going anywhere permanent.
We have forged passports, guaranteed, worth the price.
GILEAD
CANADA
PASSPORT

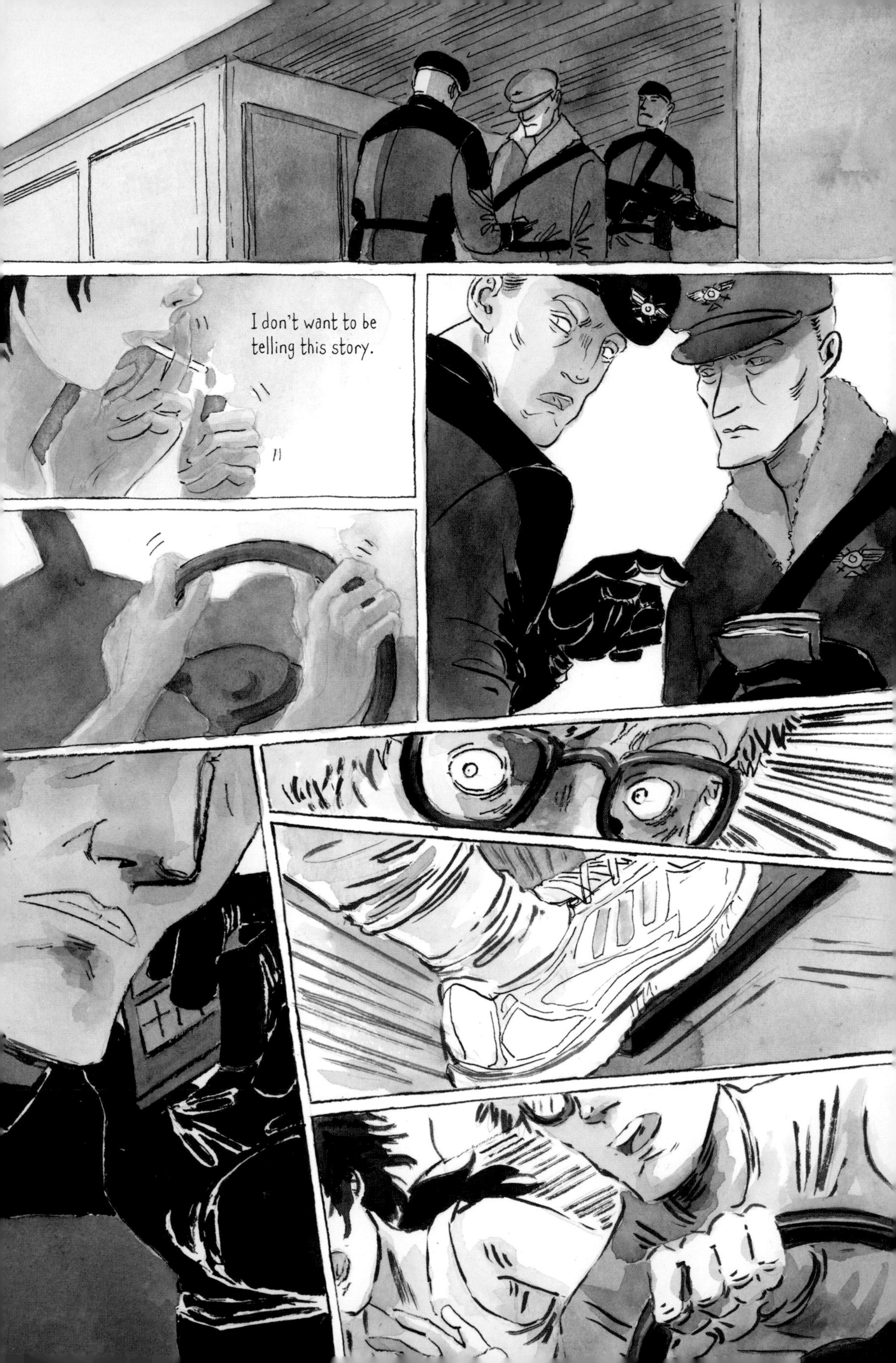
I don't want to be telling this story.

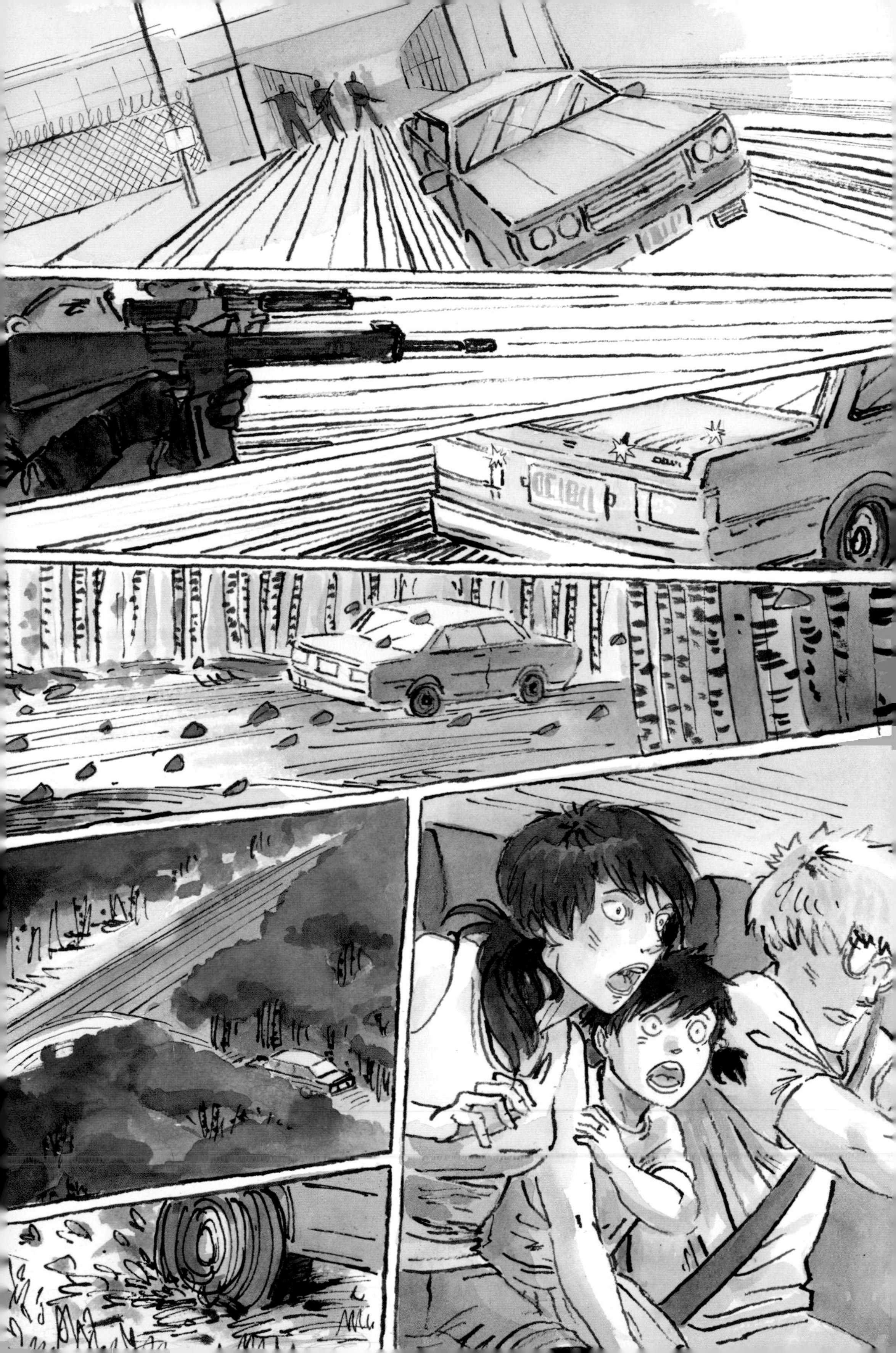

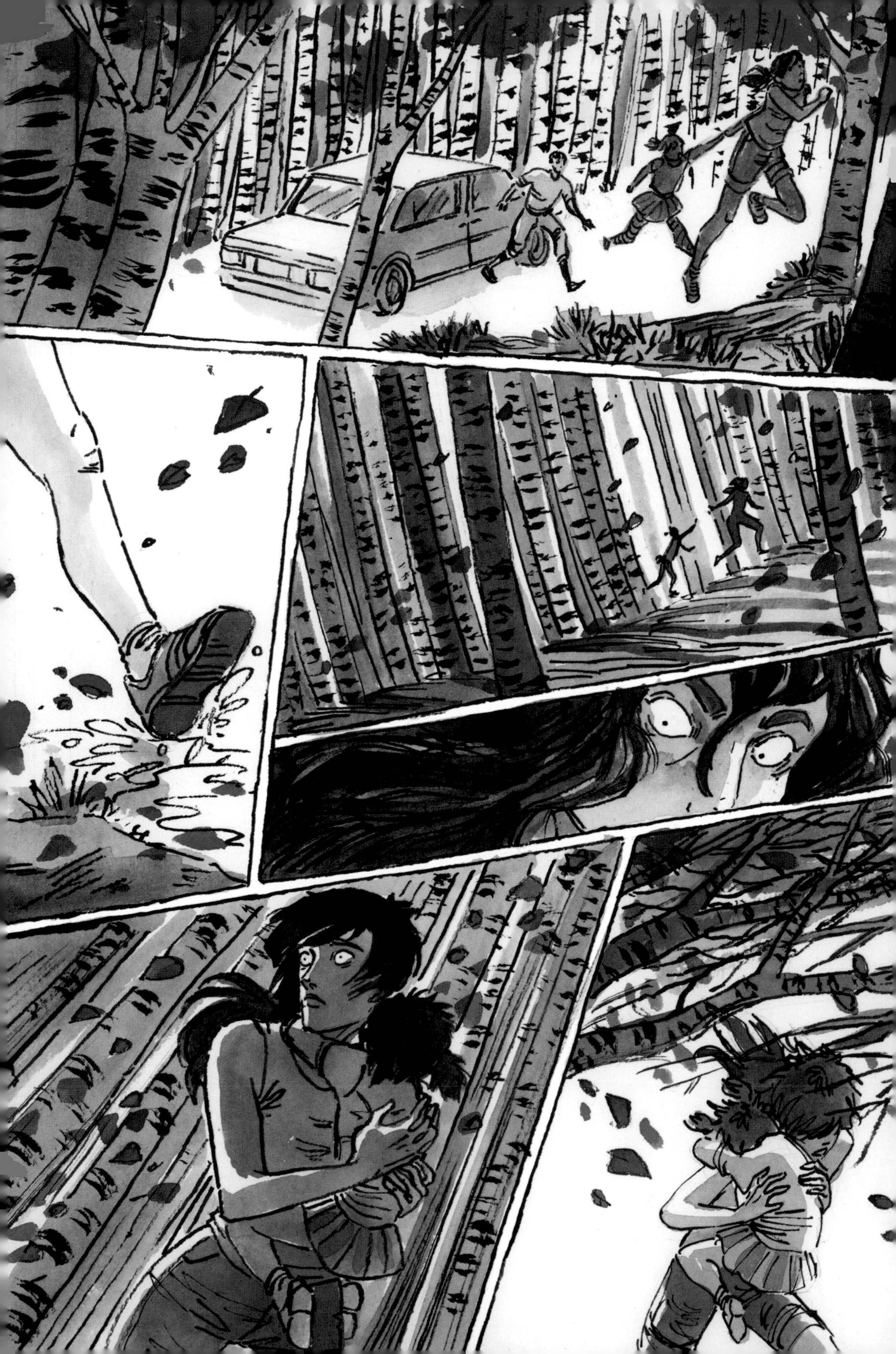

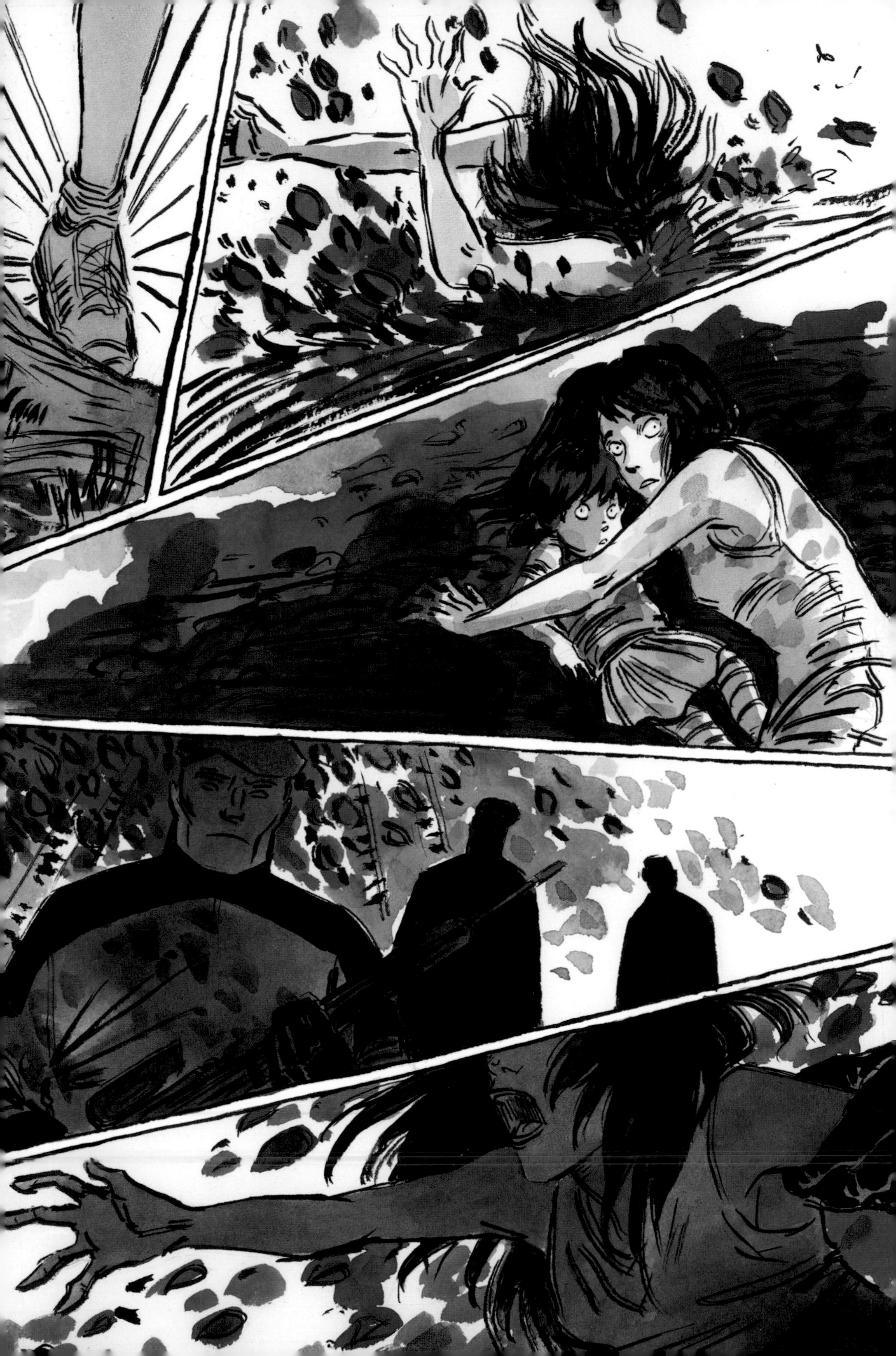

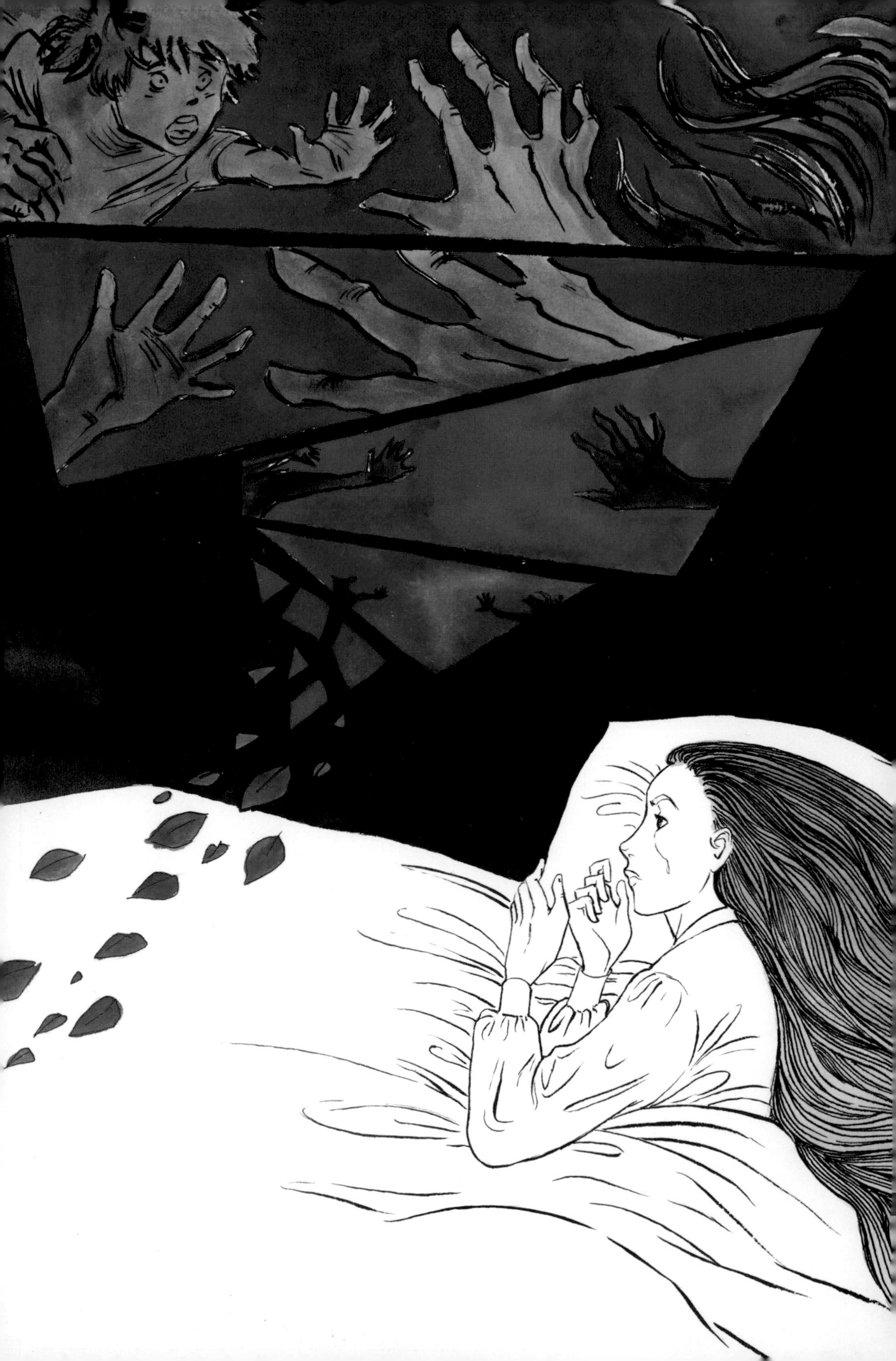

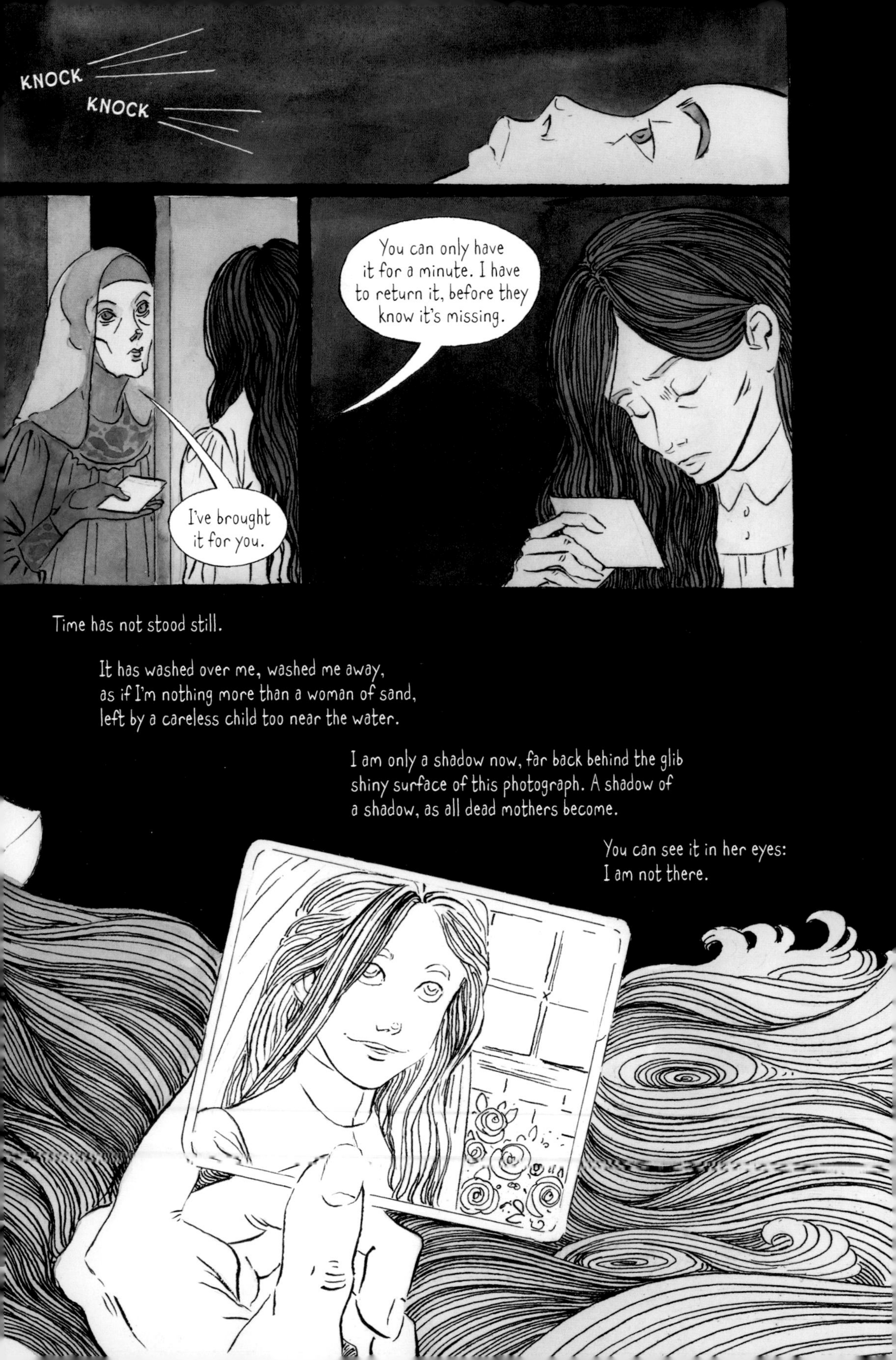
KNOCK
KNOCK
I've brought it for you.
You can only have it for a minute. I have to return it, before they know it's missing.
Time has not stood still.
It has washed over me, washed me away, as if I'm nothing more than a woman of sand, left by a careless child too near the water.
I am only a shadow now, far back behind the glib shiny surface of this photograph. A shadow of a shadow, as all dead mothers become.
You can see it in her eyes: I am not there.

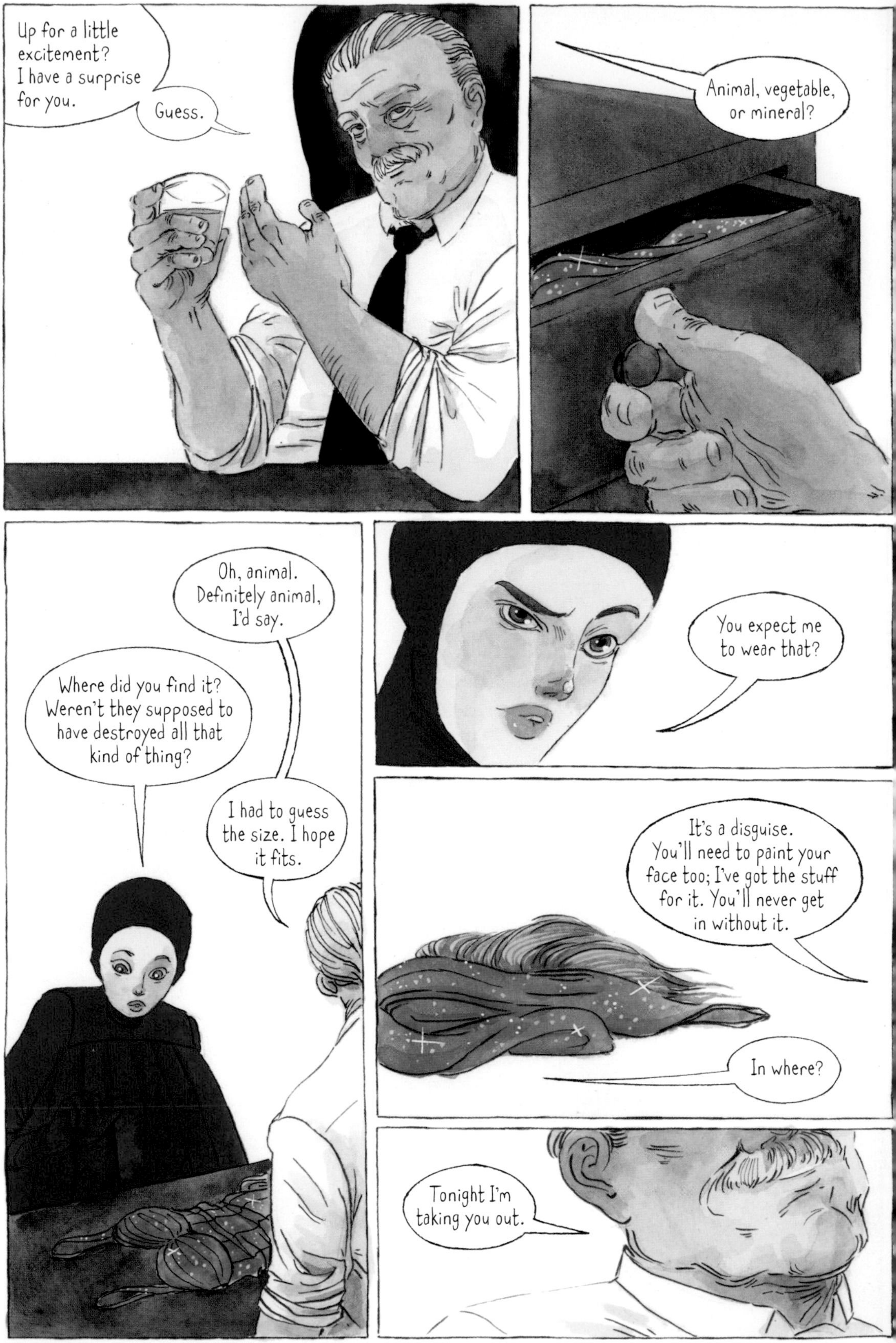
Up for a little excitement? I have a surprise for you.
Guess.
Animal, vegetable, or mineral?
Oh, animal. Definitely animal, I'd say.
Where did you find it? Weren't they supposed to have destroyed all that kind of thing?
I had to guess the size. I hope it fits.
You expect me to wear that?
It's a disguise. You'll need to paint your face too; I've got the stuff for it. You'll never get in without it.
In where?
Tonight I'm taking you out.

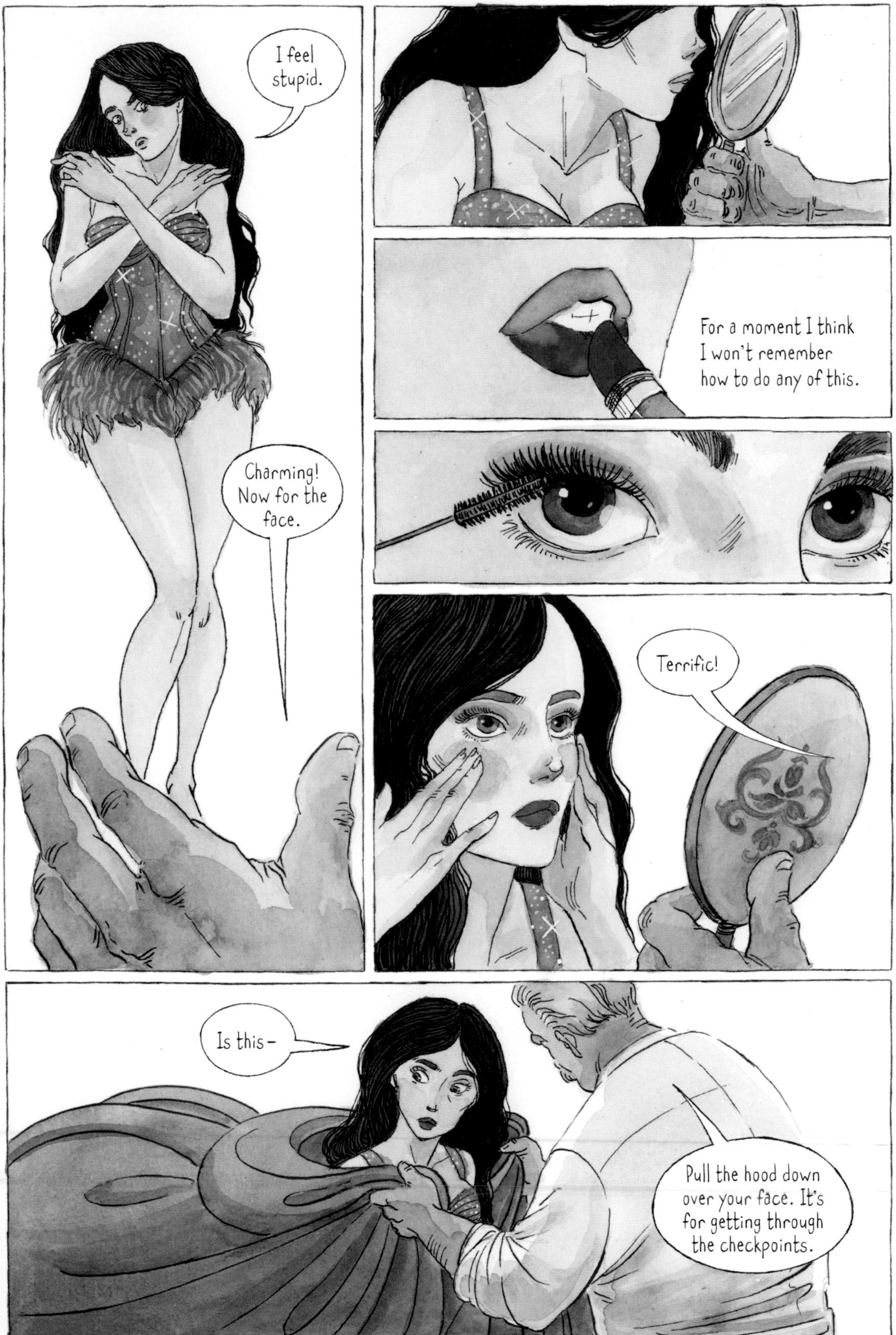
I feel stupid.
Charming! Now for the face.
For a moment I think I won't remember how to do any of this.
Terrific!
Is this-
Pull the hood down over your face. It's for getting through the checkpoints.

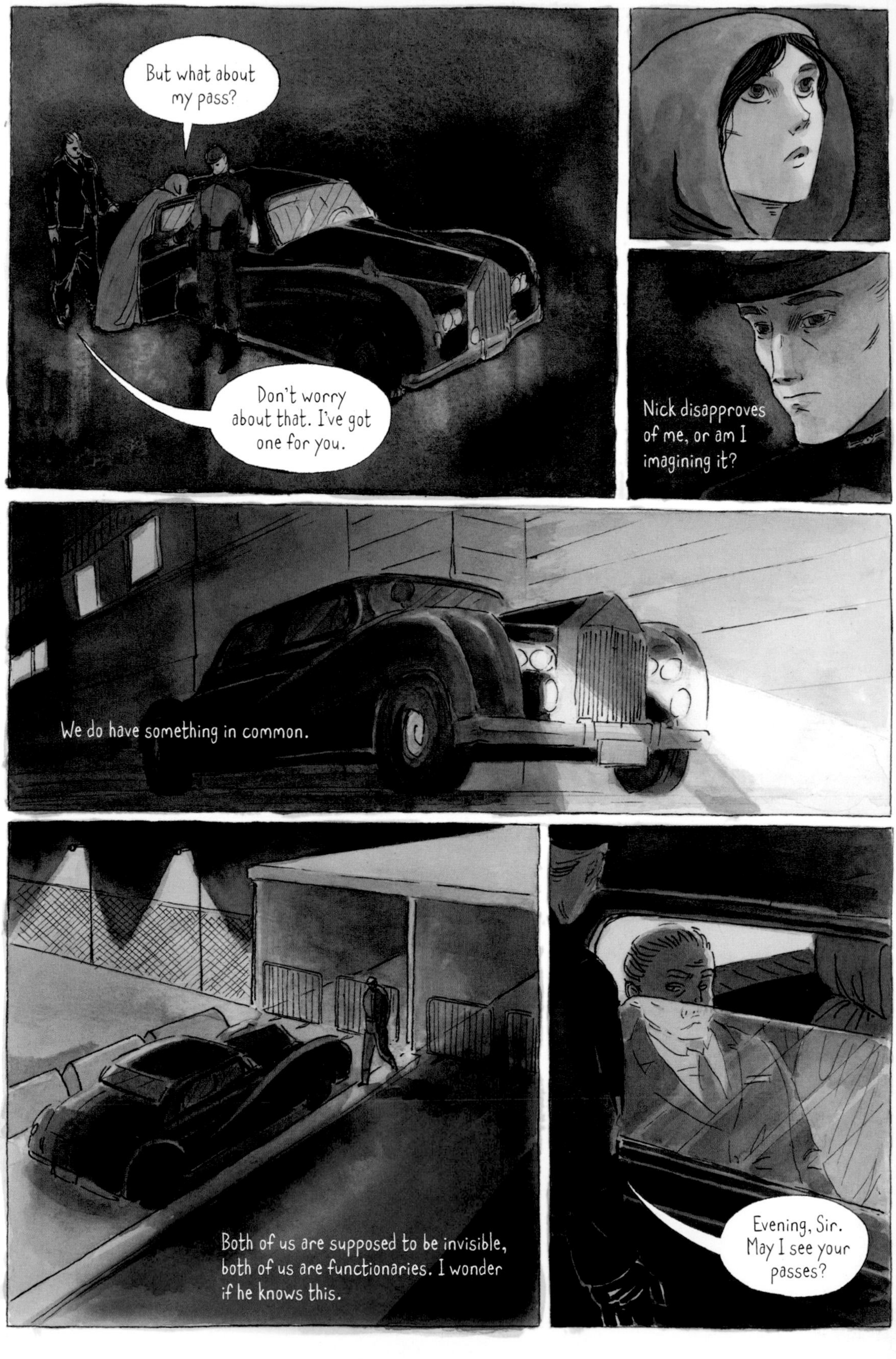
But what about my pass?
Don't worry about that. I've got one for you.
Nick disapproves of me, or am I imagining it?
We do have something in common.
Both of us are supposed to be invisible, both of us are functionaries. I wonder if he knows this.
Evening, Sir. May I see your passes?

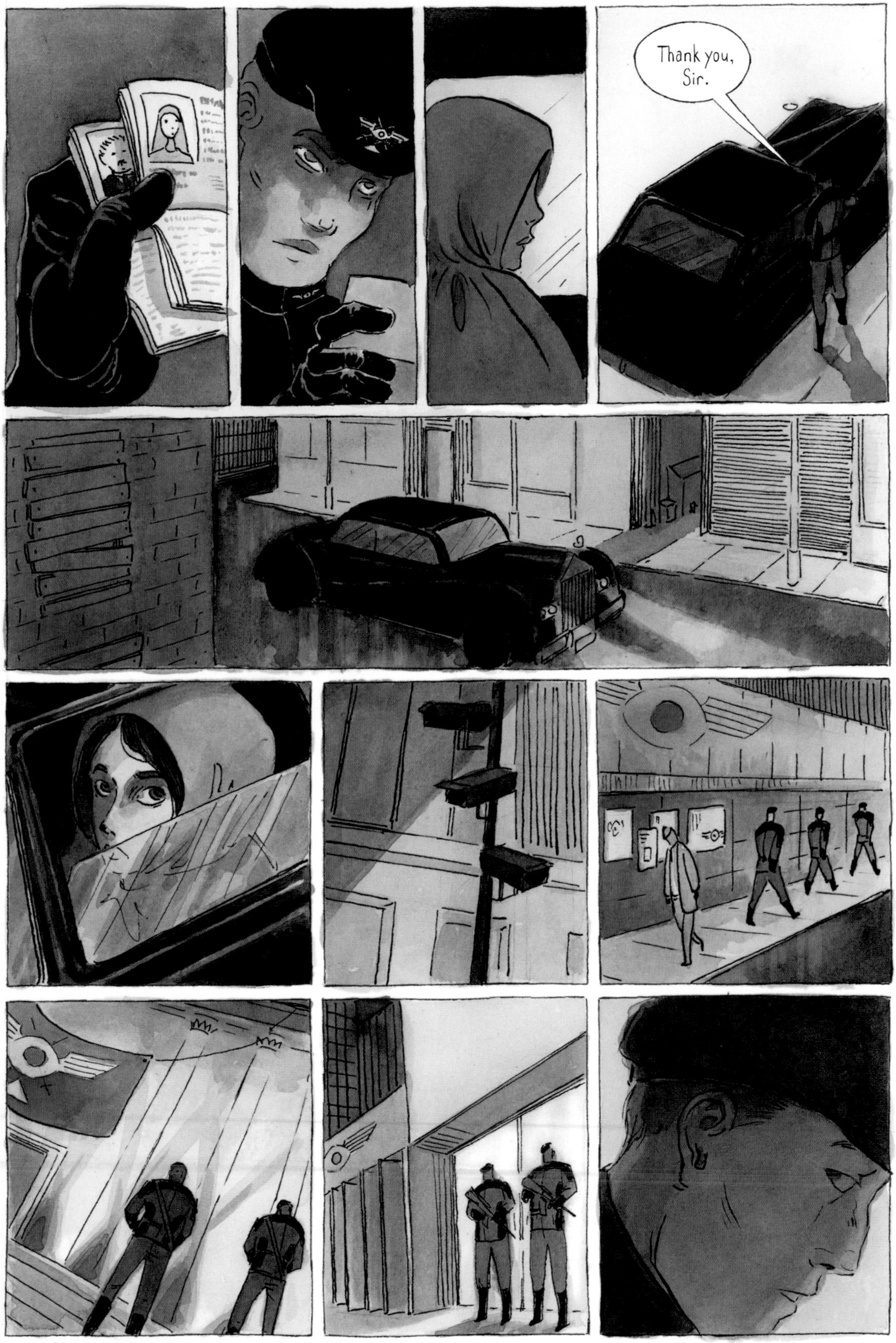
Thank you,
Sir.

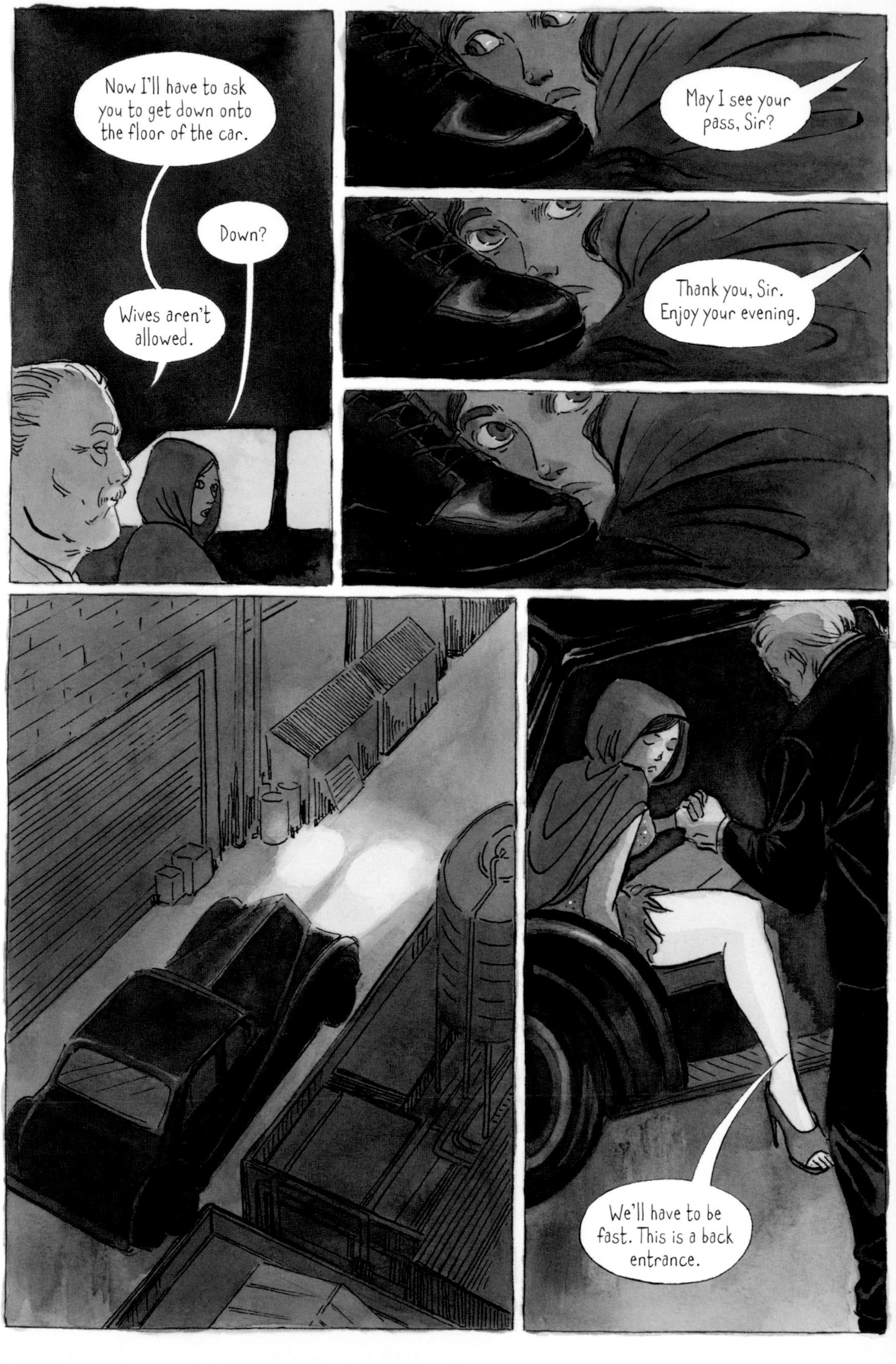
Now I'll have to ask you to get down onto the floor of the car.
Down?
Wives aren't allowed.
May I see your pass, Sir?
Thank you, Sir. Enjoy your evening.
We'll have to be fast. This is a back entrance.

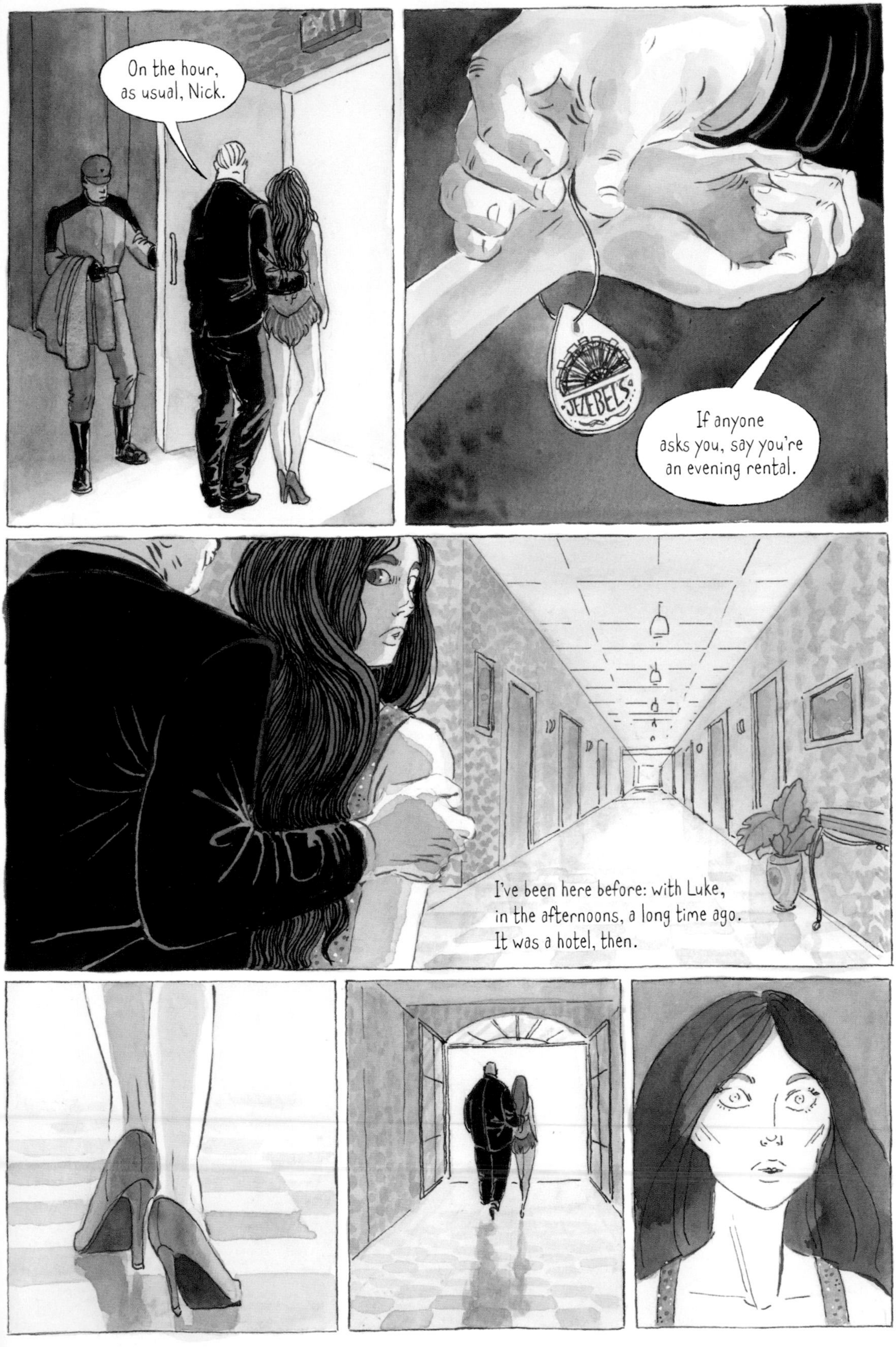
EXIT
On the hour, as usual, Nick.
JEZEBEL'S
If anyone asks you, say you're an evening rental.
I've been here before: with Luke, in the afternoons, a long time ago. It was a hotel, then.

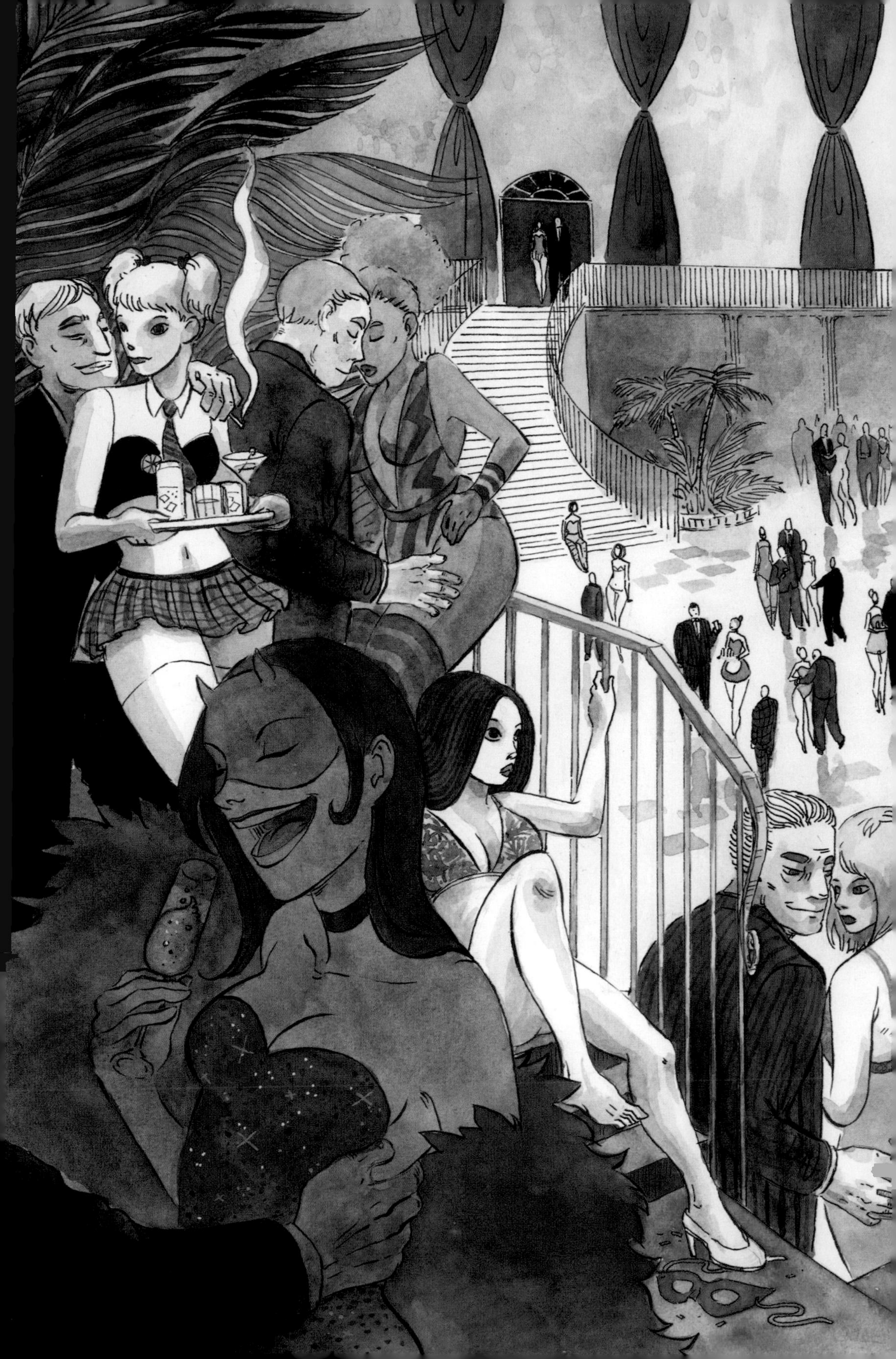

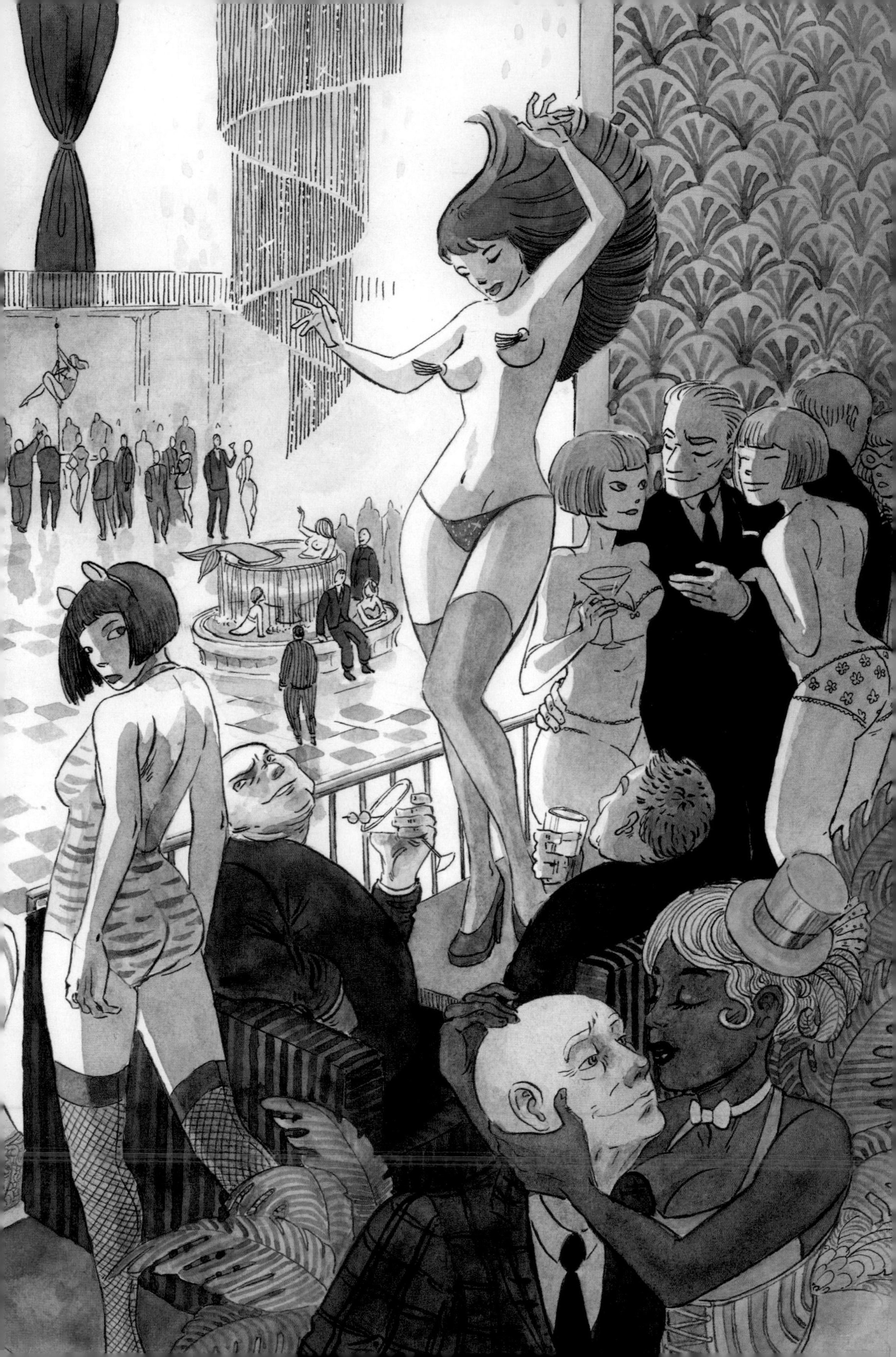

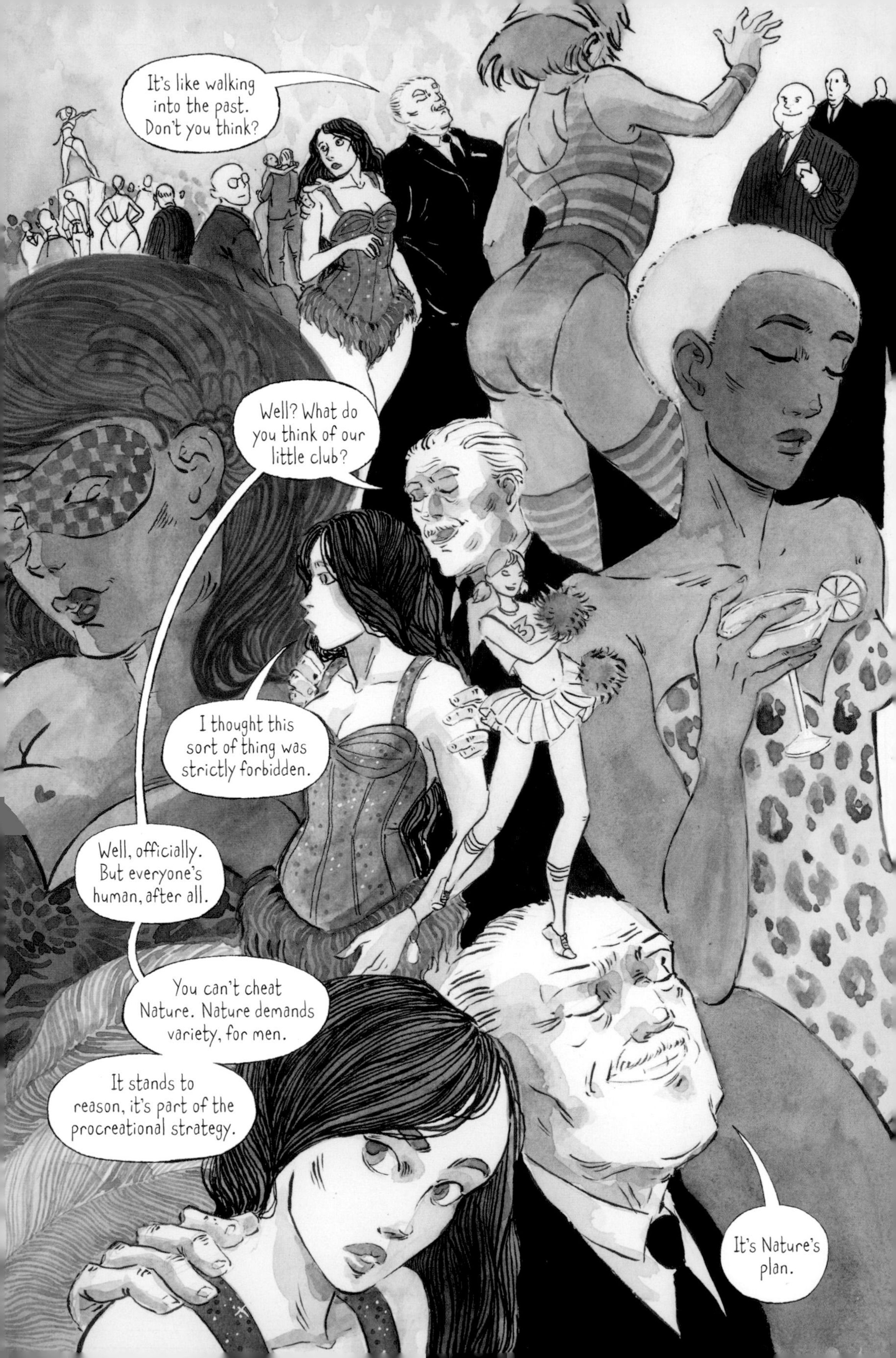
It's like walking into the past. Don't you think?
Well? What do you think of our little club?
I thought this sort of thing was strictly forbidden.
Well, officially. But everyone's human, after all.
You can't cheat Nature. Nature demands variety, for men.
It stands to reason, it's part of the procreational strategy.
It's Nature's plan.

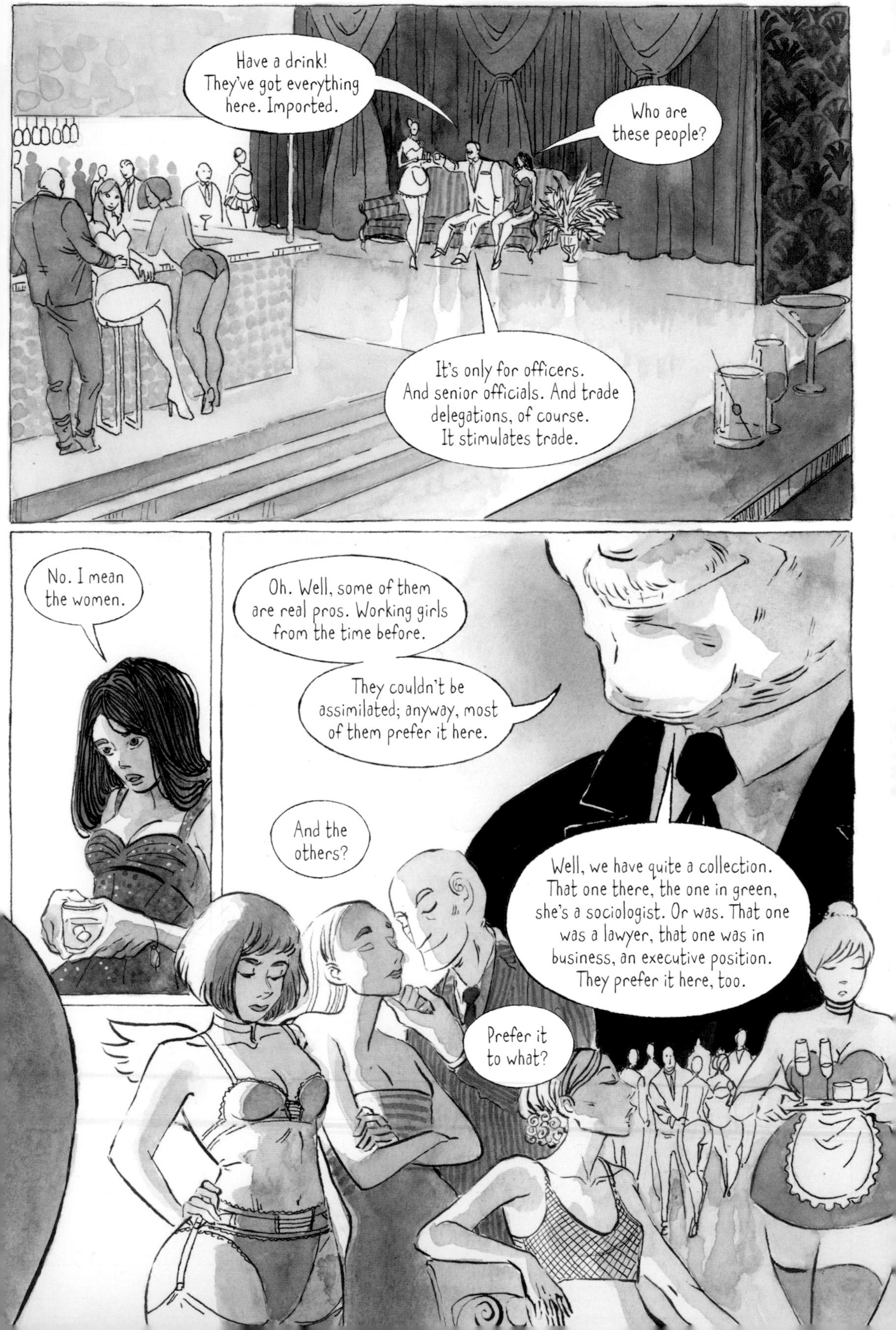
Have a drink! They've got everything here. Imported.
Who are these people?
It's only for officers. And senior officials. And trade delegations, of course. It stimulates trade.
No. I mean the women.
Oh. Well, some of them are real pros. Working girls from the time before.
They couldn't be assimilated; anyway, most of them prefer it here.
And the others?
Well, we have quite a collection. That one there, the one in green, she's a sociologist. Or was. That one was a lawyer, that one was in business, an executive position. They prefer it here, too.
Prefer it to what?

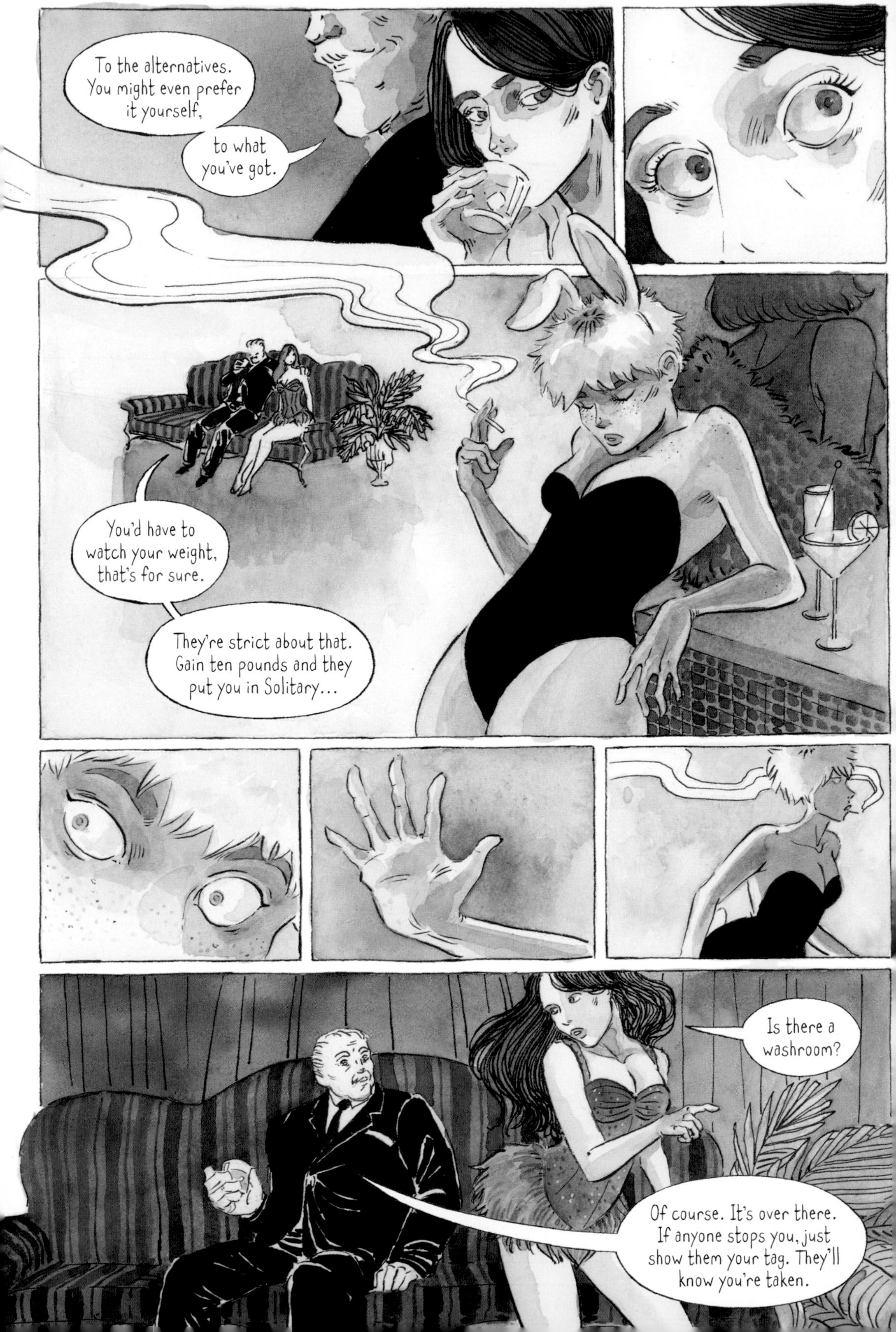
To the alternatives. You might even prefer it yourself,
to what you've got.
You'd have to watch your weight, that's for sure.
They're strict about that. Gain ten pounds and they put you in Solitary...
Is there a washroom?
Of course. It's over there. If anyone stops you, just show them your tag. They'll know you're taken.

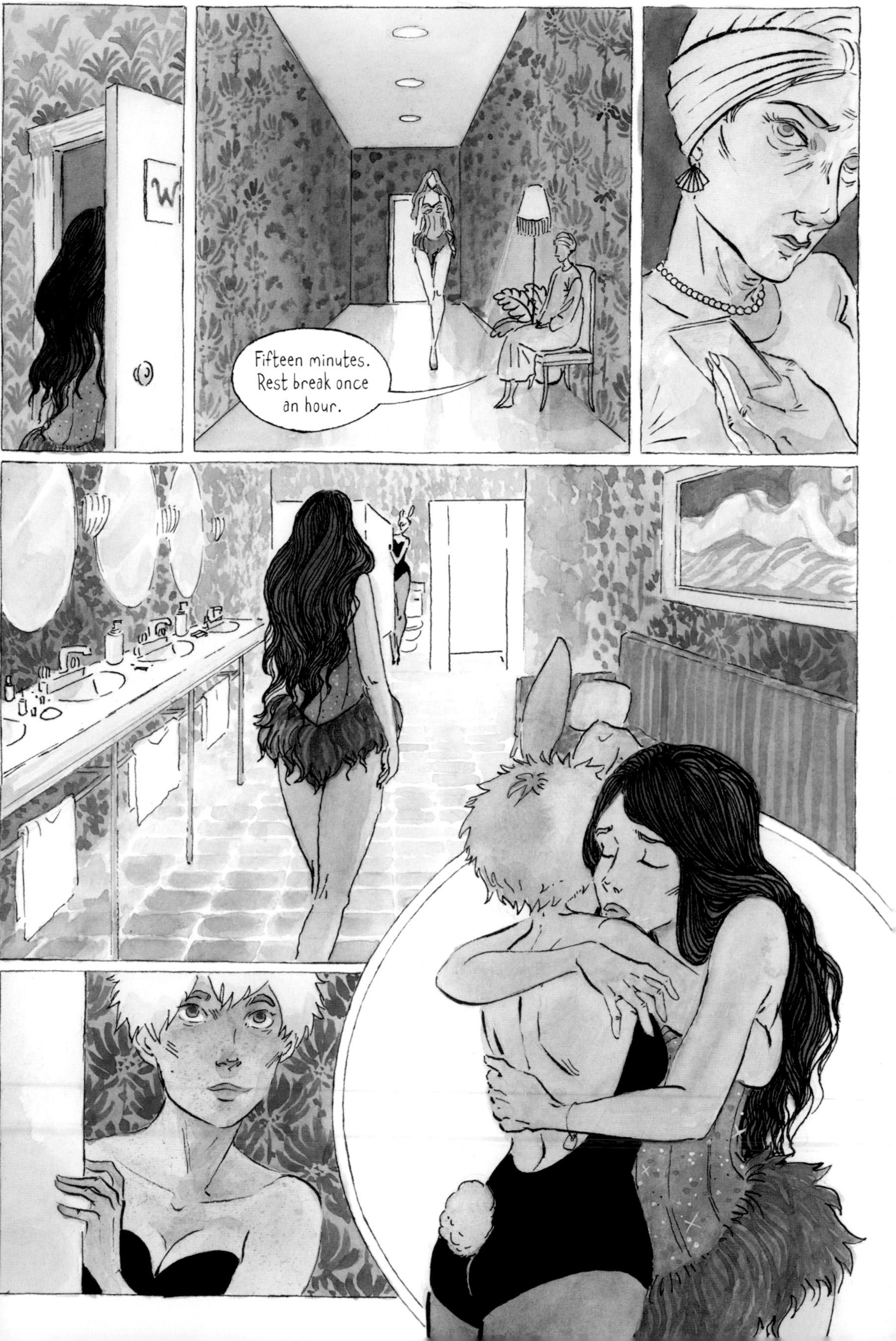
Fifteen minutes. Rest break once an hour.

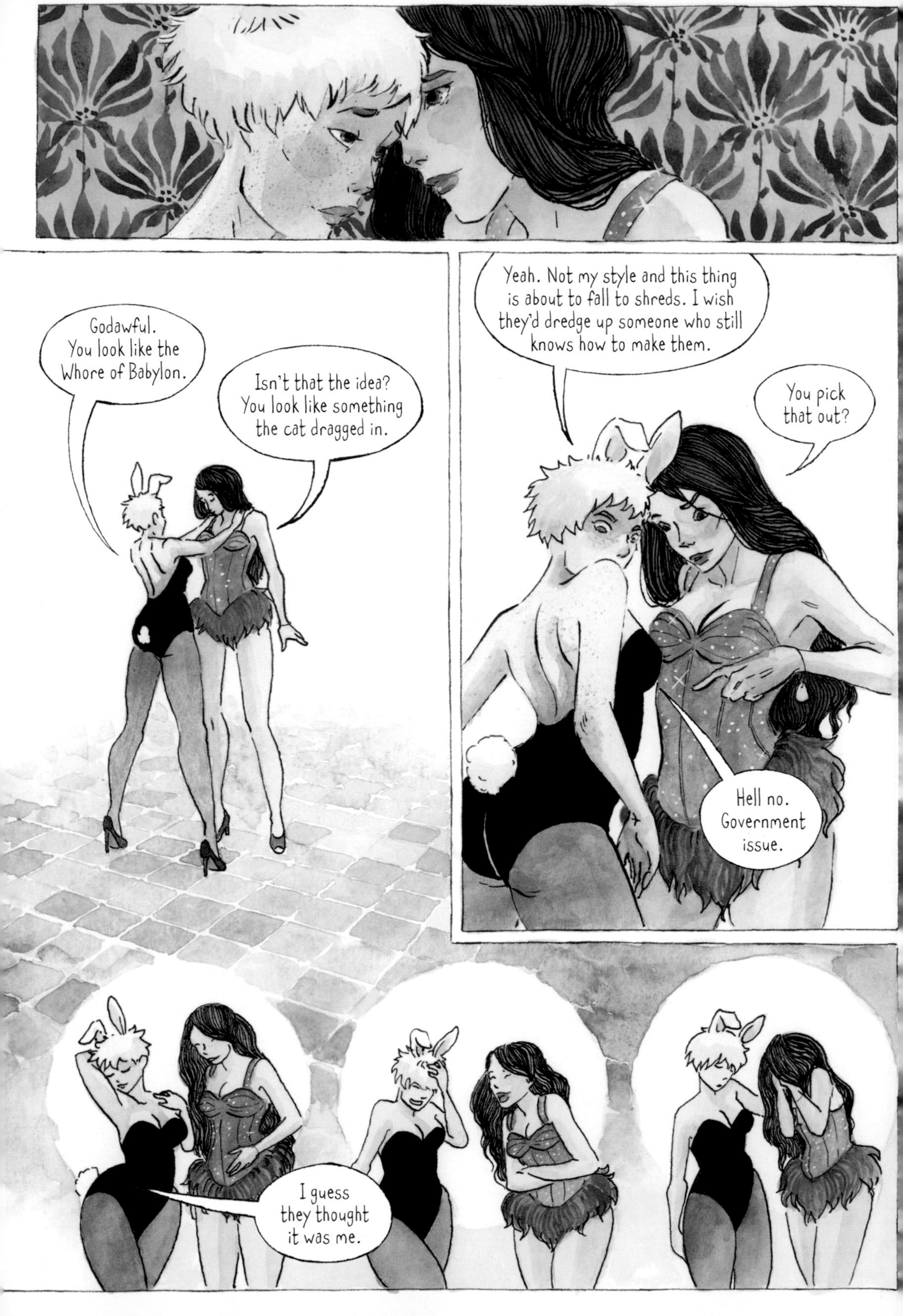
Godawful.
You look like the Whore of Babylon.
Isn't that the idea? You look like something the cat dragged in.
Yeah. Not my style and this thing is about to fall to shreds. I wish they'd dredge up someone who still knows how to make them.
You pick that out?
Hell no. Government issue.
I guess they thought it was me.

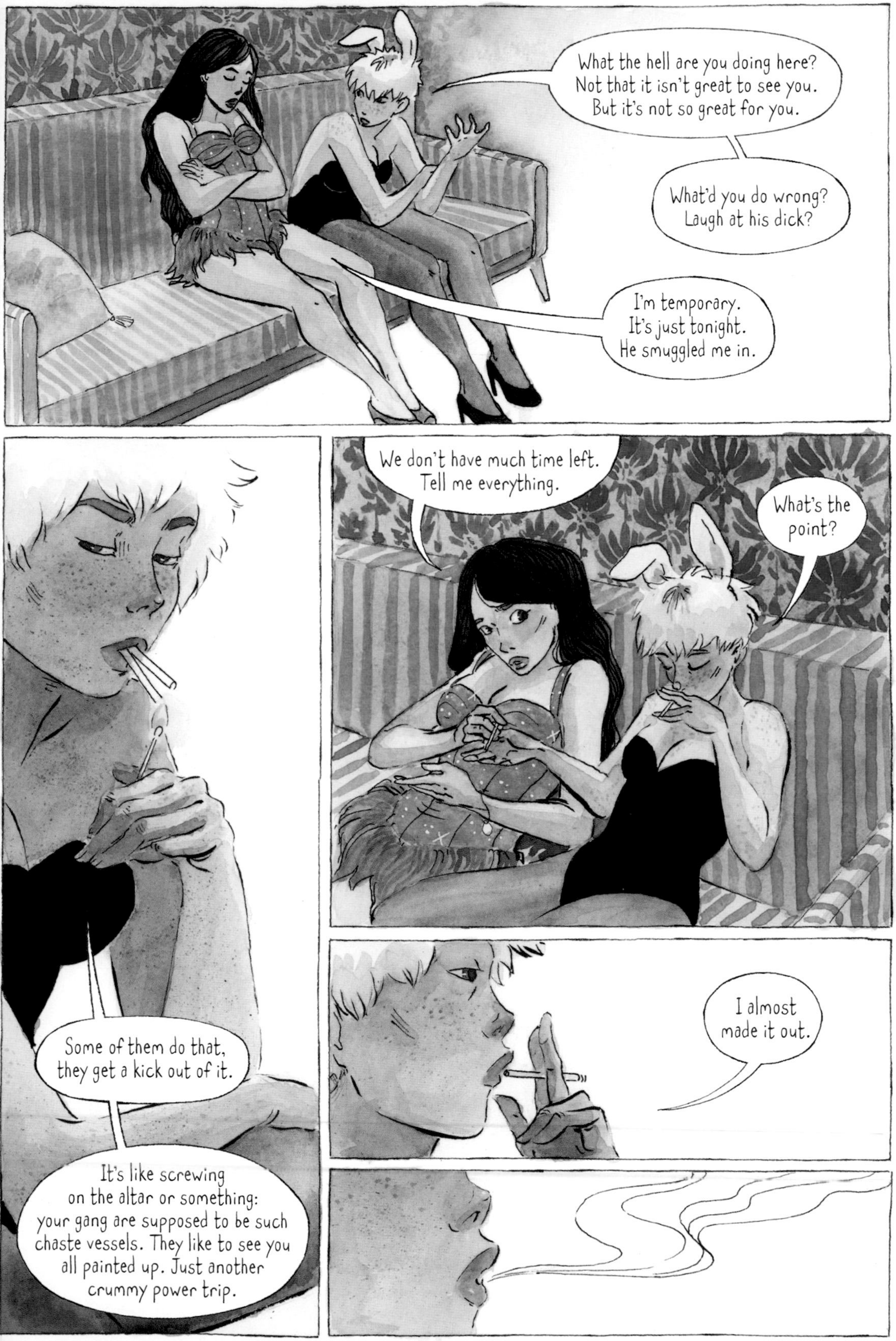
What the hell are you doing here? Not that it isn't great to see you. But it's not so great for you.
What'd you do wrong? Laugh at his dick?
I'm temporary. It's just tonight. He smuggled me in.
We don't have much time left. Tell me everything.
What's the point?
Some of them do that, they get a kick out of it.
It's like screwing on the altar or something: your gang are supposed to be such chaste vessels. They like to see you all painted up. Just another crummy power trip.
I almost made it out.

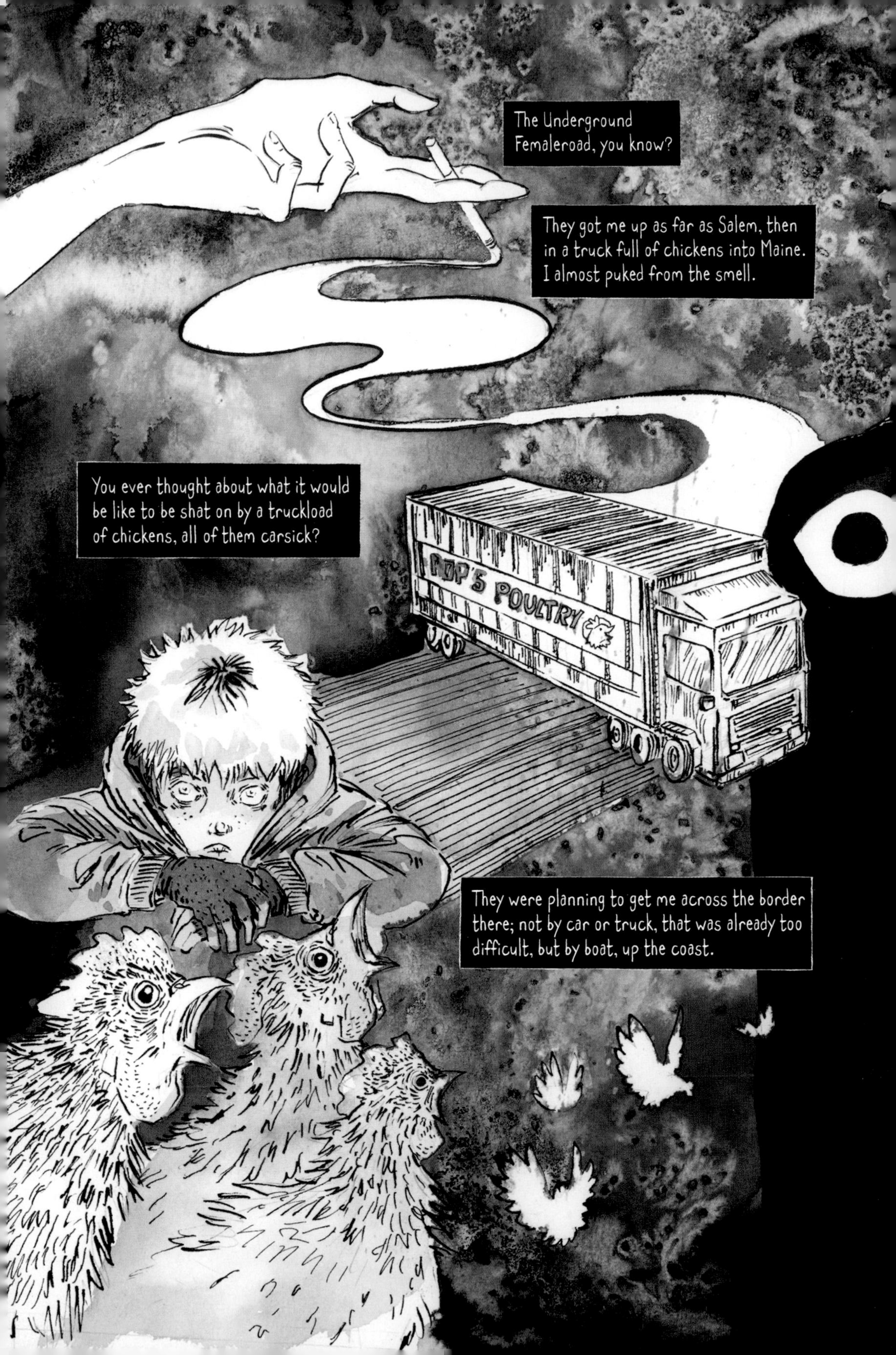

The Underground Femaleroad, you know?
They got me up as far as Salem, then in a truck full of chickens into Maine. I almost puked from the smell.
You ever thought about what it would be like to be shat on by a truckload of chickens, all of them carsick?
POULTRY
They were planning to get me across the border there; not by car or truck, that was already too difficult, but by boat, up the coast.

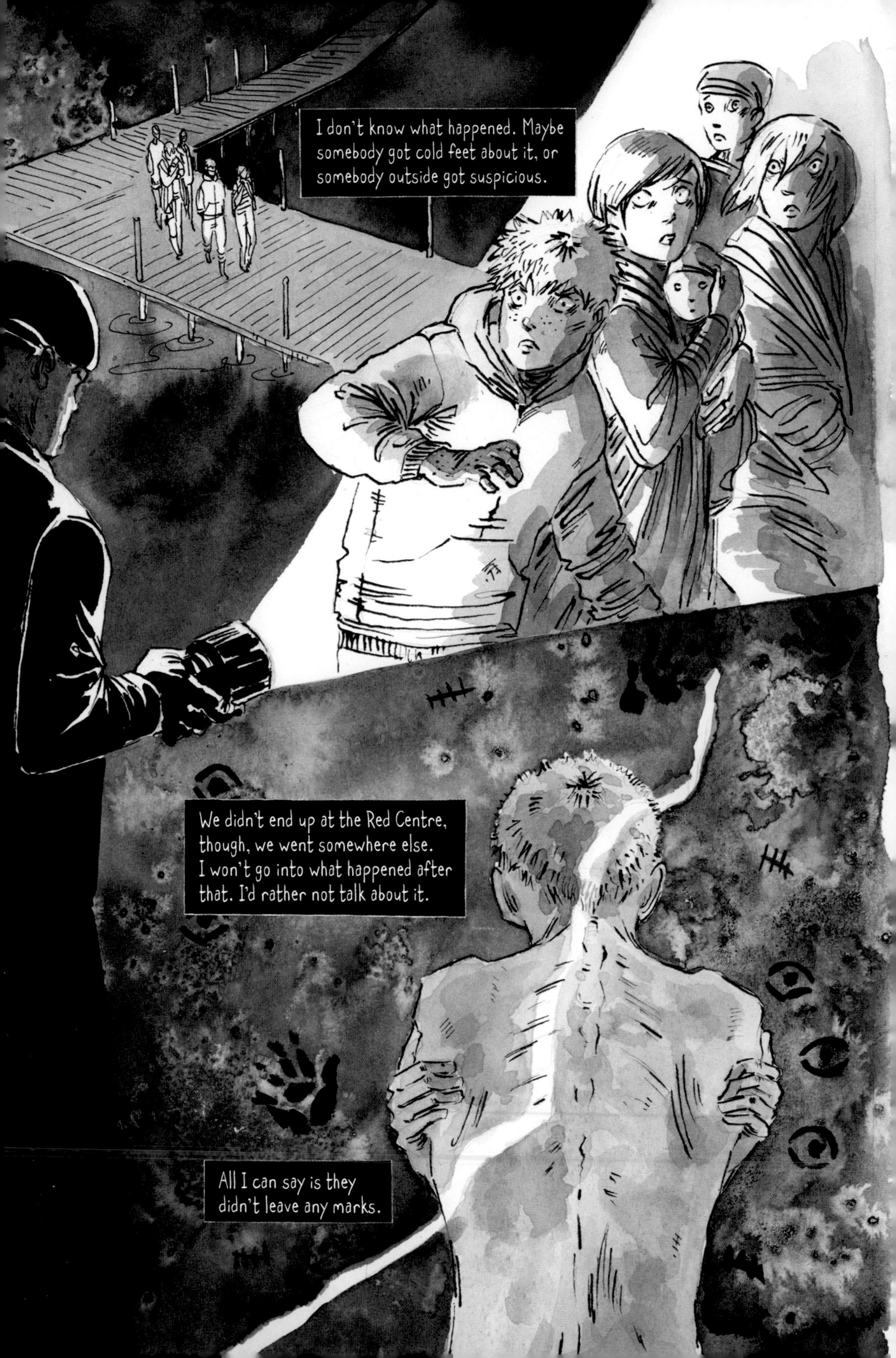
I don't know what happened. Maybe somebody got cold feet about it, or somebody outside got suspicious.
We didn't end up at the Red Centre, though, we went somewhere else. I won't go into what happened after that. I'd rather not talk about it.
All I can say is they didn't leave any marks.

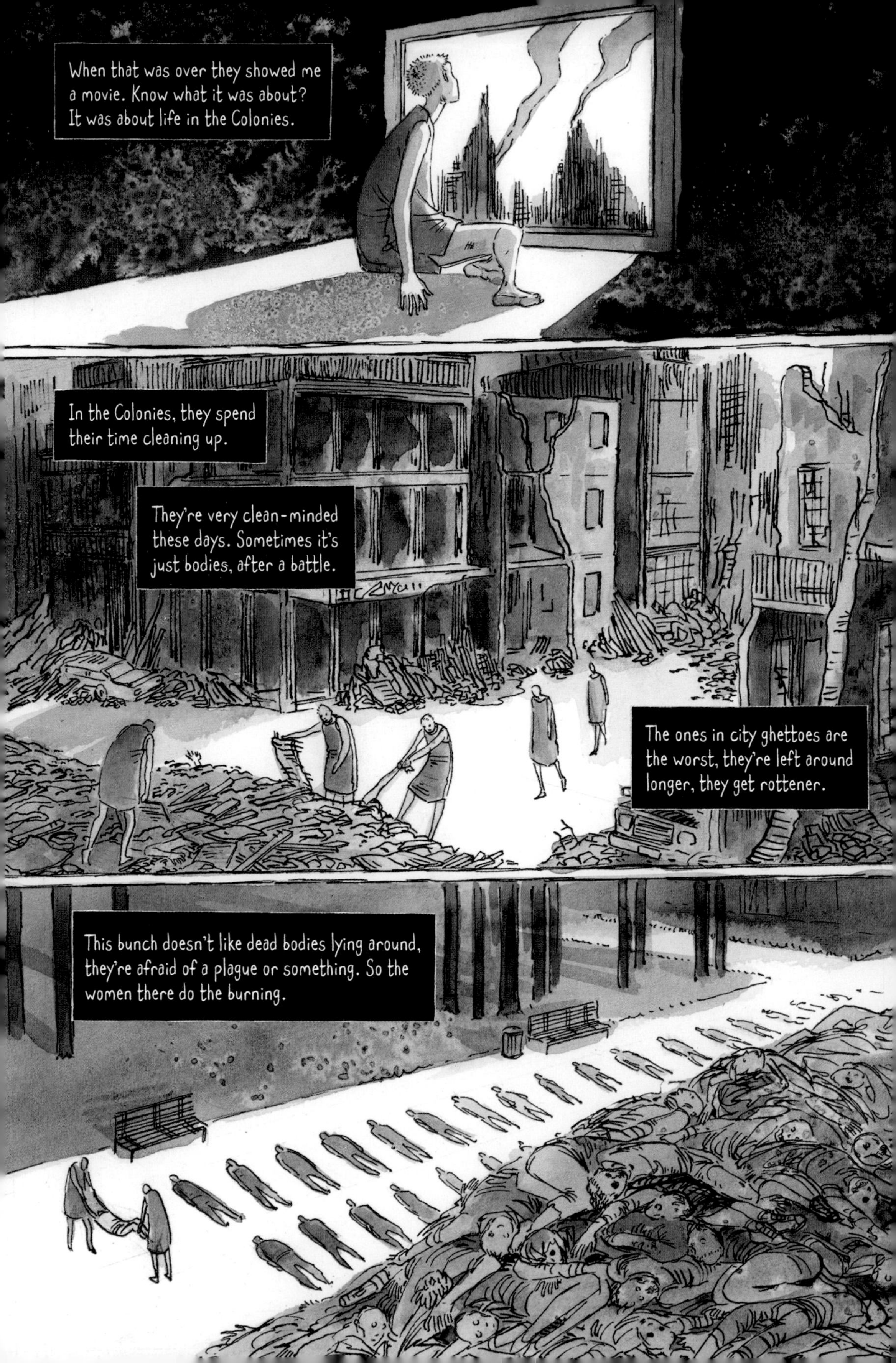

When that was over they showed me a movie. Know what it was about? It was about life in the Colonies.
In the Colonies, they spend their time cleaning up.
They're very clean-minded these days. Sometimes it's just bodies, after a battle.
The ones in city ghettoes are the worst, they're left around longer, they get rottener.
This bunch doesn't like dead bodies lying around, they're afraid of a plague or something. So the women there do the burning.

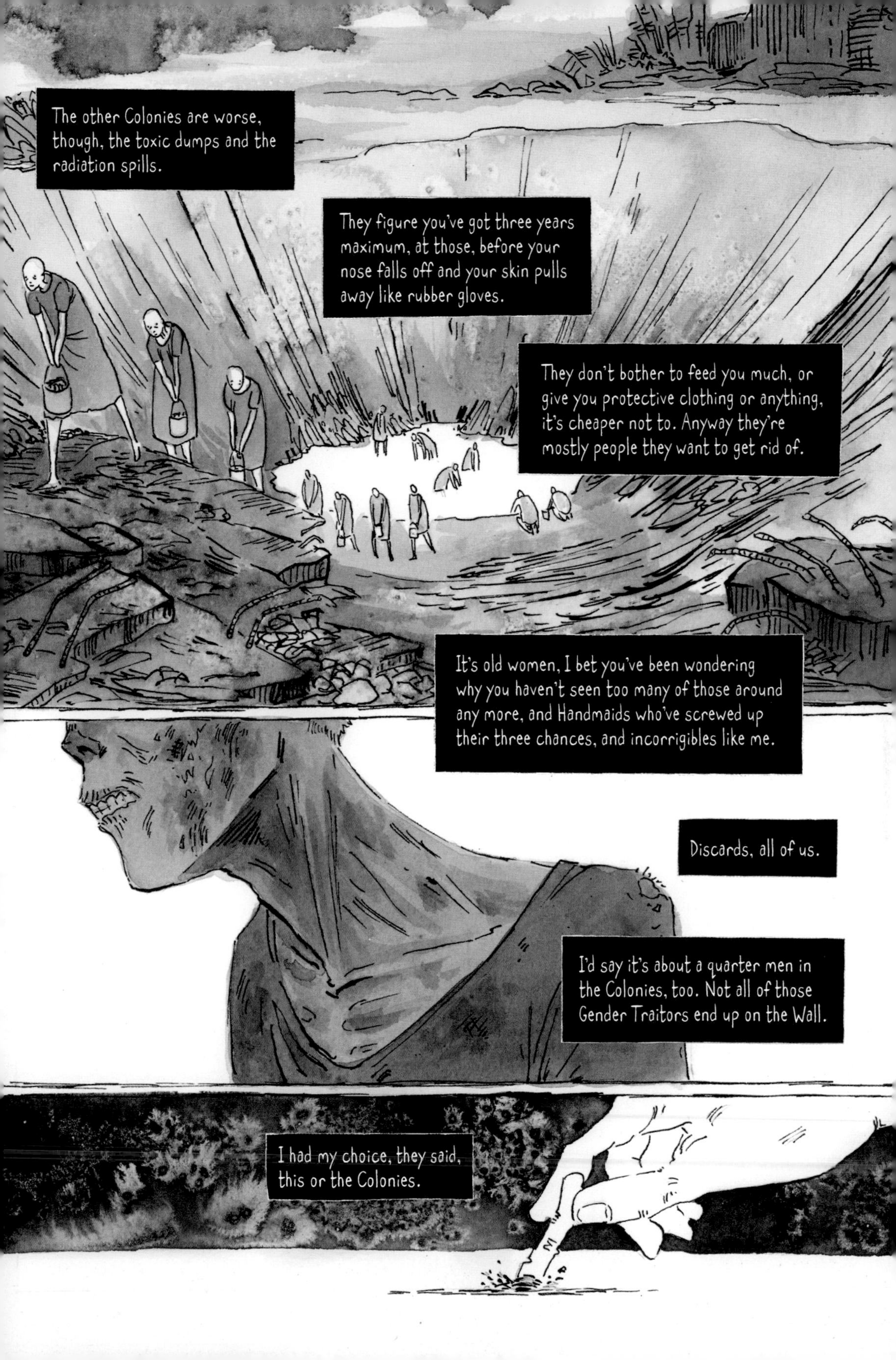

The other Colonies are worse, though, the toxic dumps and the radiation spills.
They figure you've got three years maximum, at those, before your nose falls off and your skin pulls away like rubber gloves.
They don't bother to feed you much, or give you protective clothing or anything, it's cheaper not to. Anyway they're mostly people they want to get rid of.
It's old women, I bet you've been wondering why you haven't seen too many of those around any more, and Handmaids who've screwed up their three chances, and incorrigibles like me.
Discards, all of us.
I'd say it's about a quarter men in the Colonies, too. Not all of those Gender Traitors end up on the Wall.
I had my choice, they said, this or the Colonies.

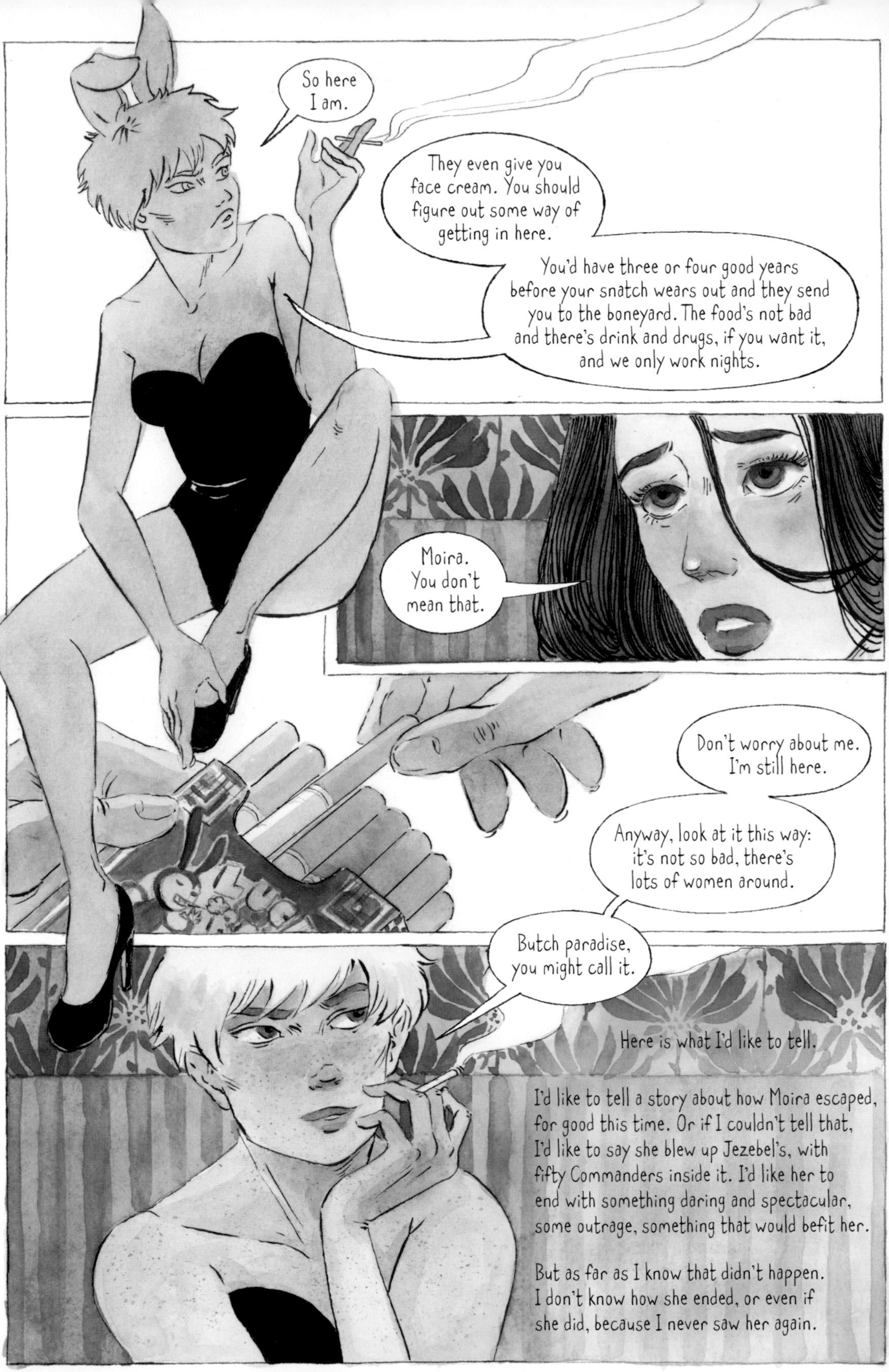
So here I am.
They even give you face cream. You should figure out some way of getting in here.
You'd have three or four good years before your snatch wears out and they send you to the boneyard. The food's not bad and there's drink and drugs, if you want it, and we only work nights.
Moira. You don't mean that.
Don't worry about me. I'm still here.
Anyway, look at it this way: it's not so bad, there's lots of women around.
Butch paradise, you might call it.
Here is what I'd like to tell.
I'd like to tell a story about how Moira escaped, for good this time. Or if I couldn't tell that, I'd like to say she blew up Jezebel's, with fifty Commanders inside it. I'd like her to end with something daring and spectacular, some outrage, something that would befit her.
But as far as I know that didn't happen. I don't know how she ended, or even if she did, because I never saw her again.

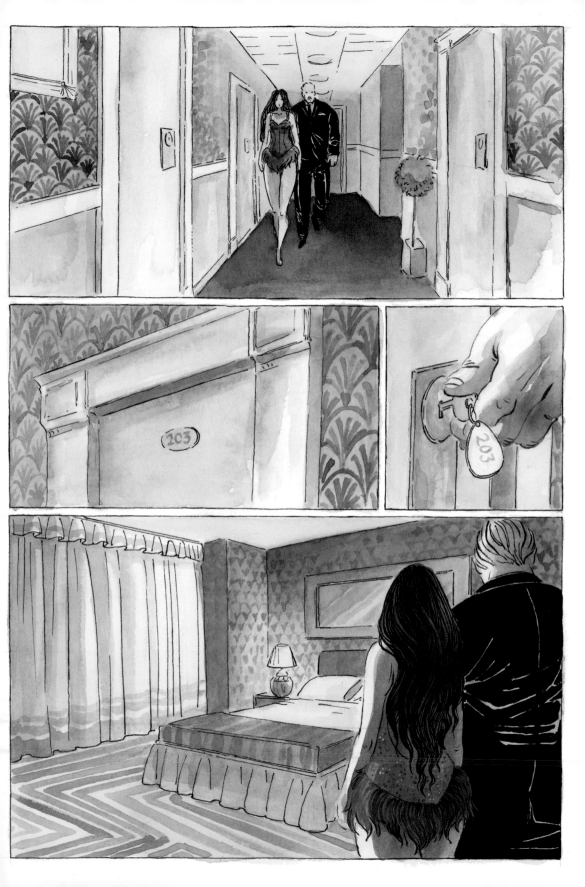

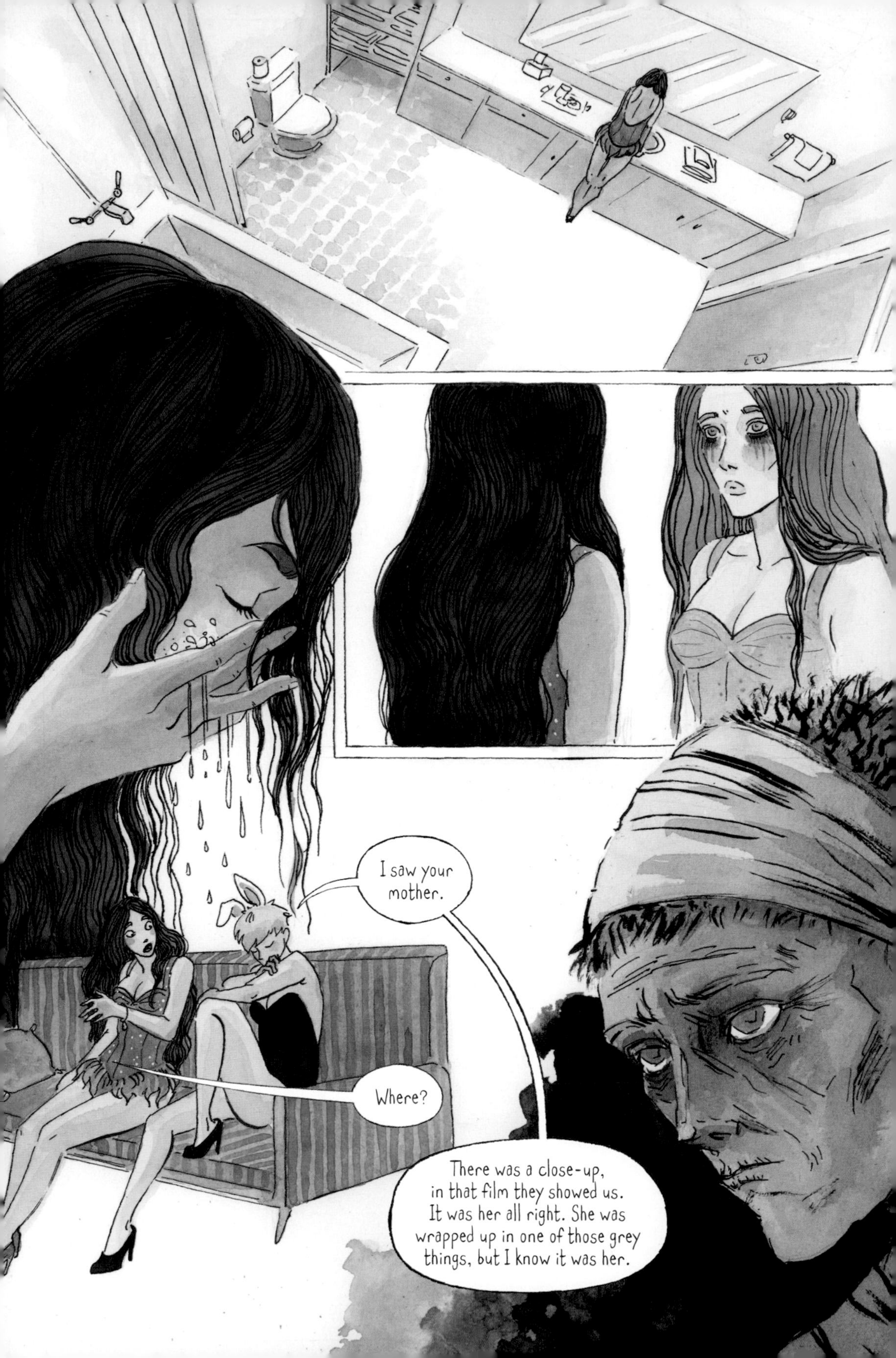
I saw your mother.
Where?
There was a close-up, in that film they showed us. It was her all right. She was wrapped up in one of those grey things, but I know it was her.

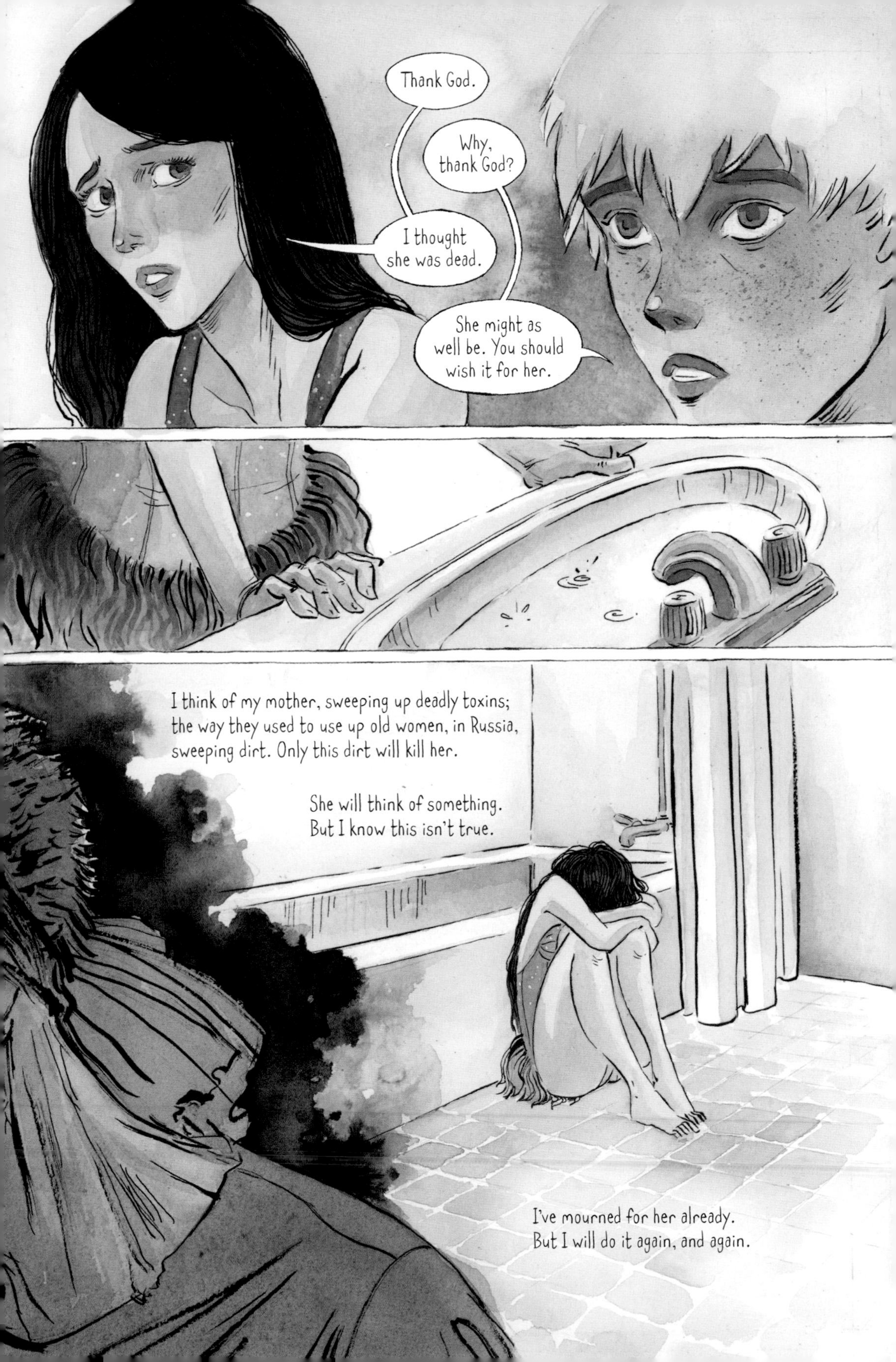
Thank God.
Why, thank God?
I thought she was dead.
She might as well be. You should wish it for her.
I think of my mother, sweeping up deadly toxins; the way they used to use up old women, in Russia, sweeping dirt. Only this dirt will kill her.
She will think of something. But I know this isn't true.
I've mourned for her already. But I will do it again, and again.

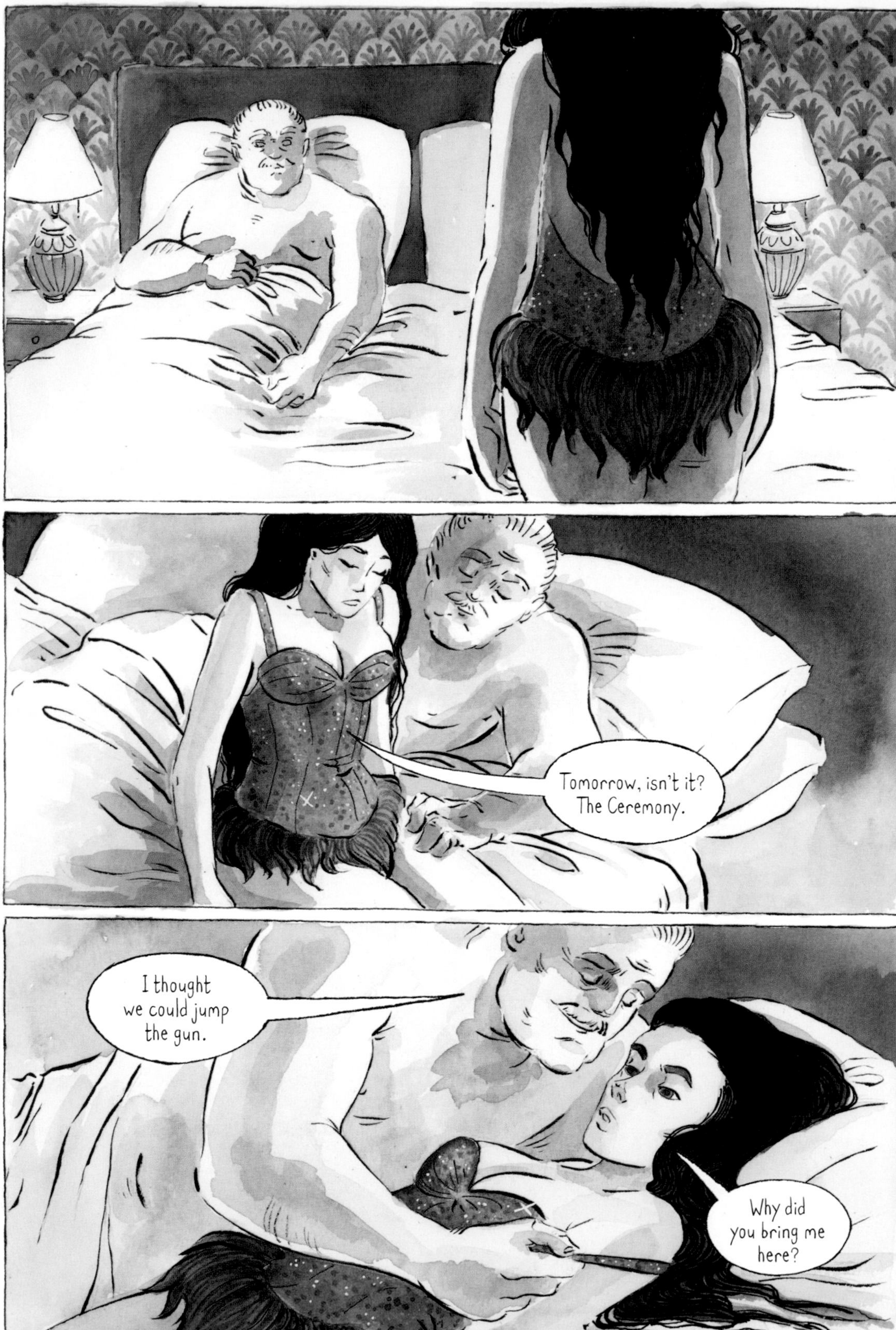

Tomorrow, isn't it? The Ceremony.
I thought we could jump the gun.
Why did you bring me here?

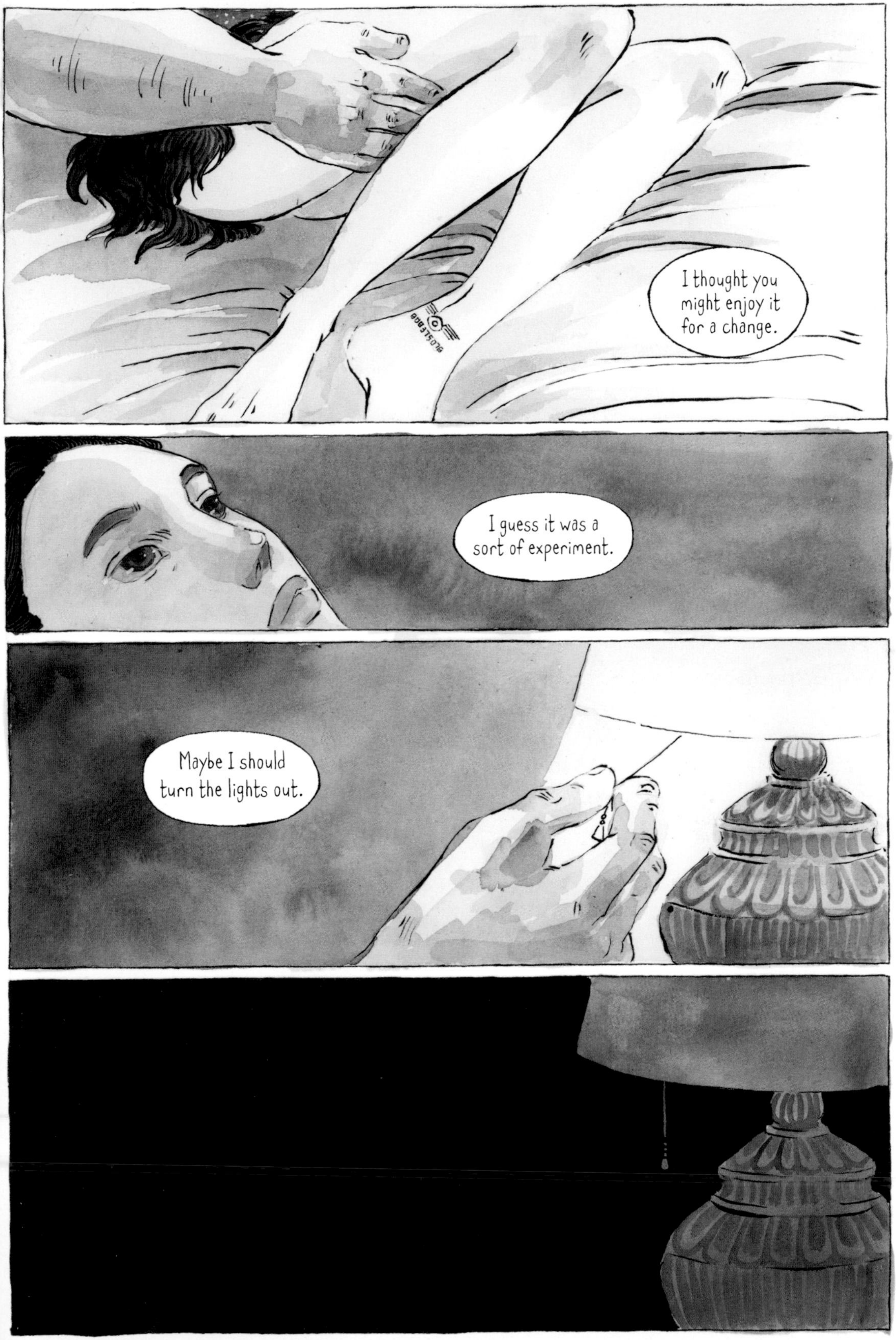
I thought you might enjoy it for a change.
I guess it was a sort of experiment.
Maybe I should turn the lights out.

XIII

N I G H T

Serena Joy is here at midnight, as she said she'd be.

I have shed the spangles, scraped off the lipstick with toilet paper.
I hope nothing shows, I hope I don't smell of it, or of him either.

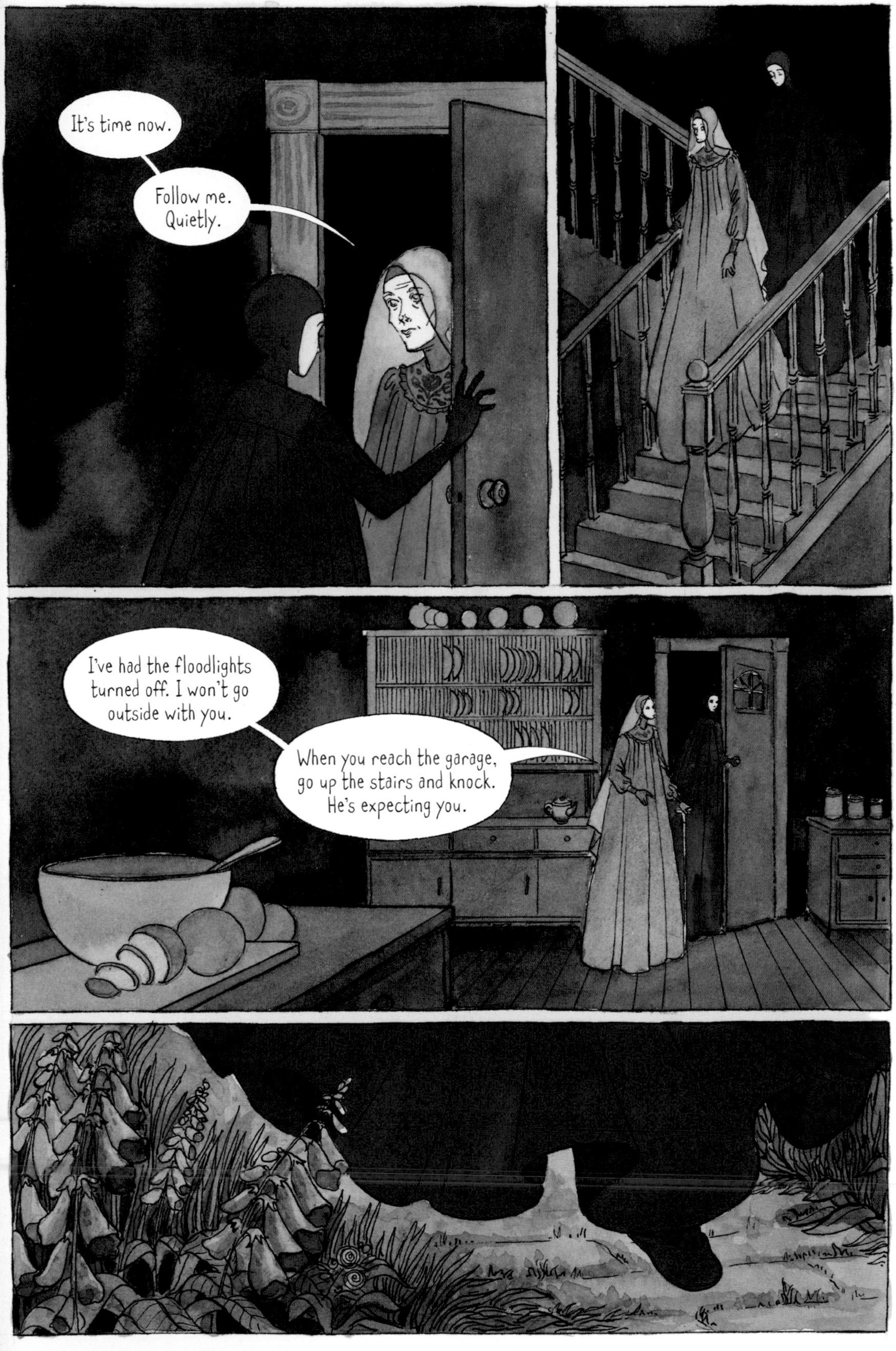
It's time now.
Follow me. Quietly.
I've had the floodlights turned off. I won't go outside with you.
When you reach the garage, go up the stairs and knock. He's expecting you.

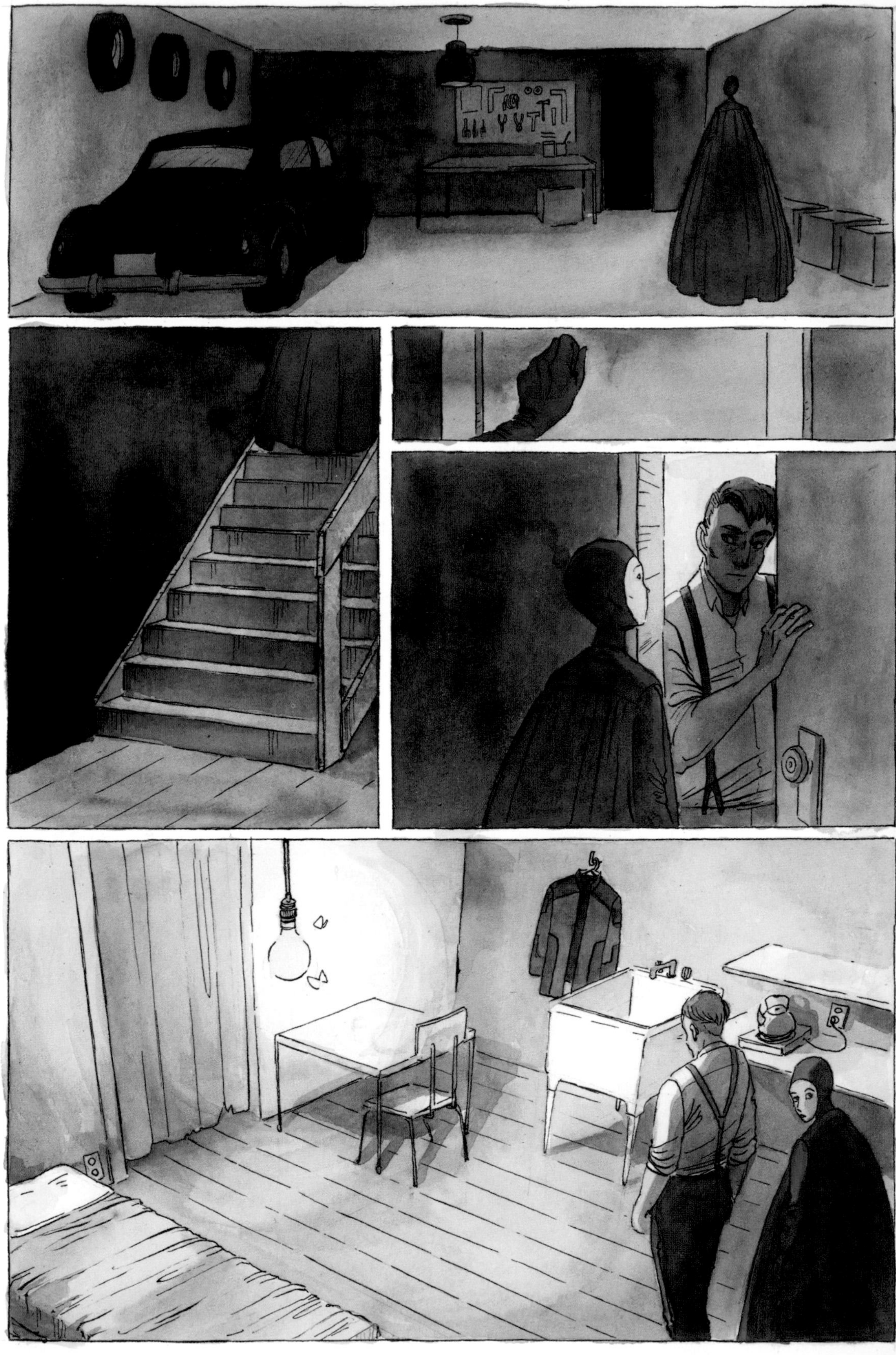

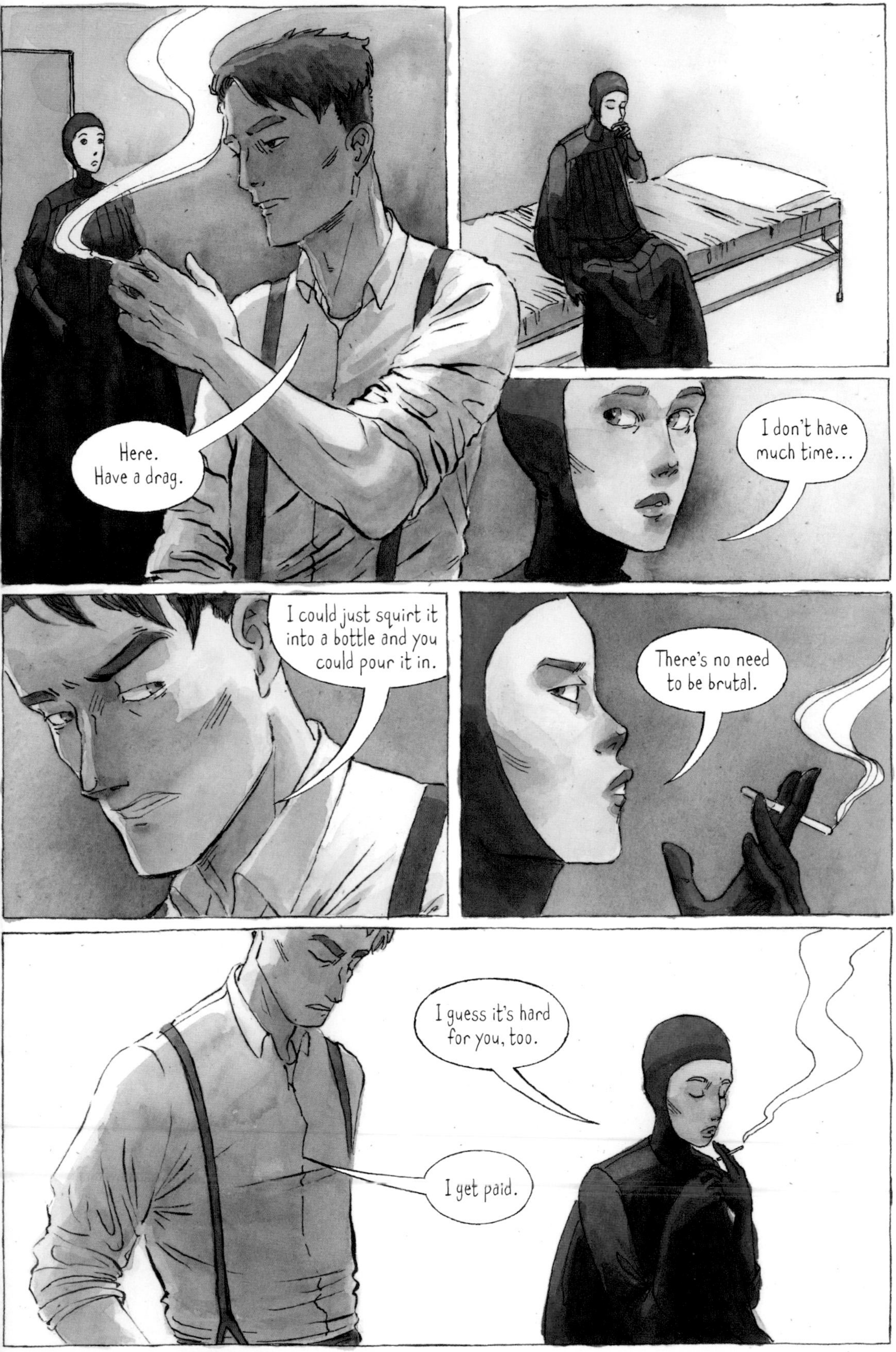
Here.
Have a drag.
I don't have much time...
I could just squirt it into a bottle and you could pour it in.
There's no need to be brutal.
I guess it's hard for you, too.
I get paid.

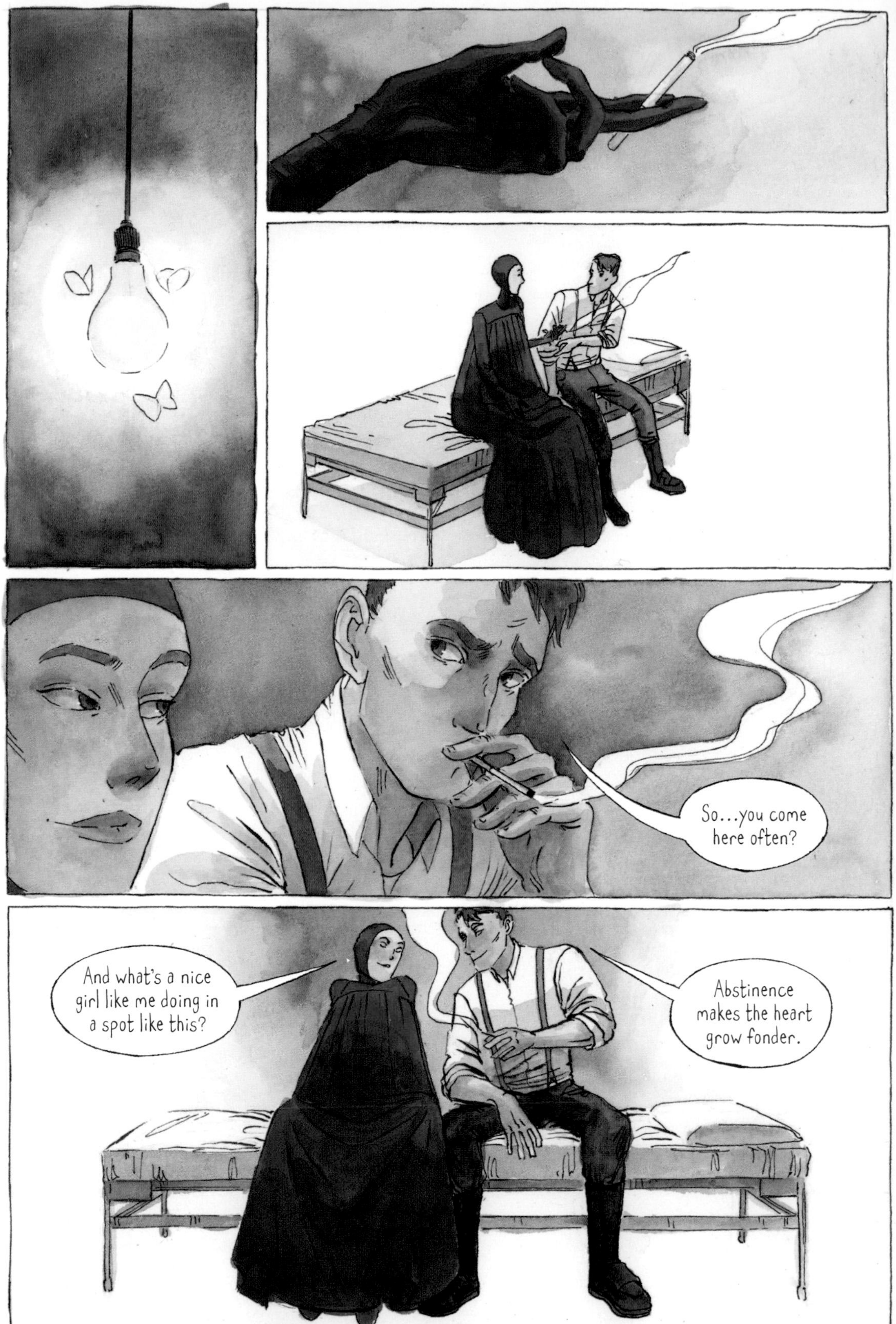
So...you come here often?
And what's a nice girl like me doing in a spot like this?
Abstinence makes the heart grow fonder.

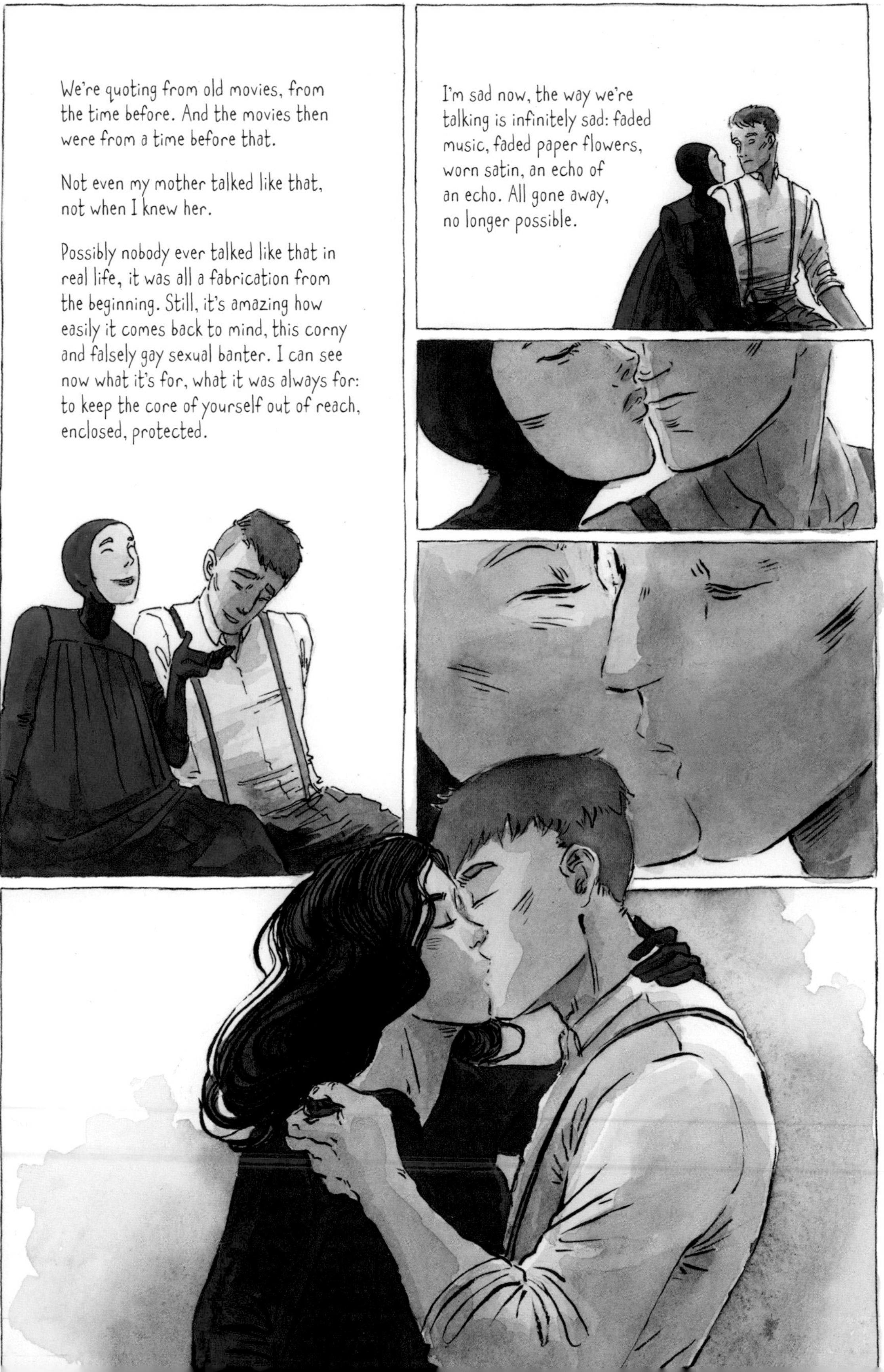
We're quoting from old movies, from the time before. And the movies then were from a time before that.
Not even my mother talked like that, not when I knew her.
Possibly nobody ever talked like that in real life, it was all a fabrication from the beginning. Still, it's amazing how easily it comes back to mind, this corny and falsely gay sexual banter. I can see now what it's for, what it was always for: to keep the core of yourself out of reach, enclosed, protected.
I'm sad now, the way we're talking is infinitely sad: faded music, faded paper flowers, worn satin, an echo of an echo. All gone away, no longer possible.

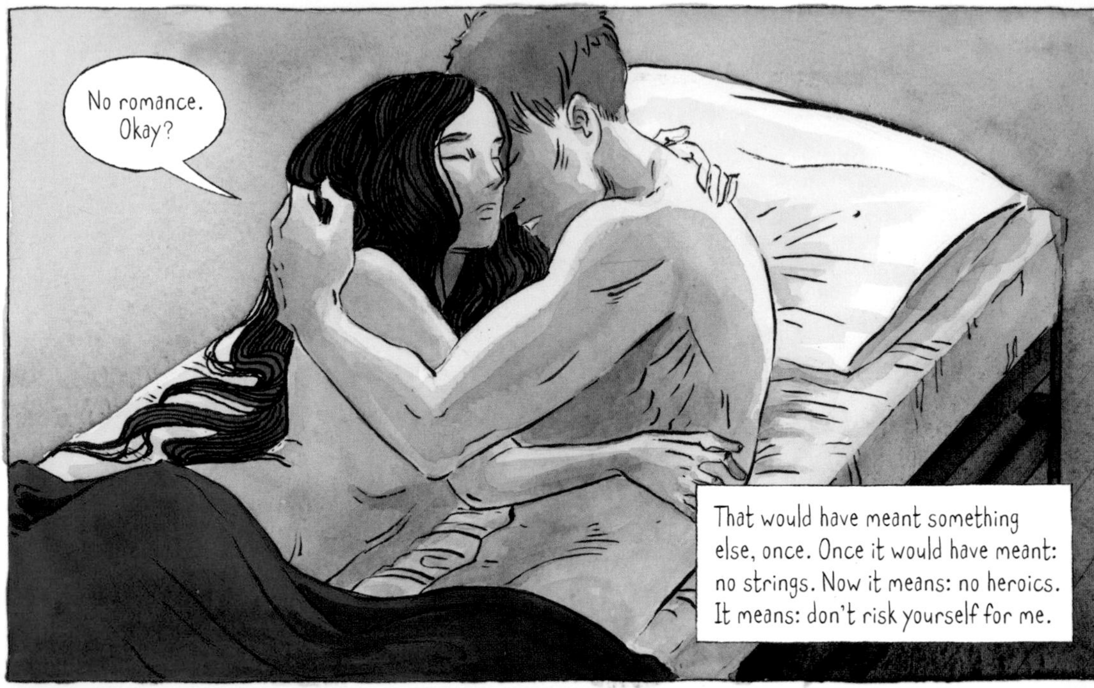
No romance. Okay?
That would have meant something else, once. Once it would have meant: no strings. Now it means: no heroics. It means: don't risk yourself for me.

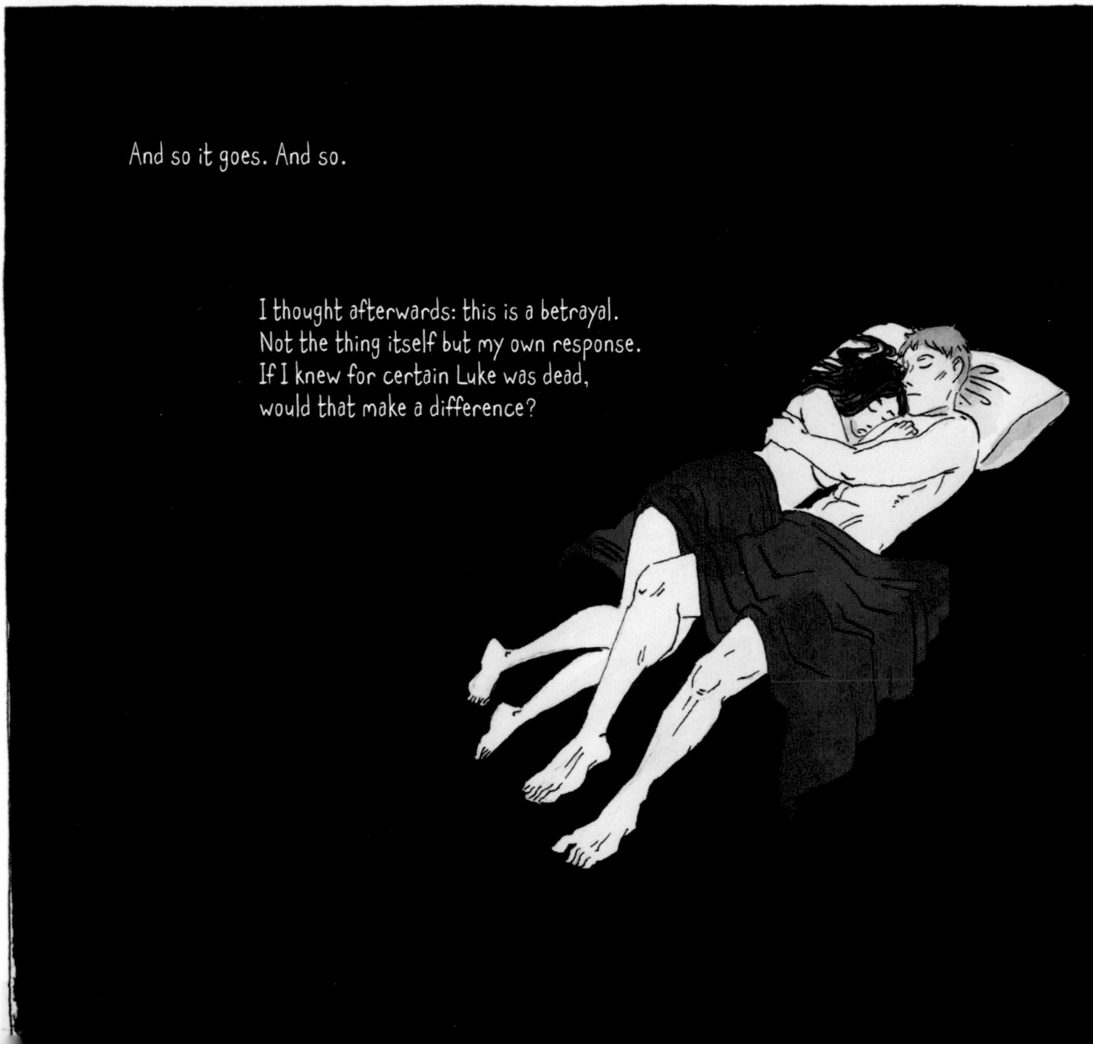
And so it goes. And so.
I thought afterwards: this is a betrayal. Not the thing itself but my own response. If I knew for certain Luke was dead, would that make a difference?

XIV

SALVAGING

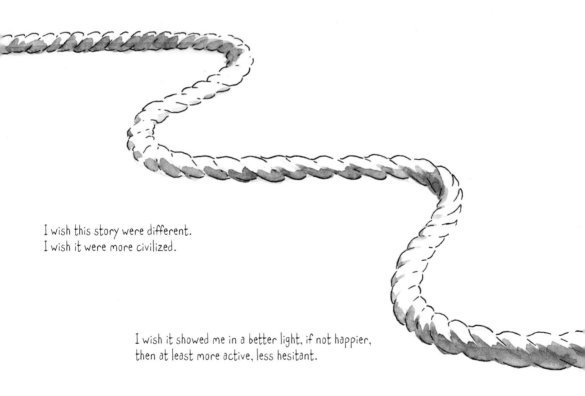

I wish this story were different.
I wish it were more civilized.

I wish it showed me in a better light, if not happier,
then at least more active, less hesitant.

I wish it had more shape.

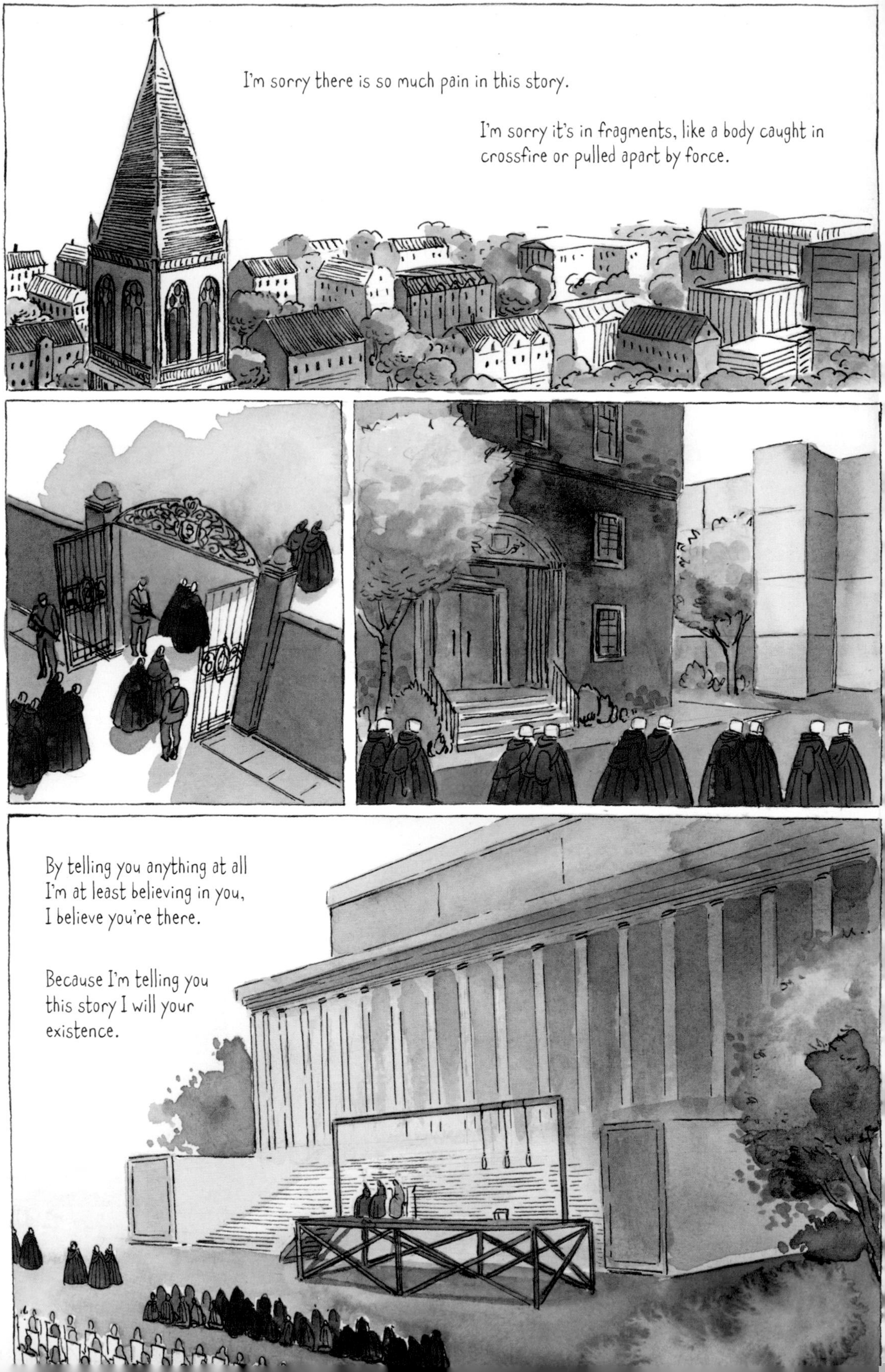
I'm sorry there is so much pain in this story.
I'm sorry it's in fragments, like a body caught in crossfire or pulled apart by force.
By telling you anything at all I'm at least believing in you, I believe you're there.
Because I'm telling you this story I will your existence.

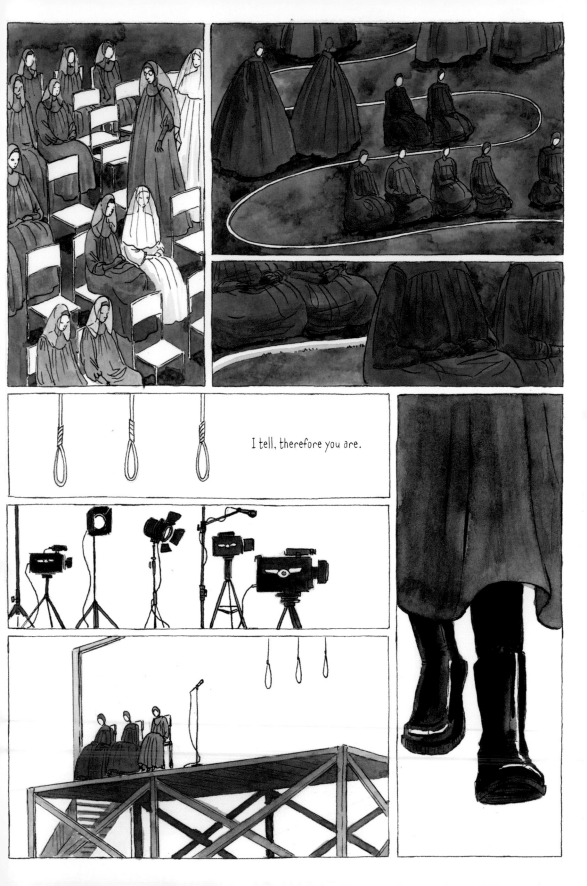

I tell, therefore you are.

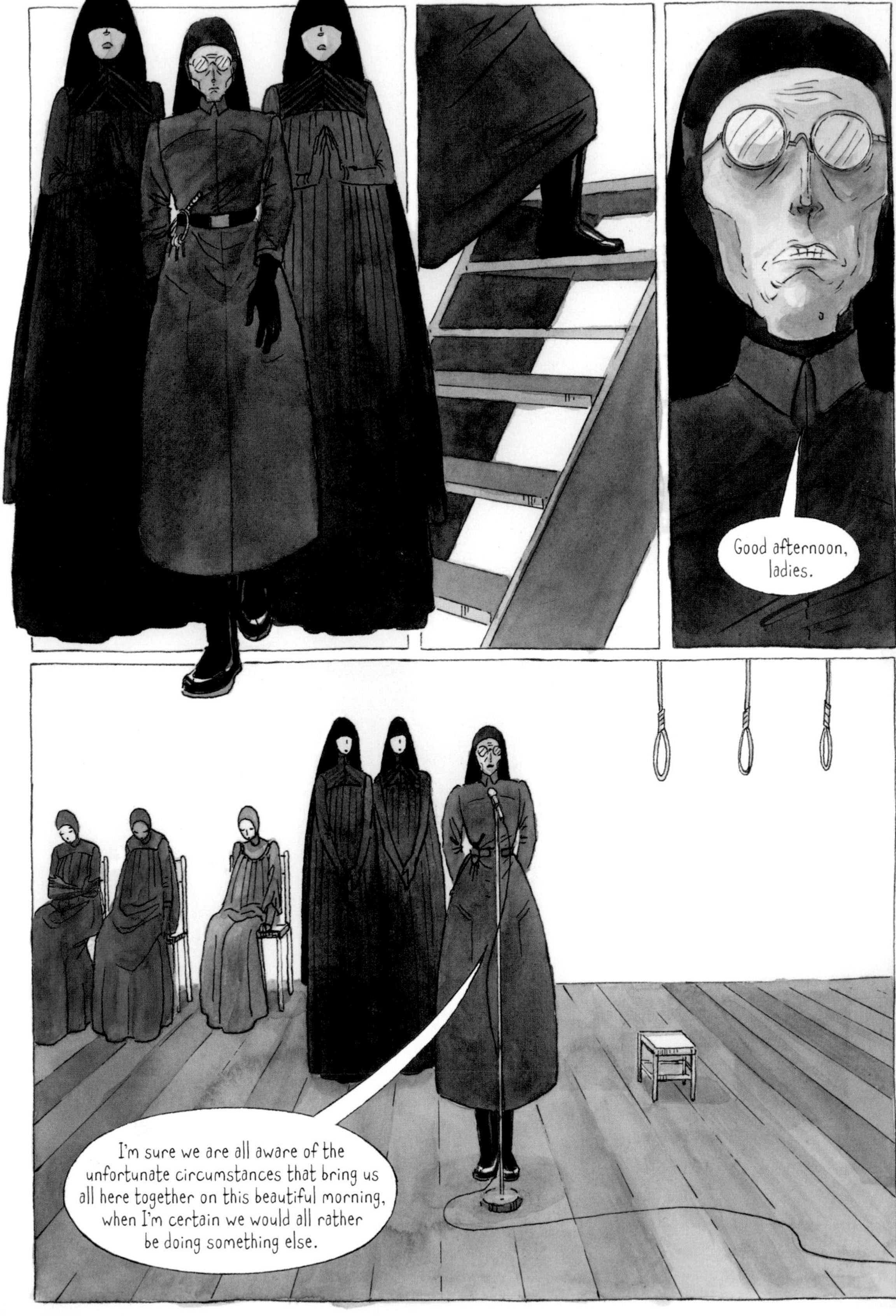
Good afternoon, ladies.
I'm sure we are all aware of the unfortunate circumstances that bring us all here together on this beautiful morning, when I'm certain we would all rather be doing something else.

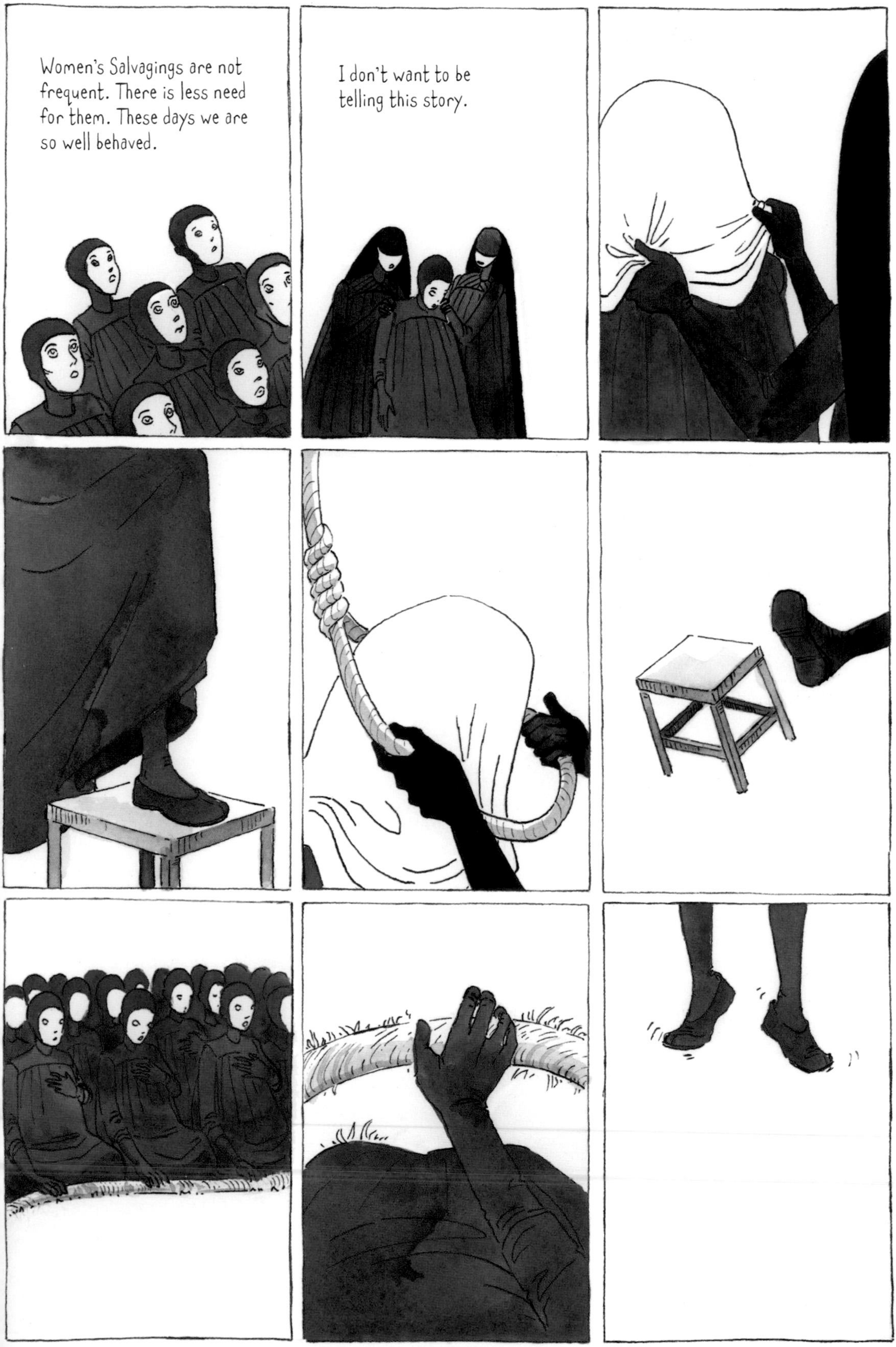
Women's Salvagings are not frequent. There is less need for them. These days we are so well behaved.
I don't want to be telling this story.

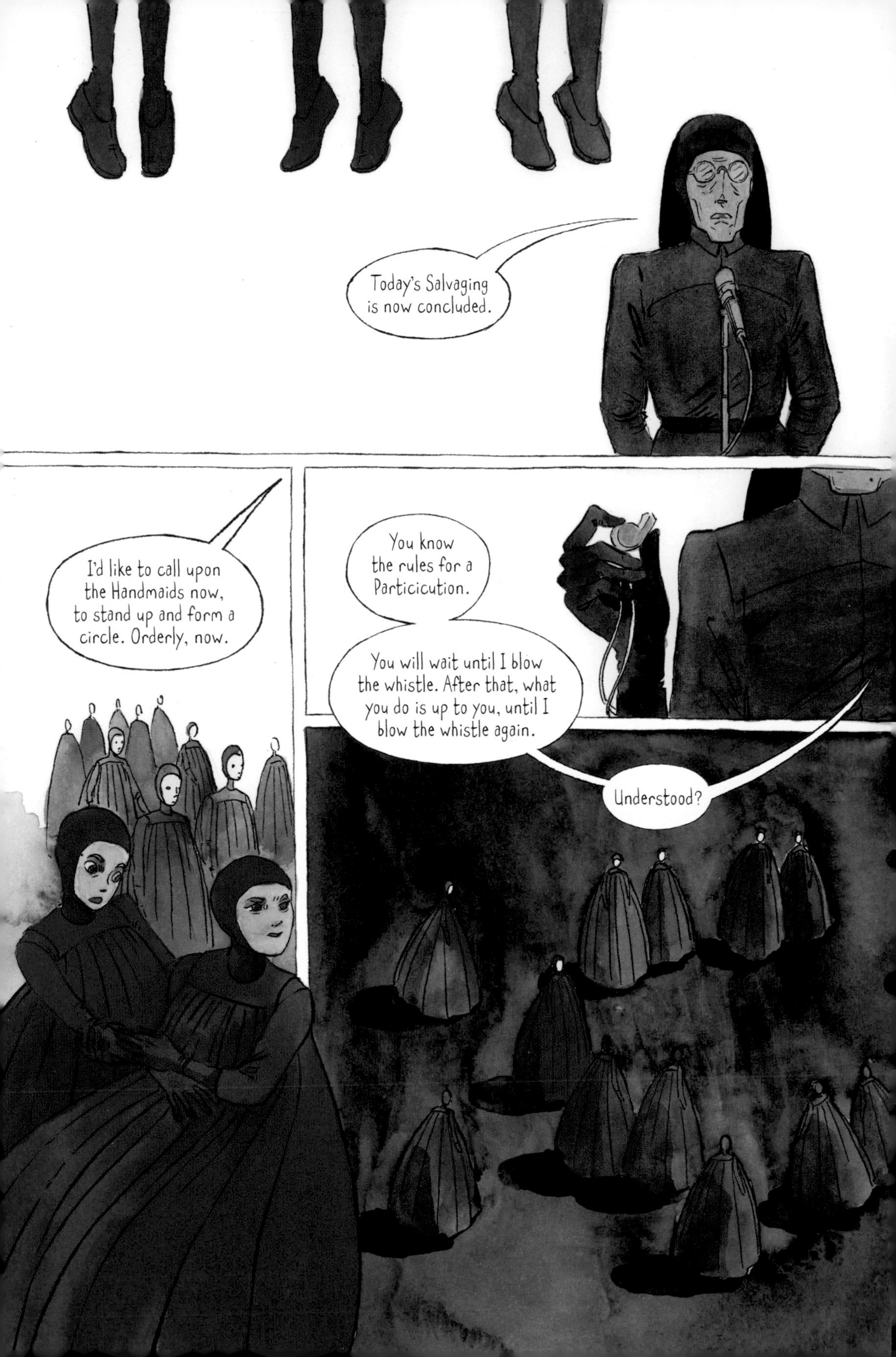
Today's Salvaging is now concluded.
I'd like to call upon the Handmaids now, to stand up and form a circle. Orderly, now.
You know the rules for a Particicution.
You will wait until I blow the whistle. After that, what you do is up to you, until I blow the whistle again.
Understood?

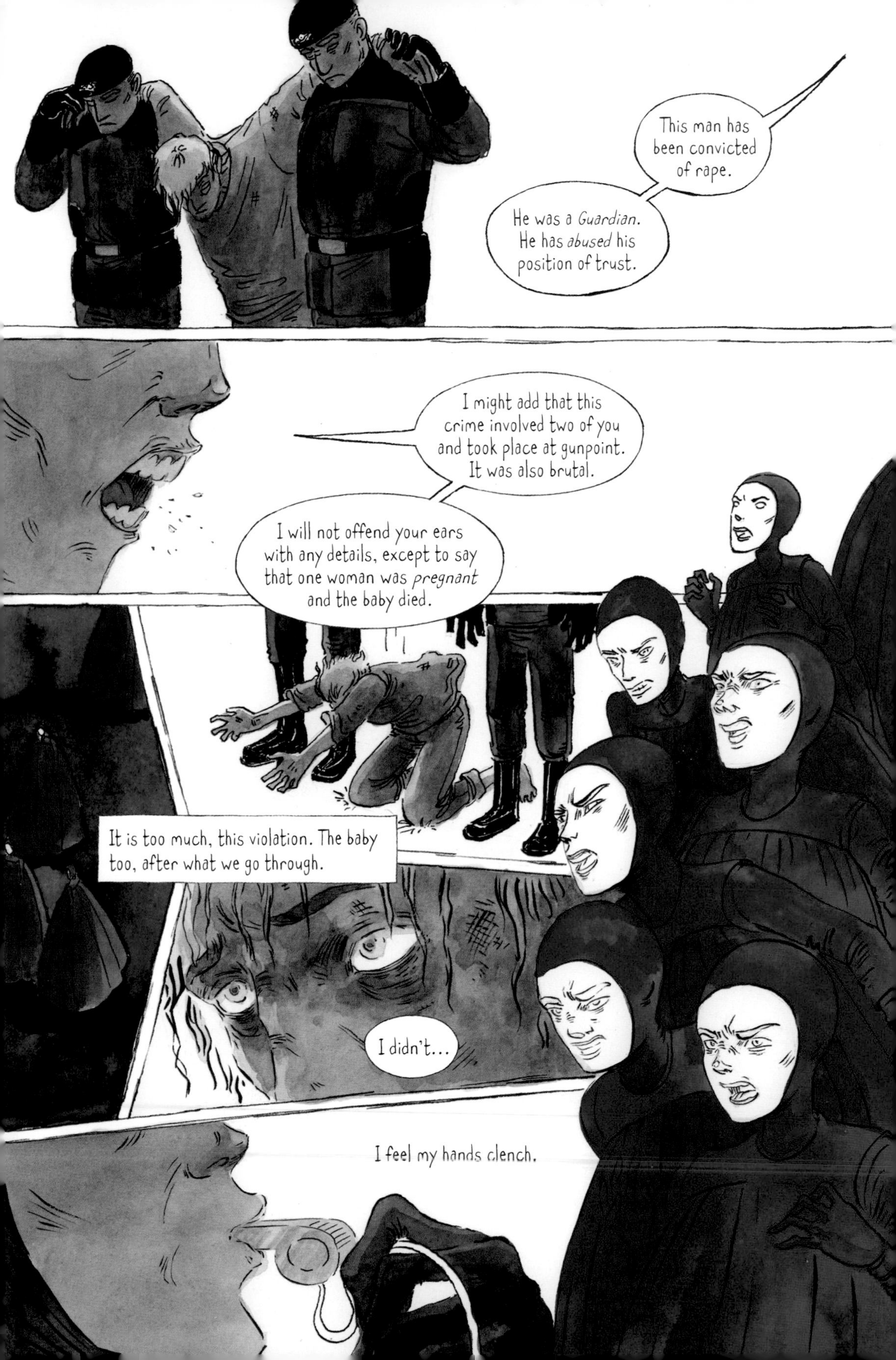
This man has been convicted of rape.
He was a *Guardian*. He has *abused* his position of trust.
I might add that this crime involved two of you and took place at gunpoint. It was also brutal.
I will not offend your ears with any details, except to say that one woman was *pregnant* and the baby died.
It is too much, this violation. The baby too, after what we go through.
I didn't...
I feel my hands clench.

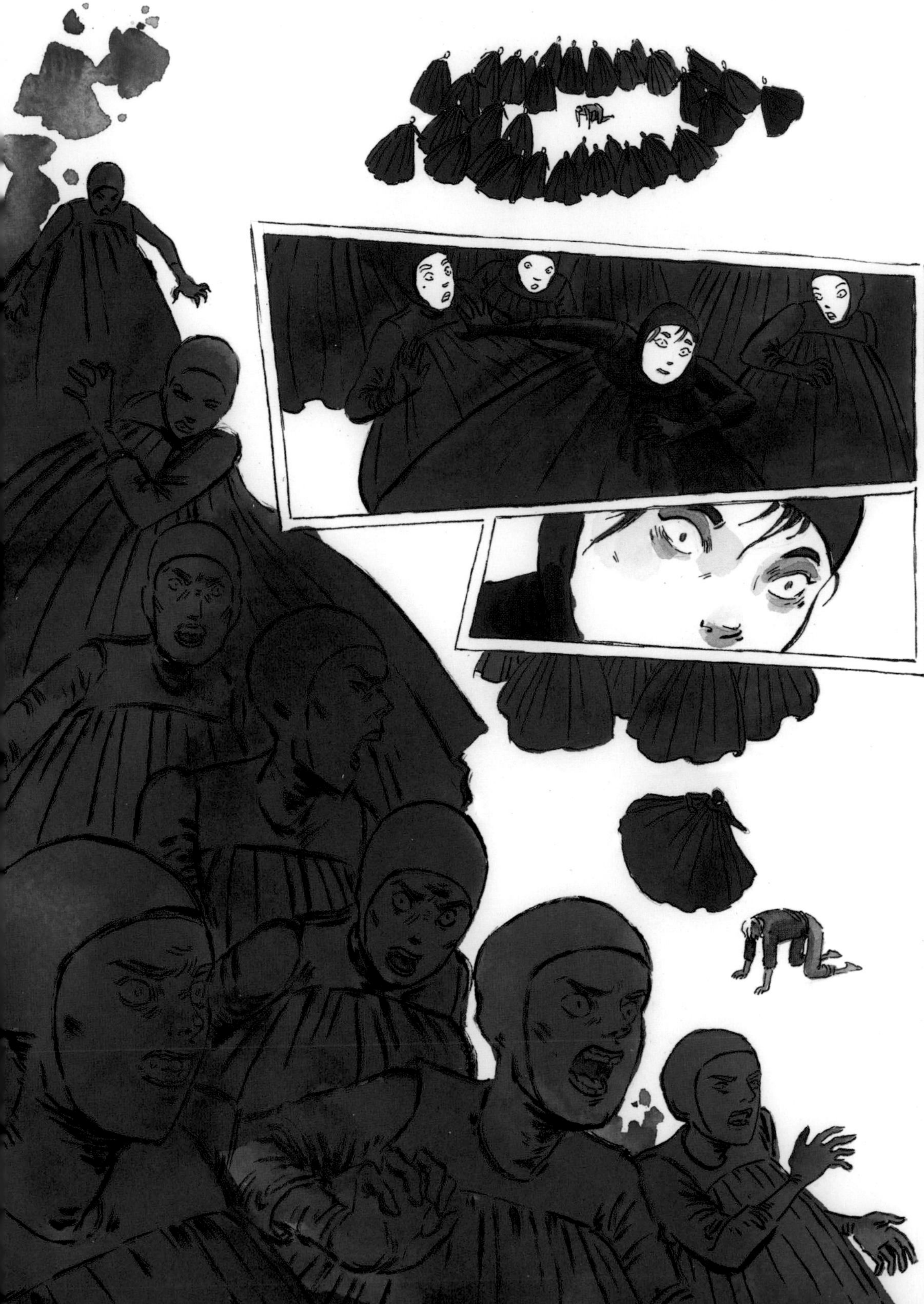

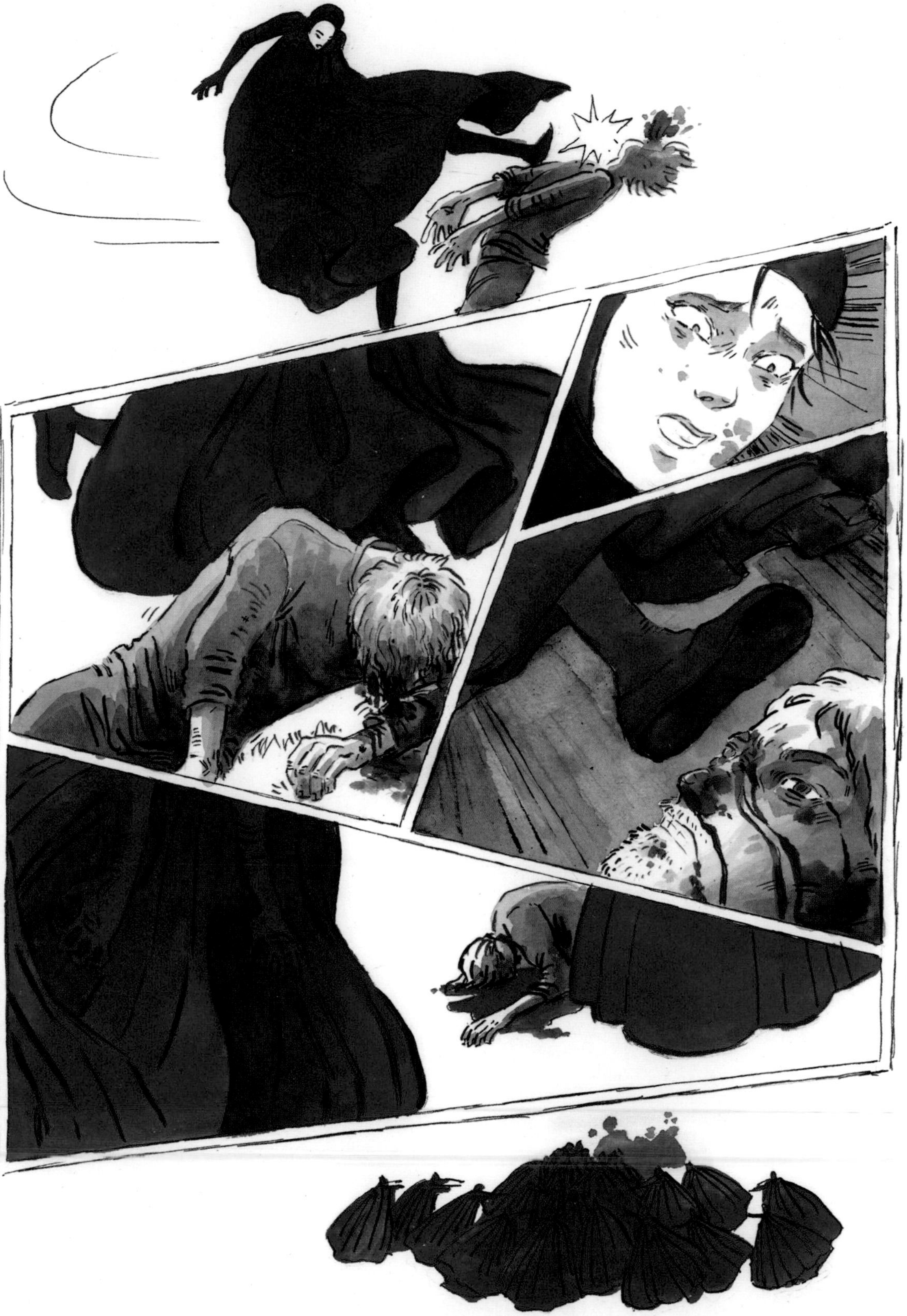

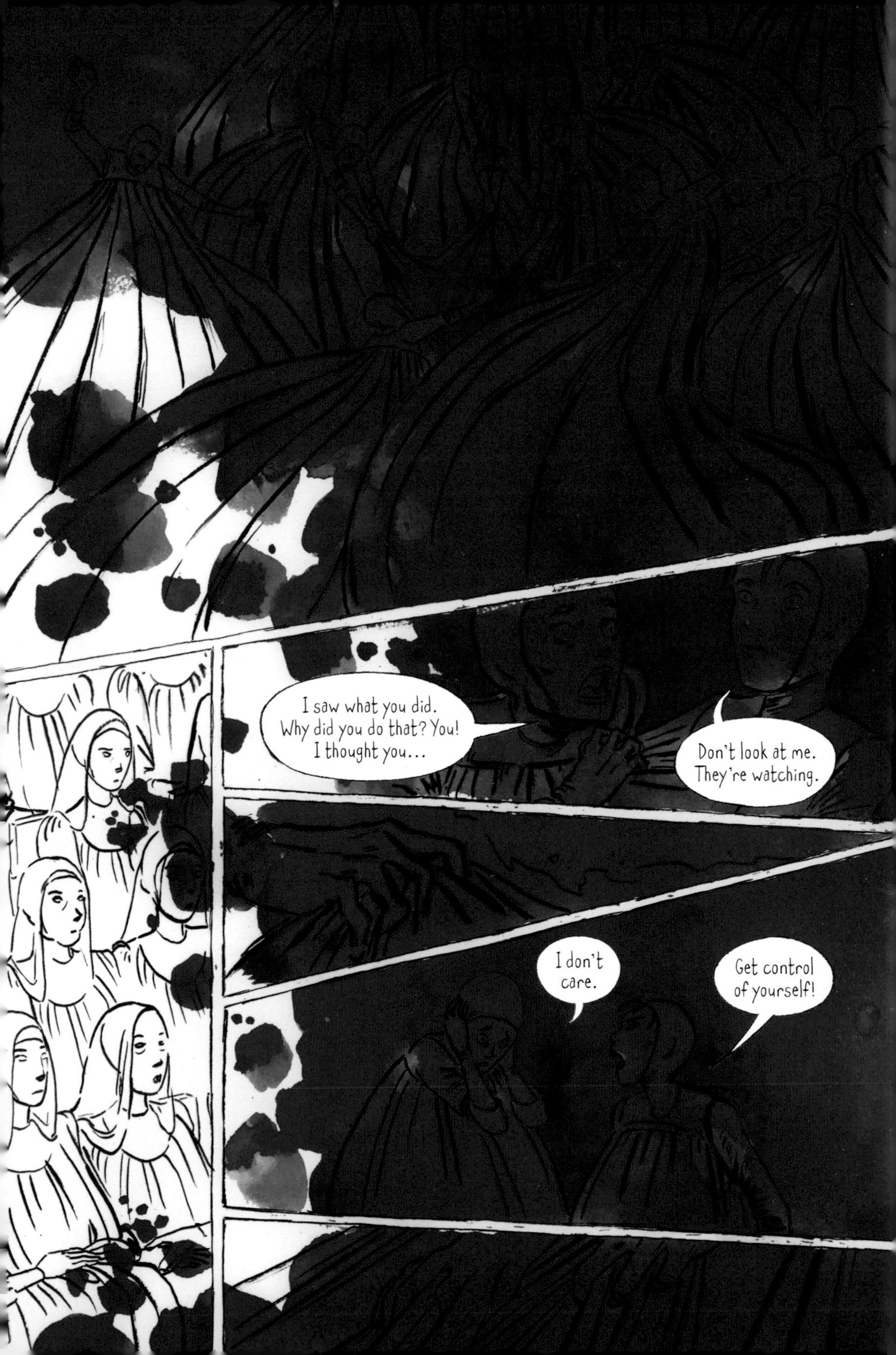
I saw what you did.
Why did you do that? You!
I thought you...
Don't look at me.
They're watching.
I don't care.
Get control of yourself!

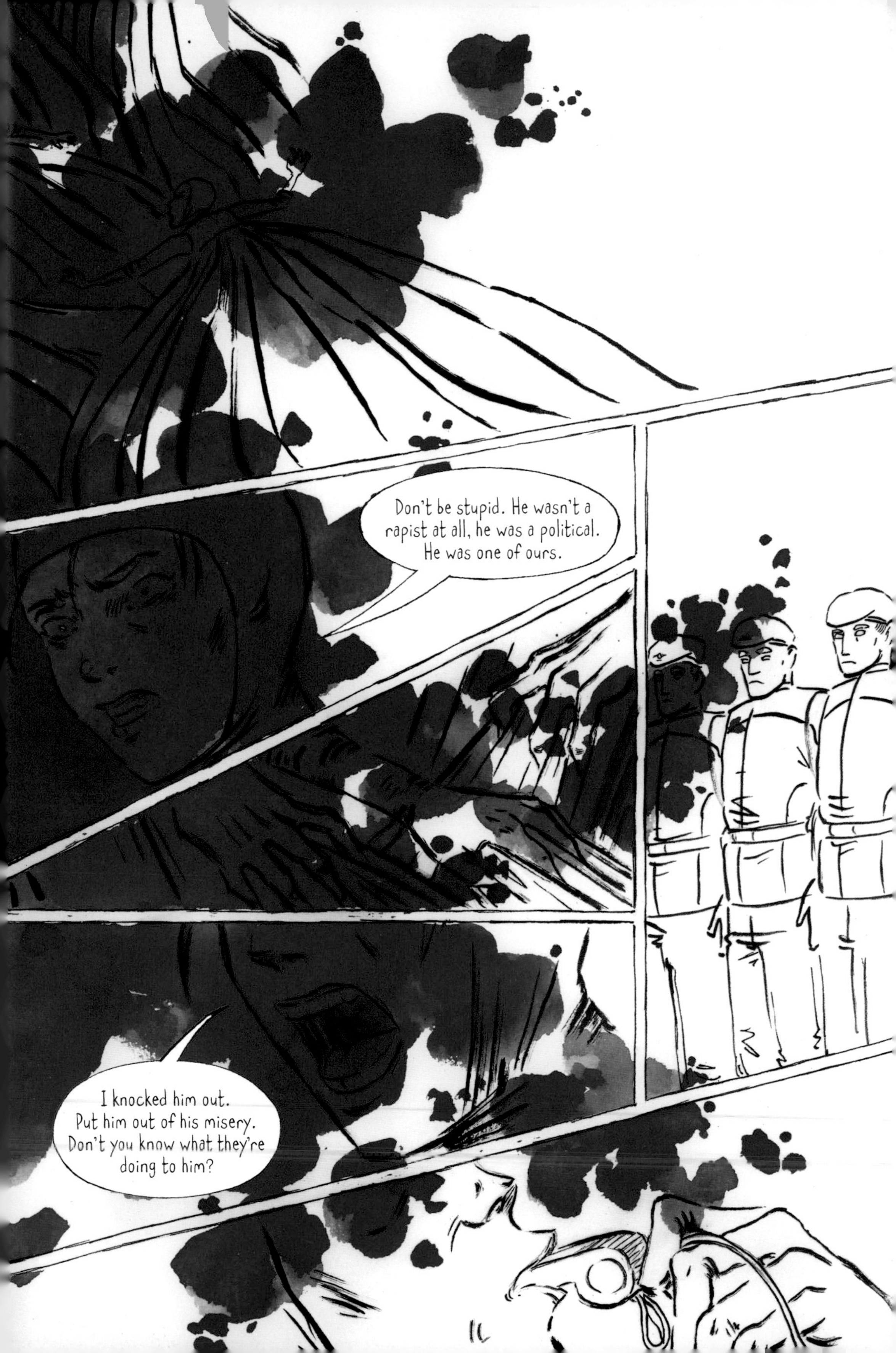
Don't be stupid. He wasn't a rapist at all, he was a political. He was one of ours.
I knocked him out. Put him out of his misery. Don't you know what they're doing to him?

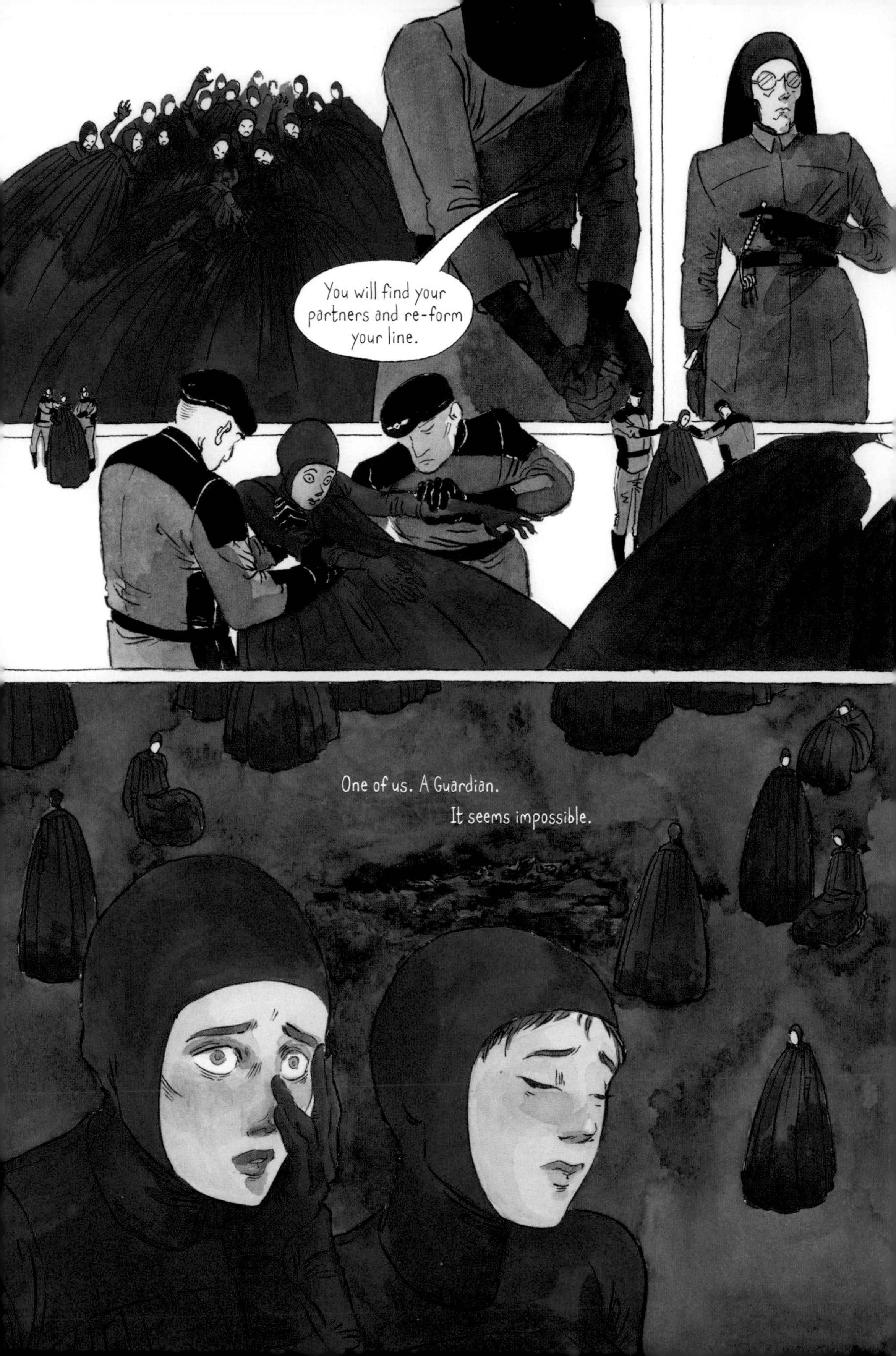
You will find your partners and re-form your line.
One of us. A Guardian.
It seems impossible.

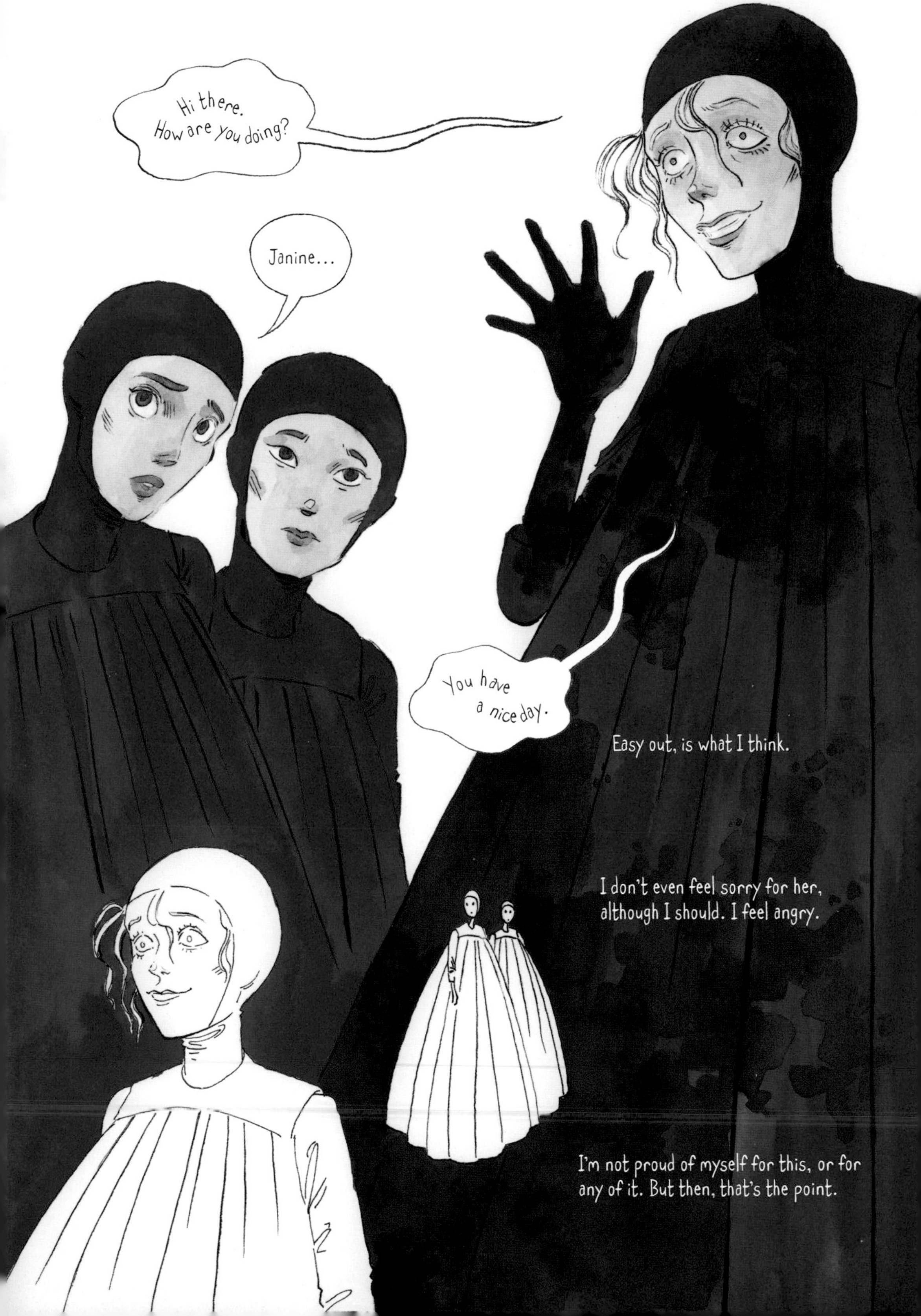
Hi there.
How are you doing?
Janine...
You have a nice day.
Easy out, is what I think.
I don't even feel sorry for her, although I should. I feel angry.
I'm not proud of myself for this, or for any of it. But then, that's the point.

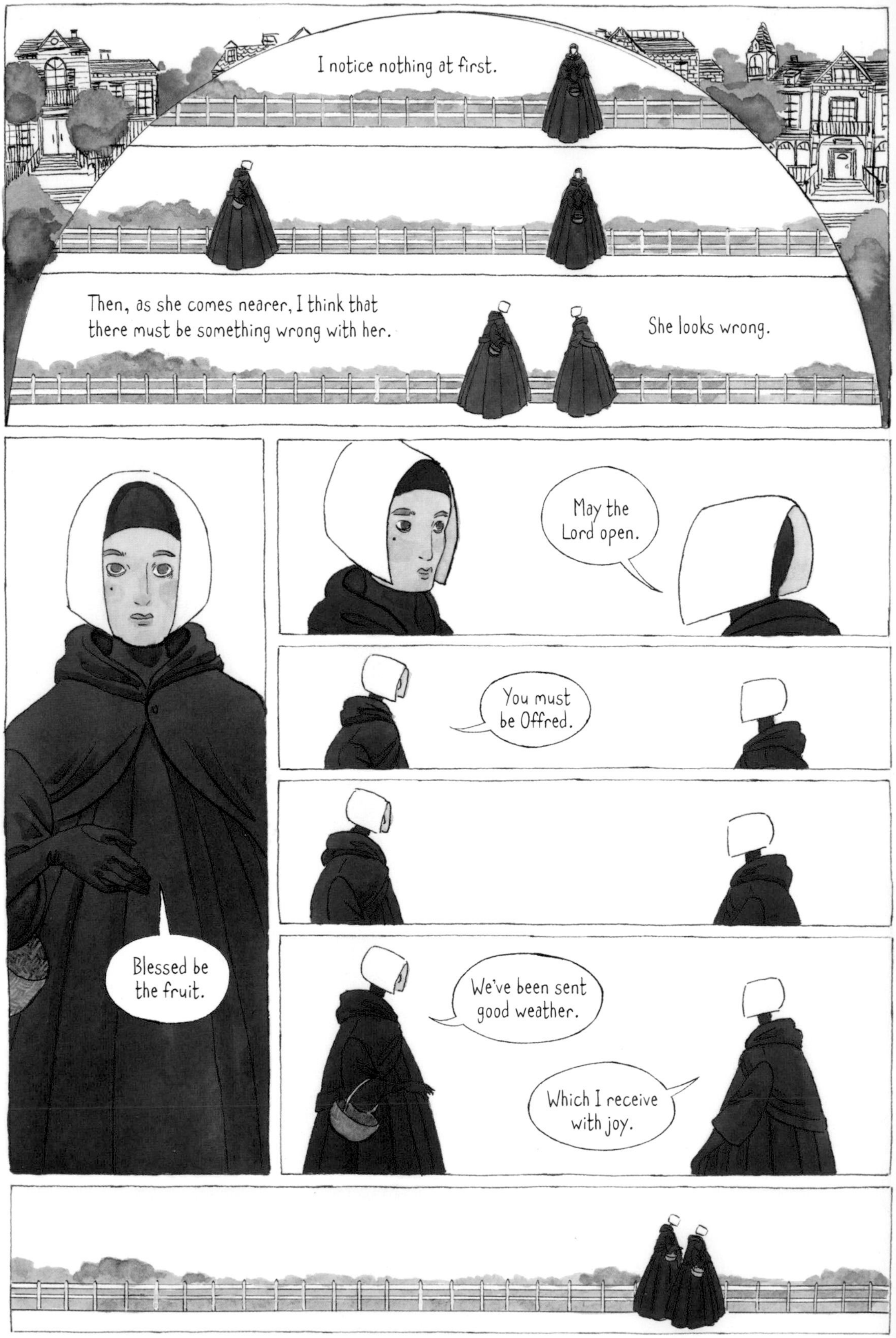

I notice nothing at first.
Then, as she comes nearer, I think that there must be something wrong with her.
She looks wrong.
Blessed be the fruit.
May the Lord open.
You must be Offred.
We've been sent good weather.
Which I receive with joy.

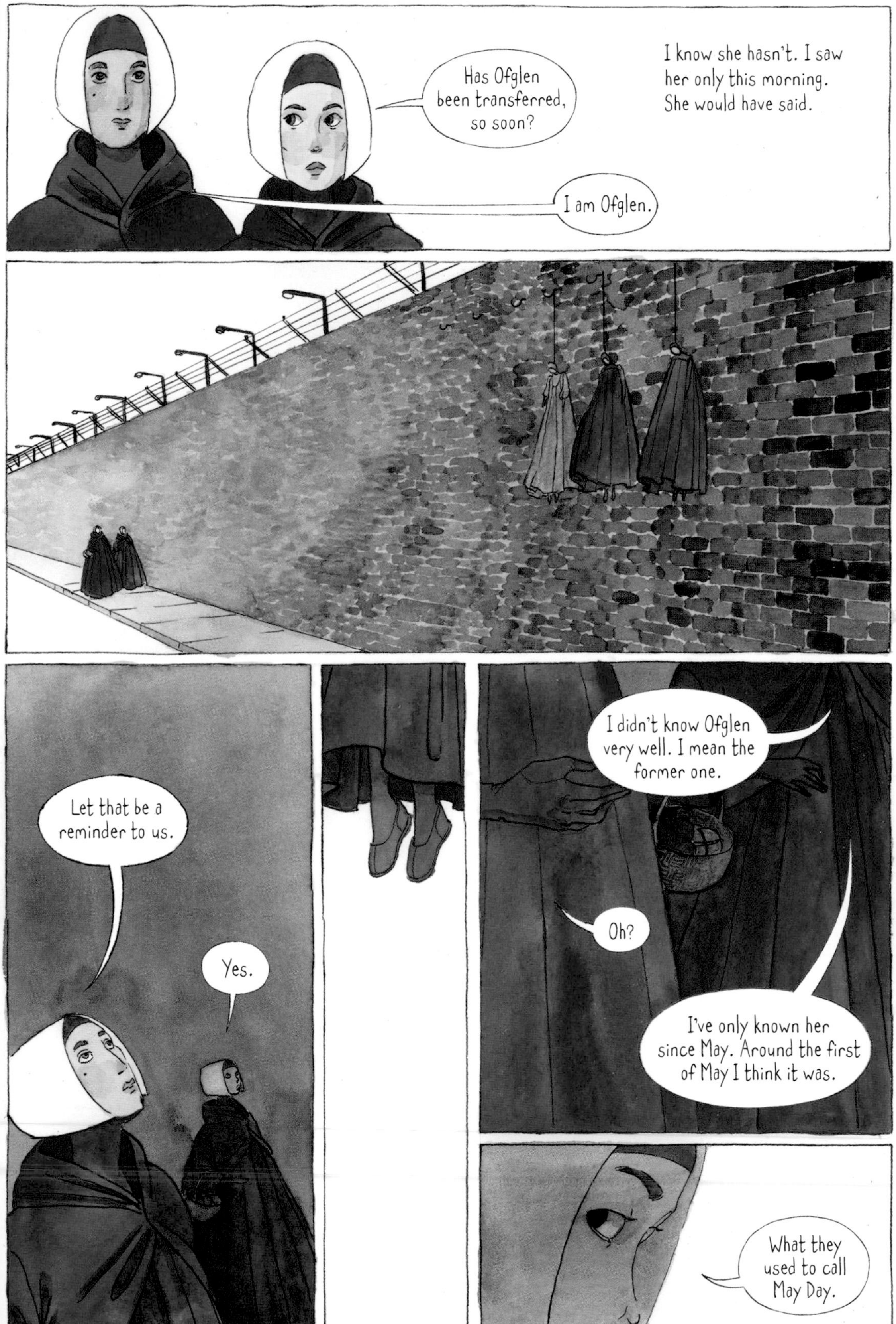
Has Ofglen been transferred, so soon?
I am Ofglen.
I know she hasn't. I saw her only this morning. She would have said.
Let that be a reminder to us.
Yes.
I didn't know Ofglen very well. I mean the former one.
Oh?
I've only known her since May. Around the first of May I think it was.
What they used to call May Day.

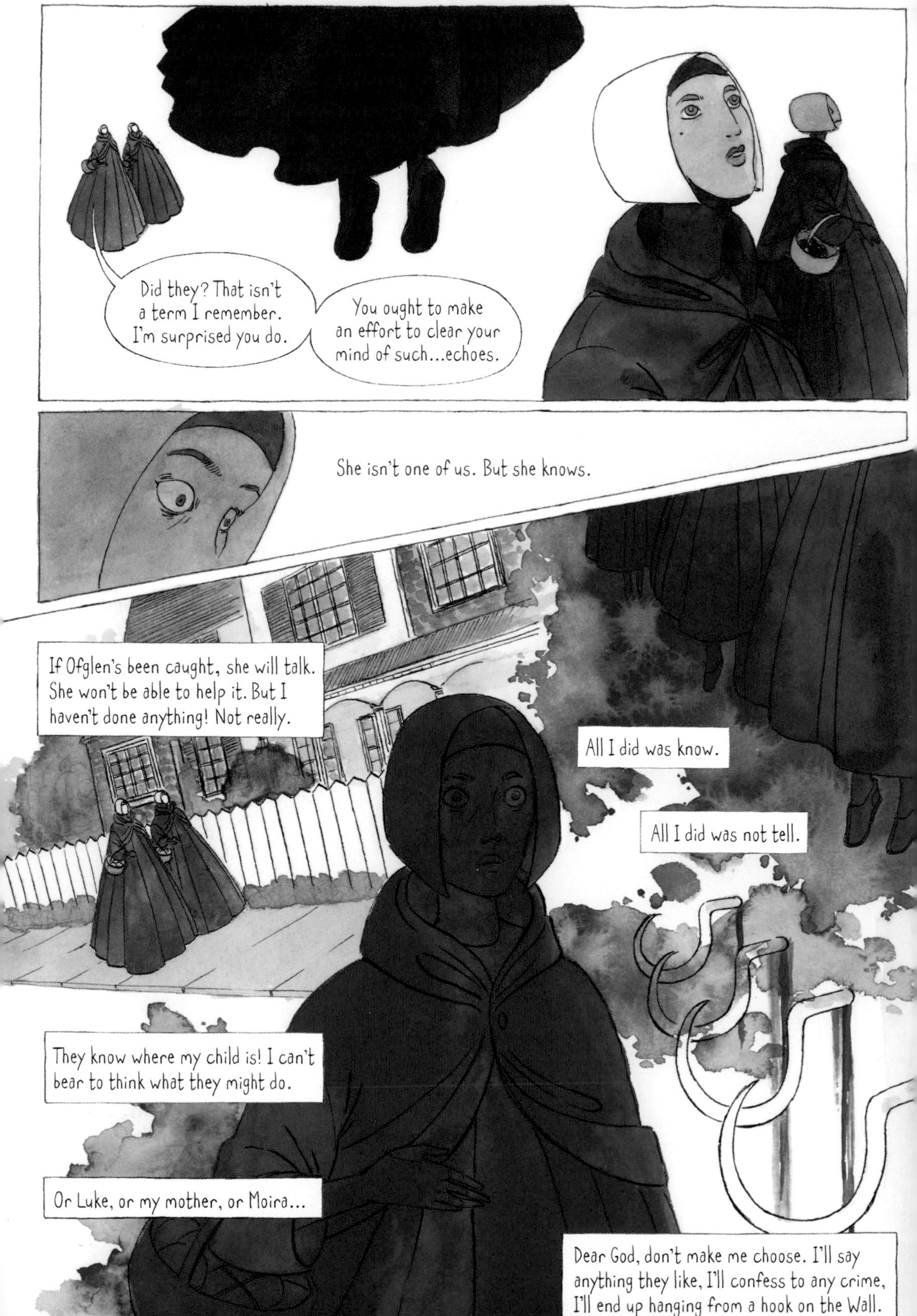
Did they? That isn't a term I remember. I'm surprised you do.
You ought to make an effort to clear your mind of such...echoes.
She isn't one of us. But she knows.
If Ofglen's been caught, she will talk. She won't be able to help it. But I haven't done anything! Not really.
All I did was know.
All I did was not tell.
They know where my child is! I can't bear to think what they might do.
Or Luke, or my mother, or Moira...
Dear God, don't make me choose. I'll say anything they like, I'll confess to any crime, I'll end up hanging from a hook on the Wall.

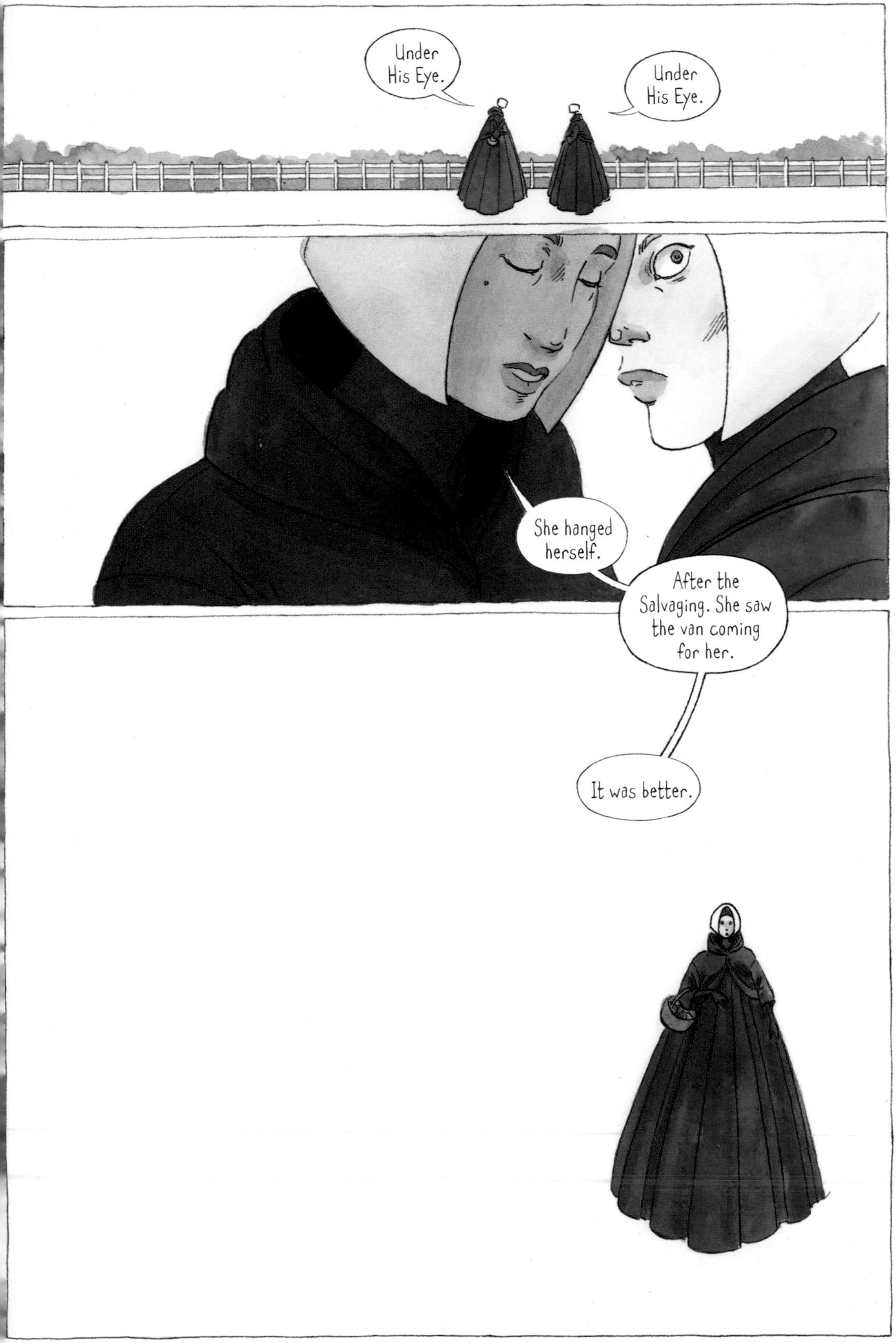
Under His Eye.
Under His Eye.
She hanged herself.
After the Salvaging. She saw the van coming for her.
It was better.

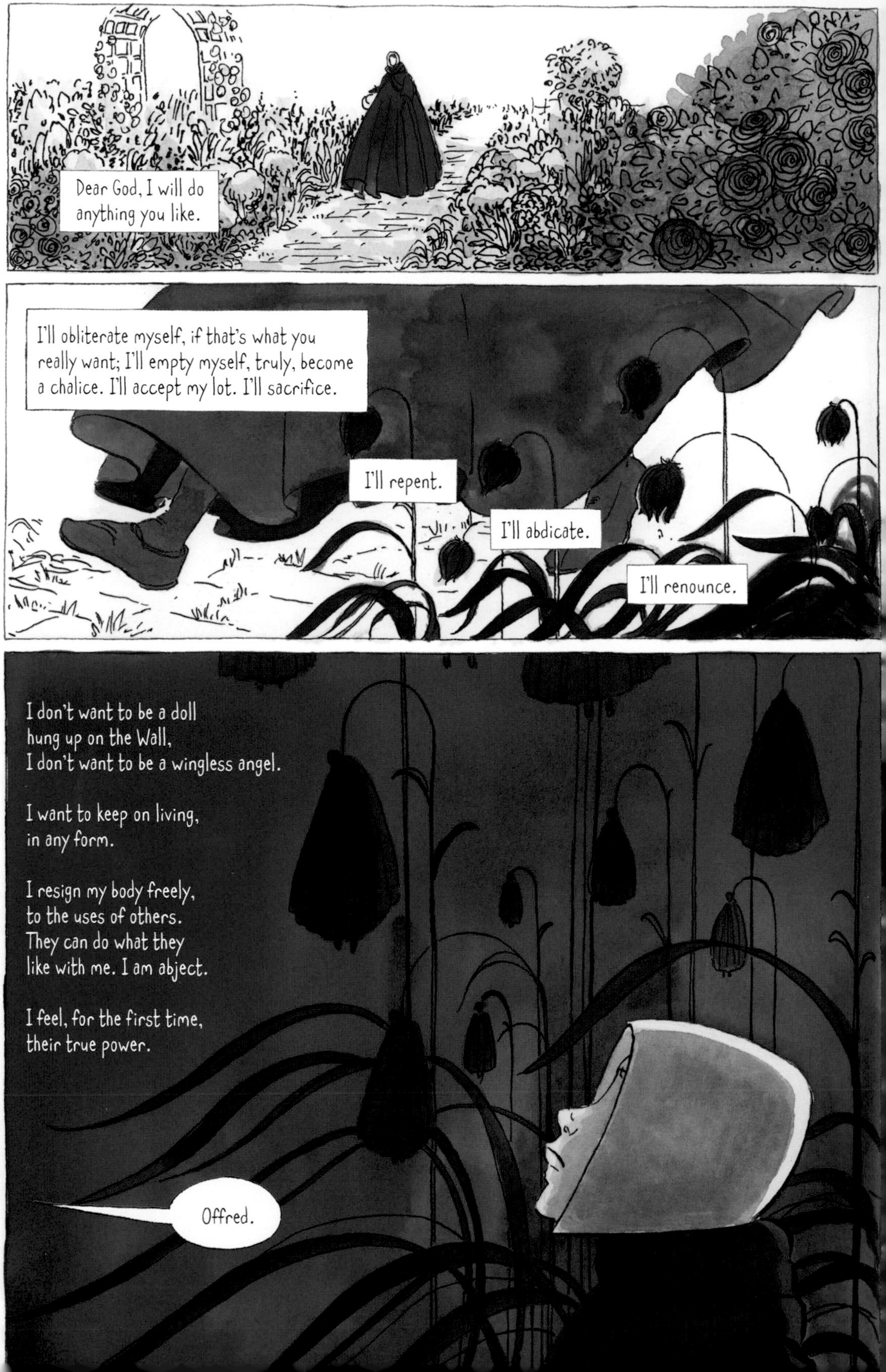
Dear God, I will do anything you like.
I'll obliterate myself, if that's what you really want; I'll empty myself, truly, become a chalice. I'll accept my lot. I'll sacrifice.
I'll repent.
I'll abdicate.
I'll renounce.
I don't want to be a doll hung up on the Wall, I don't want to be a wingless angel.
I want to keep on living, in any form.
I resign my body freely, to the uses of others. They can do what they like with me. I am abject.
I feel, for the first time, their true power.
Offred.

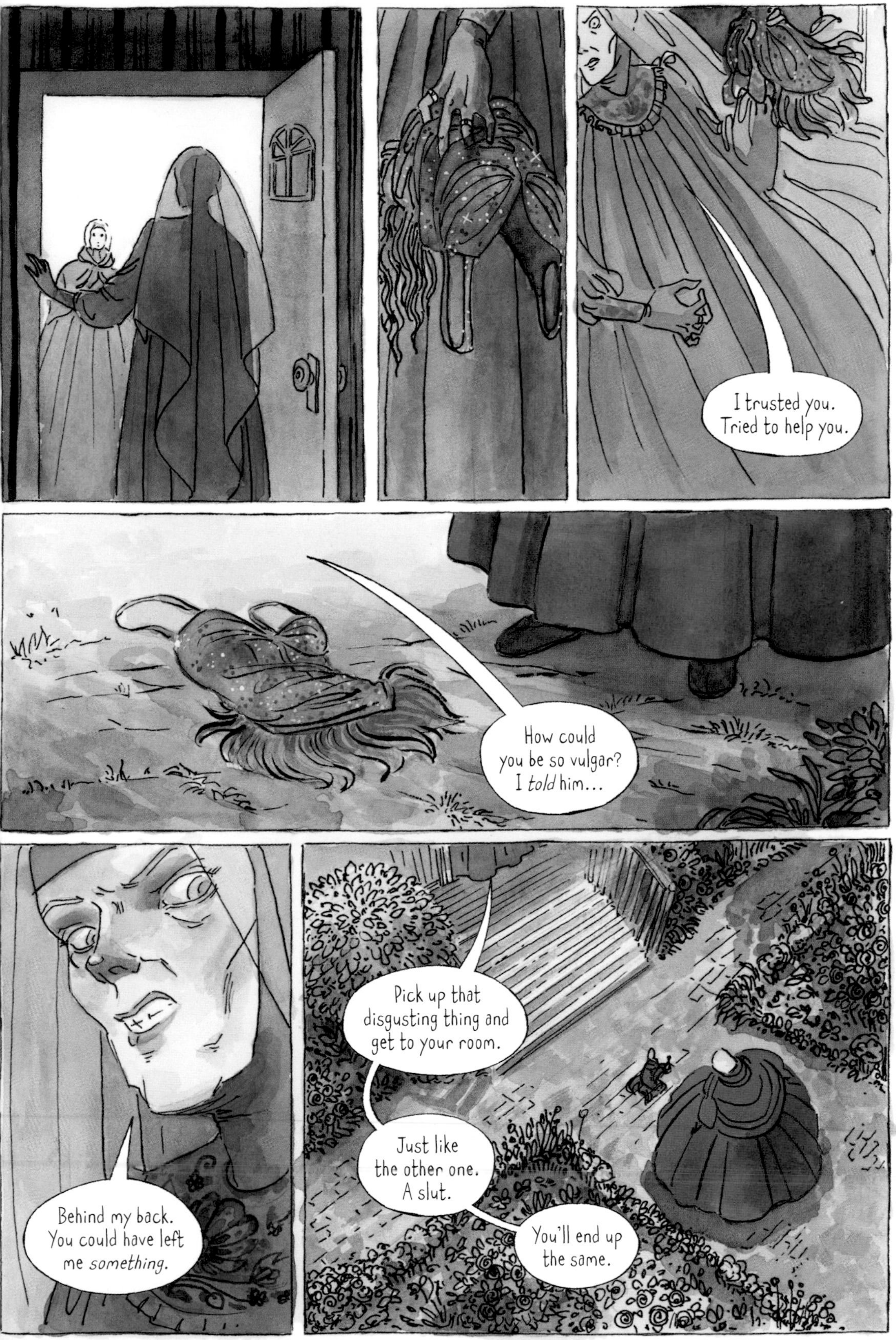
I trusted you.
Tried to help you.
How could you be so vulgar? I *told* him...
Behind my back. You could have left me *something*.
Pick up that disgusting thing and get to your room.
Just like the other one. A slut.
You'll end up the same.

XV
—
NIGHT

This could be the last time I have to wait.
But I don't know what I'm waiting for.

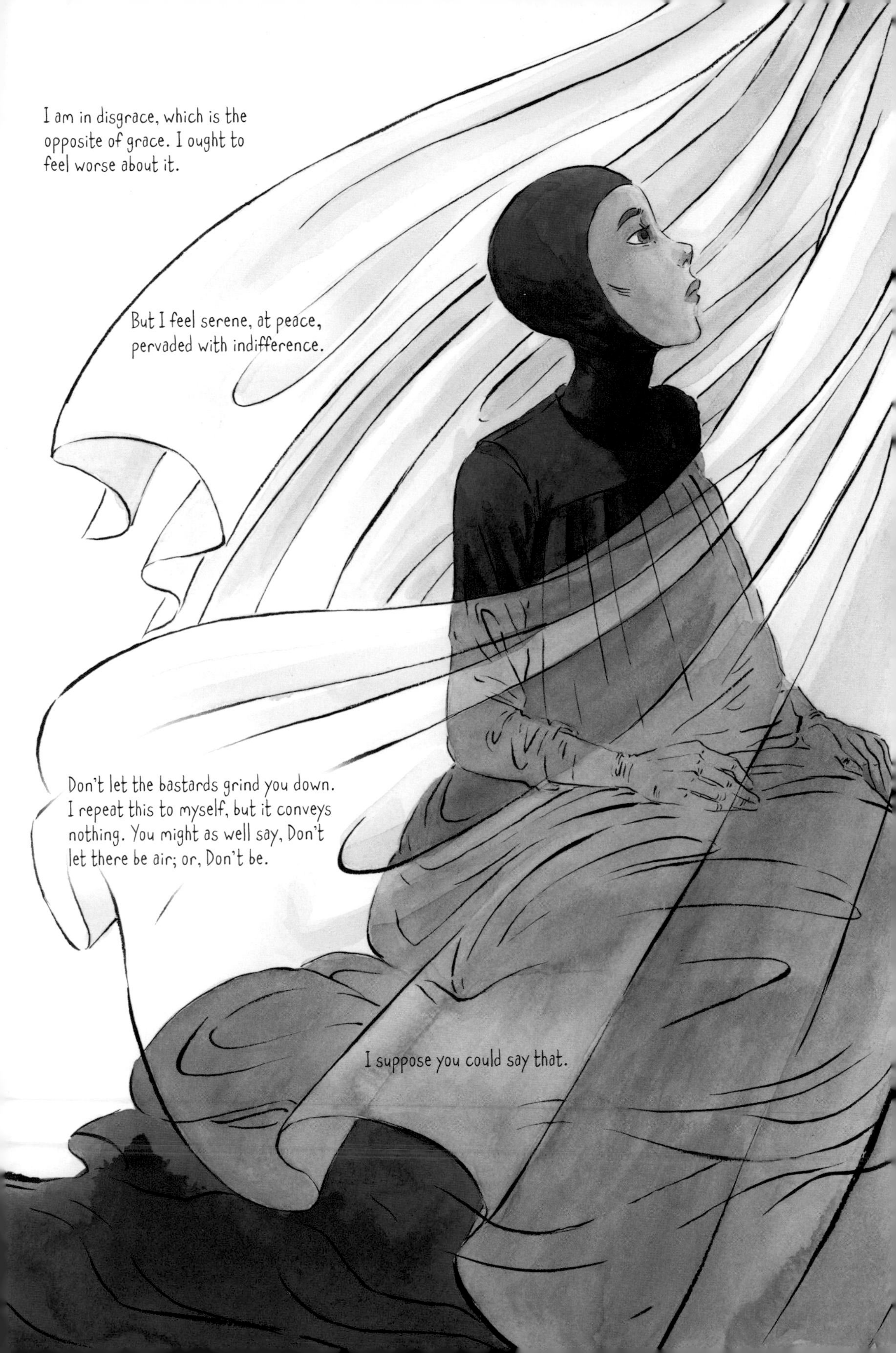
I am in disgrace, which is the opposite of grace. I ought to feel worse about it.
But I feel serene, at peace, pervaded with indifference.
Don't let the bastards grind you down. I repeat this to myself, but it conveys nothing. You might as well say, Don't let there be air; or, Don't be.
I suppose you could say that.

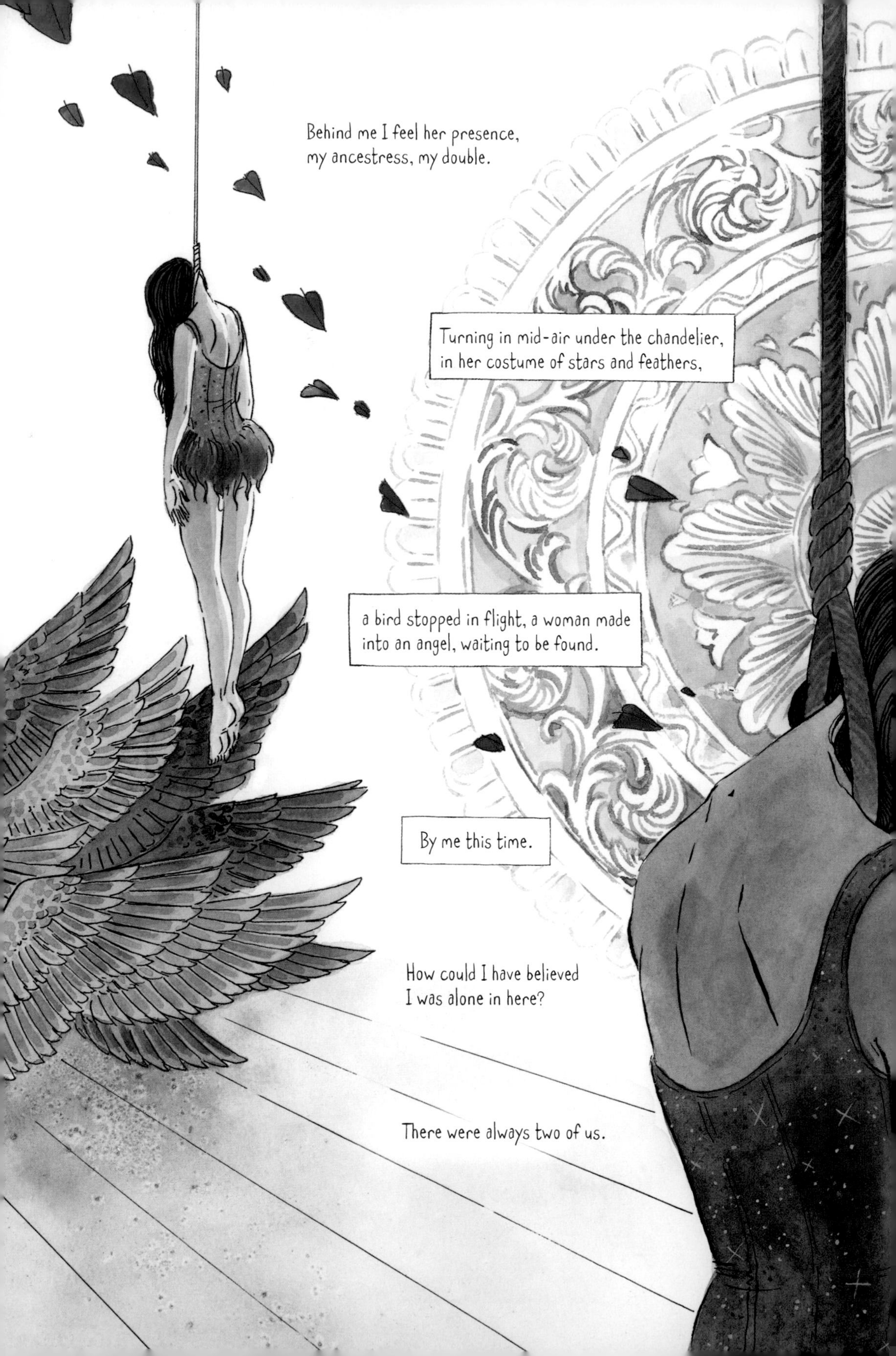
Behind me I feel her presence, my ancestress, my double.
Turning in mid-air under the chandelier, in her costume of stars and feathers,
a bird stopped in flight, a woman made into an angel, waiting to be found.
By me this time.
How could I have believed I was alone in here?
There were always two of us.

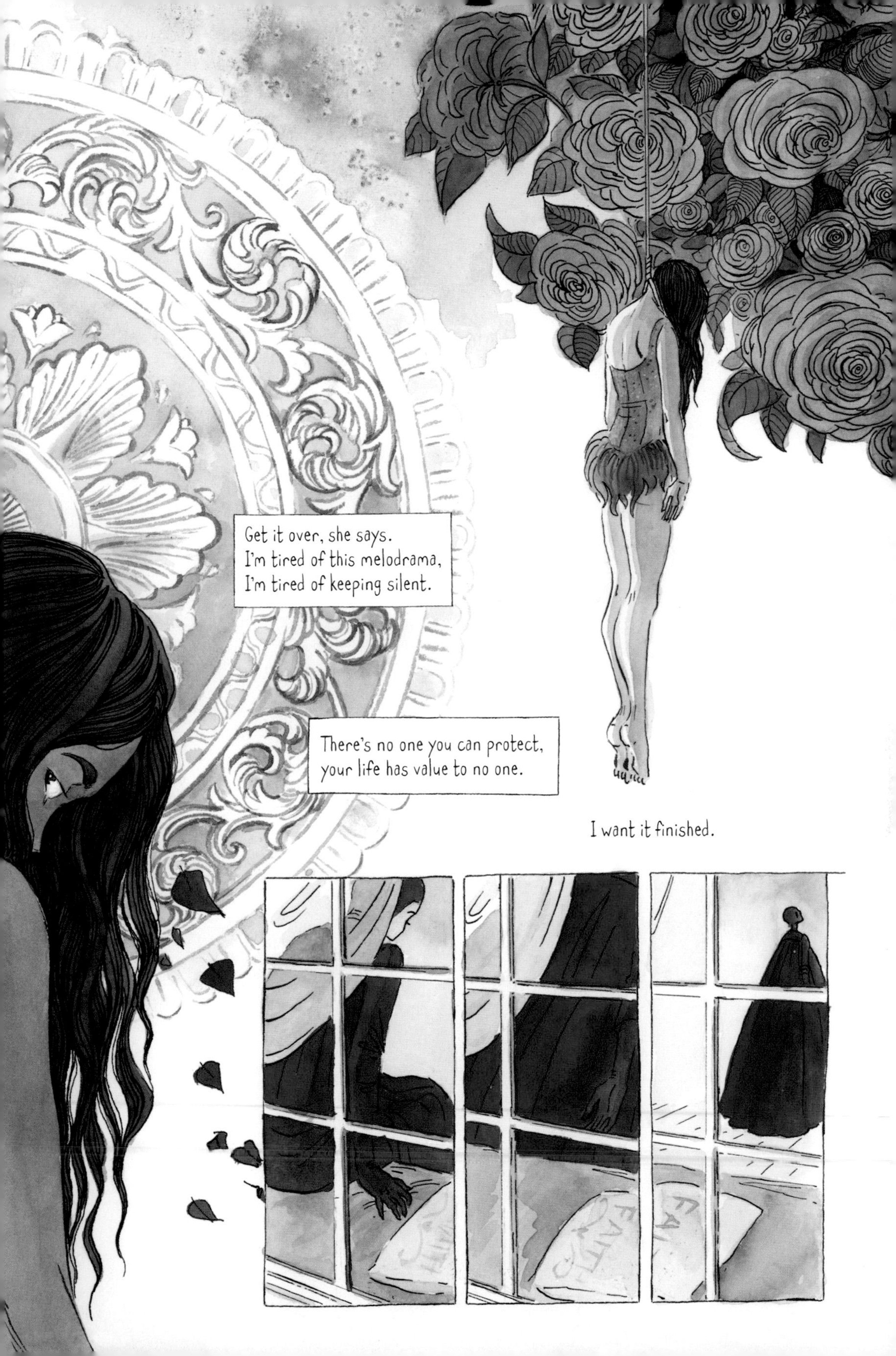
Get it over, she says.
I'm tired of this melodrama,
I'm tired of keeping silent.
There's no one you can protect,
your life has value to no one.
I want it finished.

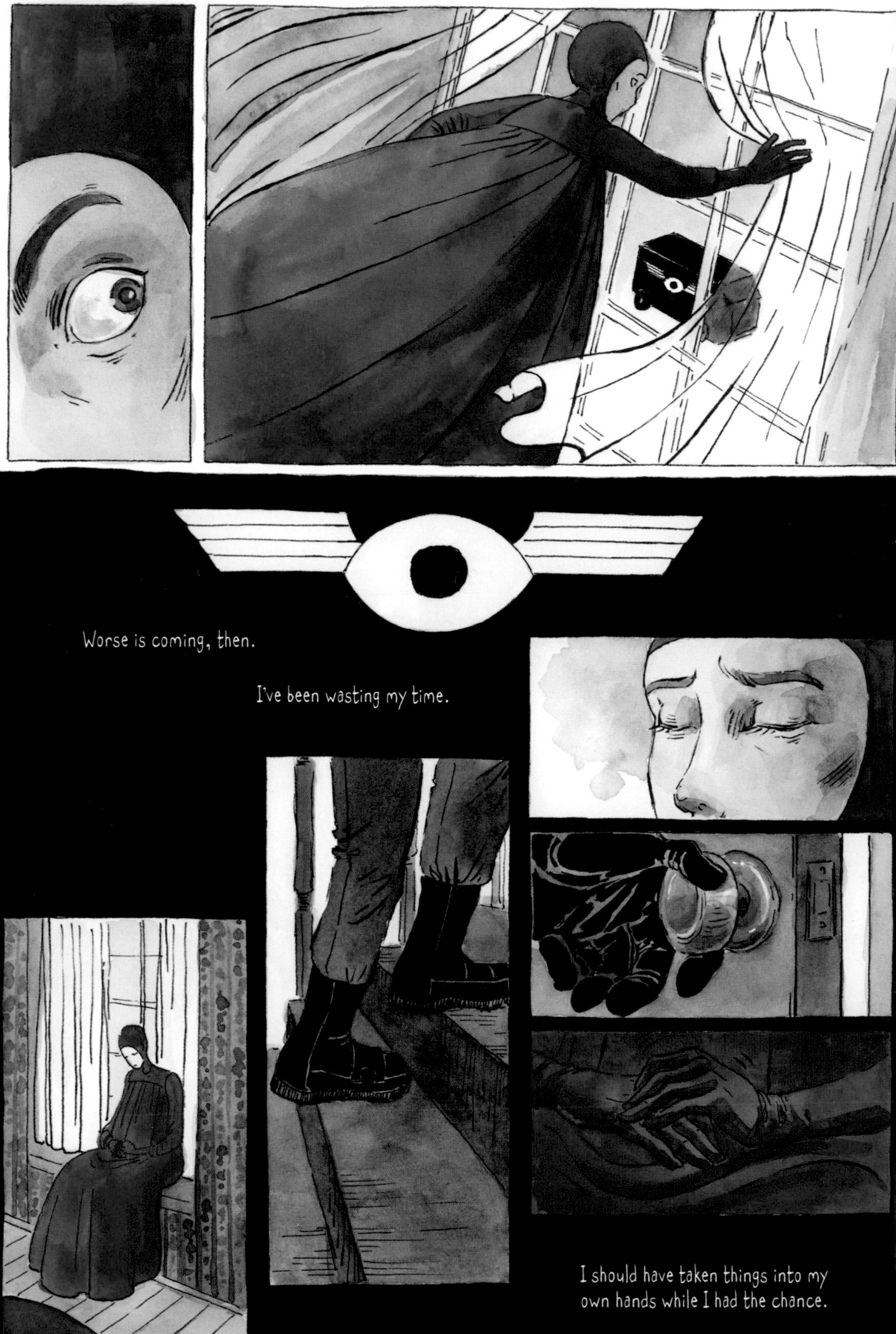
Worse is coming, then.
I've been wasting my time.
I should have taken things into my own hands while I had the chance.

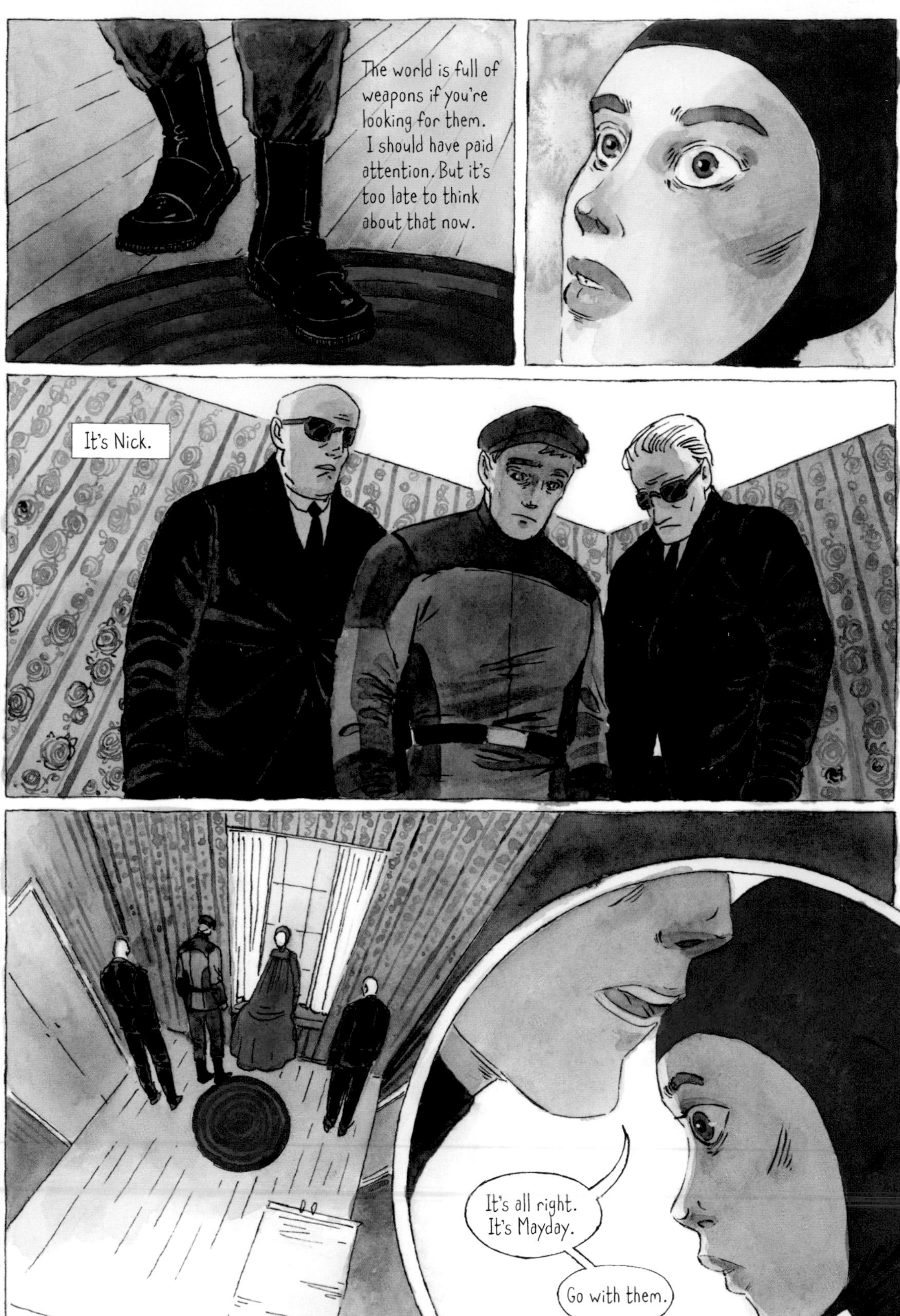
The world is full of weapons if you're looking for them. I should have paid attention. But it's too late to think about that now.
It's Nick.
It's all right. It's Mayday.
Go with them.

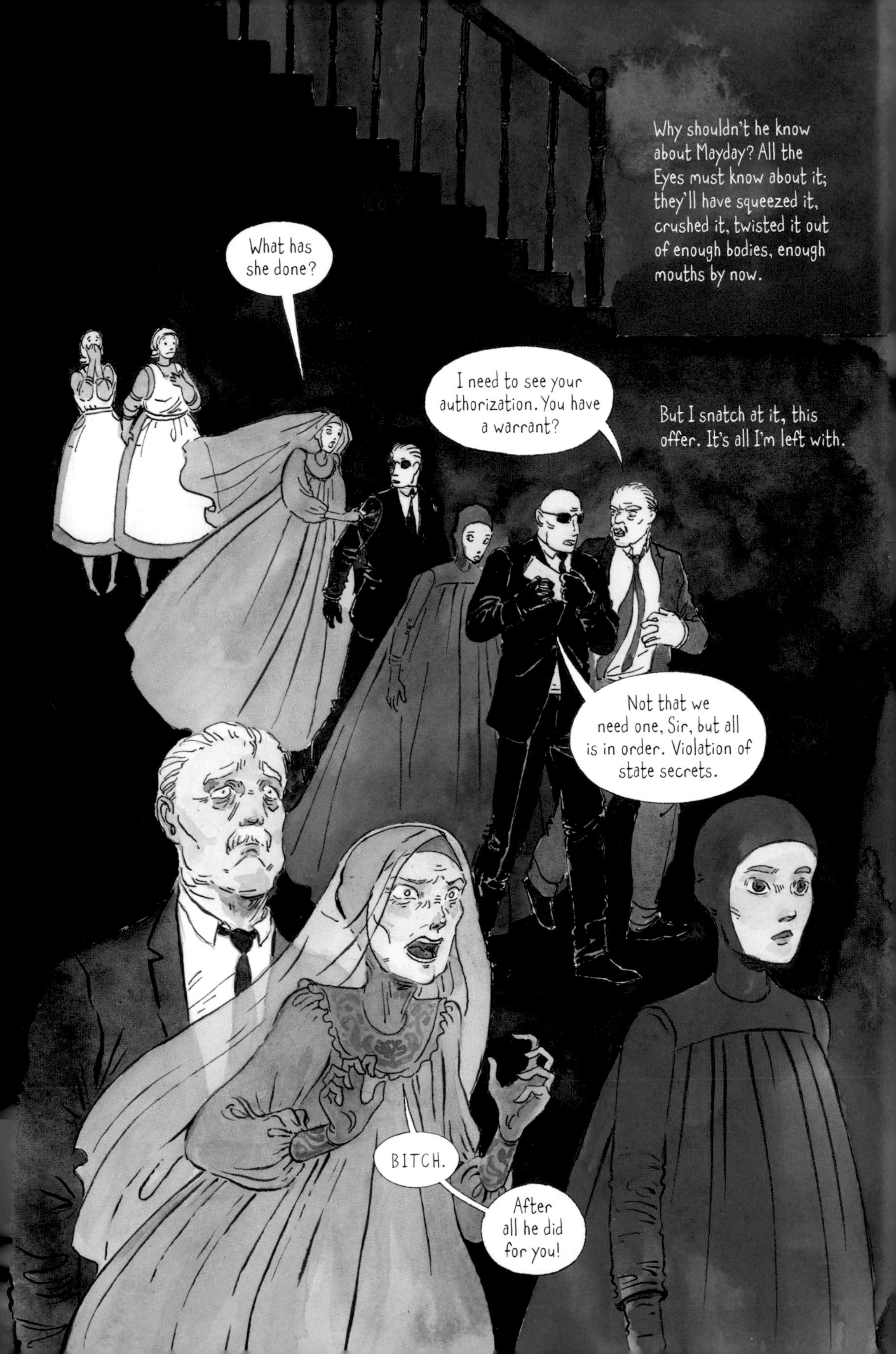
Why shouldn't he know about Mayday? All the Eyes must know about it; they'll have squeezed it, crushed it, twisted it out of enough bodies, enough mouths by now.
What has she done?
I need to see your authorization. You have a warrant?
But I snatch at it, this offer. It's all I'm left with.
Not that we need one, Sir, but all is in order. Violation of state secrets.
BITCH.
After all he did for you!

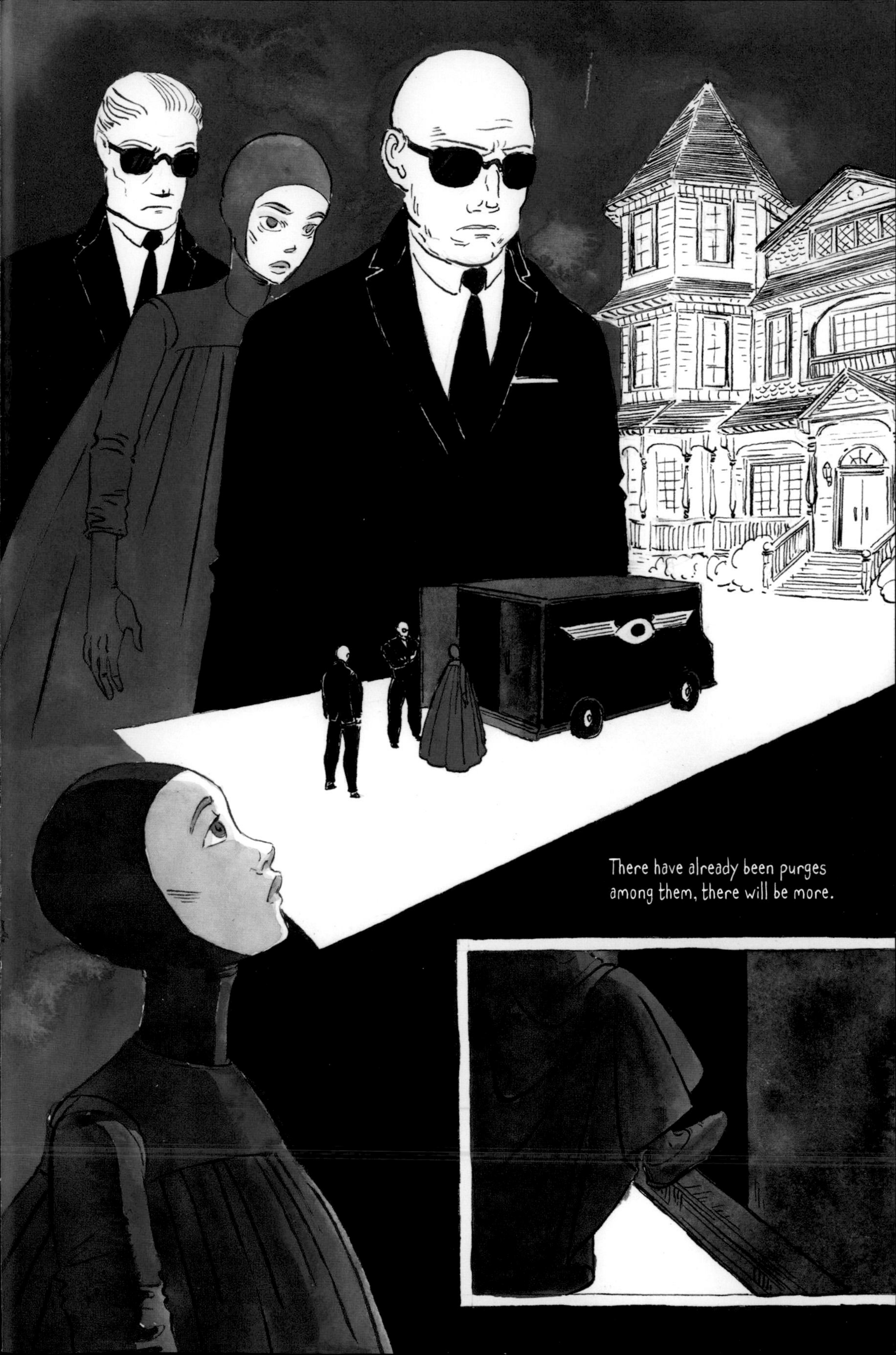
There have already been purges among them, there will be more.

Whether this is my end or a new
beginning I have no way of knowing:

I have given myself over into the hands
of strangers, because it can't be helped.

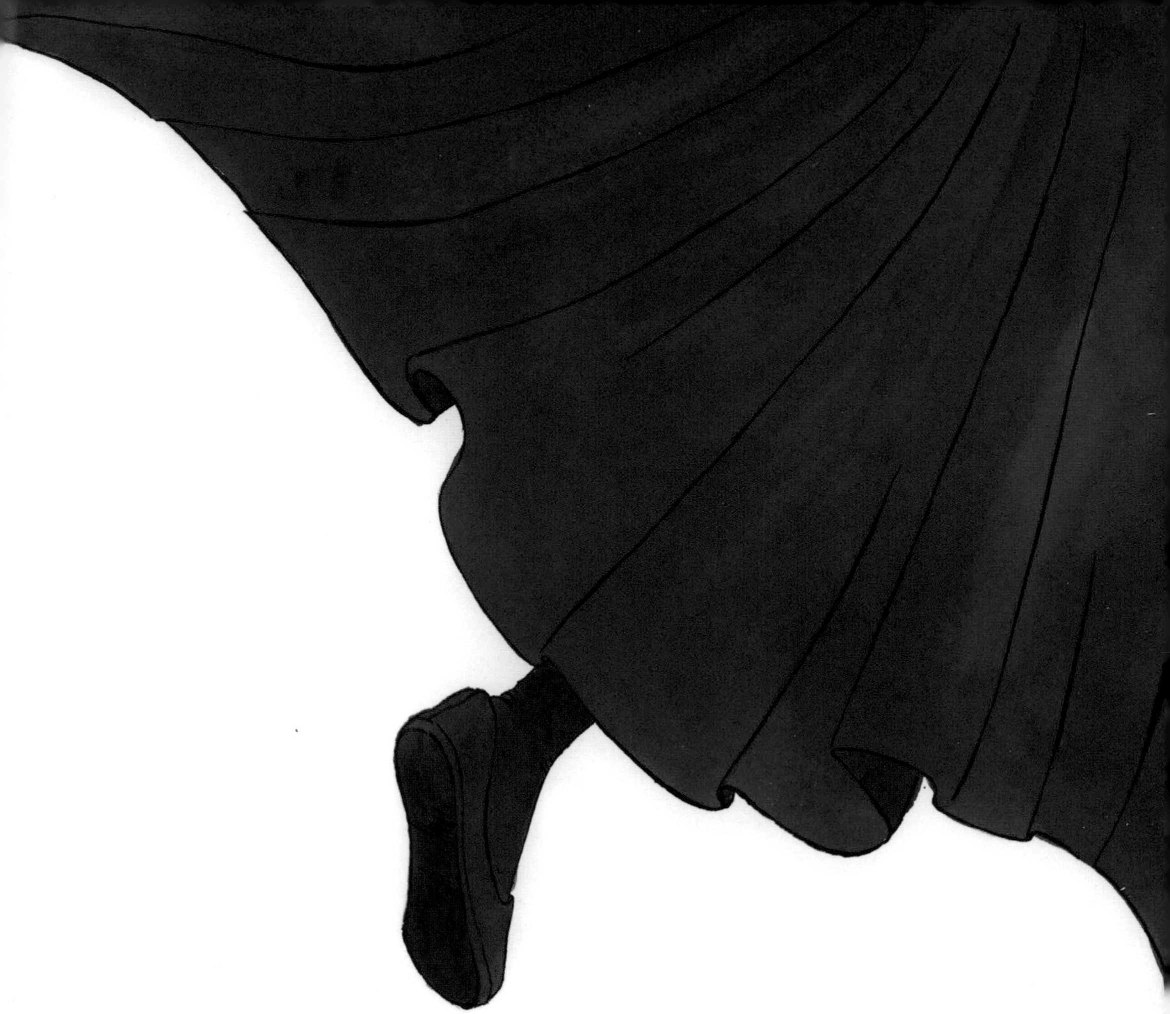

And so I step up, into the darkness within; or else the light.

H I S T O R I C A L
N O T E S

...This item was unearthed
on the site of what was once the city
of Bangor, in what, at the time prior to
the inception of the Gileadean regime,
would have been the State of Maine.

There were some thirty tapes
in the collection, with varying proportions
of music to spoken word. In general, each tape
begins with two or three songs, as camouflage
no doubt: then the music is broken off
and the speaking voice takes over.

The voice is a woman's
and, according to our
voice-print experts, the
same one throughout.

We held out no
hope of tracing the
narrator herself.

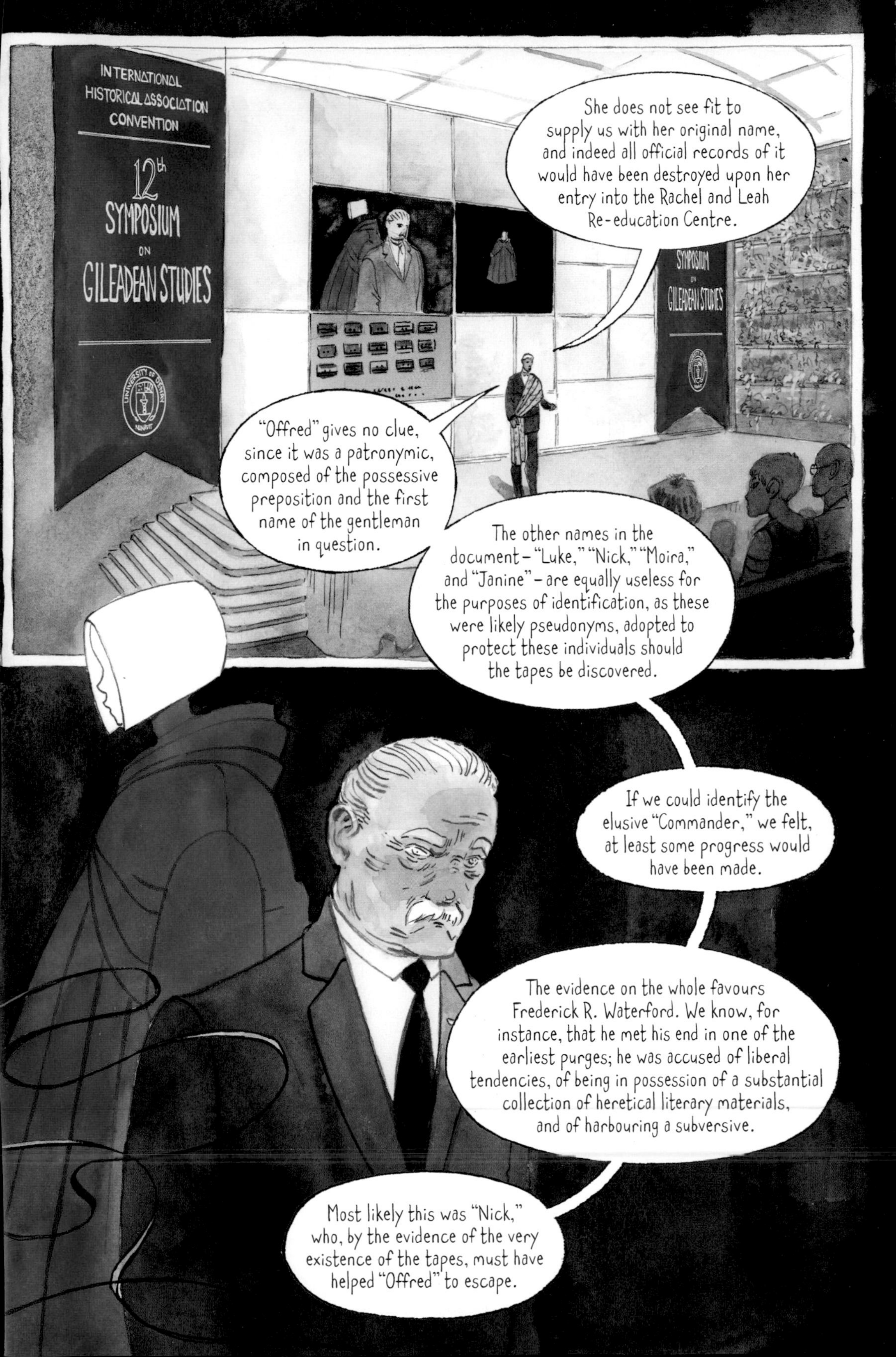
INTERNATIONAL HISTORICAL ASSOCIATION CONVENTION
12th SYMPOSIUM ON GILEADEAN STUDIES
SYMPOSIUM ON GILEADEAN STUDIES
She does not see fit to supply us with her original name, and indeed all official records of it would have been destroyed upon her entry into the Rachel and Leah Re-education Centre.
"Offred" gives no clue, since it was a patronymic, composed of the possessive preposition and the first name of the gentleman in question.
The other names in the document – "Luke," "Nick," "Moira," and "Janine" – are equally useless for the purposes of identification, as these were likely pseudonyms, adopted to protect these individuals should the tapes be discovered.
If we could identify the elusive "Commander," we felt, at least some progress would have been made.
The evidence on the whole favours Frederick R. Waterford. We know, for instance, that he met his end in one of the earliest purges; he was accused of liberal tendencies, of being in possession of a substantial collection of heretical literary materials, and of harbouring a subversive.
Most likely this was "Nick," who, by the evidence of the very existence of the tapes, must have helped "Offred" to escape.

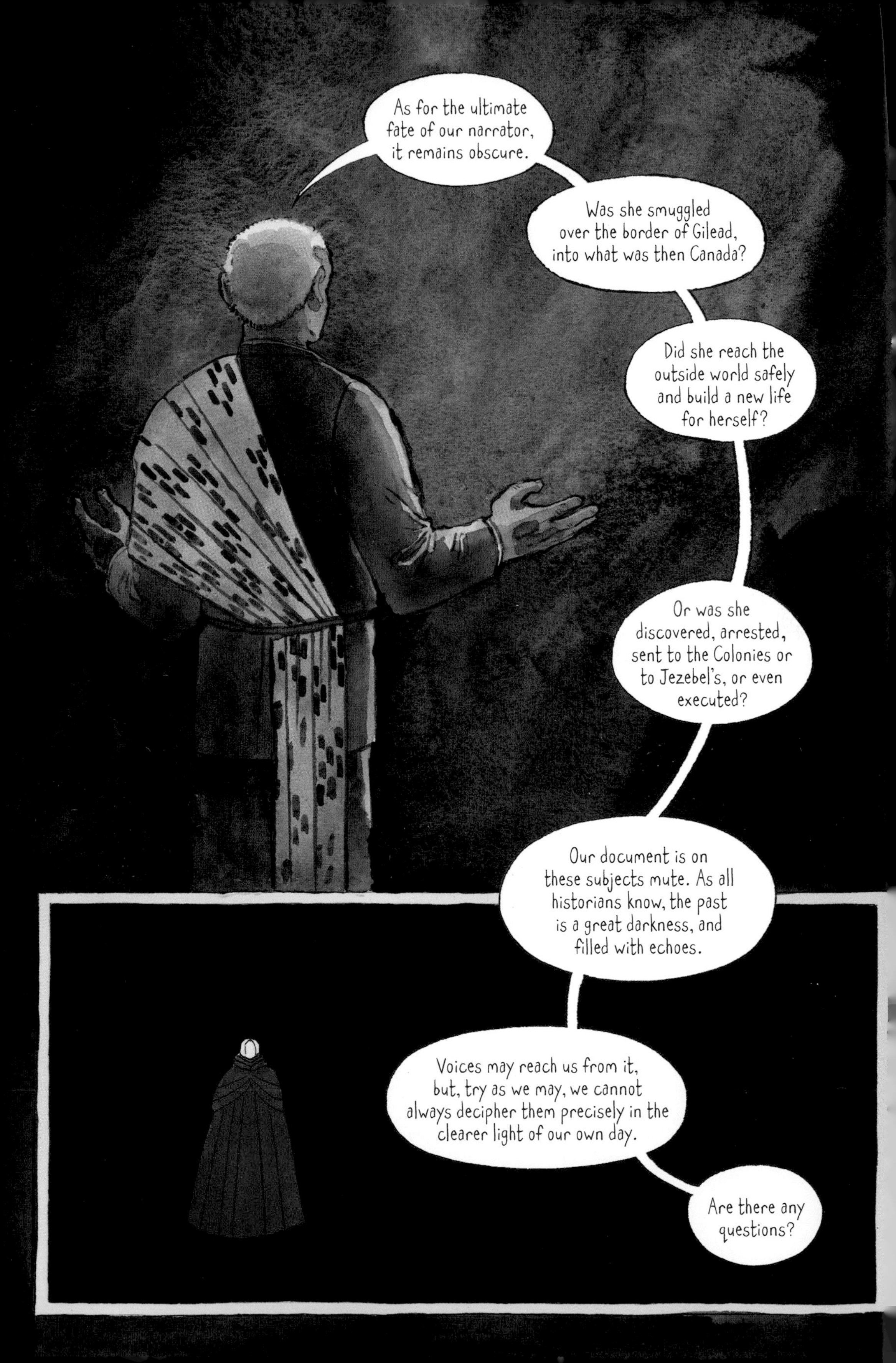
As for the ultimate fate of our narrator, it remains obscure.
Was she smuggled over the border of Gilead, into what was then Canada?
Did she reach the outside world safely and build a new life for herself?
Or was she discovered, arrested, sent to the Colonies or to Jezebel's, or even executed?
Our document is on these subjects mute. As all historians know, the past is a great darkness, and filled with echoes.
Voices may reach us from it, but, try as we may, we cannot always decipher them precisely in the clearer light of our own day.
Are there any questions?